# SOVIET VETERANS
# OF THE SECOND WORLD WAR:
# A POPULAR MOVEMENT
# IN AN AUTHORITARIAN
# SOCIETY 1941-1991

# SOVIET VETERANS OF THE SECOND WORLD WAR:

## A POPULAR MOVEMENT IN AN AUTHORITARIAN SOCIETY 1941–1991

MARK EDELE

OXFORD
UNIVERSITY PRESS

British Library Cataloguing in Publication Data

Data available

Library of Congress Cataloging in Publication Data
Edele, Mark.
Soviet veterans of the Second World War: a popular movement in an authoritarian
society: 1941–1991 / Mark Edele.
p. cm.
Includes bibliographical references and index.
ISBN 978–0–19–923756–2 (alk. paper)
1. Veterans—Soviet Union. 2. World War, 1939–1945—Veterans—Soviet Union. 3.
Soviet Union—Social conditions—1945–1991. I. Title.
D810.V42S687 2009
305.9'0697094709045—dc22
2008039122

Typeset by Laserwords Private Limited, Chennai, India
Printed in the UK
on acid-free paper by
the MPG Books Group.

ISBN 978–0–19–923756–2

1 3 5 7 9 10 8 6 4 2

Dedicated to the memory of Herbert Edele (1936–2007).

# *Preface*

This book was written by a German with a partially American education, living in Australia. I am of a generation too young to have personally experienced war and totalitarianism, growing up in a stunningly long period of peace and unprecedented prosperity in Europe, in a functioning welfare state with a vigorous public discourse, and a democratic government. For my cohort of West Europeans it takes a leap of imagination to connect to what it means to live in a totalitarian dictatorship, an authoritarian society, an economy of scarcity, or to fight for life and death for this very order. If any of the few surviving Soviet veterans happen to read these pages, I can only hope they will forgive me for my lack of comprehension.

The little insight there might be I owe to research but also to the many people who have educated, nourished, and sustained me. My parents, Herbert and Brigitte Edele, brought me up in an environment of love for discussion and respect for learning before they sent me out into the world. That this book is dedicated to my late father is more than just a gesture of a mourning son. It was this essentially self-educated man who taught me the most basic attitudes of the scholar by regularly jumping up during sometimes heated dinner conversations, running into his study only to return with a book or a volume of his encyclopedia, to share with the family what the actual fact of the matter was.

After I left my parents' house and eventually their country as well, I was fortunate to find other people who felt in similar ways about the world. Hubertus Jahn, Susan Morrissey, Jörg Baberowski, Tobias Holzlehner, and the late Nikolaus Wenturis helped me grow in their very different ways during my university years in Germany. Without them I would never have had the chance to become a graduate student at that singular institution of higher education, the University of Chicago. Here I met people who would deeply influence the way I think and act. Richard Hellie, Ron Suny, Michael Geyer, Mie Nakachi, and Charles Hachten were formative during my years at Chicago—sometimes in contradictory, but always in interesting ways. Sheila Fitzpatrick had a particularly deep and enduring influence on the doctoral dissertation which grew into this book. To put it in German terms, Sheila was a real *Doktormutter* to this project and a role model to me. There was also, as it were, a 'doctoral sister'. Debra McDougall came into my life later (and in a very different role than my adviser), but her scholarship, ethics, politics, grammar, censorship, endurance, friendship, and love made this into a better book and me, sometimes, into a slightly better person.

I had the good fortune to be able to immerse myself for altogether fourteen months full-time in the archives and libraries of Moscow, Voronezh, Nizhnii Novgorod, and Ekaterinburg, for no better reason than trying to find out what happened to Soviet veterans after the war. This luxury would not have been possible without the generous support of four institutions: the University of Chicago (which provided funding for a scouting trip in 2000), the German Academic Exchange Service (DAAD, which funded a year of doctoral research in Russia in 2001–2), the University of Western Australia, and the Australian Academy for the Humanities (whose Research Grant and Humanities Travelling Fellowship, respectively, funded another research trip in 2006). Thinking, writing, rewriting and further research were made possible by a Century Fellowship and a Mellon Dissertation Year Fellowship at the University of Chicago, a University of Western Australia Research Grant, a Humanities and Social Sciences Publication Grant of the Faculty of Arts at UWA, and a host of smaller travel stipends by the latter institution.

During research, Donald Filtzer, Elena Zubkova, Jean Lévesque, Vladimir Aleksandrovich Kozlov, and Catherine Merridale shared their knowledge of the sources. Don and Jean also gave me then unpublished work to read, as did Ben Zaijcek, Charles Hachten, Christopher Burton, and Beate Fieseler. The influence of the latter on my thought will be apparent to readers of Chapter 4. Amir Weiner's remarks at a conference in Chicago in 2000 sparked my interest in veterans in the first place. Chris Burton showed the greenhorn the archival ropes, read and commented on my work during the gestation of both the dissertation and the book, and supplied me with the phrase 'epic of return'. Fellow 'archive rats' Lorenz Lüthi, Wolfgang Mueller, Paul Stronski, Eleonor Gilburd, Julia Landau, Gero Fedtke, Simon Ertz, Juliane Fürst, and Polly Jones made research in Moscow better and continued to point me to relevant literature in the years to follow.

The veterans' representatives of Voronezh answered my questions, quickly transformed their office into a living room to serve me tea, and—after producing 'something stronger' for a toast to peace and to the friendship of the peoples—gave me a stack of memoirs as a farewell gift. They knew that I was German and I am still in awe of their generosity. The librarians in the Russian State Historical Library, the Russian State Library (both Moscow), the Bavarian State Library (Munich), the Joseph Regenstein Library at the University of Chicago, the Reid Library at the University of Western Australia, as well as the archivists of all the institutions listed in the Bibliography were invaluable. In particular, I would like to acknowledge the enormous help from June Farris, Regenstein's Slavic bibliographer. Research assistance was provided by Leith Passmore, Sally Carlton, and Julia Fein.

Nikolai Mitrokhin has been a companion, Russian teacher, and guide to Moscow's nightlife. Without him my time in Moscow would have been much less productive and more dull (if, maybe, more sober). Kolia knows the published sources on the postwar Soviet Union like nobody else, and was happy to share. I could not have written about religious veterans without his help. Particularly memorable was one evening in the winter of 2001/2 in the small grubby apartment he then rented close to Chistye prudy metro station, just a block from the always smoky intelligentsia hangout Ogi, which practically functioned as his living room. We were about to go to dinner, and I impatiently waited for Kolia to fire off a couple of emails. Noticing the hungry look on my face, he handed me a book: '*Vot smotri*, might be interesting.' It was the memoir of D'iakov—the centrepiece of Chapter 4.

The process of turning a dense, excessively empirical dissertation into a somewhat more readable book took place in large parts under the blue skies of Western Australia and partially under the not-so-blue skies of South Bend, Indiana. I would like to thank the Department of Anthropology of the University of Notre Dame for generously providing office space for the visiting not-yet spouse of a visiting assistant professor. My colleagues and friends at the University of Western Australia have made me feel at home and were a constant source of intellectual and emotional support. In particular I would like to thank Richard Bosworth, Andrea Gaynor, Jamie Moir, Jeremy Martens, Ethan Blue, Rob Stuart, Norm Etherington, Giuseppe Finaldi, and Sue Broomhall for friendship and scholarship.

As one of the first readers of the book manuscript, Richard Bosworth copy-edited and commented in record time. His red-inked outbursts at poor writing ('NoNo!' 'Eeeeek!') have helped immensely in improving my rather heavy-handed prose. That my soldiers still travel in 'cattle cars' rather than 'carriages' (the 'proper English word') is entirely due to my stubbornness. In one instance, Richard also served as a rather high-level research assistant, translating a section of an Italian memoir for me. Sheila Fitzpatrick and Debra McDougall read everything I wrote, several times. I cannot thank them enough. I also profited from the suggestions by Christopher Wheeler and by three anonymous readers for Oxford University Press as well as from meticulous corrections by Hubertus F. Jahn.

This book has developed in dialogue with many people at conferences and seminars. Bits and pieces as well as full drafts were presented at the Social Theory, the Russian Studies, and the Modern European History Workshops at the University of Chicago; at the Midwest Russian History Workshops at the University of Illinois and Miami University; at the History Postgraduate Seminars at the University of Western Australia; at the Annual Conventions of the American Association for the Advancement of Slavic Studies in 2002, 2003, 2005, 2006, 2007; at the Biannual Conference of the Australasian Association for European History at the University of Melbourne in 2005; at the Sheila Fitzpatrick Festschrift Conference at the same institution in 2006; the Russian History Workshop at the Institute of Advanced Studies at UWA in 2006; at the Institutskolloquien für Geschichte Osteuropas at Humboldt Unversität Berlin (2002), Universität Bielefeld (2002), and Tübingen (2000, 2006); and at the Committee for Russian and East European Studies, University of Cambridge (2006). Parts of the Introduction and sections of Chapter 8 were first published in *Slavic Review*, 65/1 (2006): 111–37.

# Contents

# List of Tables and Figures

# PART
# I

## Reintegration

# Introduction

## Consequences of War

The first half of the twentieth century was a period marked by mass armies and mass death; its central experience was war. Never before have so many people been under arms; never before have so many people been killed by their fellow humans as during this half century. According to one reconstruction, the First World War cost Europe sixteen times and the Second World War fifty times as many military deaths as the Thirty Years' War; even compared to the carnage of the Revolutionary and Napoleonic wars, the factor is still two and seven, respectively.[1] Such cataclysms could not remain without serious impact on the societies caught up in them. This book is about one of the results of this Age of Violence, which engulfed Europe and the world between 1914 and 1945—the rise of war veterans as a new social and political force in Soviet society.[2]

When the German army attacked on 22 June 1941, Stalin's empire was a pariah state with massive internal problems, stemming from its turbulent history. The world's first successful socialist revolution in 1917 had been a result of the large-scale changes brought about by the spread of the industrial revolution and the birth of mass politics in the nineteenth century—an upheaval exacerbated by the destruction of the First World War (1914–18) and the following bloody civil war (1918–21). The Union of Soviet Socialist Republics, which rose out of this cauldron of violence and disturbance, struggled with international isolation, institutional weakness, and economic underdevelopment. The regime had lost much of the popular support it had commanded in 1917 and faced hostility by large sectors of the population instead. In the late 1920s and throughout the 1930s the Bolshevik Party's most radical members—now under the leadership of the callous Iosif Stalin—tried to overcome their society's technological and military backwardness and eliminate internal enemies in order to prepare for what they thought was an inevitable and necessarily violent confrontation with the capitalist world. In a few years and at the price of incredible human suffering, a militant minority dragged Old Russia, kicking and screaming, into the Bolshevik version of modernity.[3]

The society which would withstand the Nazi invasion in 1941–5 was the result of this aggression against the majority of the population—an onslaught which had two stages. First came what contemporaries called the Great Break (*velikii perelom*) of 1928–32, today better known as Stalin's revolution from above. It combined an attack on traditional elites and the training of new cadres from the working class with breakneck industrialization and a civil war against the peasantry. The rural population was forced into collective farms, in order to subdue those who were meant to pay for 'primitive socialist accumulation'. This first assault on Old Russia petered out as catastrophic drops in productivity, famine, and increasing opposition within the ruling Communist Party encouraged a partial retreat to a more sane pace of social change. The attack on society was renewed during what is known as the Great Terror of 1936–8, when Stalin engineered a bloody cleansing of the entire population from actual and potential enemies, including many supporters of his rule.[4]

The results of these revolutionary upheavals were contradictory. On one hand, they caused social anomie, or what one historian has termed a 'quicksand society'—broken lives, personalities, and families; social relations in severe flux; a high level of social and geographic mobility.[5] Many citizens had good reasons to resent the Stalinist order and thus hope for deliverance from this regime—a hope the *Wehrmacht* seemed to embody for a short while in 1941.[6] On the other hand, the revolution resulted in a rigid social organization according to rank and status—very much a peacetime version of a war economy.[7] It is well known that this was a police state which used terror and intimidation as well as propaganda and surveillance in its quest to remake society according to its wishes. What sometimes gets lost in discussions about state violence and ideology as central aspects of the Soviet system of domination is the economic aspect of regime stability.[8] Most of the consumer goods and services were produced and distributed by the state, and this state gave according to its own needs—the more important a citizen seemed to the regime, the better his or her life chances. Members of the new service class—many of them trained during the

Stalin revolution and promoted to now empty positions during the Great Purges—lived much more comfortably than most workers or even peasants. But even among those lower orders a rigid stratification was in place, ensuring that some did better than others, tearing the ruled apart. The planned economy, then, was one of the central mechanisms to encourage compliance with and participation in the Bolshevik project—those who did not contribute to official society were not supposed to eat. The severe dysfunctions of this centralized economy of scarcity, however, ensured the persistence of a second economy of semi-legal and outrightly illegal market, pseudo-market, and reciprocal transactions. This shadow economy made it possible, despite empty stores, for people to survive within an industrial society geared towards war production rather than consumer needs.[9]

This already mobilized society could easily be brought on a wartime footing after 22 June 1941. Indeed, in some respects the war meant laxer controls, which explains why many Soviet citizens remember the war as a time of relative 'freedom', despite the continued use of terror as a means of social control.[10] Many of those who at first were not convinced that fighting for Comrade Stalin was worth it soon fell into line—the new rulers turned out to be even worse than the home-grown butchers. It is tempting to speculate that, if only the Germans had been less brutal to the civilian population, they could have won the war in the East. They could have instrumentalized the widespread resentment against Stalin's regime and sold their conquest as a war of liberation. Such arguments ignore both the realities of warfare and the facts of ideology. The Germans had the double handicap of being racists and of having started a war which could only be won by tactics which would have bordered on the genocidal in the best of circumstances. Germany was far inferior in terms of numbers of men and materiel from the very start and the only way to win this war was through another of the lightning strikes the *Wehrmacht* had become so renowned for since 1939. This warfare relied on quick movement of armoured divisions, but was hampered by the bad roads and huge distances in the East as well as the reality that the German army remained horse-drawn in its vast majority. Military specialists had known all along that the only way to overcome these obstacles was to live off the land—an old habit of armies indeed. In a country as desperately poor as the Soviet Union this implied accepting mass starvation of the conquered. Not that this was a problem for the German High Command. Despite the many and recurrent attempts to whitewash the deeds of Hitler's soldiers, a large section of both

commanders and men accepted the Nazi view that what they dealt with
were Jewish, Slavic, or Asiatic 'sub-humans'—a preconception which was
only reinforced by the desperate poverty they found and the ferocity of the
enemy they encountered.[11]

Soviet society, under the brutal leadership of Stalin's regime and reacting
to the mortal threat of a war of annihilation by a racist enemy, rose to
the challenge. The red colossus fielded 34.5 million regular troops and
tens, maybe hundreds, of thousands of irregular forces (the 'partisans').[12]
These otherwise ordinary men and women did what nobody had done
before—stop the invincible *Wehrmacht*, make it turn, and beat it in one of
the most vicious wars of the past century.[13] This victory came at the bitter
price of mass death and horrible suffering. The Soviets lost at least 25 million
and maybe as many as 27 million people, most of them civilians, but also at
least 7.8 million of the dead were members of the regular armed forces.[14]
According to official statistics, fewer than three million service-personnel
returned 'permanently disabled', but we can safely assume that many
millions more suffered from the physical, mental, and social consequences
of this horrible slaughter.[15] This is a book about these men and women,
about the way they made do in postwar society, and how they tried to find
a place in one of the harshest social and political environments of Europe.

In all belligerent countries, veterans demanded recognition and support
once the fighting had stopped. Organized movements of the survivors of
the modern battlefield frequently exerted considerable influence on the
political process. Legislative responses varied from country to country,
as did veterans' political affiliations, but old soldiers' needs, desires, and
demands became central to political struggles nearly everywhere. Indeed,
by 1935, veterans were deemed enough of a potential 'political problem'
in the West to merit their own entry in the *Encyclopaedia of the Social
Sciences*—appropriately sandwiched between 'Vested Interests' and 'Veto'.[16]
Literature and the arts, too, are hard to conceive without the prominent
role of the survivors of combat—try to imagine the interwar years without
George Grosz, Siegfried Sassoon, Ernst Jünger, Erich Maria Remarque,
or Ernest Hemingway; imagine postwar literature without Günther Grass
or Joseph Heller; imagine cultural theory without Raymond Williams or
history without E. P. Thompson. Given this general context, one of the
central theses of this book might not be too surprising: that veterans were an
important social force in Soviet society after the Second World War. After
all, the former Russian Empire, now renamed the Union of Soviet Socialist

Republics, had to take more than its fair share of suffering, destruction, and death in that war. Of the maybe 60 million dead claimed by the furies of German militarism and racism, at least 42 per cent were Soviet.[17]

The suffering was not over with the war. Soviet veterans returned to a desolated country. To be sure, the Soviet Union had been an economy of scarcity before the Germans attacked, but the material destruction resulting from the war of annihilation can hardly be overestimated. According to Soviet data, 1,710 cities and towns as well as more than 70,000 villages had been razed to the ground. The economic cost of the devastation was estimated as totalling more than twenty times the national income of 1940. Two million people met victory day living in dug-outs rather than houses.[18] To make things worse, the ruinous policies of the 1930s were re-enacted once victory was assured. The successful war convinced the political leadership that the Stalin revolution had been the correct path and, expecting war with the United States, the dictator saw little alternative to rebuilding the country along prewar lines. The hopes of many citizens for a postwar relaxation, the abolition of the collective farms, or a more permissive cultural climate were thus doomed to be disappointed. Despite some serious discussion within the state apparatus about major economic reforms, none were forthcoming. The kolkhoz regime was rebuilt, the creative intelligentsia terrorized, and veterans were told to go back to work rather than rest on their wartime laurels. The war was over—it was time to start preparing for the next one.[19]

Whatever the regime's intentions, however, the legacy of the war could not be made to disappear. Too deep were the scars, too horrible the memories, and too massive the destruction to simply ignore what had happened. Slowly, a culture of memory developed, which proved to be an important heritage of the slaughter.[20] Postwar Stalinism was marked by an attempt to replace the memory of mass suffering and mass heroism with a narrative which focused on Stalin's role as leader and 'War-Hero-in-Chief'. After the dictator's death in 1953, a more populist storyline re-emerged as official commemoration was de-Stalinized. The cult of what the Soviets called the 'Great Patriotic War' (*Velikaia Otechestvennaia voina*) finally came into its own between 1965 and 1985, a period marked by a partial re-Stalinization and increasing bombast and monumentalism.[21]

Veterans participated in the different periods of the developing cult to different degrees. During the first period, they were by no means silent. The official representation of homecoming as the enthusiastic reintegration of the returning heroes into the hard work of building (or rebuilding!) socialism was not infrequently adopted as a self-description by the minority of veterans who took over leading positions all over the country. At times, veterans also publicly defended their right to remember the war on their own terms, including fear, panic, and frontline love affairs.[22] Representations of homecoming, while certainly full of Stalinist clichés, were also more complex than scholars sometimes make them. Even an immediate postwar classic like Petr Pavlenko's *Happiness* (1947), which stressed the heroic overcoming of disability through sheer will power, painted a quite grim picture of veterans' postwar life, including sickness, poverty, and destruction.[23]

Before Stalin's death in 1953 the party leaders among former soldiers—mostly older men who had been established in civilian life before the war—were the most vocal group. During Khrushchev's cultural liberalization from 1956 onwards (known as the 'Thaw') a different elite of veterans made itself heard: younger authors and filmmakers, who worked on their version of the war experience and the return to civilian life. They had come of age intellectually during the war, studied literature, art, or the movies in the postwar years, and started to dominate artistic production during the years of the Thaw.[24] Other veteran-intellectuals, like Viktor Nekrasov (born 1911), had been established before the war in a different profession, but changed careers under the impact of their wartime experience.[25]

Some of the best (and most complex) representations of homecoming were published during this period: Nekrasov's *In the Home Town* (1954) and Iurii Bondarev's *Silence* (1962).[26] In the movies, too, some masterpieces appeared, including Grigorii Chukhrai's take on his generation's wartime experience (*Ballad of a Soldier*, 1959), and his denunciation of the Stalinist persecution of former POWs in *Clear Sky* (1961).[27] The war now moved to the centre of artistic and intellectual production. Movies, literature, memoirs, and paintings all showed a more complex, slightly more realistic picture of the war than had been the case during Stalinism.[28] Even a 'bourgeois pacifist' like Erich Maria Remarque gained wide circulation. While before Stalin's death only two books of this outspoken German survivor of the First World War were published in the Soviet Union (*All Quiet on the Western Front*, 1929; and the sequel *The Road Back*, 1936), the years 1956 to 1961 saw a Remarque revival, which made him the second most published German author in the Soviet Union (after the leader Stefan

Zweig).[29] Works like *In the Home Town* and *Silence* paralleled the tone of mourning and depression underlying Remarque's work. Reactions to such 'Remarquism' were not unequivocally positive. Conservative critics blasted Bondarev's work for its brawls between demobilized soldiers, the depictions of the connections between veterans and the shadow economy, the stress on the centrality of the 'trench brotherhood' (*okopnoe bratstvo*)—all elements supposedly borrowed from Remarque and reflecting a foreign reality, not Soviet actuality. Instead, one critic suggested, Bondarev should have shown 'the people's heroic rebuilding effort'.[30]

Such critics were more content with the second, parallel stream of war memory—a more monolithic, heroic, and uncomplicated discourse, which would rise to dominance under Khrushchev's successor Brezhnev (1964–82).[31] The latter's years in office are often compared unfavourably with the preceding Thaw and termed the era of stagnation (*zastoi*). As far as war memory is concerned, neither the era's torpitude, nor its discontinuity with what came before should be overemphasized. For one, the basic decisions which started the state-sponsored monumentalism in war memory were made under Khrushchev.[32] Moreover, as a recent study on war films has shown, the war cult of this era was itself a much more complex and more dynamic affair than is sometimes suggested.[33] It might be more accurate to see this as a period when the 'religion of war' which had emerged since 1945 finally came into its own.[34] This quasi-metaphysical system of memory of and communion with the dead now flowered not only into a whole pantheon of heroes, saints, and villains but also a fully fledged set of rituals, large and small, of symbols and gestures suffusing everyday life and punctuating the year. That not all expressions of commemoration were reduced to black-and-white propaganda only reinforces the point that this was more than a state-sponsored cult—a living religion, deeply rooted in a population still trying to make sense of the unintelligible horror of this war.[35] As we will see in the final part of this book, the period of stagnation was also very dynamic in terms of the development of the organized wing of the veterans' movement and brought major changes in legal standing of old soldiers.

The 1965 celebrations of twenty years of Victory also show the entanglement of old and new, and of state discourse and social psychology. Popular reactions—which were overwhelmingly positive—were carefully monitored and must have convinced the leaders that they were on the right track.[36] In his Victory Day speech, just months after he had replaced

Khrushchev as first secretary (October 1964), Brezhnev did not need to invent much, as he already had the entire phraseology at his command and could draw on the full pantheon of wartime heroes, which would be repeated largely without change until Perestroika. The main novelty was the careful reinstatement of Stalin into the story of victory, and the silencing of more complex or ambiguous ('Remarquist') representations. Victory Day now became a non-working holiday again, as it had been before 1948. Significantly, the new leader also picked up the preoccupation of Thaw era art with ordinary people's contribution to the war effort by mentioning the millions of unknown 'participants of the Patriotic War' (*uchastniki Otechestvennoi voiny*)—the term which over a decade later would become the basis for the new special status of war veterans.[37]

Given the centrality of this 'Patriotic War' in the official legitimation myth, it comes as somewhat of a surprise how hard it was for these millions to gain recognition, organization, and an official legal status—despite, or maybe because of, their sizeable numbers (between 20 and 25 million by the war's end, comprising somewhere between 12 and 15 per cent of the Soviet population).[38] After these soldiers had been welcomed back with fanfare, official meetings, Stalin posters, and high-minded speeches, the minor special status they were granted during demobilization was quickly taken away. Veterans were expected not to rest on their laurels but to reintegrate quickly into the production process and to perform more heroic deeds (*podvigi*), this time in the reconstruction of the country. Pensions for war invalids were miserable, medical support and the supply of prosthetic appliances poor, and the main interest of the state was in war victims' remaining labour power.[39] During the final years of Stalin's rule, veterans who could not keep their mouths shut about the living conditions they had seen in the West were liable to be arrested for 'anti-Soviet agitation'.[40] More famous is the repression of former prisoners of war (POWs), who after their repatriation were checked by the security organs in temporary concentration camps. Those who were cleared of wrongdoing and released into civilian life were again threatened with arrest in the late 1940s and early 1950s. In the context of the xenophobia of late Stalinism, their contamination with things foreign kept them on the watch-lists of the security organs, making them into logical suspects in later campaigns.[41]

Even after the death of Stalin in 1953, in the context of the beginning liberalization and developing war cult under Khrushchev, the Soviet rulers remained reluctant to grant special privileges and representation of veterans in their own organization. A Soviet Committee of War Veterans (*Sovetskii komitet veteranov voiny*, or *SKVV*) was formed in 1956, but its explicit function was to be international propaganda in the global veterans' movement, not domestic representation of former soldiers. Only after a long struggle, and only for the decade between 1965 and 1975, was a local infrastructure allowed to develop. The institutionalization of veterans' status in law did not happen until 1978.[42]

In a comparative context, then, the Soviet experience until the 1980s is located at one extreme of the spectrum of societal responses to the emergence of veterans as a new social group. In some cases, such as Germany after the First World War, the state monopolized both welfare and the recognition of veterans' status, expelling civil society from this field of action; in others, like Britain, most of the care for former soldiers was left to voluntary associations.[43] Still others, such as the United States after the Second World War, combined a robust private-sector response to returning servicemen with official recognition through major legislation.[44] In the Soviet Union, by contrast, private-sector initiatives were illegal since the Revolution, as the Soviet party-state claimed an organizational monopoly within society. The lack of private philanthropy was not balanced by a vigorous state welfare system. In what amounted to a totalitarian version of the British path of postwar accommodation, the Soviet state expected veterans to demobilize completely, become civilians, and stop claiming special rewards for wartime service. The goal was to unmake veterans as a social group as fast as possible.[45]

Soviet veterans were not content with this approach. A constant groundswell of dissatisfaction sometimes grew into what can only be described as uncoordinated mass letter-writing campaigns. As we shall see in Chapters 7 and 8, this consistent pressure from below was eventually successful, as the Soviet leadership moved away from its original ideological preconceptions and allowed first the growth of an organized veterans' movement and then a growing field of legal privileges. By the mid-1980s, indeed, the Soviet approach had shifted from one extreme to the other: now, veterans were a corporate group with a degree of organization, legal status, and integration into the political system which went even beyond the French approach to *anciens combattants*.[46]

The history of Soviet veterans thus challenges a central assumption in the literature on veterans' movements. Much of this literature assumes that old soldiers do not form a social group unless they are organized in associations or constructed by legislation as a distinct status group. This assumption was made explicitly by the great historian of French *anciens combattants*, Antoine Prost, in his magisterial study of the French veterans' movement of the interwar years.[47] Prost argues that veterans do not form a 'real' social group, like for example 'workers', who exist before they are organized (or, it might be added, singled out by legislation). In what amounts to a reformulation of the old Marxist notion of a class in itself and a class for itself, Prost assumes that workers are a group because of their objective position *vis-à-vis* the production process. Even if they are unorganized, even if they do not have any class consciousness, workers are, for Prost, a 'real group' (*un groupe véritable*), because they fulfil a clear function in society. Veterans, by contrast, have no such objective existence. Their only commonality is their shared wartime experience, maybe enhanced by a similar age. This participation remains without consequence for society at large unless veterans organize to claim a special status. Therefore, the history of veterans is necessarily a history of veterans' organizations, the veterans' movement, and the consciousness of its participants.[48] In a language popularized later, one might summarize Prost—and with him much of the literature on veterans—as claiming that combat survivors are either an imagined community or they are nothing.[49]

Veterans of the Great Patriotic War—by contrast—existed as a socially relevant group long before they were organized and despite the fact that their special status was dismantled soon after demobilization. They kept bombarding state institutions with requests for special treatment; they assumed that their village, their family, their city—those they had defended during the war—owed them for their wartime sacrifices; they felt entitled to special status, to special treatment, to a better life. During the first postwar decade, these feelings, which were rooted in the culturally mediated experience of war, were usually not expressed as a function of membership in an imagined community of veterans: more often than talking of 'us', veterans talked of 'me'. It was the individual's wartime sacrifice which entitled to a particular status after the war. The mass expression of such individualized sentiment created a social entity which was as real as any other: a popular movement which can be called an 'entitlement group'.[50]

This might sound like an unnecessarily complicated way to state the obvious fact that veterans were a generation. For most of postwar history, this would be a misunderstanding, even if there are some similarities between these two social phenomena. Like a generation, Soviet veterans were diverse in social and cultural background, as diverse as Soviet society as a whole; like a generation, Soviet veterans were divided by gender and ethnicity, but also by political affiliation and ideology; and, like a generation, what made them from a cohort of individuals into a recognizable social entity was a shared foundational experience.[51] However, while British, German, or French men who fought in the First World War can fairly easily be treated as a cohort of coevals unified by frontline experience, Soviet veterans of the Second World War cannot.[52] True, most of the soldiers who fought in the Red Army were young men, but few of them survived.[53] Indeed, of the youngest cohorts, most were wiped out during the immensely costly campaigns against the *Wehrmacht*. Official statistics show 40 per cent of the demographic losses of the armed forces to have been 25 years or younger.[54] According to one historian, of the men born in 1921 'up to 90 percent were dead'.[55] As a result of such casualties, young veterans were a distinct minority among the survivors of military service in the wartime Red Army.

Instead of one generation of veterans, then, we can distinguish at least three.[56] The best known of these is the youngest generation of men (and, as we will see, some women) who entered the armed forces directly from the school bench or as students. These youth, born between 1923 and 1927,[57] had not been established in adult life before the war and by 1945 had learnt not much more than 'shoot, throw grenades, and creep around' on their bellies, as the veteran-author Viktor Nekrasov put it.[58] For many of them, the front became the fundamental experience of their lives, and they had often massive problems of adjustment when they came back. Their often rapid careers within the army did not give them adequate civilian competencies, and therefore demobilization often meant a step back in life-cycle stage and social standing, at least initially. We can term this group the 'frontline generation'.[59] The second generation of veterans had already been established in civilian life before the war, and thus had something to go back to. Even if their homes and families were frequently damaged or destroyed, they could still return to an established pattern of life, a profession, and frequently a job as well. Judging from official reports on demobilization, this cohort of *frontoviki* had far fewer readjustment problems than the frontline generation proper.[60] It was largely men of this and the next older generation of veterans who took over leading positions after their return from the army.[61] The least known generation of *frontoviki* can be called the 'double veterans'. Members of this oldest cohort, born in 1904 or before, had not only fought in the Great Patriotic War, but were also likely to have participated in the Civil War (and sometimes even in the 'First Imperialist War', too).[62] Many were career military men like the first three chairmen of the Soviet Committee of War Veterans Aleksandr Mikhailovich Vasilevskii (born 1895), Kirill Afanas'evich Meretskov (born 1897), and Semen Konstantinovich Timoshenko (born 1895); others were civilians like the script writer Iosif Leonidovich Prut (born 1900), who 'participated in nearly all wars of my country'—that is, in the First World War, the Civil War, and then again in the Second World War.[63]

No data exist about the exact size of these generations of veterans. Both postwar visual propaganda and the 'lieutenant's prose' of the 1950s and 1960s most often depicted young veterans, which explains why this generation dominates our historical imagination.[64] The demographic data we have, however, suggest that this prominent group was a minority among Soviet citizens who had survived combat on the Eastern Front of the Second World War. Reconstructions of the size of the respective birth cohorts at the end of the war can give a first, though inconclusive, orientation.[65]

Table I.1 strongly suggests that the frontline generation proper was a minority among veterans after the war, even if it is true that not all men were soldiers, and not all soldiers men. (Women formed somewhere between 2 and 3 per cent of veterans after the war as the Red Army had included many women, particularly in the medical services or as other support personnel, but also as snipers, tank drivers, infantry women, and bomber pilots.[66] The second wave of demobilization in autumn 1945 released most of them into civilian life, independent of their age.[67]) That the youngest cohorts of frontline survivors were in the minority is confirmed by an analysis of demobilization statistics: the first demobilization wave freed the birth years 1893 to 1905 from active duty.[68] A staggering 40 per cent of all soldiers released during mass demobilization returned as part of this wave between July and September 1945.[69] Two-fifths of those veterans who were sent home during mass demobilization until 1948, then, were 40 years or older at the end of the war. A history of the frontline generation, therefore, is not the same as a history of Soviet veterans more broadly conceived.

This book is such a broad history of Soviet veterans as a 'new social entity'.[70] Its topic is the emergence of a novel group within Soviet society. The focus is on social relations and the behaviour of veterans rather than, for

Table I.1. Male population of Soviet Union by cohorts at beginning of
1946 (000s)

| Generation | Birth cohort | Absolute | % |
|---|---|---|---|
| Frontline generation | 1923–7 | 7,891.9 | 22.9 |
| Middle generation | 1905–22 | 17,097.6 | 49.6 |
| Double veterans | 1890–1904 | 9,502.1 | 27.5 |
| Total | 1890–1927 | 34,491.6 | 100.0 |

*Source*: Reconstruction by V. S. Gel'fand, *Naselenie SSSR za 50 let (1941–1990)* (Perm':
Izd-vo Permskogo universiteta, 1992); see Edele, 'A "Generation of Victors"?', app. 1; for
reconstruction of cohorts: ibid. 69–71.

example, the political processes which led to policies affecting old soldiers.
Much more could be said about these, about the role of war experience
in the making of the entitlement community, the role of the army in the
movement, the genesis and transformation of the cult of the Second World
War, the everyday life of war invalids in the 1960s and beyond, or the role
of war survivors in literature and the arts. Demobilization or the history of
the 'young communists' admitted at the front could also provide material
for book-length studies in their own right. The organizational history of
the veterans' movement is also explored only in so far as it impinges on
the topic of this study, social integration and social disintegration of the
popular movement of former soldiers after their return.

The book is organized thematically into three parts, each consisting
of several chapters. The first two parts focus on processes of group
disintegration; the final part on group formation. These two broad processes
are separated for analytical purposes only, as in real life they happened in
parallel. In Part I we start by following veterans home on their often
chaotic journey upon demobilization. They brought with them—beside
all kinds of loot, war stories, injuries and often chronic illness to haunt them
later in life—a strong sense of a right to a good postwar life. This sense
of entitlement was further fuelled by official propaganda, which promised
exactly what the soldiers expected. Once the veterans had arrived and had
been demobilized successfully, however, these promises turned out to be
largely empty: instead of the good postwar life, veterans were treated to
the routine hassles of a malfunctioning bureaucratic machine, which are
analysed in Chapter 2. Chapter 3 then focuses on what made reintegration
into civilian life possible and, as a rule, successful: non-state social ties,
networks, and institutions.

Part II analyses some of the divisions established by demobilization and reintegration, which tore the 'frontline brotherhood' apart. War invalids (Chapter 4) had to deal with specific problems created by their disabilities and the poor welfare provisions of a state most interested in mobilization to labour. The chapter also shows that, even among members of this group, strong differences in income and life-chances—their own hierarchy of misery—existed. Chapter 5 turns to another collectivity with special problems: former POWs who faced discrimination and persecution. Chapter 6 widens our view beyond such problem groups and shows that veterans were not united by a common social trajectory after the war—as in other countries, some did remarkably well, while others did not.

Moving from processes which divided veterans from each other to those which pulled them together, the two chapters of Part III then analyse the emergence of the Soviet veterans' movement and the transformation of combat survivors from an entitlement community into a status group and, eventually, a corporate group within the late Soviet order. The argument of this book culminates in these final two chapters. As in Part I, the focus is not on the state alone, which is treated as only one—if important—aspect of the larger socio-cultural and socio-psychological process which made and unmade veterans as a social entity.[71]

This process was not completely controlled by anybody. In many ways the state yielded to—at times was carried away by—a force beyond its control. However, state decisions were still crucial: while government policy could not unmake the entitlement community, it could easily resist its demands. The centrality of the authoritarian state in the *timing* of the shifts in the larger story told in the final part of this book is evident from even a cursory look at the major periods of the history of veterans as a group and a movement. The entitlement community took shape during the war and the immediate postwar period and survived despite nearly a decade of non-recognition. The Khrushchev period brought some changes, particularly with regards to formulating war memory and shaping the cult of the war, but also to some extent as far as organization is concerned, but no institutional development of the sense of entitlement veterans consistently displayed ever since the war. Only under the pragmatist Brezhnev, who also liked to see himself as a war hero, did this latency period end. When Gorbachev came to power in 1985, veterans—their numbers thinning, their age advancing—had become a major status group within Soviet society. Despite all his 'back to Lenin' rhetoric, Gorbachev continued this course, completing the process started under his predecessors. As time went on and many of the older cohorts died, veterans became closer and closer in age to each other. While in 1945, they had been 'nebulous in generational terms', now 'they appeared much less chronologically diffuse'. They started to emerge as a distinct generation who had more in common with their coevals who had not fought at the front but shared the general experience of wartime than they had with younger Soviet citizens. By the 1970s, as a result, 'the heroes of Stalingrad and Kursk were regularly joined in celebratory public discourse by the "veterans" of the factory and the collective farm'. This process of 'the identity of "pensioner" ' hitching 'a ride on that of "veteran" '[72] was completed under Gorbachev, who united both types of veterans in one single organization and applied many of the privileges of the former to the latter. Moreover, he also formally integrated this new organization into the political system.

It was not a historical accident that the recognition of wartime sacrifice was eventually institutionalized as a system of privileges. The legal ascription of special treatment to 'deserving' categories of citizens and the uneven distribution of benefits on this principle was one of the bases of social stratification and regime stability.[73] During the inter-war years some social groups were for ideological reasons assumed to be in natural alliance with Bolshevism—workers, for one, or certain nationalities. They earned an ascribed position which, for example, made access to higher education easier for them than for groups assumed to be in natural conflict with the regime (such as former aristocrats, or well-to-do peasants, the *kulaks*).[74] Others owed their status to service to the state and the revolution—the more important this service, the higher the status, and the better the access to goods and services.[75] The special position of soldiers in Soviet life initially followed the service principle: it was determined by achievements in the service to the state. The sheer scale of this war, however, blurred the boundaries between achievement and ascription in the minds of many. The service they had rendered at the frontline was so enormous that all those who survived became part of an ascribed category of war participants who should receive special benefits independent from ongoing service. This made perfect sense within the changed symbolic universe, too: if after 1917 workers had a special status because they had made the revolution, after the war the old soldiers should receive similar esteem, as they had fought the war. The institutionalization of the cult of the Second World War as the new legitimizing myth in the Soviet polity thus logically implied the creation of a special

position for the defenders of the Homeland (*rodina*). Soviet lawmakers finally followed this logic in 1978, at a time when the War had in many ways
eclipsed the Revolution as the major foundational event of the Soviet order.

In the context of Brezhnev's war cult and within a growing redistributive
state, a new discourse took shape about the relationship between the state
and the veterans. It was a variation of what one historian has called the
Stalinist 'culture of the gift', in which citizens were obliged to serve the
state (and love the leader) because of the latter's presumed attention to
the welfare of the population. According to such representations, veterans
owed the state because of the special treatment they had already received.[76]
Starting in the 1960s such ideas were combined with a competing, and in
many ways antithetical notion: the veterans' long-held sense that they were
entitled to special treatment because of the enormity of their past wartime
service. The culture of the gift was now modified into something akin to
a reciprocal relationship between veterans and the state—the state owed
veterans, but if it kept up its side of the deal, the old soldiers owed the regime
in turn.[77] By the late 1970s this bargain was thoroughly institutionalized.
Writing in 1979, the chairman of the veterans' organization first described
the propaganda work done both within the country and in the international
arena. He then moved to what in 1956 still had to be fought over: veterans
had special interests and needs, and those needed to be addressed by
an organization. 'The SKVV also devotes a lot of attention to assistance
(*sodeistvie*) to Soviet organs in their fulfillment of the resolutions of party and
government, which are directed towards better addressing the interests and
needs of war participants, war invalids, and the families of fallen soldiers.'
He also explicitly formulated the relationship between the party-state and
the veterans as a relationship of reciprocity. Praising the 10 November
1978 decree about the further improvement of the living conditions of
war participants, he wrote: 'This obliges us to labour even more actively
for the good of the Homeland.'[78] Three decades after the guns had fallen
silent, the consequences of war had finally found their proper Soviet
expression.

On one level, then, this is a case study of one of the most intriguing
socio-political phenomena of the twentieth century (which, it appears, will
have an afterlife in the twenty-first): popular movements in authoritarian
societies. The Soviet veterans' movement was neither a simple result of
state engineering, nor an expression of opposition to the regime. Rather,
it was driven by its own logic—a logic which emerged from the peculiarly

Soviet experience of war and demobilization, but did so not in a planned, engineered, or controlled fashion. The Soviet rulers never set out to create 'veterans'; the policies which created this new social entity did not follow from Bolshevik ideology.[79] Quite the opposite—the ruling elite saw the former soldiers' sense of special rights stemming from wartime service as problematic and the regime was for four decades staunchly opposed to any veterans' organization. The relevant practices which led to the rise of the new entity were connected to the emergency of war, which forced the regime to institute special privileges for soldiers and their families. Thus, on a second level, this book is an investigation of unintended, long-term, socio-psychological, and political consequences of waging war.

These consequences had a prehistory. Violent conflict with long-lasting effects on social and political organization was nothing out of the ordinary for this society. The ruling Bolsheviks themselves, while relying on a nineteenth-century ideology which stressed violence and conflict as the motor of history, learnt to rule during the first defining moments of the twentieth: the First World War and the ensuing Civil War.[80]

What the Soviets would call the 'First Imperialist War' was crucial in the history of the notion of reciprocity between soldiering and citizenship, which the army reforms of 1874 had introduced and legislation in 1912 had reinforced.[81] The experience of total war, and the implementation of a system of privileges for servicemen and their families, popularized the link between soldier and citizen, between fighting and a privileged position in society.[82] This connection would become the basis of the militarized socialism of the 1920s and 1930s.[83] War was, thus, central for the formation and transformation of this society, which, for much of its history, remained at war, prepared for organized violence, or recovering from it. The Civil War was followed by a prolonged campaign against the anti-Bolshevik Muslim forces in Turkestan (1923–31), the Soviet-Chinese conflict in 1929, military interventions in the Spanish Civil War (1936–9) and in China (1937–9), conflicts with Japan at Lake Khazan (1938) and the River Khalkhin-Gol (1939), the campaign in Western Ukraine and Western Belorussia in 1939, and the Winter War with Finland in 1939–40.[84] The war with Germany from 1941 to 1945 was the next important crucible in the organization of society for and through war. During the enormity of what quickly became known as the Great Patriotic War (*Velikaia Otechestvennaia voina*), the link between fighting for the community and receiving rewards for this sacrifice was transformed in popular consciousness into the notion that soldiering during wartime entitled special status after the war was over as well.

The effects of this transformation of ideas about soldiering, citizenship, and privilege were not immediately institutionalized because the political leadership resisted such change—for ideological, economic, and political reasons and despite the developing war cult. Many veterans, however, wanted recognition more tangible than a mention in speeches and representation in rituals at Victory Day (9 May). As this book documents, they eventually—in 1978, when their numbers had dwindled and the youngest were in their fifties—succeeded in this quest.

# I

# The Epic of Return

Already on the platforms of Leningrad's train stations, demobilized soldiers feel the love, care and attention of their fellow countrymen (*zemliaki*). Every special train which arrives in Leningrad will be met by large delegations of the labouring population of the city.

The demobilized soldiers are brought straight from the train station to district houses of culture, where assembly points have been set up, In these points the soldiers receive their passports, military documentation, ration cards. The best movies will be shown in the movie theatres [of the houses of culture], and concerts will be performed. Colourful exhibitions will tell the new arrivals about the life of the diverse districts and enterprises of the city during the time of the Patriotic War. The exhibitions help the demobilized to study the particularities of the enterprises of the city and choose a suitable occupation. In the assembly points directors of enterprises and party organizers of the factories will give speeches.

The party, soviet, economic, and societal organizations of the city prepare housing for the demobilized.... The demobilized soldiers will have privileged access (*v pervuiu ochered'*) to heating fuel. Special shops, which sell material for the repair of apartments, are being created for them.[1]

(*Red Star*, 1945)

According to the army newspaper *Red Star*, demobilization was to be a smooth and well organized, festive ritual which would ensure the veterans a privileged status, but also reintegrate them quickly into the labour force. This was a fantasy rarely fulfilled. Experiences of demobilization differed between one soldier and the next, but most had to deal with the chaos, disorganization, lack of preparation, and scarcity of everything—from food and shelter to clothes and transportation—which were endemic in the Soviet Union of the 1940s. Most soldiers did make it back nevertheless, and some were even greeted in elaborate ceremonies such as those promised in the newspaper article quoted above. Many more arrived with less pomp and coped with the situation they found to the best of their abilities. First, however, they had to travel, which was more adventurous, messy, and complicated than one might first expect in a police state like Joseph Stalin's Soviet Union.[2]

This epic of return deserves a close look. We first follow the demobilized soldiers on their way home as they travelled on the roof of or inside train cars, on river boats, and in planes. We see them jump on the back of trucks to hitch a ride, argue with officials to get transportation, ride horses, or simply walk. We hear them complain and swear, and see some of them vent their anger—and the drinks they consumed during the trip—in sudden explosions of violence. We analyse one major problem they had to solve: how to bring back home what they had acquired as 'trophies'—from a suit or a watch to grand pianos, hunting rifles, and cars. Finally we listen closely to what the Communist Party's agitators and newspapers had to say to released soldiers about their status and their rights and duties in postwar society. Despite all the chaos and confusion, the experience of demobilization and the rhetoric surrounding it suggested to veterans of the 'Great Patriotic War' that they had earned a new status in Soviet society—a status which entitled them to special treatment by all levels of social organization: the family, the village or neighbourhood, the regional party and soviet institutions, and, ultimately, 'the people' and 'Soviet power' in general.

War invalids were among the first veterans to return to civilian life. During the war 3.8 million soldiers were dismissed due to illness or wounds, 2.6 million of them remained permanently disabled.[3] In addition, above 200,000 soldiers were discharged 'for various reasons', a similar number deserted and were not found, and 3.6 million were sent to work in industry, in local anti-aircraft outfits, or as armed guards in the rear.[4] These wartime arrivals included enlisted men of the oldest age groups, that is, those born between 1890 and 1892, who had been called up in the emergency of 1941.[5] After the war's end these returnees were joined by at least 8.5 million soldiers who were demobilized by age group in several waves between 1945 and 1948 (see Table 1.1).[6] About 1.8 million former POWs were repatriated as a separate group.[7]

In the chaos of war and its immediate aftermath, the released soldiers' return tended to be far from comfortable. In 1943 an enraged member of the Supreme Soviet wrote to Central Committee Secretary Georgii

Table 1.1. Reconstruction of the demobilization waves with birth cohorts (rank
and file, ground troops)

| Legal act and date | Dates | Age groups | Birth cohort |
|---|---|---|---|
| Demobilization law 23 June 1945 | 2nd half of 1945 | 13 oldest | 1893–1905 |
| Decree of Presidium of Supreme Soviet, 25 September 1945 | By end of 1945 | next 10 oldest* | 1906–15 |
| Decree of Presidium of Supreme Soviet, 20 March 1946 | May–Sept. 1946 | next 6 | 1916–21 |
| Decree of Presidium of Supreme Soviet, 22 October 1946 | Nov. 1946–Jan. 1947 | 1 age group | 1922 |
| Decree of Presidium of Supreme Soviet, 4 February 1947 | Mar.–June 1947 | 2 age groups | 1923–4 |
| Decree of Presidium of Supreme Soviet, 12 February 1948 | Feb.–Mar. 1948 | 1 age group | 1925 |

*Also demobilized in the second wave: those with more than three wounds; specialists, former
teachers and students; women; and others.
Source: The legal acts in question are published (among other places) in Vedomosti Verkhovnogo Soveta
SSSR (30 June and 3 Oct. 1945; 28 Mar. and 31 Oct. 1946; 12 Feb. 1947). The ukase of 12 Feb.
1948 was, to the best of my knowledge, not published. A short note on this legal act appeared in
Vedomosti Verkhovnogo Soveta SSSR (21 Mar. 1948). The act itself can be found in GARF, f. r-7523,
op 40, d. 45, l. 1–2. The legal acts hide the actual birth cohorts, which had to be reconstructed using
published and archival sources. For this reconstruction see Edele, 'A "Generation of Victors"?', 62–8.

Malenkov about what he had witnessed during a train ride from Tashkent
to Moscow—a situation which was typical according to several conductors
on the train. About 300 war invalids who had been released from the
hospital and were on their way home stood in line for the express train
no. 73 from Tashkent to Moscow. As the boarding started they were
muscled aside by healthy passengers, who rushed to take over the two train
cars reserved for the old soldiers. Wounded servicemen were pushed over
and fell. Casts broke. Wounds reopened. Many disabled veterans remained
without a seat.

They had to try to find a space in different, equally packed carriages. To
make things worse, during a stop in a later station one car full of invalids
was separated from the train because it was supposed to remain in that
station. Again the disabled had to crowd into other, already full wagons.

The food they were supposed to get at supply points for servicemen in train stations also did not materialize. In Orenburg, Kuibyshev, and Riazan refreshments were located in the furthest corner of the station and no special arrangements were made to ease access for the wounded. As a result, many went for days 'without even a piece of bread'. No wonder that the invalids got annoyed: 'They write in the newspapers about the sensitive and attentive approach to wounded soldiers, and then they pack our brothers into the train car like pieces of wood', noted one. 'Well, when we were healthy and fought, we were useful. But now we are crippled and nobody cares about bringing us home like human beings (po chelovecheski).'[8]

This horror story of return was typical for those who had to make their way home on their own. Besides those who were invalided out during the war this included released officers, and those demobilized individually (for example, because they were requested as specialists by their former enterprise)[9]—all those who did not return home in the organized trains of mass-demobilization. One veteran who was medically discharged at the end of 1945 remembers how he was stuck in the last Romanian station before the Soviet Union with thousands of other demobilized soldiers hoping for a train. He found one with dismantled industrial equipment heading east. The space between the machines was filled with standing soldiers catching a ride over the border. He managed to join them.[10]

'Our train had a weird and pretty frightening look', noted a travelling party propagandist reporting similar experiences in early September 1945. The carriages of the train from Stanislava to L'vov and on to Briansk were packed. Released soldiers crowded the platforms between the cars, stood on the footboards at the entrances. The roofs were full of people with their luggage. 'At the train stations traders threw all sorts of food up there, and from the roofs flew money in return.' People openly bribed the conductors in order to get seats. In Kiev and some other stops the local military authorities forced passengers off the roofs, which only temporarily changed the situation. Soon, the train's top was full of travellers again. Because of all this commotion, the train arrived five hours behind schedule. During a stop in L'vov the propagandist also witnessed soldiers on their way home celebrating victory. 'A large number of severely drunk officers and soldiers were out on the street, singing.... They looked unruly. Until deep in the night I heard noise, drunken songs, shooting.' A similar scene awaited him in the opera, which he visited to hear La Traviata (in Ukrainian). 'There were many drunken officers and soldiers. Two completely drunk sergeants boasted and sang songs during the break for everybody to see [*sic*]. Two colonels stood nearby without doing anything.'[11]

In Rostov 205 demobilized soldiers stood in line for several hours because they had been told (incorrectly, as it turned out) that they needed to get their boarding passes stamped. Civilians managed to buy tickets for wagons reserved for returning soldiers. 'As a result, the demobilized have to travel in regular train cars, on the foot-steps, and on the roofs.'[12] Such scenes remained common in 1946:

> The roofs were already covered with sacks and human bodies, which the train, jerking every now and then, tumbled onto the platform like ripe apples. Men scrambled to their feet to fight once more for their hard-won places. I saw many uniforms and caps, without the stars. These were recently demobilized men.
>
> As soon as the train started the roofs, footboards, and buffers crowded again with non-paying passengers. And so they traveled from station to station.[13]

Trains were not the only means of transportation. One veteran, who hitchhiked home from Berlin in 1945, left the following description:

> Day and night a human stream moves in different directions across our immense country. Soldiers return from the front, evacuated return home. And all have the same thought: Just somehow get on a train or a passing car, and there, on the way, everything else will find itself.... Loud animation not only in towns, at rail junctions, but also on country roads: a half-ton truck arrives in a cloud of dust, and on it a soldier impatiently waits for his crossroad. Without waiting for the truck to slow down he jumps off, waves good-bye to the driver. He looks from side to side, mischievously like a little boy: are people around paying attention to the shiny orders and medals on his chest?[14]

Within the general disorder, there was a more organized way of coming home as well. Those who were released *en masse* in the context of demobilization of older age groups from the summer of 1945 travelled back in special trains (*eshelony*). The first left in early June.[15] In July newspapers reported about their arrival, the scenes at the stations full of women waiting for brothers, husbands, and fathers, and the reception by officials and representatives of local factories.[16] What was reported less frequently was the entire epic of travel and the mismanagement haunting soldiers on their way back home. On 10 August 1945, for example, the special train no. 45117 on its way to Tashkent was restructured at the train station Arys'. Ten cars with demobilized soldiers were forgotten as a result. They stood for twelve hours until a new locomotive was found. Hours were lost by other trains because of the lack of engines, or—if one could be found—a lack of oil to keep them greased. On 15 August 1945 special train number 45702-A stood for six hours without apparent reason at a train station. When it finally moved, it kept moving. It did not stop at a couple of stations where some demobilized soldiers were supposed to get off. Instead they ended up in Tashkent. It took another nine hours to find yet another train to take them back. 'Naturally,' noted the party comptroller for Uzbekistan in his report, 'this led to the expression of justified discontent on the side of demobilized and their families.' This was not a singular occurrence. In other special trains, too, veterans could see their home pass by on the train without a chance to get off.[17] Some of these were passenger trains, but most were much less comfortable.[18]

As a rule these special trains were made up of heated freight cars (*teplushki*):

> The bunk beds inside the train car were completely covered with German carpets, sometimes as big as the entire car. Grey smoke of Cuban cigars (for some reason there were plenty in Germany). Somebody always played falsely on German accordions—on 'Homers' and even expensive Italian makes. What dexterous folks: After two or three days (the way home was long) these people who never before in their life had held a musical instrument in their hands, whose hands had seemed to be for ever attached to machine guns, quite tolerably played [their favorite songs] ...

> This ghost-train drove at full speed away from the war and across the border of Europe, a border that did not yet belong to anybody and was not yet guarded. With its mad music this train frightened German and Polish villages on both sides of its historic march—the war on its way back.[19]

The locals might have been frightened by more than just the strange music coming out of these 'ghost trains'. Fuelled by the boredom of the long travel, and enhanced by the ready availability of guns and alcohol, violence broke out suddenly and with little warning. On 21 October 1945 the special train no. 45481 stopped at Kuznetsk station, in Kuibyshev region of the Ukraine. While the train was waiting for a new locomotive, a group of drunken officers and soldiers got off, threatened the station master with guns, and demanded that the train leave immediately. When they received the answer that this depended on the arrival of the locomotive, they started to insult the railway personnel and severely beat one of them. A small group of troops of the Commissariat of Internal Affairs (NKVD) which came to restore order arrested the commander of the train. This led to further violence. As the demobilized soldiers learnt of this arrest they assaulted the local garrison chief and the city NKVD boss with rifle butts. After that they proceeded to the office of the military commander of the city and freed their chief by force. Returning to the station they got into a gunfight with the NKVD troops, which left four dead and four wounded.[20]

On 27 October 1945 special train no. 445803s arrived with 968 demobilized soldiers at Medvedevo train station in Kalinin region. The train was accompanied by still serving soldiers of the 67th Guard Rifle Division. Three drunken men of this division, who were armed with machine guns, approached three independently travelling demobilized soldiers who were standing on the platform. They claimed to be a military patrol and ordered them to follow them to the military commander's office in the train station. The released soldiers refused. One of them, demobilized Lance-Corporal Gusev, was hit with the butt of an automatic rifle. Shots were fired. Gusev alerted a real patrol unit, which tried to re-establish order on the platform. It was attacked by the drunken pseudo–patrol. The patrol called for backup. The backup arrived and managed to disarm and arrest 'the drunken sergeant Voropaev'. When they took the automatic rifle from him a 'group of drunken demobilized Red Army men' tried to get hold of the weapon, an attempt which was frustrated by the patrol. At the same time, two other soldiers of the accompanying unit broke into the commander's office. An intervening patrol soldier was stabbed to death with a Finnish knife, while three others were wounded by automated rifle shots. In order to prevent similar occurrences in the future, the local NKVD increased security at train stations which special demobilization trains passed through. A local NKVD officer reported to Stalin's lieutenant Lavrentii Beriia about this problem and proposed to institutionalize similar steps in the rest of the country.[21]

The security organs were well advised to take the problem of violent returnees seriously. Even disabled veterans could cause serious disturbances. On 6 December 1945 a medical train with wounded and sick soldiers from Germany on their way to Novosibirsk, stopped at Kropachevo in the Southern Urals. The invalids left the train, broke into a shop in the nearby settlement, threw the salespeople out on the street, and stole 20 litres of vodka and 7,000 rubles. Then they returned to their waiting train which took off. In order to arrest the thieves, the railway militia, together with state security (NKGB) officers, and local army and NKVD troops waited at a later station. Twenty-two people were arrested. Under investigation, they confessed that before returning to the Soviet Union they had beaten up a Polish station master and raped his wife and daughter. A unit of the Polish army had tried to arrest the perpetrators, but the invalids fought back and travelled on. Once back in the USSR, they continued to behave as they had on foreign soil, committing up to thirty robberies and raping a nurse serving on the train.[22]

With the arrival of a special train at its final destination the travel was not over for most, who did not live near a rail line. Transport to the many villages and towns was seldom provided.[23] Sergeant-Major Gapon, for example, arrived at Lubny train station in Poltava region on 23 June 1945. Together with five other demobilized soldiers he tried to figure out how to make the final forty kilometres to their home village. They went to the local military conscription offices, to the local party and government institutions to ask for assistance. 'All refused to help and advised that each demobilized soldier organize his trip himself as well as he can and as well as he can afford. It took a long time to find transportation and then it cost 100 rubles for each of us to get home.'[24] The distance Gapon had to cover was within walking distance, comparatively speaking. In other regions, distances were greater. In Ivanovo province the transportation of demobilized soldiers to places located fifty to ninety kilometres from the railway line worked only in fits and starts.[25] In Komi Republic the majority of settlements were between 150 and 500 kilometers from the next railway line. The only available means of transportation were cars and horses, both in short supply, and there was a lack of gasoline in the republic as well. In the end, people had to walk, while the horses hauled their baggage.[26]

Those who returned to Iakutiia used river-boat traffic on the River Lena—until frost set in and navigation ceased. By early October the only way to get from Bol'shoi Never into Iakutiia was the 1,200 kilometres of the Amur-Iakutsk Magistrale. The agency which was responsible for the transportation of the demobilized soldiers over this stretch of the road had only twenty-five trucks, which were tied up in a task of high priority—transport for the gold industry. As a result the train station was crowded with released servicemen. About a hundred arrived every day. No food was organized for them and they had to make do with the three days of rations they had received. The supplies of warm clothing which had been prepared for the returnees turned out to be insufficient.[27] By late November, the situation had changed only slightly. Now the regional military administration had taken charge of transporting the arriving veterans from the train station to Iakutiia—or rather nearly there; they did not go further than the town of Aldana, 500 kilometres from the city of Iakutsk. The military administration refused to leave its own jurisdiction and provide transportation into a neighbouring military district.[28] By January 1946 the problem was still not solved. Despite clear orders from the People's Commissar of Defence to bring demobilized soldiers all the way to the city of Iakutsk, the local military authorities continued to transport them only as far as Aldana. To their annoyance, masses of demobilized soldiers were stuck in this town in the middle of winter.[29]

Similar problems occurred in Siberia. When the second wave of demo-bilized soldiers arrived in the city of Tiumen in late 1945, navigation on the frozen waterways had ceased. The local authorities encountered 'huge dif-ficulties' in trying to organize transportation to Tobol'sk and to the regions of the far north. The secretary of the regional party committee (obkom) sent a telegram to Moscow in order to secure an airlift.[30] After Malenkov's intervention the airlift started with local planes, but was hampered by bad weather and the limitations of the Tobol'sk airport which did not allow some of the larger planes to land. Nevertheless, by 15 November—two days after the secretary's telegram to Malenkov—eighty demobilized sol-diers had already been flown to Tobol'sk. Additional planes (two German Ju-52s) were sent from Alma-Ata to help with the airlift, especially to places with small airfields. Two Soviet S-47s waited for the River Ob to freeze over to be used to land.[31] The weather continued to ground the planes. By 4 December 600 demobilized soldiers were still stuck in Tiumen.[32]

Transportation problems were not confined to the so-called 'provinces'. The final leg from one of the Moscow train stations to a village in Moscow region posed a problem as well, even if no airlifts were necessary here:

> I was demobilised and came to Moscow. From there I had to go by bus some way and then walk several kilometers to reach my place. There is a metro station there now but at that time there were cherry orchards and deep ravines. One of them was really big and I had to cross it. It was already dark when I reached the place.... As luck would have it, a lorry came passing by and I decided to ask for a hike.
>
> The lorry stopped.
>
> 'Where to?'
>
> 'Dyakovskoye,' I said.

'Me too,' the lad laughed.

I climbed into the driver's cab, he put my suitcase in the back and we set off.

He took in my uniform and decorations and asked:

'How many Germans have you killed?'

'Seventy-five.'[33]

As the suitcase of this accomplished female warrior suggests, the existing problems of transportation were increased by many veterans returning with more than war stories. Often, the odd suitcase was not enough to carry all the loot, especially when coming back from Germany or Austria. This was officially encouraged: Initially, demobilized soldiers and repatriated citizens were subjected to customs controls. As a reaction, they sold their trophies before crossing the frontier, on Polish soil. A report to Stalin on 10 July 1945 stressed that this state of affairs only benefited 'speculators of Polish border towns'.[34] By the time Stalin received this information, the controls had already been discontinued. A resolution of 14 June 1945 freed demobilized soldiers from customs controls, a rule which was in effect at least until 1949.[35] As a result, lots of 'trophy goods' made their way into the Soviet Union. An investigation by a local party plenipotentiary found watches, motorcycles, pianos, radios, furniture, paintings, cloth, things made of gold, and 'other property'.[36]

On 16 September 1945 special demobilization train no. 45780 from Vienna arrived in Uzbekistan. Many of the travellers had a lot of luggage, so much indeed that no more than eight or ten of them could be packed together with their belongings on the back of a five-ton truck. One demobilized veterinarian's luggage weighed 'not less than 60 pood'—983 kilograms. On the same day another special train arrived. One of the demobilized soldiers had both arms full of gold watches, in addition to a 'large number of suitcases and bags'. When asked why he was wearing all these watches he said: 'It is more secure to have them on the arms. The suitcases might get stolen.'[37]

Theft was not the only way in which trophy goods disappeared during the prolonged travel home. Somebody might kick suitcases from an overcrowded train-car in order to make space for a comrade.[38] The travelling soldiers' needs also had to be met in some way.

I ... had a small accordion, I don't remember where it came from. It was always in my way ... So in Warsaw the little accordion was sold for a couple of bottles of Polish moonshine ... and several packs—about a hundred—of 'Pani' cigarettes. That's how my only possibility to join the world of music burned and went up in smoke.[39]

In 1945 a Western journalist reported on the habit of Red Army soldiers in the West of exchanging trophies for alcohol: 'one Russian major offered us a motor-cycle in exchange for two litres of cognac'.[40]

After the return, trophy goods had to be exchanged for the necessities of civilian life, such as clothes. The markets of Tashkent were full of 'foreign things' in 1945, as were those of Moscow.[41] Sometimes, local authorities confiscated trophy goods. Such incidents of (illegal) mass searches of demobilized soldiers and the seizure of 'various things and objects, which belong to them personally', were reported in September 1945 from Kazakhstan.[42]

Not everybody came back with booty, though. The majority of the army did not see Germany or Austria, which would have given soldiers the possibility to acquire 'trophies' in the first place. By the end of the war the armed forces counted 12.8 million.[43] Clearly, not all of them made it to the West. Even if we imagine that all army personnel crowded into Germany and Austria at the end of the war, or that the entire army circled through the zones of occupation, these would still only be about half of the total number of war participants. In reality, the share must have been much lower, possibly closer to 10 per cent.[44] And while Eastern Poland (one of the poorest regions of Europe at the time) seemed like a land of material plenty to Red Army soldiers in 1939,[45] it was the huge difference in material wealth between the Soviet Union and Germany or Austria, combined with the hatred towards the enemy and the leniency of the authorities towards plunder (and sometimes their cooperation), which led to the massive 'requisitioning' of goods there.[46]

Being at the right spot at the right time, then, was one of the factors which determined whether or not a veteran could bring home 'trophies'. A second factor was access to means of transportation. The goods, after all, needed to be brought east. Smaller items could be sent by regular field-post mail. Once a month, soldiers and non-commissioned officers (*serzhanty*) could send home free of charge a parcel of up to 5 kilograms. Officers and generals received larger weight allowances.[47] Military authorities handed out special coupons for parcels home—and a lively trade in these developed within military units. As a result, some wives of frontline soldiers received 'a large quantity of valuable parcels'. One wife of a *frontovik* received thirty-two parcels in 1945. Among the things her husband sent from the West were four radios and two accordions. Other wives received up to forty-three parcels in 1945. One reportedly made 250,000 rubles—a huge amount—by selling what she had received in twenty-one parcels.[48] The problem with this way of transportation of trophy goods, however, was twofold. Only relatively small items could be shipped. Bikes and motorbikes, for example, were by their size excluded from such attempts. Such parcels did not always arrive unopened and complete. Postal workers made sure that they got their fair share of the loot.[49]

What was needed, then, was access to means of transportation. And this access largely coincided with rank. Privates could carry the suits, presents for their loved ones, or harmonicas themselves. But what about bicycles or motorbikes? 'Thousands of bicycles and motorbikes—try to transport them across Europe. After all, the special demobilization trains consisted of goods cars—[each had space for] forty people or eight horses.' Officers and generals, by contrast, found 'more cunning ways' to bring their bikes and motorbikes home.[50] On 9 June 1945 the state regulated what would be tolerated: generals were allowed to acquire a car, a piano or grand piano, a radio set, a hunting rifle, and a watch. Officers of the field army could send home free of charge one motorcycle or bicycle. Both officers and generals were also allowed to buy ('in the amounts necessary') carpets, tapestries, furs, dishes, and other consumption goods.[51] The limits imposed were frequently ignored. The habit of high-ranking officers and generals of carting large amounts of goods out of Germany was used by Stalin and his henchmen to slap down the generals once the war was over. In 1947 Marshall Zhukov himself was accused of pillage and looting in Germany.[52]

Such accusations against the high brass were not without basis in reality. In 1945 one regimental commander had all 'trophy goods' and foodstuffs confiscated from his subordinates—only to take a portion for himself. He also illegally 'requisitioned' a car, which he subsequently sold for 15,000 rubles. A general-major had his subordinates steal things for him in Germany, which he then sent by train to his family in Moscow: 1,700 metres of diverse cloth, 'a lot of leather', paintings, furniture, sugar, and half a kilogram of gold. While during the war generals rarely got into disciplinary action within the party, between the end of the war and 1946 eighty-five generals were sanctioned, twenty of them were excluded from the party. Three reasons were behind these disciplinary proceedings: 'unworthy behaviour in everyday life' (i.e. drunkenness and sex-scandals), abuse of their power position for personal gain, and 'illegal acquisition of trophy goods'.[53] It was not an accident that it was a captain and not a rank and file army man who managed to find space in the special train from Berlin for a grand piano, upholstered furniture, paintings, dishes, as well as 'female adornments and other things'.[54] Defector Peter Pirogov reported in 1950 how the political commissar of his regiment had used a plane to bring 'all kinds of female trash' to his wife in 1945.[55]

Most likely, then, those who refused to work in 1945 because they had brought back 'enough to live for one to twenty years' were officers rather than rank and file soldiers.[56] The majority of veterans must have experienced the material side of victory like the *frontovik* and later song-writer Mikhail Tanich: 'grey coats/rosy dreams/was all we managed/to bring back from the war'.[57] Some returned from Germany with nothing more than an old military coat—if they found looting distasteful or if they did not want to touch anything which had belonged to the hated enemy.[58]

However little the 'average veteran' brought back, these few things were quite prized in an economy of extreme scarcity which had suffered some of the worst destruction of the Second World War. The authorities announced that more benefits would follow. Demobilization was embedded into a major agitation effort on the part of the party and the state, which tried to counter one of the implications of the trophy goods phenomenon—that life outside of the Soviet Union was materially better than within the land of Socialism. The authorities worried that such experiences could breed political discontent. At times, they even feared the birth of a new liberation movement similar to the Decembrists—officers who had rebelled against the Tsar in 1825 and 1826, after Napoleon's disastrous Russian campaign of 1812 and the following fall of Paris to the united Russian and Prussian armies in 1814.

> After the war of 1812 our soldiers, who had seen French life, compared it with the backwardness of life in tsarist Russia. At that time the influence of French life was progressive, because it gave Russian people the possibility to see the cultural backwardness of Russia, the tsarist oppression, and so on. This was the basis of the conclusion of the Decembrists regarding the necessity of the fight with tsarist injustice (*proizvol*). But now the situation is different. It is possible that an estate in Eastern Prussia is richer than the one or other kolkhoz. And from there a backward individual makes a judgment regarding estate economy as compared with Socialist forms of economic organization

(*khoziaistvo*). This is already a regressive influence. Therefore one has to fight such moods without mercy.[59]

One way to fight such 'moods' was to hammer home again and again that the Soviet Union, supposedly unlike its capitalist former allies, cared for veterans. 'Only in our socialist country is such care for demobilized warriors possible. This attentive, sensitive relation to the defenders of the Homeland is a result of the character of our Soviet social structure (*obshchestvennyi stroi*), of the policies of the Soviet government as a truly popular government.' Under capitalism things were different. There, 'the transition from war to peace leads to a slump in the level of production, the closing of enterprises and the rise of unemployment. In capitalist countries demobilized soldiers enter the army of millions of unemployed.'[60]

In the Soviet Union, by contrast, veterans were to be reintegrated into productive life within a month of their return. Their job was supposed to take into account 'the experience and profession (*spetsial'nost'*) acquired in the army', and had to be on the same level or higher than the work before army service. By law, demobilized soldiers also received some celebrated but actually quite limited benefits, such as a uniform (but no civilian clothes) and a pair of shoes, transport home paid by the state, food during their journey, and a lump sum depending on rank and length of service. Republican and regional governments as well as the heads of enterprises, institutions, and organizations in city districts were supposed to supply returning veterans with both housing and heating fuel. Rural government and kolkhoz administrations were told to provide 'utmost help' to demobilized peasants who returned to the village. They were to be set up to work and should get material assistance in re-establishing their household. In regions which had been under German occupation, demobilized soldiers who had to repair or rebuild their dwellings were supposed to get wood free of charge and loans for the work.[61]

The propaganda machine made sure that the meagre benefits of the demobilization law were published again and again, and reinforced by the agitation network.[62] These benefits were celebrated as an expression of 'how highly our people values the warrior-victors'. The people, like Soviet power in general, were said to relate to the homecoming heroes with 'fatherly, Stalinist love' (*otecheskaia, stalinskaia liubov'*). There was 'no other country in the world, where state legislation is imbued with such care about service-personnel and their families'. The returning defender of the Homeland was declared 'the most honourable person in the Soviet country. He defended our free, happy life, and he deserves the gratitude and respect of the whole people.'[63]

On the basis of this propaganda, veterans could thus expect privileged treatment after their return. This special status, however, did not come without duties. Many veterans imagined a reciprocal relationship between their wartime sacrifice for the community and privileged treatment by the community thereafter. Official discourse during demobilization also implied that a special status had been earned—a status which bound the veterans to be model citizens. As such, they would not rest on their laurels, but would get back to work, rebuild the villages, cities, and the economy. In public rituals the new position of veterans in Soviet society was directly linked to continued service to the state: 'to the fatherly care for them by the whole Soviet people, the Soviet government and personally by comrade Stalin, every demobilized soldier answers with heroic deeds (*podvigi*) in labour, with selfless work in industry, agriculture, and transport'.[64]

Official discourse treated demobilization benefits both as a reward for the frontline service rendered during the war, and as a gift veterans had to repay by renewed service.[65] The latter part needed to be laboured, as veterans often did not listen. Consequently, the central task (*glavnaia zadacha*) of agitators was to ensure that 'the glorious soldiers carry the high calling of a citizen of the Soviet Union during peaceful and creative work with the same dignity as they have done during the battles at the frontline, in order to increase the honour and the might of their Homeland'. On whatever job the soldier ended up, 'he' was 'obliged to be a model of selflessness, organization and discipline'; he was expected 'to work well himself and to inspire others to heroic deeds in labor (*trudovye podvigi*)'. As if that was not asking enough of soldiers exhausted from a long and brutal war, they were also expected to organize circles for military education in order to ensure the production of new generations of 'defenders of the Homeland'.[66] On top of this the veteran was meant to be 'a faithful helper of the local organs of Soviet power and a passionate propagandist of the ideas of the party of Lenin-Stalin'.[67] Exemplary old soldiers were celebrated in the press and by agitators as role models. These *Über*-veterans returned to civilian life and immediately started to fulfil and over-fulfil the plan, to agitate and organize their community for the rebuilding of Socialism.[68] In conformity with this general line of an immediate return to work, the 'central task' for local authorities was said to be the work-placement of the former *frontoviki*, which was to take into account the qualifications acquired in the army.[69]

The propaganda effort surrounding demobilization thus transmitted a decidedly mixed message. On the one hand it acknowledged that veterans had a right to expect material and symbolic benefits from their wartime service for the community; on the other hand, they were not supposed to express any feeling of special status or entitlement to special treatment. In a famous speech to women soldiers the chairman of the Presidium of the Supreme Soviet Mikhail Kalinin made this point very clear: 'don't give yourself airs ... Don't talk about your merits, but let people talk about you—that's better.'[70] Men were warned against arrogance or insistence on entitlements, too. Independent of gender, veterans were admonished to be modest. Yes, they could expect good treatment, but they were not to insist on it:

> The soldier-victor who returns form the front does not need to worry about tomorrow.... With open arms and embraces, the workers of the Soviet home front welcome the hero of yesterday's battles into their harmonious family. It is only important that the hero himself behaves in a manner befitting a real hero: with dignity but without arrogance, without unnecessary vanity, free and easy, but with the decorum befitting a ward (*vospitannik*) of the Red Army. That, too, has to be explained now to every single [soldier] who gets demobilized from the army.[71]

The official interpretation of veterans' status and demobilization benefits was supposed to be inescapable. The returning soldiers were to be completely surrounded by this discourse and agitation was to accompany the returning veteran during the entire process of demobilization. Ideally, agitators and officers talked to soldiers individually while they were still in their units. Such talks were to focus on 'their new tasks (*zadachi*), on the preservation of [our] fighting traditions [i.e. a heroic rendering of the history of their unit], about exemplary labour for the good of the people'. In addition, the soldiers were offered lectures on topics such as 'Care of the Soviet government and the Bolshevik party for the soldiers of the Red Army'; 'Help and privileges (*l'goty*) for demobilized soldiers'; 'Always remember the traditions of your regiment'; 'What awaits you at home'. Veterans returning to the village were to get additional training in party resolutions about agricultural work. Following such preparation, they were sent on their way. After a farewell ceremony the released soldiers were to be accompanied by agitators and party organizers on their special train back home. This train was supposed to be 'festively decorated' (*prazdnichno ukrasheny*) and, if possible, equipped with radios in every car.[72] Along the way, agitation was to be conducted at train stations, based on 'agitation points' (*agitpunkty*).[73] The arrival of the train was again marked by a ceremony and festivities, followed by individual consultations about the rights and duties of demobilized soldiers and the possibility (and necessity!) of finding work.[74]

In the chaos and messiness of real Soviet life, however, propaganda and agitation were far less ubiquitous than the reports of propagandists or the newspaper reporting about these efforts would make one believe. Returning soldiers by no means constantly immersed themselves in official discourse. Newspapers were prized, to be sure. Toilet paper was one commodity the Soviet economy was renowned for not producing in sufficient quantities. Cigarette paper was another. Propaganda materials could substitute for both. Asking if the soldiers under his care had already read the newspaper, one agitator got the reply: 'There was one, but we smoked it already (*Byla odna, da skurili*).'[75]

Before using the paper in such profane ways, demobilized soldiers managed to learn what they needed to know from it, even if this was not always what the propaganda machine wanted them to internalize. Veterans were especially eager to absorb the promises of special treatment and understand the rules involved in receiving them. Party agitators were asked frequently about the technicalities involved in replacing lost military decorations, which conferred not only status, but also material and financial benefits. The agitators, in turn, wrote to journals published for their orientation, and the journals replied.[76] They also answered questions about how soldiers were to be taken care of once they returned to their home village, town, or city:

> I held my first talk [as an agitator] in Eastern Prussia, after victory over Hitlerite Germany, as the soldiers of the older age-groups started to leave with demobilization. From our group four people left. I told them about the privileges (*l'goty*) for demobilized, explained, with what care our government surrounds the defenders of the Homeland.[77]

Veterans listened when they were told by agitators, their officers, or the newspapers that they had a right to expect special treatment. In dialogue with each other—and there was a lot of time to talk during the prolonged travel home—they tended to inflate these privileges far beyond what the state was actually willing and able to provide. These conversations proved crucial in the development of the strong feeling of entitlement veterans shared even after they had split up to re-enter civilian life—a sentiment forming the deepest level of commonality among veterans. It had been forged during the war and was now reinforced, as official discourse during demobilization used these feelings to appease a potentially troublesome group.

As so often in Soviet history, the logistics of demobilization of the wartime army were insufficiently worked out, and the infrastructure not extensive enough to cope with such an enormous population movement (which happened in the context of other dislocations, such as repatriation and re-evacuation). Amid the general chaos, improvisation, and crisis management, however, the authorities largely stayed in control. The security organs kept the lid on the boiling pot, moving in to mop up any overflowing violence where it did occur. The propaganda apparatus also made sure that, as long as they were together as a group (and still partially armed), the former soldiers' expectation for special treatment was met, at least on a symbolic level. The constant reiteration that 'no other country in the world cares for the defenders of the Homeland' as Stalin's Soviet Union, the playing up of the rather meagre provisions of the demobilization law, the bombastic receptions of the first groups of veterans and their celebration in the newspapers—all this created the impression that a special status had been gained by the wartime sacrifice and heroism of the frontline soldiers. The provisions to allow soldiers to send trophy goods home and to bring them in person as well added some actual material benefits to these symbolic gestures, benefits, to be sure, which did not cost the state anything. One needed a good ear to hear the second line over the thunder of the victory salutes: 'do not rest on your laurels! Get back to work!' The official line became less ambiguous once—by 1948—the regime had survived demobilization without major interruptions of the political order. Now the 'do not rest on your laurels' message became dominant. During demobilization the admonishment not to mention the rendered services was still supplemented by promises for special treatment—promises most veterans took quite seriously.

# 2

# Welcome to Normalcy

The expectations raised during and immediately after the war were bound to be disappointed.[1] Some of them were impossible to realize under the best of circumstances, such as daydreams about life after the war as a continuing feast. Fantasies of boundless abundance could be projected to the inaccessible 'countries abroad', where some maintained work was restricted to three months a year while still supporting a lavish lifestyle.[2] They could not, however, be satisfied in reality—on neither side of that border soon to be known as the 'iron curtain'. Less unrealistically, many expected the unloved kolkhoz regime to go as a reward for the peasants' service to the regime.[3] Such a change (in principle as possible and imaginable as a legalization of the black market) would have amounted to dismantling one of the pillars of Stalinism—exploitation of the peasant majority for the good of industrialization. And while there were discussions about economic reform behind the scenes, the lesson that Stalin had learnt during the war was what he had known all along: that his revolution from above had been historically necessary. Predictably, then, the loosening of the collective farm regime during the war was quickly reversed, and most of the small economic and cultural freedoms of wartime rolled back.[4] In effect, Stalin and his regime attempted to restore 'the Soviet order to the template he had more or less imposed before Operation Barbarossa'.[5] This had far-reaching consequences, not only for veterans, but for Soviet citizens in general, who had to return to 'normal Stalinism'—an everyday life experienced as abnormal by most; a normalcy dominated by a malfunctioning but unavoidable bureaucratic apparatus.[6]

Under such conditions, even the least utopian expectations turned out to be rosy dreams for most—assistance during the difficult process of readjusting to civilian life and a special status after the war. Simply put, the benefits promised during demobilization could not be delivered.

There were not enough resources devoted to the task; there were many, far too many veterans with a claim to them; the administrative apparatus was too dysfunctional, understaffed, and overburdened to deliver welfare to millions; and rebuilding of the desolated country took precedence. The economic situation was bad, to say the least, even in comparison with the rest of postwar Europe. A famine in 1946–7 further worsened living standards, and the regime quickly focused on the developing global conflict with the United States, and thus preparation for a possible new war.[7]

To be sure, the same regime continued to celebrate its help to veterans throughout the years of mass-demobilization (1945–8) and it did deliver some assistance. The figures cited in both published and archival sources in this period sometimes look impressive at first glance. However, a comparison of data on material help with demobilization statistics in four regions for which both sets of numbers are available for roughly the same time period demonstrates how miserable this aid really was (Table 2.1). In the autonomous republic of Bashkiria the demobilized received on average 1 ruble, 2 kilograms of bread, a tiny piece (one centimetre long) of cloth, and no heating fuel. Only one demobilized person in a thousand received a head of cattle, twelve in a thousand a pair of shoes, and six in a thousand one piece of clothing. Moreover, such averages hide an extremely uneven distribution of benefits—some received much more than the statistical middle, many others nothing at all. In order to receive financial aid or help in kind, veterans had to convince the authorities in charge that their privileges were more important than those of hundreds or even thousands of their peers. Anybody who did not want to end up empty-handed needed to actively and aggressively seek assistance, employing two well-established practices: public letter writing and personal petitioning.[8]

Veterans and their families were among the most active citizens launching complaints on a local level—81 per cent of all supplication and complaint letters received by the welfare administration of Sverdlovsk region in 1944 came from war invalids.[9] During a review of 481 organizations in Kazakhstan during the third quarter of 1945, the procuracy found that 2,691 complaints had been filed. Among them 60 per cent came from families of serving soldiers, 31 per cent from war invalids, and 8 per cent from the demobilized.[10] The quest to receive assistance in the rebuilding of a civilian existence usually started on the local level, but veterans frequently had to get higher level authorities involved if they wanted to get things

Table 2.1. Material help to demobilized in context

| Region | Demobilization | | Material help (average per person) | | | | | | | | |
| --- | --- | --- | --- | --- | --- | --- | --- | --- | --- | --- | --- |
| | reporting period | no. of soldiers | money (rubles) | bread (kg) | cattle (heads) | shoes (pair) | clothes (pieces) | linen/cotton textiles (cm) | linen/cotton textiles (pieces) | Fuel (kg) |
| Stalinskaia obl. | 1945–1946 | 105,246 | 17 | – | 0.018 | 0.240 | 0.452 | 200 | – | 694 |
| Zaporozhsk. obl. | Aug. 1945–Aug. 1946 | 62,891 | – | – | 0.012 | – | – | – | – | – |
| Bashkirskaia ASSR | Aug. 1945–Aug. 1946 | 90,151 | 1 | 2 | 0.001 | 0.012 | 0.006 | 1 | – | – |
| Kemerovsk. obl. | 1945–1946 | 52,047 | – | 3 | 0.007 | 0.007 | 0.239 | 100 | 0.172 | – |

*Sources for raw data*: RGASPI f. 17, op. 88, d. 699, l. 6 (material help); V. N. Donchenko, 'Demobilizatsiia sovetskoi armii i reshenie problem kadrov v pervye poslevoennye gody', *Istoriia SSSR* 3 (May–June 1970), 99 (demobilization numbers). The average for Stalin. and Kemerov. oblasts are lower limiting cases, because the demobilization numbers include the second half of 1946, while the numbers for material help do not.

moving. Consider the seemingly simple problem of family reunification. One soldier was about to be demobilized, but his wife, who had been evacuated in 1941, was not allowed to return home, because Odessa was a restricted access city. Together with his commander this man wrote letters to the city soviet, asking for his wife to be allowed back. The answer was negative. He asked other local state actors for assistance: 'I appealed for help: in the executive committee of the province, in the party committee of the province, in the party committee of the city, in the provincial military state prosecutor's office, but nobody wants to listen. [They are] soulless people (*bezdushnie liudi*).' Having accomplished nothing on the local level, he appealed in a letter to the State Prosecutor of the Soviet Union.[11] He had finally found the right address. The procuracy reacted, forwarded the letter back to Odessa, and by September 1945 the city soviet had issued the necessary documents to allow the family to be reunited in the city.[12]

Another veteran, a war invalid from Stalin province, described his own march through the institutions (the metaphor can be taken quite literally):

> I came home and up to this day I live in very bad circumstances, I go every day to the executive committee of Budennovskii district, to the procuracy of Budennovskii district, to the party committee of Budennovskii district, I regularly appear at the militia station, in the city executive committee and nowhere can I obtain justice (*dobit'sia pravdu*), that they give me and my family an apartment ... at the front I lived alone in wet trenches, but at home I live with my family under the open sky.[13]

Because local structures were frequently overburdened, veterans had to queue for days on end only to be told that they were in the wrong institution, needed other papers, or should come back a week later. In Cheboksary, the capital of the Chuvash autonomous republic, supplicants not infrequently waited in the city housing administration for the whole morning (reception hours were 9 to 12) for the head of the operation to show up.[14] In Suma province in Ukraine officers sat in the waiting room while the chairman of the city soviet used his office hours to get a haircut and shave.[15] In the housing administration of the city of Baku the reception of demobilized veterans who came for help in housing questions was not organized at all. To their great annoyance veterans stood in the halls of the administration for days on end without receiving any reaction to their applications.[16] In Kalinin province no waiting rooms were provided in the

executive committees of local soviets, and supplicants stood for hours in the
corridors. On 22 March 1946 demobilized soldier Zuev started to queue to
see the chairman of the executive committee of Central district at 9 a.m.,
and was admitted only in the afternoon. This was comparatively good.
Demobilized Voskoboinikova tried to be seen in the regional procuracy,
where no admission times were posted. On 26 March she waited for seven
hours, followed by three hours the next day. The report does not mention
if she gave up or was finally admitted.[17] Invalids who depended on pensions
from the city welfare administration of Kizlovodsk had to be ready to
write two or three times if they had a complaint, and then they did not
always receive an answer.[18] One demobilized soldier, a kolkhoz peasant
from Kalinin province, desperately needed help to feed his family including
two children and a sick wife. He appealed three times in one month to the
local soviet but failed to get a reaction.[19]

Given the destruction of the country, housing was a priority for many.
If their homes had not been flattened during the war, they were often in
severe disrepair. To make them inhabitable again might involve years of
persistent and stubborn activity. One demobilized citizen, V. S. Tsatskin of
Moscow, had to nag authorities for three years until finally an intervention
from the office of the Chairman of the Supreme Soviet got things moving
in 1948. He frequently wrote to Moscow City Council, which forwarded
his letters to the Moscow housing administration. He appealed five times
to the housing administration, at least once to the procuracy of his district
in Moscow, wrote three times to the local newspaper *Moskovskii bolshevik*,
and had four commissions review his housing situation (all of which
decided that repairs were to be done 'immediately'). During his three-year
campaign he collected 'more than ten' decrees of the district housing
administration about the immediate repair of his apartment, without ever
seeing a repairman.[20]

Others had to fight long bureaucratic battles to have the documents
necessary to receive an invalid's pension sent from one employer to the
next if they returned home after release from labour mobilization.[21] A
letter could also travel from the regional executive committee, to city
executive committee, to district administration, where it finally landed in
the archive, because the veteran had meanwhile moved elsewhere. Other
veterans became victims of overworked bureaucrats. One war invalid wrote
a letter of complaint to the district welfare administration. His kolkhoz
chairman had mobilized him to go logging. He had refused to go because

he was physically incapable of hard labour, a group II invalid (who by law were not required to work). In response the chairman had taken away his right to receive bread. The veteran tried to get help by appealing to the local welfare organs, but the inspector in charge of answering his letter had settled into writing one answer to all the requests for help: 'Comrade Krylov, with regard to your application the district welfare administration declares that your request will be honoured at the first possibility.' And, of course, applications got lost altogether.[22]

The frustrations over this process finally led veterans to Moscow, where they crowded the waiting rooms of various institutions. First, however, they tended to resort to letter writing. Veterans sent supplications and complaints to all levels of the administrative and party hierarchy. The archival holdings of the Supreme Soviet alone include thousands of letters from demobilized soldiers. The office which was supposed to deal not only with supplicants who showed up in person but also with incoming letters nearly drowned in this flood of paper. Another important address for complaints was the central newspapers. In August and September 1945 *Izvestiia*, for example, received many letters of complaint from demobilized soldiers. The authors usually had already unsuccessfully appealed to the district soviets, the district housing administration, or their city soviet.[23]

The results of all these efforts were highly contingent. Professional con men, who exploited the availability of benefits to war veterans immediately after the war, show what could be possible. One of the most intriguing tricksters we know of was Veniamin Borukhovich Vaisman. His example provides an extreme case of what supplications could achieve, if executed skilfully.[24] Originally a thief, Veniamin Borukhovich turned to conmanship in 1946 after a professional injury had ended his career (he lost both legs and a hand from frostbite as he tried to escape from labour camp). Instead of making a living in the provinces like most of his colleagues, he worked in the centre until he was arrested in 1947. Equipped with an attestation claiming the status of a double Hero of the Soviet Union, seven orders, and three medals, he went directly to the offices of central agencies and sought help. He was amazingly successful:

> He almost always managed to get in to see the minister or a deputy minister, no mean feat in itself, and persuaded them to contribute tens of thousands of rubles and similar values in goods. A total of 27 ministries succumbed

to Vaisman's wiles, and his victims included a whole raft of top Soviet administrators, among them I. T. Tevosian (minister of ferrous metallurgy), V. M. Malyshev (minister of transport machinery), and A. G. Zverev (finance minister).[25]

From these sources he obtained money, clothes (including a 'dark blue American suit'), shoes, cloth, and other manufactured goods. He also obtained an apartment in Kiev, a plane ticket to get there, and the necessary furniture for his new home.[26]

Fake or otherwise, some veterans were thus very successful in their quest for state assistance, while others were not at all. As Table 2.1 shows, the supply of 'soft money' and 'soft goods' available after the war for the express use of veterans was absolutely insufficient on a per capita basis. There was a clear hierarchy of who would receive what slice of the pie. Demobilized soldiers got more money per head than the average supplicant and the highly decorated got more than normal soldiers. War invalids got very small sums on average, probably because there were so many of them.[27] The effect of an appeal also depended on the social skills of the supplicant, the whims of Soviet administrators, the rumblings of the bureaucratic machine, and the decision of a case worker that a certain letter was worth to be given to the bigwig in charge. Most correspondence to the highest authorities was simply sent back to the localities with the instruction to deal with the problem. Only if the higher level workers decided that a problem was worth following up did they audit (kontrol) further developments. In such cases veterans might get what they had a right to. The war invalid V. N. Nikitin from Sverdlovsk had the following experience. When in 1946 he left the hospital and travelled back home, his army pay book with the sum of 7,180 rubles and 82 kopeks was stolen in Moscow. He immediately informed the administration of the State Bank in charge of military pay about the loss. Gosbank told him that his deposit would be renewed within six months. 'I wrote several letters but did not get a definite answer, they all drag their feet (vse tianut).' In December 1946 he went to Moscow in order to resolve the problem. He was now told that he would get his money in March of the following year. By April he had still not received anything. He wrote another letter to Gosbank and received a disquieting answer: 'Account closed, money received, we are trying to find out who received it.' At this point Nikitin decided that he needed help from higher up in order to get this straightened out. He wrote to the Chairman of the Presidium of the Supreme Soviet. The

officials there found his matter worthy of attention and contacted the
military procuracy. This finally got things moving and Nikitin received his
money.[28]

On some occasions, privileges could be pushed through with the support of central actors, even if their resolution was far from pragmatic and
bordering on the absurd. Such was the affair of Iakov Nikitich Ozerov,
which created quite a headache for the Moscow education administration
(*Mosgorono*) in the spring of 1946.[29] On 23 June 1941, Ozerov had volunteered to fight in the Red Army and a volunteer had a right to get his
prewar job back—exactly the same job, not just a job at the same or a
higher level, as was the case for other demobilized soldiers.[30] Ozerov seems
to have been intent to have this privilege applied no matter what. Before
the war, he had been the director of the fourth school for sick children
(*ozdorovitel'naia shkola*) of Mosgorono. This institution, like others of its
kind, was closed during the war and the building used by military units.
Upon his return from the army, Mosgorono invited Ozerov to resume his
post as a school director. 'In the interest of the cause', as the boss of the
administration Orlov put it, he was asked to direct school no. 8, which
was reopening, instead of school no. 4, which was still closed. Mosgorono
issued the necessary order to appoint Ozerov.

However, the veteran was not content. After all, he had a right to
*the same* job, not a similar one. He did not show up at work and thus
delayed the opening of this school, much to the annoyance of the education
administrators and to the detriment of sick schoolchildren of the Moscow
region. He ignored pleas by the administrator to accept the appointment.
Instead, he wrote a letter of complaint to the state prosecutor.[31] Surprisingly,
the latter did not endorse the completely pragmatic argument of the
education administration that there was no school no. 4 and that Ozerov
should accept the similar position in school no. 8. In a letter to the deputy
Commissar of Enlightenment of the Russian Federation, the procuracy
pointed out that the law was clearly on Ozerov's side, and should be
enforced: 'Please give categorical instructions to the head of Mosgorono
comrade Orlov about the reinstatement of Ozerov in his former position.'[32]
This settled matters. Ozerov was appointed director of school no. 4, which
presumably had to be reopened exactly for that purpose.[33]

Even if a veteran managed to get the support of higher level authorities
involved, every supplication, application for help, or letter of complaint
remained an open-ended game. Local authorities could decide that there

were no resources available,[34] that the veteran in question did not, in fact, need any assistance,[35] or that the complaint was not merited.[36] Local authorities simply did not have enough resources to adhere to every veteran's privileges or entitlements. That there were too many of them to help them all was a sentence veterans heard frequently.[37] On any level of the bureaucratic hierarchy, the support of those higher up would not necessarily ensure that resources were actually available. In June 1945, for example, the war invalid Doktorov wrote a supplication letter to the chairman of the executive committee of the city council of Cheboksary. He needed housing. The chairman agreed and noted on the letter 'comrade Dmitriev! The request is to be complied with.' The head of the city communal affairs department (*gorkomkhoz*) Dmitriev also approved the request and scribbled a note to the head of the city housing administration: 'Comrade Abramochkin! Add to the list.' However, comrade Abramochkin demurred. Knowing the housing situation, he added a final resolution to the letter: 'Request denied because of the absence of an apartment.'[38]

Another annoyance was getting help, but the wrong things. A war invalid could, for example, ask the local welfare administration for a pair of trousers and a coat and receive a skirt and a woman's overcoat instead, while one of his peers asked for clothes for his wife and received trousers.[39] The understanding of the local bureaucrats was that if the needed item was not available, another item allowed exchange at the flea market.[40] Other help was in principle provided, but in fact inaccessible. After long bureaucratic hassles, for example, the war invalid I. A. Polovikin of Kostroma province finally received wood to fuel his stove—which he would have needed to pick up twenty kilometers outside of the city and transport was not provided.[41]

The resolution of problems could also be blocked because there were competing parties in the scramble for scarce resources, who would not give up their own claims. The most frequent conflicts of this kind were about housing. The vast majority (73 per cent) of the complaints which demobilized filed with the procuracy of Moscow region in July and the first half of August 1945 were about this problem. Many veterans attempted to get tenants thrown out of the rooms or apartments that they had inhabited before the war, and to whose return they had a legal right.[42] While as a rule the eviction process worked to the advantage of veterans, there were cases when they had to fight for years for their housing. Such cases occurred if the apartment or room which the veteran had inhabited before the war was occupied either by an individual with competing legal rights, with superior connections, or by an institution which could claim to be more important than an individual veteran.

On 28 June 1945 the Council of People's Commissars of the Soviet Union allowed its Ukrainian counterpart to make an exception to the rule that returning soldiers should get their housing back. If their homes were occupied by the top reaches of the Soviet intelligentsia they would not regain their prewar apartments. Instead, they should get, 'if possible', different housing space in Kiev or in the cities of L'vov or Chernovitsy.[43] Similar status clashes occurred when a veteran's prewar housing was occupied by a prominent Red Army commander.[44]

While in cases such as these veterans lost out in the official and legally institutionalized hierarchy of distribution, in the second category of cases they lost out in the *de facto* hierarchy created by the realities of power, not the constructions of law. One example is the case of Major L. L. Turkiia, who, in order to get his housing back, had to fight against a boss of the Commissariat of Internal Affairs (NKVD)—part of Stalin's powerful security forces. Turkiia, a medical doctor, was drafted to the front and his wife went as a volunteer. Under current legislation their home—a private house (*sobstvennyi dom*) with three rooms and a kitchen, which they owned in Sukhumi—should have been protected and returned to them no matter how it was used during the war. They left the house under the care of one of their relatives, who rented one room, while the others, with the personal belongings of the family Turkiia, were locked up. Soon the acting chairman of the city executive committee, a comrade Gokhokidze, searching for ever scarce living space for the deputy of the People's Commissar of the NKVD of Abkhaziia, comrade Enukidze, evicted the person looking after the house, broke open the closed rooms, and threw out the personal property which relatives of the owners could only partly cart away. Turkiia's relatives were threatened with 'repression' if they wrote about this to the major.

When they finally informed him nevertheless, Turkiia in October 1944 wrote a letter to a military state prosecutor who started the process of evicting the illegal tenant. For reasons that are obvious but remain un-stated in the archival document, this did not work, and he handed the case over to the procuracy of Abkhaziia. The Abkhazian state prosecutor duly informed the city executive committee that the illegal tenants had to be evicted and also talked personally with local party bureaucrats and even with the People's Commissar of Interior of Abkhaziia. All this was to no avail because Enukidze simply ignored any formal resolution and went on living where he did. The prosecutor in charge had a problem now—who should expel the second man in the region's NKVD? He tried to use the local military procuracy, since Enukidze formally served under its jurisdiction. The military procuracy flatly refused to cooperate. The prosecutor of Abkhaziia did not want to employ administrative measures against Enukidze, arguing that since nobody had returned from the war yet the decree of 5 August 1941 did not apply. Instead he kept trying to pass the hot potato on to others. He wrote a report to the Abkhazian government which 'took the appropriate measures'—again leading nowhere. Nobody wanted to touch the NKVD man. Most likely to the relief of all involved, the question finally resolved itself whens Enukidze moved on to another job.[45]

This resolution came after years of persistent effort by Turkiia, who, as everybody agreed, was completely supported by existing law. Following his initial complaint in November 1944, he wrote to the state newspaper *Izvestiia*. After his demobilization, now a war invalid (second group), he remained 'without housing wearing a Red Army uniform' in Tbilisi. As letters of complaints led to nothing, he tried to sue. But the decision of the People's Court to return his property was ignored for one and a half years, as were further letters of complaint. In 1945 he described his material situation as 'bad'. He lived in a kitchen.[46]

It was not only people higher in the formal or informal hierarchy of power and consumption who could compromise a veteran's rights. Institutions could also override the privileges of veterans with regard to their housing space. If, for example, a hospital had settled in a house during the war, neither the status of demobilized soldier, nor resolutions of the regional soviet, nor appeals to the Supreme Soviet helped. As long as there was no other building available for the hospital, the veteran had grudgingly to pay rent in another apartment, even though he not only owned a house, but also had a clearly recognized right to return to it. Such cases must have been especially frequent in the heavily destroyed western regions of the Union.[47] Finally, clashes of privilege could occur if one demobilized soldier was put into an empty apartment which belonged to another demobilized soldier. Given the housing scarcity, such cases also must have been frequent.[48]

Supplication for entitlements was not the only practice linking veterans with the state. One important step in the process of return to civilian life was registration, the handing out of documents, the reception of a residence permit, and getting orders, medals, and wounds properly recorded. These issues involved again dealing with overburdened and understaffed institutions, often to Kafkaesque effect. Stalingrad veteran Viktor Nekrasov described the beginning of civilian life in his 1954 novel *In the Hometown*:

> It started with a run through the institutions (*begotni po uchrezhdeniiam*). One had to register with the military authorities and receive the pension book, in the militia office one had to hand in some questionnaires and photographs in order to receive a passport and a ration card. Everywhere lines, and one always needed to wait for somebody, or some paper was missing, or one had to take it to a notary public to get it certified, and there, too, were lines, or one again had to wait for somebody ...[49]

If one did not return to the region of one's birth even more red tape could follow. One veteran sent several requests within half a year to the registry office (ZAGS) in his birth region to send him a copy of his birth certificate, which he needed to get an internal passport after demobilization. He received no answer, and thus remained without proper ID. He was not alone. Upon demobilization soldiers received a temporary passport which after some time had to be replaced by a new one. The temporary passport was handed out on the basis of military documents, but the new document needed, among other things, a birth certificate. If this record had been destroyed during the war, an official statement was required from the ZAGS of one's birthplace that no such document existed. With these credentials in hand, the veteran was then sent to a medical commission which established the returnee's age. To get either of these papers was immensely complicated. ZAGS'y were completely overburdened by the task of having to prepare so many documents. Requests went unanswered for months and even personal travel to one's place of birth did not help in many cases. This caused incredible problems with residency registration (*propiska*) and even with finding work.[50]

The imperfect rumblings of the administrative machine thus created much nuisance for returning veterans. However, the same imperfections allowed ample opportunities to better one's lot, if one managed to play it right. Vaisman was only the most spectacular case of the more widespread phenomenon of claiming to be in a certain category of veterans in order either to escape repression or gain the privileges of this group. Especially during demobilization such identity fraud was widespread. Deserters tried to pass themselves off as demobilized soldiers whose papers were stolen during their travel back. Soldiers who were too young to get demobilized tried to pass as older in order to get out of the army.[51] Already during the war, military decorations 'with all the corresponding documents, regularly stamped and signed' could be bought at bazaars, allowing the purchaser's name to be inserted and an unearned status claimed—and in some cases material rewards as well.[52] After the war was over, veterans appeared with forged party cards and sometimes escaped after their arrest, leaving the state security to wonder if the person was 'only a con man or a spy' (*prosto aferistom ili shpionom*). In March 1946 a 'demobilized' man with false party documents even managed to become acting state prosecutor of a district in Belorussia.[53]

Another veteran tricked the party organization in Gor'kii. In order to hide that he had been excluded from the party and sacked as a division commander in April 1946, he forged a letter from the political administration of the troops under the Ministry of Internal Affairs in the Caucasus, which claimed that his party card had been burnt and that, according to an order by the Chief Political Administration of the Armed Forces from 19 February 1947, this 'document' would be sufficient to allow the handing out of new party papers. He wrote the letter with the typewriter of a factory (that he had somehow managed to use) on cigarette paper with no letterhead, which bore instead an illegible seal of a housing administration of the same factory (which, again, he had somehow 'obtained'). He dropped this letter in the regular mail, in a mailbox right next to the district party committee (*raikom*) which he hoped would give him a new membership card. The second secretary reviewed the 'document', found it sufficient, and started the process of issuing new papers. The veteran also supplied fictitious certificates claiming that he had worked in 1939 as a director of a machine-tractor station (MTS), that he had received the order Red Banner of Labour, and that he had graduated from the agricultural institute in Odessa. These 'accomplishments' greatly helped in his application for the job of a director of a machine-tractor station. He also invented other details about his life, claiming to have been in the party before the war, whereas he had entered it at the front. He made his father a victim of the battle of Berlin, while in fact he had been sentenced as a collaborator with the Germans.[54] There was one flaw in his scheme—he had not changed his name. So when his personal file arrived from the military administration (*gorvoenkomat*), the scheme was uncovered.[55]

These stories illustrate how chaotic the environment of returning veterans was. Local party organizations were frequently overburdened with the many communists returning from the army. During 1945 this influx reached up to 19 per cent of the membership in civilian party organizations.[56] As late as 1947, the Gor'kii party organization lacked registration cards for 1,800 communists.[57] The situation was made worse (from the perspective of the authorities) or better (for those reinventing their past in order to build a brighter future) by the actual destruction or loss of much paper. During the war the documentation of 199 local party committees in the western regions was not evacuated but either destroyed or captured by the Germans. Among the lost documents were 41,800 registration cards. In addition, the army party organizations destroyed or lost 19,000 registration cards. Confronted with this situation (and with the large influx of demobilized communists immediately after the war) local party organizations often could not determine who actually was without a registration card, and who just claimed to be. 'As a result', complained an internal report, 'con men and all kinds of rogues (*prokhodimtsy*) sometimes manage to obtain party cards with false documents.'[58]

The transition to civilian life thus had a distinctly Soviet flavour—not only because of the severe destruction of the country, but also because of inherent traits of this social order. Comparison puts this specificity into sharp relief. North American servicemen often experienced their induction into the army as the takeover of their lives by a ridiculous bureaucratic machine, producing unnecessary hassles, incomprehensible red tape, and unintelligible rules—what the grunts called 'chickenshit'.[59] Demobilization, then, was a process of escaping this world of meaningless bureaucratism and a return to a world of sanity. Soviet veterans often felt the opposite. For them the 'chickenshit' started once they came back into the world of civilians:

> Instead of a holiday after four years of military travels, instead of collecting one's strength for future life and work, instead of allowing the wife to reconstruct the destroyed household, [instead of all of this] one has to be nervous, one has to fret oneself and fight with the homefront types, with soulless people, with narrow minded people.[60]

The return to Soviet normalcy—dominated as it was by an inescapable but malfunctioning state running an economy of scarcity—might explain part of the sometimes severe 'frontline nostalgia', the longing for the trenches, which at least in retrospect appeared like a world devoid of red tape and 'homefront types'.[61]

These types were hard to avoid. Material and monetary matters, pensions, legal documentation, and legal status, including resident permits, housing registration, orders and medals, and, for invalids, the question of establishing the category of invalidity—all of these led to frustrating interactions with a rumbling bureaucratic machine. Housing was also high on the list of troubles: certain groups of veterans had legal privileges involving interactions with the state to receive the benefits; much of the housing stock was controlled by state agencies; and the scarcity of housing led to conflicts with other citizens as well as with institutions, for whose resolution the state was needed as a judge and arbiter. A final key aspect of the reconstruction of civilian life could involve the state as well: finding a job. 'I ask the Supreme Soviet to review my complaint and help me in finding work,' wrote one veteran who had lost a leg during the war and was unable to perform hard work, 'because the local authorities do not provide any help. I have already complained to the district, but they took no measures there. I complained in the regional [administration], but received absolutely no answer, and also no answer from the republic.'[62]

Despite its totalitarian ambitions, then, the Soviet state was still far from an efficient bureaucratic machine capable of thorough surveillance but also of providing welfare. The promises propaganda had made to veterans—whether or not they had ever been more than hot air to start with—could not be kept: too underdeveloped was the administration, too strained the resources, and too big the problems faced by a country devastated by war and facing a new, global confrontation with the USA. To extract any kind of service or material benefit from this distracted and limping behemoth was hard work. Only skilful negotiation with the various levels of the bureaucracy—and luck!—brought success to some. Most had to make do without state aid, and manage in spite of the petty red tape produced by what official discourse called 'our dear government and our dear party'. Such disappointments led to resentment and frustration: 'After the war they promised us a good life, but in reality they increased taxes, and life became worse and worse all the time. And for what we fought we don't know ourselves.'[63] At the same time, the march through the institutions, the writing of supplications, the entire process of lobbying on one's own behalf also reinforced a sense of special entitlement. During the years of mass-demobilization in particular, veterans constantly encountered each other in offices, queuing in corridors. The long waits provided ample time to talk, to reassure one another of the right to a better life.

# 3
# Becoming a Civilian

If veterans had relied exclusively on state assistance, they might have barely made it home during demobilization; once back, reintegration would have failed spectacularly, had this complex task been under the control of the limping behemoth alone. At the same time, most veterans did return, first home, and then to civilian life. In fact, they had little choice but to reintegrate as ordinary citizens, because of the weakness of state support. For the time being, the meagre welfare provisions of postwar veterans' legislation, and the even smaller actual benefits, prevented the fusion of former soldiers into a special status group distinct from both the military *and* the rest of civilian society. The re-entering into 'normal' Soviet life was possible because of their own resourcefulness and the assistance from people around them—friends and strangers, acquaintances and kin (and their friends, families, and acquaintances). A variety of relations of exchange—formal and informal, ongoing or restricted to the moment—allowed necessary goods and services to be acquired, shelter and work found. The criminal and semi-criminal shadow economy helped many over temporary difficulties, and for some it became a home for longer. Legal, illegal, and semi-legal religious communities also provided support, resources, and constraints in the rebuilding of civilian existence. In short: veterans were embedded in a variety of networks and institutions which often overlapped with but were never reducible to state action alone.[1]

In fact, the state was relatively unimportant in resolving the problems of food, shelter, and belonging posed by the return from the army. Take housing, for instance. In late 1945 Moscow only 1 per cent of demobilized soldiers had received housing or had been registered to that end. The remaining 99 per cent had found shelter on their own.[2] The search for employment provides another example of the extent to which non-state social ties and practices were important in the reintegration into civilian life. Demobilized soldiers, because they were supposed to be assisted in finding jobs on the same or a higher level than they had held before the war, could mobilize various levels of state actors in this search. However, as Figure 3.1 shows, most veterans did not use the infrastructure (the local bureaux of labour reserve) which was supposed to assist them. Instead, the majority (growing from 51 to 61 per cent as time went on) utilized other channels—the topic of this chapter.

One central institution in Soviet everyday life was the family.[3] It was part of the solution to the psychological problem of belonging after the homelessness of war, an economic unit as well as a survival organization, which became a crucial base for the further reconstruction of postwar life. Reconnecting with surviving kin or establishing new family ties was, therefore, one of the first problems to be solved upon return. Sources produced by state institutions tend to obscure the role of spouses and families in the integration into civilian society. The evidence for this central aspect of everyday life is more likely to be found in memoirs, literature, or movies than in state or party archives—strictly speaking, sources for public culture and shared memory rather than for the past they

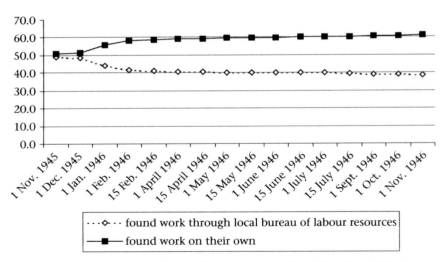

Fig. 3.1 Frequency of use of state infrastructure by job-seeking demobilized soldiers in urban areas (since start of mass demobilization; %)
*Source for raw data:* GARF f. r-9517, op. 1, d. 56, ll. 125,115, 88, 78, 73, 58, 53, 47, 44, 39, 34, 31, 26, 15, 10, 7

claim to represent. Nevertheless, they include a wealth of unintended information available to critical historical examination.[4] After Stalin's death, moreover, and as part of the unfolding war cult, memoirs, literature and films often functioned as *Ersatz*-history in a context where academic history writing was very tightly controlled. Simply put, during years of relative cultural relaxation, artistic representations of the past could discuss matters still beyond the domain of Soviet historians.

Today, historians do not have the problem of censorship and can study the formerly secret archives relatively uninhibited. However, the once hidden records might also lead us astray. The party-state, which produced these files, took note of the everyday world of Soviet citizens largely where things did not work and somebody therefore appealed for help, or when the daily activities of the population were seen as problematic by the regime. We thus still need to use non-archival evidence when attempting to reconstruct past life-worlds. At the same time we can turn the bias of the archives to our advantage. For example, we can draw conclusions about the importance of relatives in civilian life from the cases where there were none. War invalids—the legally most privileged group of veterans—were thrown into a life of misery if kinship ties were missing or their families unable to support them, as their letters to the Supreme Soviet attest:

My relatives perished during the occupation, only my wife is left, and she is sick and cannot work at all.[5]

I do not have relatives.[6]

... I am a war invalid, my family cannot work.[7]

I have a father who is not able to work, he is 60 years old, a sister born in 1935, and a mother of 57 who cannot work.[8]

My family is not able to work, and prior to my arrival they did not build anything, there was no house ...[9]

... but how should I live. I do not have relatives, my relatives were shot by the Germans. I live in a private apartment [i.e. he rented the place privately], I live in bad circumstances.[10]

... there is no help coming from anywhere, my family is unable to work—six souls ...[11]

More generally, where integration into social networks was missing and veterans thus had to rely on the state for help, the reconstruction of private life tended to become a miserable process. Where this social integration was present, life was a little bit 'more cheerful', even if still dire by most standards. It was not untypical for a veteran 'with nerve damage from the war' to live with his sister, his adult niece, her husband and child in a communal apartment room of sixteen square metres.[12] In fact, this was a comparatively comfortable arrangement. Others lived in dugouts 'not fit for habitation', were struggling to get heating fuel, and were obliged to have their children sleep on the bare floors.[13]

Where the family could not help, or where it did not exist, networks of friends and acquaintances, and the families of friends and acquaintances, frequently stepped in. Raban Idiev returned to a completely destroyed family: during the war his wife, two children, and his two sisters had perished. Only his 6-year-old son was left, living in a battered tent or a covered wagon (*kibitka*). For two weeks Idiev and his son lodged with a female neighbour until finally the intervention by a representative of the regional party committee got them their own housing space.[14] Others lived for six months with various acquaintances who let them (and their family of four) stay for the night.[15] Chukhrai's first place to live in Moscow was provided by the family of a childhood friend.[16] More clearly reciprocal private interactions were used as well. One demobilized soldier worked for four days for a fellow *kolkhoznitsa* for 4 kilograms of grain in order to feed his family.[17] Others sought credit from private sources if the government housing-construction loan proved insufficient.[18]

Veterans thus resumed life in a social world where nuclear families and wider kin were interconnected and sometimes overlapped with diverse institutions and organizations of the party-state on the one hand, and were embedded in wider networks of friendships, mutual assistance, and reciprocal exchange on the other.[19] Often, demobilization simply meant a return to one's prewar social circles.[20] In addition, bonds which had developed during the war were kept alive and new connections emerged between strangers on the basis of similar war experiences. One site for this to happen were the drinking places which are sometimes called 'Blue Danubes', and which in most sources appear as *zabegalovki* and *pivnye* ('drink-and-run-counters', beer bars).[21] The future poet and song-writer Mikhail Tanich, for example, had a circle of friends who met in a beer bar in Rostov-on-Don, which was knit tightly enough to be mistaken by state security for an anti-Soviet gathering.[22] Such circles could expand through the principle of 'a friend of my friend is my friend'. They served many functions: they kept wartime memory alive, recreated the feeling of the 'frontline brotherhood', nourished 'frontline nostalgia', and helped coming to terms with war and postwar experience. They had more practical functions as well. Somewhere between 1945 and 1956 Iosif Prut made friends with the writer Emmanuil Kazakevich. They were introduced by their shared comrade Venia Riskind, another *frontovik*. In 1956 Kazakevich and Prut pooled resources to allow Riskind to buy a suit, because they thought he could not perform his songs in the only outfit he had—his decade-old army uniform.[23]

Yet, the history of veterans' connections is far from straightforward. Often, postwar life pulled wartime comrades apart: geography became an obstacle to daily interactions, as did social difference. Only in rare instances did wartime friendships mean more than the occasional letter on Victory Day.[24] Many veterans lost contact with their combat comrades altogether and reconnected only in the 1960s, 1970s, or 1980s—in the context of the establishment of a veterans' movement which organized meetings of the survivors of specific units.[25] The first postwar meeting of the Third Stalingrad Guard Mechanized Corps, for example, was in 1963, and some of its remaining members did not meet until 1975.[26] The members of Tanich's 168th anti-tank regiment did not see each other for forty years, until a meeting in 1985 finally brought the survivors back together.[27]

The veterans' networks which emerged in the immediate postwar period were usually confined to a period of transition when soldiers were demobilized but not yet fully reintegrated into civilian society.[28] This period of strong bonding was likely to be more important for younger veterans who had not been established fully in adult life before the army than for those who could return to more-or-less familiar roles and social circles. However, even the young tended to be divided by civilian life. The three *frontoviki* Aleksei Petrovich Okhrimenko, Sergei Kristi, and Volodia Shreiberg, to give another example from the better documented world of the artistic intelligentsia, composed war songs together in the immediate postwar years.

> Then, unfortunately, our troika was shattered. That does not mean that we, God forbid, fell out with each other—we were friends and continued to be friends, but for Volodia it was time for his diploma ... Serezha moved to the Moscow suburbs (*v Podmoskov'e*), where he then worked in the newspaper in Voskresensk. And after 1951 we never again wrote anything together.[29]

Why were veterans' networks so fragile in the postwar world? One answer is state repression. I have already mentioned the arrest of Tanich and his drinking buddies, who had not kept enough of a leash on their tongues. Others suffered similar fates. The Moscow University student Vladimir Kabo and his fellow *frontovik* Iurii Bregel, also not very good at keeping their mouths shut, were arrested on similar charges (they were also Jewish, which did not help in the postwar atmosphere of xenophobia towards 'rootless cosmopolitanists').[30] In fact, veterans are a quite prominent group among those arrested and tried for 'anti-Soviet agitation' (article 58-10 of the criminal code) in the postwar years.[31]

There were more mundane reasons as well, as in the case of the troika of war-song composers. Postwar life was hard. It required networks which helped in the resolution of basic problems like housing, food, and a means of existence. Such networks implied contacts to people in power positions in order to get access to state-distributed goods and services. Many of these positions were in the hands of non-veterans, making connections across the front–homefront divide highly necessary.[32] While horizontal, more or less symmetrical, and reciprocal relations (friendship) did play an important emotional role in the process of transition to civilian life, the practical problems this new life posed required the vertical, often asymmetrical relationships between patrons and clients.[33] This, in turn, made ties between veterans less stable in the postwar world—they were simply less useful in resolving the problems of postwar existence than those with non-veterans. Wartime networks proved more stable where they included vertical relationships after the war. If an officer became a leading civilian cadre he might bring along his wartime subordinates and recreate (to the annoyance of their civilian colleagues) a spirit of frontline work in civilian administration.[34] In other cases subordinates simply followed their former commanders, because they had no kin left and did not know where else to go. Even the arrest of his former commander did not prevent Aleksandr Solzhenitsyn's sergeant-major (*starshina*) travelling to Rostov-on-Don where he rented a corner in the apartment of the wife of the 'enemy of the people'.[35]

A second category of veterans' connections are those which emerged between strangers after the war on the basis of shared war experience. Often they were rather fleeting encounters in bars or at beer kiosks. Kazakevich's diary notes such a meeting on 9 May 1950—Victory Day: 'I went to a beer bar. Two invalids and a plumber... were drinking beer and reminiscing about the war. One of them wept and said: If there were another war, I would go...'[36] In the novel *In the Home Town*, Nekrasov describes a very similar scene: two veterans meet by chance in a drinking establishment and start talking war (which in this case was still going on). In contrast to Kazakevich's encounter, this one develops not only into a night-long drinking bout between the two, but also into an ongoing, if sometimes strained, friendship, which helps both in emotional and practical ways in their reintegration into civilian life.[37] An important factor in the long run was, again, the compatibility of such relations with the requirements of postwar life. Some veterans who obtained administrative posts after their demobilization felt that they should recruit other veterans to their work or study environment, because they did not trust non-veterans. These feelings might have been stronger in the formerly occupied regions (where one was surrounded by potential 'traitors'), but they can also be found in representations of postwar life in Moscow.[38] An overlap of veterans' bonding with positions within the state structure—and thus with access to goods and services as well as simply to jobs—ensured the longevity of such relations.

Another context where postwar connections between veterans proved long-lived was in higher education. Veterans were a distinct group within the student body. They were (mainly) men in a largely female environment and they were a little older than the rest of the students. Thus, both age and gender difference reinforced the discrepancy in war experience, which made veterans' identity a strong component of the culture of higher education in the postwar years. Veterans also took over large parts of the political structure in these institutions (the Komsomol and party cells) and thus became a dominant force in the student body.[39] In addition, they tended to share dorm rooms with other veterans, which gave them the opportunity to reinforce their relationships with one of the traditional practices of male bonding—heavy drinking and drunken conversations.[40]

One place where war experience overlapped with postwar living arrangements was institutions set up to house war invalids.[41] Here, however, the situation was not one of empowerment of the veterans as in higher education, but one of shared deprivation. The resistance of enterprise directors to the employment of invalids, the underdevelopment of the welfare state, and the often horrible conditions in such institutions, together with their relative immunity to prosecution, made alternative job choices such as trader ('speculator'), beggar, or thief attractive for war invalids. While I could not find an instance of veterans-only criminal gangs, war invalids not infrequently were the leaders of such groups.[42]

The popularity of semi-legal and outrightly illegal jobs among veterans shows the extent to which the shadow economy revolving around markets and market exchanges provided an alternative channel of access to goods, relative well-being, and social status expressed through things. Despite all the 'planned economy' rhetoric, market mechanisms remained crucial to the working of Soviet society. Distribution could not function without an entire sphere of semi-legal ('grey') and illegal ('black') exchange. Legal bazaars and the kolkhoz-markets (where collective farmers could sell excess produce from their garden plots) also played a very important role in supplying the population, particularly during the war and its immediate aftermath.[43] In such transactions, legal and illegal exchange went hand in hand, and the official and unofficial distribution networks were closely entangled. In their quest for the good postwar life, veterans drew on both the official and the unofficial 'hierarchy of distribution'.[44] Not unlike the family and networks between former soldiers, the shadow society combined material and psychological support. For some returning soldiers it provided an alternative lifestyle which satisfied psychological needs left unmet by the officially promoted life of duty, discipline, and service.[45]

Not only did this 'shadow society' provide possible employment for those who could not or would not make it in the official world of respectable jobs, it also provided a means of converting trophy goods brought from Germany into whatever one needed. Sergei in Iurii Bondarev's postwar novel *Silence* had to sell a watch he brought back and use the money to buy a civilian suit. The place for these transactions was the Tishinskii market in Moscow.[46]

> Here one could buy anything.... Here, 'on the side', they traded in bread and vodka obtained on ration cards in shops, in penicillin and lengths of cloth stolen from warehouses, American jackets and condoms, and in 'trophy' bicycles and motor-cycles. Here they sold fashionable 'Macintoshes', cigarette lighters of foreign make, bay leaf (*lavrovyi list*), home-made shoes with rubber soles, German hair-growing preparations, watches, false diamonds, old furs and forged references and diplomas about graduation from any kind of educational establishment. Here they traded in everything which could be traded, anything which might be bought ...[47]

While for Sergei the shadow society of the black market was a resource used only once, for others it became a home and an alternative to life along respectable lines. For this process archival documents give only scant evidence. Again, the best sources are memoirs and artistic representations.

Iurii Nagibin's 1982 novella *Patience* provides one illustration. The war invalid Pasha refuses to go home after the war. After some unsuccessful attempts to learn a new profession he turned his back on official society, starting an odyssey through the subcultures in the shadows.

> With masochistic fury, he continues the tale of his degradation—how he sold rotten cigarettes, how he spent his measly earning with drunkards, whores, and thieves who employed cripples in their enterprises; how he took part in brawls, how he learned to use a knife mercilessly—never touching another cripple—and how in a bizarre way he hoped to be murdered by these criminals. But it came to an end without blood. With shame instead. He got into a fight with a young woman who had furnished him with stolen cigarettes. She had cheated him. It wasn't a question of money; it was her flagrant arrogance that made him take after her in his small four-wheeled cart (*telezhka*), which he was using at the time. She mocked him. He tried to hit her and fell out of his cart. Helpless, he rolled down the steps between two steep streets. And that's when he decided to get himself to Bogoyar.

In the novel, the island Bogoyar 'served as a terminal shelter for those who were maimed by war and who either had not wanted to return to their homes or who were refused acceptance there'. Here, war cripples had created their own subculture, helping each other and forming a 'brotherhood' with Pasha as their 'commanding officer'. Nagibin took his cues for the fictional Bogoyar from the real-life island of Valaam in Lake Ladoga, outside Leningrad, a place he had visited himself, and which was a well-known destination for war disabled.[48]

The connection to the shadow-society of Stalinism (the black market and criminal subcultures) was not unique to war invalids. Non-invalided war returnees also worked as 'speculators', sometimes refusing to take any other job.[49] Part of the demobilized soldiers in Krasnodar region in 1947 'do not desire to work and engage in trade on the bazaars and in other places'.[50] Some veterans actively sought out positions which allowed them to siphon off goods from the official network of distribution and sell what they did not consume themselves on the black market. Jobs in 'economic' administration of enterprises, in food kitchens and cafeterias were highly popular.[51] In Rostov-on-Don the party committee (*gorkom*) discussed in late 1945 the fact that 'many' demobilized soldiers 'agree to work only in trade organizations or cafeterias even if they did not work in such jobs before, or they demand leadership positions with higher rations'.[52]

Besides 'leading' and 'administrative' positions, any job in trade was sought after by returning veterans.[53] The profession of driver was highly saturated with former soldiers who had learned to drive while in the army. They continued in this profession not only because driving a car is pleasurable in itself, but also because it allowed a person to make a good living on the side by using the vehicle for private hauling of black market goods.[54] A lot of goods regularly 'fell off the truck' and could be 'picked up' by the driver. 'Trophy goods' which had been brought in from the occupied areas in the West could provide starting capital for a career as an illegal trader. In late 1946 the militia confiscated 4,622 furs from an enterprising veteran from Tambov. He had stolen them at the end of the war from a Berlin fur shop and now wanted to sell them in Moscow.[55] One of his colleagues drove a car full of trophies from Germany in October 1946. His brother-in-law took over the sale of the goods. He was arrested in the spring of 1947.[56]

The reintegration into civilian life could also be facilitated by religious organizations and religious practice, which both played an important role in the lives of many Soviet citizens—despite the long-standing hostility of state and party to such 'superstition'.[57] In this secular Bolshevik state, the leading strata of communist party members were supposed to be militantly atheist. For Bolsheviks—as for most Marxists—religion was part of the 'superstructure', the 'opium of the people' as Marx had famously put it. This sedative made life under capitalism bearable, but also deluded the exploited into consenting to their subjugation. Such irrationality would wither away after the revolution had destroyed its 'objective base'. Religion would be replaced by a rational and scientific worldview. This basic approach never changed, but the concrete policies did according to tactical considerations. Thus, periods of aggressive atheist activity (1917–21, 1929–39, 1959–64) were interspersed with more pragmatic approaches to faith and religion, phenomena which, despite everything, stubbornly refused to wither away.[58]

Late Stalinism was one of these periods of relative liberalism. With the annexation of eastern Poland in 1939, millions of practising Christians and their church organizations became part of Soviet society. In order to not cause too much unnecessary upheaval in what came to be known as the western borderlands, militant atheism was put on the backburner. The Soviet Union even reverted from the five-day week back to the seven-day calendar in 1940. During the war, policies towards religion were relaxed, and the Orthodox Church coopted as part of the mobilization campaign. Stalin received church leaders in 1943, allowed the opening of orthodox churches, monasteries, and seminaries as well as Muslim academies.[59] The church now blessed tank columns and prayed for victory. This more permissive approach towards the church was also maintained after the war, until Khrushchev started a new onslaught against religion in 1959. Until then, religion could be practised relatively freely unless one was a candidate or member of the communist party—this vanguard was still supposed to be staunchly atheist.[60] Believers now massively lobbied for the reopening of their churches and practised their religion openly.[61]

Religious communities became important for veterans because they took over commemorative and welfare functions which the state fulfilled only haphazardly. Local religious communities took care of war invalids and war orphans.[62] In several localities of Voroshilovgrad region in the Ukraine 'representatives of Soviet organizations address church and [other] religious communities with requests to help orphans and invalids of the Patriotic War'.[63] Despite the disapproval from the centre, hard-pressed local leaders in other regions, too, 'turned to the priests and religious communes with requests for assistance to the families of soldiers, invalids, and orphans'.[64] In Krasnodarskii krai priests and other church activists organized the building of memorials for war heroes.[65] In April of 1949 the senior students of the musical school for war invalids in Moscow province found themselves without the necessary instruments to work in their new trade as accordion players (*baianisty*). Correctly judging the likelihood of the supply of instruments from the state, they appealed to the Moscow Patriarch for financial aid to buy thirteen accordions.[66]

The percentage of men among churchgoers increased during demobilization. In Kuibyshev province in 1945 maybe 10 per cent of churchgoers were men. In the first quarter of 1946 this number rose to 30–40 per cent, many of whom were between 20 and 40 years of age.[67] Especially important were religious rites of passage. Marriage—an important step in the establishment of a civilian existence—was a case in point. In March 1945 a senior lieutenant of the tank forces, a decorated war hero with five wound stripes, married in full uniform in a church in Kazan. He was excluded from the party for this display of backwardness and lack of enlightenment.[68] The same happened to Iulian Alekseevich Dulevskii, who had entered the party in 1943. After demobilization he lived with his parents and did not work. However, he wanted to marry. Since the wedding was to happen in church he went to the district committee of the party to ask for permission. The secretary explained to him that a party member could not marry in church. Comrade Dulevskii obviously did not understand why and went another two times to ask for permission. He received the same answer. Finally, he married in church anyway, which led to his exclusion from the party.[69] In the autonomous republic of Mordva one rural activist and war veteran (born in 1922) married in January 1945 in church.[70] The Council of the Affairs of the Russian Orthodox Church reported on similar church weddings between well-educated Komsomol members (teachers) and veterans.[71]

These cases were part of a larger problem within the party. Eighty per cent of those excluded for participation in religious rites from the party organization of Voronezh region in 1946 and 1947 were war veterans.[72] The drive to ease admission at the front had brought many believers into its ranks, making such 'young communists' ('young' not necessarily in years, but in experience of party life) very likely to be excluded for religious activity.[73] Many communists, complained an obkom official in the summer of 1947, 'have forgotten the instructions of our party that religion is not a private matter' (ne iavliaetsia chastnym delom). This was especially true for those who had joined during the war.[74]

The existence of religious veterans of all age groups should not be too puzzling. After all, in the 1937 census a large percentage of men of the future draft cohorts identified themselves as religious believers—especially among the poorly educated. Even in the most 'atheist' group (literate men born after the revolution) a quarter defined themselves as religious (Table 3.1). Given these figures, it is not surprising that a secret police report about reactions of Red Army soldiers to Stalin's 1943 meeting with top representatives of the Orthodox Church noted 'general satisfaction' and only some discontent.[75]

The wartime relaxation of policies towards the church was not likely to convert religious soldiers to atheism. This relaxation went so far as to make sermons to meetings of Red Army men possible:

> At large gatherings of officers, Metropolitan Nikolai spoke about faith, religion, and the meaning of life. The officers listened to him with deep attention and interest and with much sympathy. He made quite an impression on them, and very interesting conversations then took place.[76]

Table 3.1. Percentage of men in draft cohorts identifying themselves as religious believers in 1937

| Age in 1937 | Birth cohort | Literate | Illiterate |
|---|---|---|---|
| 16–19 | 1918–21 | 24.8 | 60.8 |
| 20–29 | 1908–17 | 28.2 | 66.0 |
| 30–34 | 1898–1907 | 35.9 | 73.6 |
| 40–44 | 1888–97 | 45.6 | 78.1 |

*Source*: V. B. Zhiromskaia, *Demograficheskaia istoriia Rossii v 1930-e gody* (Moscow: Rosspen, 2001), 198.

For a minority of demobilized soldiers, religion and the community of co-believers provided more than just a help in readjustment and an orientation about the meaning of existence. For some they became sites of active participation or even a central life choice. While the Christian communities were dominated by women, the leading organs of these institutions—including (besides the priesthood) the church councils and the revision commissions—were overwhelmingly in male hands.[77] A reregistration of members in early 1949 found in these institutions 5,585 decorated persons (8.4 per cent of the total), most of them former rank and file soldiers and holders of civilian decorations, but also 107 veterans who had formerly held officer rank.[78]

Some veterans chose the priesthood after demobilization. L. L. Poliakov from Leningrad graduated in 1939 from the medical institute and served for a decade as an army doctor. During this time he also graduated from a part-time course (*eksternom*) at the Leningrad spiritual academy. In September 1949 he became a priest at the Preobrazhenskii Cathedral in Leningrad.[79] The best known veteran-turned-religious leader is today's archimandrite Kirill of the Holy Trinity Sergiev Monastery (Sviato-Troitskaia Sergievaia Lavra), born in 1919. Kirill, at that time still sergeant Pavlov (not to be confused with the famous defender of Stalingrad of the same name), found God under the rubble of destruction, in the form of a Bible he pulled out from a destroyed house in Stalingrad—'balm for the soul' during the incomprehensibility of war. Pavlov was demobilized in 1946, in Hungary. He travelled to Moscow and asked in the Elokhovskii Cathedral if there were any 'spiritual institutions'. Yes, he learned, a seminary had opened in the Novodevichi Monastery. He went right there, still wearing his army uniform. After some time of study and preparation he was admitted, by no means the only *frontovik* in the monastery.[80]

The veterans in Novodevichi were not alone. A Captain Ermolaev, a demobilized commander and party member, entered an institution of theological education in 1946.[81] In 1947, 'up to 50' demobilized soldiers studied in the newly opened academy and seminary in Moscow, as the *Journal of the Moscow Patriarch* proudly reported. They were all decorated and most of them were former officers.[82] By 1 January 1948, fifty-nine demobilized soldiers were enrolled in spiritual educational institutions, where they constituted 10 per cent of the student body.[83] Former army officers were among the new deacons and priests whose ordination the Council for Affairs of the Russian Orthodox Church (the state surveillance institution) opposed.[84] Many other examples could be added.[85]

We can distinguish two groups of men of God among veterans. On the one hand are those who served the church before the war, fought, and returned to what now was an officially recognized institution. Some were demobilized from active military duty during the war if they 'consented to return to church service'.[86] Others returned to the church after their regular release after the end of hostilities. Petr Seregin, for example, was born in 1895 in Penza province into a deeply religious peasant family. Following the example of his father (who sang in the church choir), Petr served as a psalm reader in the local church from 1921. A year later he became a deacon, and already in 1925 he was made an elder (*presviter*) of the church in the neighbouring village. Then came the repressions of the 1930s. Petr was arrested in 1931 and sent to Karelia as forced labourer in the construction of the Belomor–Baltic canal. He was released in 1935 and joined by his family in Karelia, where he worked in secular jobs. In 1941 he was drafted into the army. He ended his war service in 1945 in Budapest, demobilized and returned to his family which the chaos of war had moved to Petrozavodsk. In 1946 he returned to the church career interrupted by the terror of the 1930s and the war: he started to serve in the Cathedral of Christ's Assumption (*Krestovozdvizhenskii sobor*) in Petrozavodsk.[87]

The second group were men like Pavlov/Kirill: they had not been members of the church hierarchy and sometimes not even active practitioners. They were part of the revival of church activity after the shift in state policy from repression to supervised recognition during the war. Vasilii Ivanovich Afonin was born in 1926 into a peasant family. He went to the front as a

16-year-old volunteer in 1942, rose through the ranks to become a junior lieutenant and was about to be promoted to senior lieutenant at the end of the war when his superiors learnt of his plans to become a priest. As a result he was demoted instead. After demobilization he worked as a worker in Leningrad (1947–50). He then received an education in the Stavropol' Seminary and became a priest in 1954.[88]

Veterans were not only drawn to the official church organizations—a problematic but completely legal choice. Some were also attracted to informal and illegal religious communities.[89] Officials in charge of surveillance of religious institutions and practices linked the epidemic of supplications to open churches to the activities of freelance preachers, many of them veterans: 'Unattached clergy and monks play an important role in the organization of believers for supplications... Often one finds invalids of the Patriotic War among these persons.'[90] In May and June 1946 a freelance religious activist and war invalid in a village in Penza province organized several public prayers for rain, which attracted 150 people.[91]

In May of the same year the freelance preacher Boris Samoilov organized a three-day procession and prayer for rain with between 300 and 400 participants in a village in Voronezh region. He was born in 1923 in Lipetsk, had five years of schooling, and volunteered for the front in 1943. He was demobilized for health reasons and worked as a military educator. In March 1945 he started to 'lead the lifestyle of a tramp' (vesti brodiachii obraz zhizni), soon causing much trouble as a freelance preacher. Late in the first day of the procession, at 11 p.m. on 16 May 1946, the local authorities tried to break up the unauthorized assembly and arrest Samoilov. When the authorities arrived, some in the crowd ran away, while the rest resisted the breakup attempt, and beat one of the policemen involved. Later the procession dispersed for the night, but about 100 of the participants went to Samoilov's house which they had converted into a church. During the service in his house, Samoilov called the local authorities drunkards and hooligans, and asked the crowd to protect him and his church. The crowd answered: 'we will not go anywhere and we will protect Boris and the church'. This seems to have settled matters for the next day. On 18 May new troubles started. A car arrived in front of Samoilov's unofficial church and six men got out: the local state prosecutor, the local MVD boss, and four MVD policemen. Samoilov barricaded himself in his house in order to escape arrest. The officials tried to open the door with an axe, but were stopped by a large crowd who ran to defend Boris. The crowd forced the local representatives of the Soviet regime to leave. Boris came out of his 'church' and again addressed the crowd. He threatened to call in people from the surrounding villages if the authorities tried to use troops to arrest him. The crowd yelled that they would defend him no matter what. A guard of 100 people during daytime was organized for Samoilov. At night, up to 400 people joined him in prayer and religious song. The authorities now shifted tactics, brought in a priest from the town of Borisoglebsk, who held church service in a different part of the village. This diverted most believers from Samoilov, and only a small group remained faithful to their Boris and his 'church'. At the end of July the Voronezh obkom secretary reported to the Central Committee that Samoilov 'did not lead a church service after 22 May'. Apparently, he still had not been arrested.[92]

Samoilov was not the only religious leader among veterans. In 1946 a highly decorated former tank-man returned to the 'Proletarskii' factory in the town of the same name. Within three years 'he fell under the influence of the sect of evangelical Christians and actively participated in it, started to preach and became the sect's spiritual leader'.[93] In December 1951 the Rostov province court sentenced a group of fourteen people for 'anti-Soviet agitation' to labour camp sentences between ten and thirty-five years. They were found guilty of being part of the anti-Soviet religious underground of the monarchist wing of the sect of the Ioannites (*sektanty-ionisty tserkovno-monarkhicheskogo tolka*), a part of the larger movement of the 'Flagellants'.[94] Between 1945 and the day of their arrest they had, according to the verdict, held secret meetings in apartments, agitated against the policies of the regime, fabricated lies about Soviet reality, and attacked (presumably verbally) members of the Soviet government. Moreover, they had also recruited new members to the sect.[95] One of the older men in the group was a veteran of the Patriotic War, Grigorii Ivanovich Putilin, born 1893 in Rostov province of peasant background. He had two years of schooling, was married, not a party member, had never been tried before, and had been decorated with the medal '*For Battle Merit*'. Before his arrest on 27 June 1951 he had worked as a guard (*okhrannik*). In court he said that he had been a member of the Ioannites since the 1920s. Putilin was accused by the Ministry of State Security (MGB) of being the organizer of the group, an accusation he denied in a letter of complaint after his sentence.[96]

Most veterans struggled to become civilians. Their reintegration depended on their skill in obtaining state aid, the support they could get from their families, and the extent to which they managed to establish (and re-establish) ties with other veterans, with co-religionists, neighbours and work colleagues, acquaintances and friends. Women, in particular, were crucial—as mothers, sisters, wives, or lovers; as the major labour force in postwar society; and as the centre of most families. Without their contribution, the reintegration of both male and female veterans into civilian life would have never succeeded.[97] Women were not only 'healers of wounded souls' as portrayed in postwar literature but also providers and everyday assistants of veterans in real life.[98] War invalids provide a particularly clear example for this phenomenon, as they frequently needed support in their daily lives which the underdeveloped welfare state could not provide.[99] Working wives also contributed large shares to the family budget of non-working war invalids. One 35-year-old unemployed war invalid received a pension of 180 rubles, while his wife contributed a salary of 300 rubles.[100] The monetary income of the family of another war survivor (who lived and worked on a kolkhoz) consisted in the pension of the invalid (96 rubles), welfare payments for large families to his wife (100 rubles), and the income of his daughter (400 rubles).[101] Again, the major share of the family budget (84 per cent) came from the female family members. War invalids also had something to offer in return beyond the simple fact that as men they were scarce goods on the marriage market. For students in any of the major cities, such a marriage was beneficial, because as wives of war invalids they were defined as 'immobile', that is, were exempt from the necessity to go to the provinces to work after graduation.[102] For those engaged in illegal activities such as trade ('speculation'), a bond with a war invalid was also attractive because until the anti-parasites campaign of the early 1950s, the war invalid's (informal) status provided some protection against police harassment.[103]

Relations between men and women, then, were at the very centre of reintegration into civilian existence, and the postwar years, as a result, were a period of heightened gender conflict. 'Many fathers', reported the office of the Presidium of the Supreme Soviet in 1947, 'who have been cut off from their families for several years, do not return to them after the war and at the same time do not file official divorces from their wives, because in this case they would have to tell their families where they live and pay child support.'[104] The fog of war was manipulated relatively easily. One soldier stopped writing letters to his wife in 1942. Despite all her efforts to find out, she did not know until 1945 whether her husband was among the living or among the dead. Finally, she received a letter stating that 'your husband is alive, he lived in Baku, got married, left his wife, took another one and is now in Poland'.[105] Such behaviour was made possible by the limited reach of the state. Until 1947 the state prosecutor had a hard time locating such child-support evaders because of the unhelpful bookkeeping practice of local military registration offices.[106]

Unwillingness to pay child support was not the only reason for the non-return to the former spouse. The mere possibility of jumping from partner to partner, or having several families at once, played a role. This was a well-established male practice since at least the 1930s, further facilitated by the drastic scarcity of men in the postwar years ('there were no men, the men had perished in the war'). The family law of 1944 also contributed by freeing fathers from financial responsibility for children conceived out of wedlock.[107] Another reason was social mobility in the army. One veteran was drafted in 1939, made a career during the war, and decided (in the words of his wife) that his family no longer corresponded to his new status and 'obviously, found himself a new, frontline family'. He sent his wife a note about his own death. She did not buy this trick, found his field post number, and unsuccessfully wrote to request child support. Her further inquiries yielded contradictory results: he had been jailed for hooliganism in Bobruisk; he was demobilized and lived in Khar'kov; he was demobilized and lived in Poltava. As of 1947, he managed to evade her search. A similar case was described by Igor' and Stella, two children of another runaway veteran from Alma-Ata in a letter to the Supreme Soviet:

> Our papa was in the ranks of the Soviet Army since 1928, as part of the cadre soldiers (v kadrovom sostave). In the first days of the Great Patriotic War, holding the rank of captain, he was sent to the front. In 1943 he was already promoted to the rank of colonel of the artillery. It seems that he already had a new family, with whom he lived since 1942 in Moscow, but he deceived us at the time, claiming that he lived alone. He wrote his last letter on 25 March 1947 from Moscow, in which he asked us not to write to him in Moscow, because he is not there, and that he would be demobilized and that he will come to us. However, the Stalinskii VK [voenkomat, or military registration office] summoned Mama on 3 April and warned that papa had already been demobilized for two months and that we had received 800 rubles too much support for him and they threatened to take the case to court.... Until right now our papa hides from us, but mama is unable to pay for our education.

When we said farewell when papa went to the front we were convinced that he was fighting for our happy childhood, but it turned out that he fought for his own new happy life (*zavoeval sebe novuiu schastlivuiu zhizn'*) with a new family, while he threw us to the mercy of fate, without a corner [in which to live] and without money.[108]

Postwar didactic fiction took on the problem, quoting the arrogance of those who had seen the wider world as a reason for a non–return to prewar girlfriends or spouses:

He has seen the wide world, Budapest, Königsberg, Vienna... before the war he did not even know these names. Such guys don't like anything at home: neither the towns, nor the girls, nor our affairs. He turns up his nose. Don't you see that he is used to [something] different![109]

Disabled veterans often did not come back for reasons other than those already suggested. A culture which worshipped the lean, muscular body of the athlete and the feats of healthy Socialist supermen did not make the trauma of physical mutilation easier to bear. While positive role models of invalids overcoming their physical limitations did exist, the same examples also illustrate how hard it was to develop such a positive attitude.[110] Confronted with serious doubts about their manliness and with a society where daily life was hard even for the physically fit, many war invalids decided that they could not expect their spouses or their parents to put up with a 'cripple' (*kaleka*).[111] Others were dropped by their wives for more promising mates.[112]

In some cases the non–return was prompted by a decision to stay with a woman who had shared frontline experience with the male veteran. 'In 1945 he abandoned me, and brought with him another woman—a frontline woman (*frontovaia zhenshchina*).'[113] Sometimes, such attachments ended tragically. A high-ranking officer (*general-maior*), who was married with two children, lived from 1944 with a frontline nurse, who had a child with him. In May 1946 his son (also a demobilized soldier) and his wife came to live with him as well. Not surprisingly, this arrangement led to conflict. In one of these fights the son shot his father's new wife.[114]

This extreme case was part of a wider phenomenon of hostility towards female veterans, who were stereotyped as 'camp followers'. They were nicknamed 'Mobile Field Wives' (*Polevye Pokhodnye Zheny*, or, in the pseudo-military shorthand, P.P.Zh.). Putting on one's medals in public provoked cries of 'A ha! There goes a frontline whore!' If one wanted to be a 'marriageable girl' it was better to hide the fact of war participation, not take public pride in it, and never wear military decorations.[115]

But victimization is not the full story of female veterans.[116] While they were stigmatized by popular assumptions about their sexuality, they were also honoured. At the end of the war and during the years of demobilization, the official media continued to mention the role frontline women had played in the defeat of Nazi Germany. 'Soviet women went fearlessly into battle', wrote *The Agitator's Notepad* in 1945.

> They were active participants [in the war] and loyal assistants to the fighters of the Red Army in all phases of the gigantic battle with the Germans.... They were in the first units of our forces, which went on the offensive outside of Moscow in the bleak winter of 1941. They fought in the battle of Kursk, went together with the advancing troops to the West. They forced the Dnepr and the Visla. Today, you can see them in the fields of Eastern Prussia, Silesia, Brandenburg. Modest warriors, they are always ready for a heroic feat, for self-sacrifice in the name of the Homeland.[117]

Demobilization stories in *Red Star* mentioned the heroism of female medical personnel,[118] as well as the hero's welcome the 'girl-warriors' (*devushki-voiny*) received upon their return to Leningrad in late July 1945.[119] In 1947, at a time when the vast majority of women had long been demobilized, the army's propaganda journal had not forgotten that 'many Soviet women' had fought as volunteers in the Red Army: 120,000 of them received decorations 'for heroism and courage ... in battles with the enemy', and sixty-nine were elevated to the status of 'Hero of the Soviet Union'.[120] Outside of military publications, too, the role of frontline women continued to be mentioned by the late 1940s,[121] and Khrushchev took up the theme in his 'secret speech' of 1956 ('many women participated directly in the Great Patriotic War at the fronts').[122] Female warriors continued to be present in war movies—one of the central media of the developing War Cult throughout the 1960s, 1970s, and 1980s and beyond.[123]

Popular assumptions were not restricted to vilification of frontline women. Some believed they were the ideal partners for male veterans since only they could understand what it meant to be a civilian after years of fighting.[124] Some men abandoned their wartime partners for 'civilian' women in beautiful dresses to escape memory of combat. Others preferred to stay with their wartime spouses, and a third group saw them as desirable partners. Consider the following encounter of the journalist and oral historian of women's frontline experience Svetlana Aleksievich with two male veterans in the late 1970s or early 1980s in a train compartment.[125] One of them had been opposed to women at the front during the war, and still held this position. He was especially disturbed by snipers, whom he suspected to have acquired a taste for hunting down and killing men, which disqualified them as potential brides. The other veteran, however, was full of respect for the heroism he had witnessed and called them 'our friends', 'our sisters', and 'wonderful girls'. He was sorry about what he saw as their typical postwar fate. 'We longed for something beautiful after all the filth, lice and deaths. We wanted beautiful women...We tried to forget everything. And we also forgot our wartime girl friends...'[126]

Popular hostility and attempts to create a clean break with the war in private life were countered by a second, more positive approach, which left prominent traces in wartime and postwar literature dealing with the reintegration of veterans into civilian life. In Pavlenko's *Happiness* the protagonist first leaves his frontline love because he cannot stand the idea of being a cripple cared for by her. In the long run, however, his attempt to establish a relationship with a non-veteran fails and in the final pages of the novel the couple is reunited.[127] One central plot in Victor Nekrasov's *In the Home Town*, to quote another well-known example, focuses on the hero's postwar love life as well. Captain Nikolai Mitiasov returns to find that his wife Shura has been unfaithful with another veteran. After some painful back and forth he moves back in with her, but never feels at home. The years of war have opened up a gulf between them which seems impossible to bridge. He leaves her again for a companion who can understand him: Valia, a veteran with frontline mannerisms and lacking femininity. In sharp contrast to the tortured communication with his wife, talking to Valia 'was easy...They shared a common language—the slightly rude language of the front.'[128]

Both poles of the discourse about women veterans—the ideal partner and the whore—are represented in Zhanna Gausner's 1947 novel *So Now We're Home (Vot my i doma)*, which has a demobilized frontline nurse as one of the main protagonists. Early in the novel an older woman comments on the alleged morals of *frontovichki*: 'In the war, they say, the girls did not live a very boring life' (*devitsy ne ochen' skuchno zhili*). At the same time, however, the nurse is portrayed as a positive character. When she falls in love with another veteran, one of the protagonists comments: 'A good couple, they are the same age, both fought. All is in the right order here' (*vse v poriadke*).[129]

This stress on the suitability of veterans' love was not just a fantasy of novels divorced from actuality. One veteran remembers her own popularity, but also her own priorities after the war:

> I impressed those around me with my energy (*aktivnost'*), love of life, steadfastness. Yes, we who returned from the war as victors could not be different. I also think that my outer appearance made a good impression. I wore a uniform (I had nothing else) with a pretty order on my chest (the Red Star). I was healthy, with curly hair and a proudly raised head. No wonder, that the Head of the Regional Education Administration (*raiono*) fell in love with me and proposed to me at the end of the academic year. This did not conform to my plans. Moreover, it seemed to me that it did not behoove a *frontovichka* to marry somebody who had spent the war at the homefront.[130]

Another veteran recalled the predictions that nobody would marry this 'lady with a dagger', noting with satisfaction that instead 'the handsomest officer' had become her husband.[131]

Might it be that some of the hostility against frontline women was caused not only by their transgression of gender roles during the war but also by their self-assertiveness and their very popularity with at least a segment of the male population? This would explain some of the brutality with which other women treated *frontovichki*:

> In the evening, when we sat down for a cup of tea, his mother took my husband in the kitchen and burst into tears: 'Who have you got married to? An army girl... Why, you have two younger sisters. Who will marry them now?' ... Imagine, I had brought a gramophone record with me which I was very fond of. There were the words 'you have the right to walk in the most fashionable shoes...' It was about a girl from the front. I put it on the gramophone and my husband's eldest sister smashed it before my eyes: I had no rights whatsoever, she said. They destroyed all my wartime photographs.[132]

Another veteran was humiliated in public by her boss, 'also a woman', who 'for some reason objected to my wearing my military decorations'.[133]

Despite this sometimes nasty environment, unions between veterans were often successful. 'Back then I thought they were simply whores', noted one veteran who had been romantically unsuccessful at the front, 'but it turned out that these relationships lasted for the rest of their lives.'[134] Many 'good and strong families' developed on the basis of frontline love.[135] A former sniper, who met her husband during the war, remembers the advantages of shared war experience. 'There was no need to explain to him that my nerves were frayed.'[136] Other veterans interviewed by Aleksievich were also married to men they had met at the front. They were still partners at the time of the interviews in the late 1970s or early 1980s.[137]

Hiding war participation was only one tactic to deal with this ambivalent situation. Another was aggressive affirmation—'I am proud that I was at the front, proud about how I lived during the years of war.'[138] A third tactic was to embrace the stereotype but turn it against other frontline women. In her partially fictionalized 1948 war memoirs the military doctor Ol'ga Dzhigurda described in detail a colleague whom she named 'doctor Wind' (Vetrova). This doctor has an affair with a high-ranking officer, becomes his field wife, enjoys all sorts of undeserved privileges, and ignores military hierarchy. The just punishment for these transgressions of moral, sexual, and hierarchical boundaries is swift to follow: Vetrova gets dropped by her lover, shunned by her superiors and colleagues, and finally is demobilized in disgrace for the pregnancy which resulted from her affair. Dzhigurda waivers between pity for the naïveté of her colleague and final moral outrage: 'We don't need women like you here!'[139] Other women also condemned the 'frontline whores' in order to underline that they were not like them. One early volunteer stressed the influx of such 'loose women' from the middle of the war in order to underline her own difference. In a letter to Politburo member Kliment Voroshilov in late 1945 she wrote: '[In 1943] more women appeared at the front. I was unpleasantly struck by the fact that among them were also those who "established themselves" very well, who dressed up, engaged in gossip, and flirted.' In sharp contrast to such 'unpleasant' women, however, she insisted on going right to the frontline, a desire which resulted in a severe injury, disabling her for life.[140]

To stress the ambivalences of the situation of female veterans after the war thus does not mean to deny the real difficulties and disadvantages women had to face. Pregnant veterans had the worst return. One of them was arrested in 1945 because she had tried to kill her newborn child.[141] Another veteran killed herself after an obviously serious run-in with her mother about her pregnancy. She was 21 years old, had survived the war in the army, and had just been demobilized.[142] One veteran who had been left with a baby after demobilization forged a 'counter-revolutionary letter' in the name of the new partner of her child's father to the Chairman of the Presidium of the Supreme Soviet in order to get her out of the way. She was caught, though, and ended up in prison for seven years.[143]

Another group of frontline women facing massive problems in postwar life were the disabled. Often perceived as 'damaged goods' they had a very limited chance of finding a husband on the tight postwar marriage market.[144] Some *frontovichki* tried to hide their invalidity, and even destroyed the papers which made them eligible for state support—depriving themselves of what little aid they could have received otherwise.[145] Because they had less chance of receiving help from life partners and depended entirely on state aid, female war invalids were among the most disadvantaged subgroups of veterans in the postwar years.[146]

# PART
## II

# Victors and Victims

# 4

# 'A Great Profession'

Party and government surround invalids of the Patriotic War with care
and attention.

(Resolution of the Central Council of Trade Unions, 8 July 1944)[1]

—You are a pilot?
—I used to be.
Pause.
—And now?
—Invalid of the second group. A great profession.
—One must not talk like that, said Shura.

(Victor Nekrasov, *In the Home Town*, 1954)[2]

Anywhere between 10 and 19 per cent of surviving soldiers were
officially recognized as 'war invalids'. The vast majority were of lower
rank and had been injured in arms or legs. This meant not only that their
chances in postwar life were limited because of their military background
(rank and file soldiers tended to get worse jobs than demobilized officers),
but also because their ability to work in many professions—and frequently
their ability to move around in the first place—was severely restricted.
This group was marginalized considerably. Insufficient state aid, scarce
and poor-quality artificial limbs and wheelchairs, the perceived need to
mobilize any able (and not so able) body into the workforce, institutional
underdevelopment, and a general preoccupation with idealized supermen
rather than with the problems of real people of flesh, bone, and blood all
combined to make life miserable for many invalids throughout the postwar
period.[3]

According to official statistics, 3.8 million soldiers were medically discharged during the war and 2.6 million remained 'permanently disabled'.[4]

These numbers understate the real size of this group of veterans, because
Soviet authorities were reluctant to grant invalidity status to wounded
soldiers.[5] Most importantly, psychological casualties of war—those who
suffered from what now would be called post-traumatic stress disorder
(PTSD)—were frequently ignored if their suffering was not expressed in
outright physical symptoms.[6] The disabled were categorized into three
groups according to the level of mutilation and their ability to work.
Veterans in group I had the most severe defects and could not work 'under
any conditions'; those in group II were also severely handicapped (they
had for example lost more than one limb), but could work if special conditions were provided; those in group III had 'suffered loss or impairment
of one limb or organ'. They were considered able to work in a regular
environment, if often not in their old professions.[7] From the point of
view of the state, this was the preferred category, if a categorization as a
war invalid could not be avoided altogether. One of the basic functions
of the labour-medical boards (VTEK) in the postwar years was to classify
as many invalids as possible as 'third group' because the incentives to go
back to work were highest here.[8] As a result, group III invalids comprised
68 per cent of non-officer invalids in Russia after the war, followed by
group II with nearly 31 per cent. Less than 2 per cent were classified into
group I.[9]

Because of their official status, the postwar lives of the war disabled
are better documented archivally than those of other veterans, making it
possible to recapitulate many of the processes analysed in Part I of this
book.[10] Take the enraging interactions with the bureaucracy, described in
Chapter 2. Losing a pension-book might deprive the invalid of payment for
two years, especially if ill health prevented consistent efforts at supplications
in various institutions. The mandatory (semi-)annual examination by the
labour-medical board to confirm invalidity status was originally even
demanded from those who had lost a limb at the front—'as if it would
grow back', veterans remarked bitterly. This absurd rule was changed in
1948, when certain unalterable mutilations and illnesses, including blindness,
certain amputations, and paralysis of two or more limbs were exempted
from regular re-evaluation.[11] In later decades, only group III invalids needed
to undergo this process every five years.[12] This approach would have made
life easier for everybody involved in the earlier years as well, when VTEK
worked under complicated conditions. The commission of the city of
Molotov occupied a corner of a hallway in the central polyclinic, behind a

wooden partition, where invalids had to undress, were examined, and the documents filled out. A commission in the city of Kuibyshev at least had a single room in a hospital, but there was no waiting room. When higher level authorities checked up on its work in 1950 they found twenty-six invalids standing in front of the door, many of them on crutches. In the countryside things were even grimmer. One commission was reported to work in an unheated room of 7 to 9 degrees Celsius. Waiting lists for appointments were long—from two weeks to two months.[13] Many more hassles caused by institutional underdevelopment could be cited.[14]

Given the relatively dense archival material on this group, disabled veterans also provide a good starting point for a discussion of one of the major results of reintegration which forms the central problematic of the second part of this study: the establishment of social hierarchies among former soldiers. Such stratification has two aspects which can be analysed particularly well in this case: economic position and status. The former is the result of the uneven distribution of goods, services, and life chances among a given population, the latter of the uneven ascription of esteem, often inscribed in law. In most capitalist countries, economic stratification is of greater consequence and status often follows wealth. In the Soviet Union, the relationship was reversed because a large sector of the economy was under state control. Only the shadow economy added an element of stratification relatively independent of status, but as a rule a person's material position tended to be determined by the level of officially granted esteem.[15]

In the case of war invalids, economic position and status combined into a hierarchy of misery created by complex interactions between prewar social differences, gender, the effects of state policies and of economic strategies employed by individuals and their families. Welfare legislation created gradations of support based on a veteran's classification according to degree of disability (I–III), prewar income, and wartime rank. An invalid's position within the matrix of access to goods, services and—in the final analysis—life chances also depended on the extent to which his or her family could function as an economic unit. The ability to convince medical boards that one should be classified into a group eligible for more benefits, or the skill in working the system to actually receive benefits, also played its part, as did the sheer physical aspect of disablility—after all, it made a difference in everyday life if one was blind or not, or if one had lost one or four limbs, independent of the judgement of doctors.

Like veterans more generally, and the society they were a part of, war invalids were thus socially differentiated to a high degree. Notwithstanding such stratification, they shared a common status—despite the internal classifications, they were all 'Invalids of the Patriotic War' (*invalidy Otechestvennoi voiny*). This category had a meaning beyond the material aspects of welfare. War invalids remained the only group of war veterans whose entitlement to special treatment was recognized at least in principle beyond the end of mass-demobilization in 1948. This is the third reason to closely observe wounded soldiers after their return: their example points to the central theme of the third and final part of this book, which focuses on the transformations of the new social entity of veterans. In this history, war invalids played a prominent role. The continued affirmation of their special status clashed even more violently than in the case of their healthier comrades with the real-life experiences of frustration and abandonment, a dialectic between discourse and experience central to the mass psychology of the entitlement community which formed the basis of the later veterans' movement.

The category 'war invalid' (*invalid voiny*) had already been created in the interwar period, when welfare for disabled soldiers was seen as an important contribution to army morale.[16] Between 1940 and 1948 the group eligible for war invalids' privileges expanded, until it encompassed more or less all persons who had lost their health in frontline service (see Table 4.1). War invalids were now one of the most privileged groups of veterans. They had special pension rights, were subject to specific labour regulations, and exempt from tuition in higher education; they were supposed to get preferred access to fuel, food, and other goods as well as to housing and were granted special conditions in the repayment of housing-construction loans. A subgroup had special tax privileges.[17]

Their status also continued after 1947/8, when most other privileges for former service personnel were discontinued.[18] From then until the late 1970s, war invalids were, in effect, the only subgroup with a distinct and slowly evolving legal status. The landmark 1956 pension law unified the ad hoc legislation for war invalids, and increased the pensions for some categories.[19] It did not, however, change the fundamentals of the pension system for victims of war. In particular, and despite public discussion of this problematic issue, it kept the principle that pensions were determined through a combination of level of mutilation, military rank, and prewar income. This system severely disadvantaged war invalids from the youngest

Table 4.1. Growth of the group covered as war invalids (pension law)

| Year | Group | Resolution |
| --- | --- | --- |
| 1940 | Drafted soldiers (including draftees who became junior commanders) who had been blue- and white-collar workers with monthly income of 400 rubles or less; injured or sick as result of frontline duty | SNK, 16 July 1940, No. 1269 |
| 1941 | Career military personnel | SNK, 5 June 1941, No. 1474 |
| 1942 | Sailors of ships of civilian sea and river fleets, navigating in battle zones | SNK, 12 Sept. 1942, No. 1511; 22 Oct. 1942, No. 1728 |
| | Sailors and aviation crews of Commissariat of Fishing Industry, navigating in battle zones | SNK Directive, 22 Dec. 1942, No. 24543-r |
| 1943 | Civilians engaged in building defence lines | SNK, 5 Aug. 1943, No. 863 |
| | Civilians working on military ships | SNK, 25 Nov. 1943, No. 1312 |
| | Medical personnel on civilian ships sailing in battle zones | SNK, 7 Jan. 1943, No. 26 |
| | Frontline workers of the Commissariat of Communication | SNK, 28 Oct. 1943, No. 1181 |
| 1944 | Anti-mine commandos of Osaviakhim | Order, RSFSR Comm. of Social Welfare, 26 Sept. 1944, No. 220 |
| | All other personnel of civilian ships (sea fleet) navigating in battle zones | SNK, 20 Mar. 1944, No. 298 |
| | Frontline film crews | SNK, 20 May 1944 |
| | Officers of First Polish Corps | SNK, 6 Feb. 1944, No. 127 |
| 1946 | Former soldiers and partisans disabled after demobilization, if connection to wartime service could be shown within five years of release | SM Resolution, 9 July 1946, No. 1516 |

Source: SP SSSR 19 (1940): st. 465 (pp. 641–4); 15 (1941): st. 282 (pp. 467–73); 8 (1942): st. 131 (p. 143); 9 (1942): st. 152 (p. 160); 14 (1943): st. 249 (pp. 248–50); R. R. Kats (ed.), Material'noe obespechenie pri invalidnosti, starosti, za vyslugu let i po sluchaiu poteri kormil'tsa (Moscow: Izd-vo Minister-stva sotsial'nogo obespecheniia RSFSR, 1948), 43, 44–5, 48–9, 53; GARF f. r-5446, op. 1, d. 220, l. 358–9; d. 210, l. 51, 101; d. 228, l. 54–7; d. 224, l. 21. For the continued relevance of the Resolu-tion of 16 July 1940 see A. D. Glazunov, L'goty uchastnikam voiny (Moscow: Iuridicheskaia literatura, 1981), 5.

generation, as they had not had a prewar income and therefore received
only minimal pensions.[20]

In 1959, the pensions of group II were increased by 10 per cent, and
in 1964 new minimum payments were defined for groups I and II. In
1965 working group III invalids were guaranteed at least the minimum
pension, no matter how much they earned.[21] In 1962 and 1964 some
categories of disabled (both war victims and others) received the right
to free public transport within cities.[22] In the same year, a resolution
promised new privileges with regard to access to jobs and flexibility of
working hours, medical care, pensions, housing, access to scarce goods, and
public transport.[23] In celebration of the fiftieth anniversary of the October
Revolution, pensions were increased in 1967. In 1970, a new landmark
resolution promised 'concrete time periods for the betterment of the living
conditions of invalids'. Further pension increases came in 1973, and in 1975
the thirtieth anniversary of victory was celebrated by privileges with regard
to public transport, pensions, medical welfare, housing and the payment
for heat, water, gas, or electricity, as well as access to private cars fitted out
for use by the legless. Invalids of the Patriotic War also finally received a
special identity card, which allowed them to claim their privileges more
forcefully.[24]

A new flurry of legislative activity started in the late 1970s, in the context
of the shift of veterans' politics away from organization and towards
entitlement.[25] It led to a fully blown system of privileges for invalids of the
Patriotic War from the early 1980s onwards, which included exemption
of group I and II from agricultural tax,[26] as well as from taxes levelled
on private garages and motor vehicles;[27] special privileges with regard to
medical care, public as well as private transport, housing and everyday
life (including better access to private telephones and garden plots), and
work placement. The chaos of decrees, resolutions, directions, and laws
was ordered in new Statutes on Privileges of Invalids of the Patriotic War
and the Families of Fallen Servicemen, passed by the Council of Ministers
of the Soviet Union on 23 February 1981, which replaced thirty-five other
legal acts passed between 1942 and 1979.[28] These statutes did not end
the legislative activity towards war invalids, but from that point onward
their growing status dissolved more and more into the broader category
of 'war participant' (uchastnik Velikoi Otechestvennoi voiny), which from
1978 onwards became the basis of welfare legislation targeted towards war
veterans.

How generous were such provisions? Let us take pensions as a starting point to study the practical meaning of state assistance. The size of the payment depended on the group of invalidity (I–III), which was considered an index for physical impairment. Pensions for professional soldiers were determined by a different set of rules than those for rank and file and junior commanders of the compulsory military service.[29] Not to complicate the discussion unnecessarily, I will restrict it here to the latter, which was regulated by the government resolutions of 16 July and 12 November 1940.[30]

As can be seen from Table 4.2, war invalids received a minimum of 90 rubles and a maximum of 500 rubles of pension payments—a huge range. At the lower end of the scale, life was miserable if the invalid depended on the pension alone. 'Heroes of the "Patriotic War",' wrote Soviet defector Abdurakhman Avtorkhanov, 'cripples with numerous orders and medals, wandered over great areas of the country, begging alms in order to keep alive. The monthly pensions of the grateful government barely covered the modest cost of living for one week.'[31] Those first group invalids who received the minimum pension of 150 rubles fell into the poorest sector of Soviet urban society. About 15 per cent of blue- and white-collar workers earned 150 rubles or less by mid-1946.[32] Just to pay for the food received on the ration cards—hardly a generous allotment—amounted to 79 rubles per month for workers in Moscow, or 116 rubles for a worker with one

Table 4.2. Pensions for regular invalids of the patriotic war

| Group of invalidity | Pension as % of average prewar monthly income (150–400 rubles) | Pension if invalid had not worked or earned less than 150 rubles before the war | Pension if invalid had earned more than 400 rubles before the war |
|---|---|---|---|
| *Rank and file* | | | |
| Group I | 100 | 150 rubles | 400 rubles |
| Group II | 75 | 120 rubles | 300 rubles |
| Group III | 50 | 90 rubles | 200 rubles |
| *Junior commanders* | | | |
| Group I | 125 | 187.5 rubles | 500 rubles |
| Group II | 100 | 150 rubles | 400 rubles |
| Group III | 75 | 112.5 rubles | 300 rubles |

*Source*: SNK Resolutions of 16 July and 12 Nov. 1940. These regulations refer to people who had been workers or white-collar workers (*sluzhashchie*) before the war. Professional soldiers were covered under different regulations.

child.[33] An increase of the minimum pension for group I invalids—who by definition were unable to work—to 300 rubles per month in 1946 did not change the basic fact of severe poverty.[34] By that year a real wage (*fakticheski mer zarplaty*) of 300 rubles or less meant that half or more of the income had to be spent on foodstuffs covering 'the barest minimum necessary to feed the human being'.[35] By 1956 it meant an ability to pay for bread and some fish products, 'but not for meat, butter, or even for better clothes (other than working clothes)'.[36] The conclusion that, without supplementary income, 'it was very difficult, almost impossible, to live on a single invalid's pension' is thus especially relevant to those on the minimal pension.[37]

The maximum of 400 rubles (rank and file) or 500 rubles (officers), by contrast, put people into the higher income bracket in postwar society. In 1946, only 35 per cent of Soviet blue- or white-collar workers received between 301 and 600 rubles a month. Career officers could receive up to 900 rubles of pension payments, which was 'a very high sum' if compared with average wages.[38] Only few invalids received pensions at this upper end of the scale. By the end of 1946 under 2 per cent of war invalids in the entire Union were in the first group, 30 per cent were second group, and 69 per cent were in the unpopular third group which was forced to work under conditions of cut pensions.[39] Of all pensioners (including but not restricted to war invalids) in 1946 only 3 per cent received more than 300 rubles while 77 per cent received 150 rubles or less.[40] Most were thus in a situation where the symbolic affirmation of their status was coupled with poverty—a recipe for resentment.

Institutions set up to assist wounded returnees showed a similar pattern of big claims and severe practical neglect. Invalids' co-operatives were supposed to create specific working conditions for disabled persons in general and war invalids in particular, but performed this function only poorly. The pressures to fulfil production quotas remained of greater concern than the welfare of invalids. Disabled veterans, who were supposed to have privileged access to these facilities, reached a share of only 26 per cent of all workers in these establishments by the end of the 1940s. Moreover, the co-operatives played a rather negligible role, employing only 1 per cent of those war disabled who had an official job (see Table 4.3 below). The working conditions in the co-ops contributed to this situation. Frequently, no special arrangements were made to cater to the special needs of the disabled; the production facilities were located in dirty, wet basements without ventilation; drinking water was kept in uncovered buckets; sufferers of open cases of tuberculosis worked side by side with other workers; there was no health care available, not to mention the absence of canteens, workers' housing, or even child care. As a result of such living and working conditions, invalids fled these establishments in great numbers—departures reached 60 or even 80 per cent in some cases.[41]

The situation was hardly different in a second type of establishment meant to cater to war wounded—invalids' homes (*doma invalidov*). While the co-operatives employed largely invalids of the third group, as these were most likely to be able to fulfil the all-important production quotas, the homes were supposed to cater to those who needed special care in daily life. Predictably, however, horrible living conditions were 'by no means the exception, but the rule'.[42] To get a better idea of these, let us follow a local official into the four invalids' homes in Saratov province in 1946. The buildings, he found, had not been repaired for years. Basic items such as tables, chairs, and bedside tables were scarce. In the canteens three to four tables had to serve 100 people or more. Often there was nothing to sit on, either in the canteen or in the wards. Items of everyday use were kept 'anywhere' instead of in the bedside tables. 'Such objects as dressers [or] racks are a great rarity in the boarding schools and houses of invalids.' Availability of plates and dishes was 'exceptionally bad', there was 'not a single' invalids' house that did not need blankets, mattresses, pillows. Summer blankets were completely absent, and the thick winter blankets were used all year round, without sheets. 'It is easy to imagine their condition, and from here [it is also easy to imagine] the general hygienic condition of the establishments, which cater to people who have defended our Homeland, members of families of fallen soldiers, personal pensioners and other citizens,' remarked the indignant official asking the government of the Russian Republic for help.[43]

Not all invalids' homes were as bad as this example, but the overwhelming impression one gets from reading archival sources on these institutions is one of utter misery and despair.[44] While certainly the specific bias of state sources towards things which do not work darkens the picture, there was a lot of darkness to be found, and improvements over time were slight at best. No wonder that veterans tended to ignore the various institutions set up to 'care' for them: by 1 January 1946, the retraining schools of the Russian Commissariat of Social Welfare were unable to fill places for 585 war invalids

(12 per cent short of the plan). One school in Kalinin region, which was expected to train ninety war invalids, had filled only twenty places.[45] Most of this shortfall was due to invalids leaving the institutions—14 per cent left before they had finished their training.[46] Throughout 1947, close to half of all war invalids working within the Union of Invalids' Co-operatives (*Vsekoopinsoiuz*) abandoned these establishments.[47]

That welfare was insufficient and pension payments in most cases implied a near-starvation diet was not an accident or simply due to the circumstances of general postwar poverty and destruction—although these certainly made things worse. Soviet welfare policy tried quite consciously to create incentives to work. Work placement (*trudoustroistvo*) was seen as a 'most important state affair' (*vazhneishaia gosudarstvennaia zadacha*).[48] Official discourse assumed that the needs of the individual veteran and the need of the state coincided neatly in this respect: the state needed the invalids' labour in the reconstruction of the country; the individual was better off working because it reintegrated him or her into society and fostered self-affirmation.[49] At the same time, employers were under too much pressure to fulfil the plan to accommodate victims of war—'I have a factory to run, not a welfare institution', as one director put it.[50]

In order to make a living in such an environment many invalids combined a paid job and a pension payment with financial and other support by family members, material help by various institutions of the politico–economic system, and food gained from their own garden plots and farm animals.[51] This created a dynamic of social stratification which is impossible to quantify precisely or relate systematically to the official hierarchy of pension payment and wage or salary, but absolutely central to understanding postwar life nevertheless. War invalids were engaged in all sorts of 'alternative professions' which ranged from completely legal activities such as tending one's own garden and contributing thus to the family economy, to semi-legal private enterprises, the illegal professions of trader ('speculator' in Bolshevik) or beggar, to various criminal activities such as theft and banditism. According to data collected by the Council of Ministers of the Soviet Union by late 1946, 248,000 war invalids of the second and third groups did not work in recognized employment.[52] This substantial minority of maybe 10 per cent was only the tip of the iceberg as many war invalids either had only an official job but engaged in other activities, or engaged in both the job and 'alternative professions'.[53]

One reason to avoid working in an officially designated 'job' was skill in getting money, goods, and services out of various levels of the political-economic system. Since every level of the administrative, economic, and party apparatus was supposed to help war invalids, some managed to exploit this parallelism of access to scarce goods and money. They went on writing letters, complaining about lack of help although they did relatively well.[54]

Material help for war invalids is provided by party and soviet organizations, by labour union and Komsomol organizations, by the supply organizations (*khoziaistvennye organizatsiia*) of enterprises and institutions, by trade organizations and the organs of social welfare.

As a result, individual invalids of the Patriotic War received large sums of money from these various organizations, as well as lots of manufactured goods. So, for example:

The war invalid Shishkov, who had worked at the Magnitogorsk metal plant before becoming an invalid, received between May and November of 1944 from the diverse organizations (plant management, factory committee, city welfare administration) 14,000 rubles and 30 different types of manufactured goods. Alone from the factory committee and the management of factory No. 259 [the war invalid] Popov received 600 rubles and 10 different manufactured goods (boots, a suit, two pairs of quilted trousers, lengths of cloth, and so on) in 1944. Analogous facts took place in other inspected cities.[55]

Other veterans did not work because they were involved in their own household economy, which often included growing their own food. In a campaign which had started during the war and went on at least until 1949, many war invalids had received gardens, preferably located close to their place of residence or to a train line.[56] These plots became central in the survival strategies of those lucky enough to control them. Already during the war the welfare administration of Ivanovo region described a common reason why third group invalids did not work:

Some of them live in towns, own their own houses and personal garden plots, a cow, a goat, chickens, and so on. They prefer to work in their subsidiary gardens, to care for their cattle, to prepare fodder for it during the summer and to prepare heating fuel. Others work at home, taking private orders for making and repair of shoes, and so on...[57]

Such small-scale home production of goods (*melkoe kustarnoe remeslo*) was one of the major alternative ways to make a living among war invalids in

Vladimir province in 1945.[58] As independent craftsmen (*kustari-odinochki*) these veterans had found an important niche in the economy: the trade of shoemaker, tailor, or simply repairman for instruments of daily use produced 'a big income'.[59] War invalids with special skills, such as blacksmith, also worked for their own pocket as itinerant craftsmen.[60]

War invalids made the best of the nooks and crannies in the existing legislation. Pensions for war invalids of the third group were not only cancelled if they did not work, they were also cut if they made too much money—more than 200 rubles of income from non-agricultural work.[61] It was thus advantageous for those who lived in the city and had a garden, a cow, or some chickens to do only a part-time job, devote their energies to their private production of foodstuffs, and get the full pension on top. The state soon reacted to this strategy: a resolution of 4 October 1948 cut pensions of third group invalids in half if they had any income other than a wage, regardless of its size. This legal change put war invalids with very small incomes into a precarious situation. They could be deprived of half of their pension for as little as a potato plot of six square metres, often losing more than what their garden could make up for. This legislation destroyed the widespread strategy of making a living with a salary of under 200 rubles, a full pension, and a well-tended garden.[62]

'Speculation' was another alternative to officially sanctioned work. In Zlatousk, 50 per cent of the unemployed war invalids of the second group were engaged in trade in early 1945. In Magnitogorsk the corresponding number was 32 per cent. Of the third group invalids who refused to work in one major district of Cheliabinsk, 44 per cent worked as 'speculators'. At the city's markets every day between 70 and 120 war invalids engaged in their chosen profession.[63] Besides money, there were many reasons why maimed soldiers went into trade: their often precarious material situation and problems on the job market, their relative immunity from prosecution, the disincentives to work in a well-paid officially recognized job written into the pension law. In addition, at least until the start of mass-demobilization, war invalids were one of the least state-controlled groups. In marked contrast to workers in many enterprises and military personnel, they were not bound to one place of work and could thus move around more freely, which helped in the profession of 'speculator'.[64] Access to goods distributed by welfare organizations also led to engagement in trade: 'Often societal organizations [and] welfare administrations give invalids of the Patriotic War as material help things, which they do not need. This encourages war invalids to engage in speculation.'[65] In Moscow, war invalids received a 35 per cent discount in high-priced 'commercial' stores—a privilege which allowed them to sell scarce goods at a profit.[66]

In terms of both practice and geography, trade was connected with begging, a second illegal activity which kept many war invalids alive. One war invalid of the second group returned home without legs in the first half of 1945. He found his house destroyed and the local authorities unwilling or unable to help. During the winter he and his wife had neither wood to heat, nor bread to eat. He went to the bazaar to sing for his supper, which got the couple through the winter.[67] For others it was more than dire need that led into the world of beggars. The willingness of many to give to those who had spilled their blood and lost their limbs in the defence of the homeland played a role as well—a practice with its own and involved history.[68]

War invalids formed an important part of the subculture of beggars, vagrants, and small-time con men who lived at train stations, travelled from town to town, begged, stole, engaged in small-scale trade, and beleaguered state institutions with requests for money and help. They were often quite aggressive and sometimes went in groups to the waiting rooms of offices, where they created 'an absolutely undesirable situation'.[69] When in 1945 Moscow authorities tried to limit the number of tickets war invalids could receive to leave the city on trains (an important part of their black-market activities), 'a large group of the sick and crippled attacked the district headquarters of the militia, which issued the passes. They were in the process of making up their own passes when a detachment of MVD. troops arrived armed with sub-machine guns, fired a few rounds and arrested the surviving ex-heroes.'[70]

By the 1990s, instances like this one had solidified in the shared memory of urban Russians into the conviction that Stalin had war invalids rounded up and sent to remote parts of the country. This anti-veteran campaign is supposed to have happened 'some two years after the end of the war'.[71] Other sources put such recollections in doubt. In July of 1947, a letter writer complained to Central Committee Secretary A. A. Zhdanov that it was impossible to travel on suburban trains without being accosted by psalm-singing beggars, many of them war invalids. Looking at these scenes, he feared that foreigners could get 'the impression that our country is a country of beggars (*strana nishchikh*)'. In reaction, the Central Committee

Secretariat asked the Ministry of Internal Affairs to 'increase the battle
against child homelessness'.[72] The resolution did not mention war invalids,
though, who certainly were still there three years later, at least on the
city's outskirts. Michel Gordey, a Russian-speaking correspondent for the
French newspaper *France Soir* reported from the Soviet Union in 1950: 'In
several large railroad stations, in the waiting-rooms, I discovered crowds of
travelers who looked very poor. I was struck by the number of wounded
veterans, the most fortunate of whom were walking on crutches. Others,
who had lost both legs above the knee, were sitting on platforms with
rollers, which they propelled by their own hands.'[73] A year later, in 1951,
such scenes were still enough of a problem in the eyes of the authorities that
the Council of Ministers and the Presidium of the Supreme Soviet called
for a concerted fight against what they called 'antisocial, parasitic elements'
in the cities, who were supposed to be rounded up by the militia.[74]

It has proved impossible to either verify or falsify the widespread rumour
that there was a coordinated state campaign to round up war invalids and
hide them away in the periphery. While archival access remains incomplete
and it is possible that files were destroyed, recent research strongly suggests
that the disappearance of begging war invalids from the big cities was a
side-effect of the 1951 decree against 'anti-social parasitic elements' and
the following 'energetic campaign against beggars' of 1952–4. It does not
appear to have been a police action directed against war invalids specifically.
This interpretation is also strengthened by the fact that the famous colony
of war invalids in Valaam cloister, Lake Ladoga, started its existence in
1952, that is, right after the campaign was started. Not unlike former
POWs who were swept up in the anti-cosmopolitanism frenzy, begging
and 'speculating' veterans were swept up in this larger campaign against
'parasites'.[75]

The shadow world of trade and panhandling was part of the mix of
strategies war invalids used to survive. One could receive a pension of
220 rubles and manage to avoid 'working' (selling cigarettes on the market
did not qualify) because the local branch of the State Bank failed to ask for
a document showing employment.[76] One could gamble on the bazaar to
make a living,[77] or labour as an unregistered worker in a beer factory who
got paid in kind and then sold what his own thirst left over.[78] One could
become a member of a criminal gang specialized in the theft of grain,[79] or
armed robbery.[80] Some even tried their luck as counterfeiters.[81] Of the 160
war invalids who were prosecuted under criminal law in the autonomous

republic of Bashkiria in 1944, 23 received sentences for speculation, 77 for theft, 7 for robbery, and 23 for hooliganism.[82] In the first eight months of 1944 the militia of Novosibirsk region arrested 160 war invalids, among them 58 for theft, 17 for the theft of cattle, 12 for robbery, 2 for robbery combined with homicide, 23 for serious hooliganism, 11 for falsification of documents and trade with ration cards, and 20 for speculation.[83]

Illegal activities of war invalids might have been encouraged by the relatively lenient approach towards them during the 1940s. A directive of the People's Commissariat of Justice and of the State procuracy from 23 July 1943 stressed the need for a 'special approach' to, among others, war invalids who committed 'petty crimes for the first time'. Local courts did not always follow this line, leading the People's Commissariat of Justice to complain in October 1945 that 'the courts do not inquire into the reasons forcing the [war] invalids to commit these thefts and do not raise the question to the appropriate organs regarding their difficulties in being placed into work'.[84] Others, however, saw things a little differently. The Chairman of the Moscow City Council G. M. Popov complained in early December 1945 that 'we have no right to give a recidivist, who was sentenced two or three times a discount (*skidka*), even if he is an invalid of the Patriotic War, even if he fought'.[85] What local courts were supposed to do was figure out who had only temporarily lapsed (and needed help) and to separate them from those invalids who had chosen to 'not rejoin the Soviet economy and were settling into a life of crime'. That was certainly not an easy task, given that, as a Moscow judge reported in 1945, half of those who passed through People's Courts were war invalids.[86] Paradoxically, the judicial leniency towards crippled defenders of the Homeland sometimes worked to their disadvantage—some were denied leading positions for fear that they could not be held criminally responsible for abuses of authority.[87]

It is impossible to judge how many of the wounded veterans who took advantage of the interstices of Soviet society to make a living did comparatively well. Clearly, there were cases of more or less spectacular success—one might recall the case of Vaisman discussed in Chapter 2. Equally clearly, many others struggled for the bare minimum of existence. The shadow world, like the official world, stratified war invalids. In both worlds, some did well, while many did not. Instead of the skilled positions they were supposed to get, many war invalids worked as guards or loaders (*gruzchiki*).[88] The majority of war invalids in Sverdlovsk who could no longer work in their former professions worked as guards or 'in various other auxiliary jobs'.[89] Despite massive differences between regions and even among enterprises in the same region, the majority of disabled veterans laboured in lowly occupations. At the one end of the spectrum were cities like Leningrad, where 75 per cent worked in skilled positions in 1945;[90] at the other end were areas like Sverdlovsk region, where the author of an internal report tried to hide the fact that 82 per cent did not work in particularly good jobs by focusing on the remaining 18 per cent who occupied leading positions (11 per cent), kolkhoz chairs (2 per cent), were engineers or other technical personnel (ITR—3 per cent), or had acquired new professions (2 per cent).[91]

Health problems made things worse. Poor housing, hard work, long commutes, and an extremely poor diet did not foster physical recovery. Prosthetic appliances and wheelchairs were nearly impossible to come by. Tuberculosis, poorly healing stumps of amputated limbs, and re-opening wounds were common ailments and inhibited advancement in postwar society.[92] V. I. Gurevich, for example, a war invalid of the second group, had to return frequently to hospital for treatment. Between 1944 and 1945 he stayed in hospital four times: first for over a month from 15 December 1944 to 18 January 1945, then again from 26 February to 19 March, only to go in again for another good month from 26 May. After his release on 5 July he stayed out for less than two weeks before returning to hospital from 14 to 25 July.[93] Health issues were a problem even for young veterans who came out of the war with all of their limbs intact. Grigorii Chukhrai nearly had to abandon his dream of becoming a movie director because splinters in his lung, poor nutrition, and tuberculosis hospitalized him during the making of his diploma movie. Only the patronage of Mikhail Romm allowed him to become one of the best known Soviet movie directors.[94] If a young veteran had such problems it can easily be imagined what life was like for older and more severely wounded *frontoviki*. This is even reflected in socialist-realist fiction. Colonel Voropaev in *Happiness* is not only an amputee but also has tuberculosis. During the whole book he is sick and in large parts of the story bedridden.

Like the fictional Colonel Voropaev, some overcame such problems. There were even norm-busters who modelled themselves after the novel's hero. They formed 'something like a movement of Voropaevism—a sui generis post-Patriotic War wounded veterans' Stakhanovism'.[95] This type can be met in newspaper reporting and other official publications, but also in internal reports of state and party actors about work with war invalids.[96]

Less spectacularly, the vast majority of war invalids did work. In the regions of the Russian Republic the percentage of working war invalids varied from a minimum of 73 per cent in Kursk region to a maximum of 93 per cent in Kirov region by autumn 1945.[97] The average was 84 per cent for all war invalids, 62 per cent for those of the second, and 96 per cent for those of the third group.[98] These figures might be inflated for a host of reasons, but are unlikely to be completely forged, given that local authorities knew that their numbers could be verified by a central commission. Moreover, there is no reason to believe that the tendency to inflate these numbers worked unequally across the different sectors of the economy, which makes it possible to treat them as good indicators of the general trends of where war invalids found employment after the war (Table 4.3).[99]

Most veterans came from the countryside and most returned there after the war, including war invalids who in their majority returned to the collective farms. However, more wounded veterans found employment in cities than other veterans—indicating social mobility of a section of the former peasants. More than half of disabled soldiers worked in the countryside; only 17 per cent were employed in industry and 28 per cent in 'other organizations'—presumably in administrative jobs in the state and party apparatus. This group was larger than the equivalent among other former soldiers (Table 4.4). This comparison suggests that war invalids were more likely to move into non-agricultural professions (i.e. move up in social standing, as nearly any work outside of the kolkhoz was preferable to the misery of rural life) than their peers who left the army during mass-demobilization after the war's end. Only about 30 per cent of demobilized

Table 4.3. Employment of war invalids on the pension roll, 1 November 1946

|   |   | Absolute numbers | % of G | % of I |
|---|---|---|---|---|
| A | In industry | 365,836 | 16.7 | 16.0 |
| B | In co-operatives | 23,153 | 1.1 | 1.0 |
| C | At home (nadomniki) | 2,193 | 0.1 | 0.1 |
| D | In agriculture | 1,159,840 | 52.9 | 50.8 |
| E | In institutions (v uchrezhdeniiakh) | 31,497 | 1.4 | 1.4 |
| F | In other organizations | 611,327 | 27.9 | 26.8 |
| G | Total work | 2,193,846 | 100.0 | 96.0 |
| H | In job training (obuchaiutsia) | 91,700 | | 4.0 |
| I | Total work and job training | 2,285,546 | | 100.0 |

Source: GARF f. r-5446, op. 48a, d. 3742, l. 101.

Table 4.4. Demobilized and their job placement as of 1 November 1946

|  | Absolute | % |
| --- | --- | --- |
| Total number of demobilized since start of demobilization | 7,517,937 | 100.00 |
| Among them those who arrived in cities/towns (v goroda) | 2,487,154 | 33.08 |
| Total work in cities | 2,215,834 | 29.47 |
| Entered educational institutions | 77,122 | 1.03 |
| Are not working | 194,198 | 2.58 |

Source: GARF f. r-9517, op. 1, d. 56, l. 7.

soldiers had found work in the cities, compared to 47 per cent of war invalids who were employed in non-agricultural professions.

That a minority of war invalids moved up the social hierarchy after the war is supported by other evidence as well. Memoirists mention the important role disabled veterans of peasant background played even in such an august institution as Moscow State University.[100] Beyond tertiary education, which could accommodate only a minority, there is also evidence for some upward mobility—at least if one takes money as an (albeit poor) indicator. A review of the financial situation of war invalids in Molotov province found in February 1945 that, on average, working group II invalids did better financially after the war. Before the war they had received a salary of 504 rubles, while now, as invalids, it stood at 524 rubles and the pension at 276 rubles. Thus, their salary had increased by 5 per cent and their income (salary plus pension) by 63 per cent. As is frequently the case, this average hid a large range of gains and losses of income among the reviewed group II invalids. In fact, only 39 per cent had increased their salary, 16 per cent had the same income, and the largest group of 45 per cent had to make do with less money.[101]

Were there any regularities to the movement of war invalids up or down the Soviet social hierarchy? Severe disability tended to decrease veterans' financial situation after the war if it was very bad, meriting classification into group I. Such veterans suffered particularly if they lacked family and spousal support. Their social standing depended largely on the income of the other family members, as they could only contribute an insufficient pension. Group III invalids were usually doing a bit better than their more seriously mutilated colleagues, but the tendency to classify as many as possible into this group, combined with their problems in finding good employment, meant that most of them did reasonably well only if they supplemented their income with private (and sometimes illegal) economic activities. Best off, from a material point of view, were group II invalids. Frequently, their mutilations were similar to those in group III, but they had managed somehow to get classified into the higher group. They could often still engage in some kind of economic activity, without being forced to work in an official job or lose their pension, as was the case for their group III siblings in misery. Moreover, requalification and training efforts focused on the more badly injured, that is, groups I and II.[102]

Because of the complex interaction of official and unofficial economic processes, downward mobility on the official scale did not necessarily imply a real fall: some in fact chose unskilled work because it allowed them to obtain foodstuffs and other scarcities. Meat-processing plants and margarine factories were popular choices for war invalids for this reason.[103] In Leningrad, those 13 per cent of working war invalids who were employed in non-skilled positions had found those mainly in the food industry—in bread plants, canteens, or chocolate factories.[104] Such choices, while frowned at by officials, in effect increased the share of war invalids who found a place in Soviet society. This process is also reflected in a 1944 review of the fate of 4,310 war invalids, undertaken by the regional welfare administration of Ivanovo. It found that 20 per cent of them worked in a lower skilled job than before the war. Less than half of those did so because they were no longer able to perform the tasks of their old profession, but had not managed ('yet', as the report put it optimistically) to acquire a new one. Most of them were poorly educated. The rest did not want to work in their old profession but had successfully requested employment which gave access to food supplies: jobs in canteens, bakeries, stores, or supply departments (ORSy). This group constituted more than 10 per cent of the sample, reducing the share of the problem group significantly.[105]

Invalids of the Patriotic War were thus in a curious position. They were clearly a privileged group according to law, even beyond the 1947/8 divide, when most other privileges for veterans were abolished. This status was particularly obvious in relation to other categories of disabled citizens, even to war invalids from other wars.[106] Moreover, these policies were more than mere propaganda. They were enforced and audited by various parts of the state machinery of coercion.[107] War invalids could thus expect to get assistance in their quest to get around the red tape which filled the life of anybody in need of state assistance. Such assistance, together with the continued official recognition of their special status and the ritualistic assertion of such status necessary to benefit from it, could not but reinforce war invalids' sense that their sacrifice for the larger community entitled them to special treatment, to a special status in postwar society. This special status, however, was not matched by the delivery of actual benefits. The attempt of legislators to build strong incentives to work into the legislation, the size of the group, the heavy destruction of the country, the perceived need to continue war-like mobilization in the context of the cold war, the underdevelopment of the Soviet welfare state, and the general lack of resources in an economy of scarcity, combined to undercut whatever positive effect the legislation might have had for the mass of war invalids.

The affirmation of a special status for war invalids was thus coupled with constant frustration of expectations, leading to anger, bitterness, and resentment. 'I am still interested,' wrote one veteran in 1959, 'if there are any advantages (l'goty) for war invalids, or if the party and the government have already forgotten about the needs of those who have spilled their blood in defense of the independence of our Homeland.' One of his comrades, similarly, noted that he simply did 'not understand' if there were 'in fact any government decisions about help, care and privileges for war invalids'. The country, growled a third, 'has forgotten about us and does not want to know that we lead a sad, half-starving, beggarly existence'.[108]

The basic tension between symbolic status and frustrated material expectations persisted until welfare policies were expanded in the 1960s, 1970s, and 1980s. Even then, however, privileges continued to outpace actual benefits. The generally increased material well-being of the population and the bombastic cult of the Second World War from 1965 onwards meant that expectations increased faster than welfare.[109] While resentment created by the gap between symbolic status and actual benefits united war invalids, this psychological unity was not cemented by a shared social position. Seriously mutilated beggars were certainly one of the most visible groups of war victims, but they were only part of the overall story. Next to them lived war invalids who became kolkhoz chairmen, extra-productive workers, or other relatively high-profile members of official society. Others were less in the limelight of public veneration, but managed to make a relatively good or at least bearable living through the combination of official job, regular pension payments, and irregular handouts by the state or their enterprise, the efforts of their families, and their own labour in private garden plots, or within the second economy. The social position and material situation of war invalids varied considerably as a result of this complicated interaction of the official and unofficial economy, the category of invalidity, gender, and age, the level of integration into a family and the extent to which this family could function as an economic unit. Even war invalids—the group of veterans which shared most in terms of postwar problems and experience, but also in terms of positive legal discrimination—were pulled apart in the process of reintegration into civilian life.

# 5

# Marked for Life

The Soviet Union does not recognize Soviet POWs. We consider Soviet
soldiers who fell into German hands deserters.

(Alexandra Kollontai, Soviet Ambassador to Sweden, during the war)[1]

The Soviet country remembers and cares about its citizens who fell into
German slavery. They will be received at home as sons of the Homeland.

(General-colonel F. I. Golikov, head of the repatriation administration, 11 November 1944)[2]

A s if missing limbs, poor health, and insufficient welfare were not
enough, some war invalids had to deal with a handicap of a different,
a political kind. Former prisoners of war (POWs) who returned from
captivity needed to show that they had, in fact, been wounded in fighting
the Germans.[3] The bureaucratic battles they had to win to be recognized
as war invalids were by no means the only problem they would have to
face in a society deeply suspicious of those who had 'given themselves into
captivity' (sdat'sia v plen), as official language called capture. At the end
of the war, the Soviet repatriation organs registered 2,016,480 POWs, of
whom 1,836,562 were repatriated, sometimes against their will.[4] Another
939,700 had been recovered during the war on liberated territory, bringing
the total number to as many as 2.8 million.[5] Up to 14 per cent of war
veterans may thus have borne the stigma of captivity after the war.[6]

Official policies were suspicious at best and hostile at worst towards these
presumed deserters, as a growing literature on Soviet prisoners of war points
out.[7] POWs had to pass what through what the Soviets called 'filtration'
(filtratsiia)—screening of the returnees by the security services in a specially
created system of 'filtration camps'.[8] This process was supposed to find
potential traitors who had collaborated with the Germans. 'Collaboration'

could mean membership in General Andrei Vlasov's anti-Soviet 'Russian Liberation Army' (ROA) or one of the other units which fought on the side of the Germans.[9] But the term might also cover behaviour as innocent as work in any capacity for the Germans in order to survive in the very tough conditions in the POW camps, or even failure to attempt to escape or to organize resistance.[10] Stressing the arbitrariness of the process of filtration, some accounts leave the reader with the impression that the typical experience was the bullet in the head or the life of a concentration camp inmate (*zek*) in Stalin's Gulag.[11] This experience was, of course, real enough for many, in particular for officers; it is well worth historians' attention, not only because of the outrage of blaming soldiers for their capture by the enemy, but also because these soldier-*zeky* became an important force in the postwar Gulag. Together with other professionals of violence (Ukrainian nationalist *guerrilleros*, for example), they changed the atmosphere of the camps enormously and were instrumental in the armed uprisings of the postwar years.[12]

Nevertheless, the return to a prolonged Gulag sentence or even to face the firing squad was far from universal. Rank and file soldiers, in particular, were treated somewhat more leniently. We still do not know how many recovered soldiers were shot during the war, but a general orientation is possible. Military tribunals sentenced 157,000 army personnel to death.[13] It is unlikely that they all were recovered POWs, but even if they were, this would be 17 per cent of those recovered by the Red Army on liberated territory (939,700). The majority of returning POWs—maybe 61 to 67 per cent—went as the so-called 'special contingent' through filtration sites, which in many ways resembled concentration camps with forced labour.[14] They were not final destinations, though, but had revolving doors, with constant arrivals and departures. Only a small share of the inmates was arrested as a result of 'filtration' (3 per cent as of late 1944) or died in the camps (less than 2 per cent). Adding those who were re-enlisted into the highly lethal 'storm' or penal battalions (5 per cent) we end up with 10 per cent who either died, were very likely to die, or ended up in long-term detention (Table 5.1). A different reconstruction lists 17 per cent as 'given over to the NKVD' but does not provide details for how many ended in penal units. We might add the maybe 17 per cent who were mobilized to work under militarized conditions (see Table 5.2), although their status was not much different from the situation of much of the industrial workforce during and after the war.[15] Given the brutality of Stalin's regime and the harshness of wartime pronouncements about how to deal with 'traitors', this is still a surprisingly low percentage. What happened to the majority who escaped this fate is less well known.[16]

During the first postwar decade, state policy remained drenched in suspicion towards former POWs. Those cleared during 'filtration' were not allowed to settle in Moscow, Leningrad, Kiev, or in the 'regime-zones' around these cities, unless they had lived there before the war and still had continuing family ties there—frequently restricting their place of residence to the provinces.[17] The returnees were, thus, treated only slightly better than the millions of Soviet citizens who at some point in their lives had been convicted for any kind of criminal activity (a common experience, as it included practices necessary to survive, including petty theft or 'speculation'), and who after their release were forbidden to settle in 'regime cities', independent of continuing family ties.[18] Seen thus as undesirables, former POWs also remained on the surveillance-lists of the security agencies. During filtration, the NKVD prepared a dossier on each former POW that was sent to the local branch of the state security in his or her place of residence. From mid-1944 repatriated citizens had to register with the local NKVD upon arrival, a requirement reinforced in 1945. After registration, they received special identity documents, which were valid for only six months. These papers did not entitle holders to travel into other regions of the Soviet Union. To get a regular passport that would allow such travel was possible only with a resolution of the local filtration commission.[19] To make things worse, former POWs and those who had been in encirclement were swept up in the witch hunt for 'rootless cosmopolitanists' of the late 1940s and early 1950s.[20] Particularly after 1948, many lost their jobs or were even arrested as potential enemies of the state.

How did one live in such an environment? The postwar life of Nikolai Fedorovich D'iakov is instructive in this respect. D'iakov was a POW in Finland, who left a detailed memoir of his postwar life.[21] D'iakov was born in 1920 in the village of Zenkino in Riazan' province as the sixth of eight children. His father was a middle peasant (*seredniak*) and a local Bolshevik activist. D'iakov finished a rural seven-year school in 1937 and proceeded to the middle school in the town of Ranenburg. In the same year his father, like many other innocents, was caught up in Stalin's Great Purges, arrested, and shot as an 'enemy of the people'. One of his older brothers had been arrested before that. In May 1941 D'iakov was drafted into the army. As the son of an enemy of the people he was not allowed to bear arms at first, but was put into a 'special labour battalion' (*osobyi rabochii batal'on*). When the war began, his battalion was thrown into the defence battles, with little training or preparation. In autumn 1941 he was severely wounded and became a POW in Finland. In October 1944 he was one of the 43,040 POWs, most of them rank and file soldiers, who were repatriated following the end of the Finnish–Soviet cease-fire (19 September).[22] D'iakov was checked by the security organs in a camp in Tkvarcheli (Abkhazia). After his 'filtration' he was demobilized from the army in March 1945 and worked for a while as an unskilled labourer on the building sites of Tkvarcheli, then as a journalist in the same town. This job he held (like so many other former POWs), only until 1947, when the 'new gorkom secretary displayed vigilance and suggested that I leave this job on my own accord, but with outstanding references'.[23] This started an odyssey which brought him first back to Ranenburg, shortly to Moscow, back to Tkvarcheli, on to Sarapul and Izhevsk in Udmurtiia, to Kazakhstan, and finally—after the Twentieth Party Congress—to Moscow.

In this chapter we follow D'iakov on his odyssey. We join him as he enters the stinking cattle car which brings him from the Finnish border to a 'filtration camp' in Abkhazia; we see him negotiating his release with his interrogator, and then trying to manage his life at the margins of Soviet society during the first postwar decade to the best of his abilities. In the absence of state assistance and faced with discrimination at every step, he had to rely largely on personal relationships with family, friends, and acquaintances. As we follow D'iakov on his postwar journey we will meet, along the way, other returned POWs and will explore the extent to which D'iakov's experience was typical for those who were released into civilian life after 'filtration'. In conclusion, the chapter discusses the limits of the silent rehabilitation of former POWs after Stalin's death and the continued discrimination they had to endure into the 1990s.

Finland in October 1944: D'iakov's group was prepared for repatriation, provided with new clothes and shoes, and then transported to the border in a passenger train. At the frontier they had to board 'our dirty, old, dishevelled cattle cars' (*teliatniki*) which were equipped with bunk beds.[24] This was only a step away from how regular rank and file soldiers travelled during the war: in heated goods cars (*teplushki*). Most of the demobilization trains were also made up of such cars.[25] What was more specific, however, was the barbed wire around one of the cars, which held those who had

worked as translators and in other functions in the POW camps. Their car
was marked with the words 'Traitors to the Homeland!' It was guarded by
soldiers with automatic rifles. The rest of the train, too, was guarded. The
former POWs were not allowed to leave their cars. If they tried to do so,
the guards shot at them.[26]

They travelled for twenty-four days. Food rations got smaller and smaller
every day. It was hot in the train. The toilet was a dirty hole in a corner of
the wagon. There was no possibility to wash. The men endured lack of air,
hunger, thirst, and the stench of unwashed bodies. While making its way
south to an unknown destination, D'iakov's train had to stop frequently
to make way for military transports travelling west.[27] The longer the trip
went on, the greater the suffering.

> You wanted to drink, drink, drink. But water also became a deficit good.
> At the stops they still did not let us out of the cars. Only four of us rushed
> along the cars with buckets full of water. They shoved two buckets into the
> car and yelled: 'Faster! Give the buckets back!'—and ran on to the next car.
> But what are two buckets of water for half a company of thirsty and dried
> out mouths?[28]

Some of the cars remained in Tula region, near coalmines, while the
rest went on to Abkhazia. After some more cars were left in Tkbuli (also
a mining town), the train arrived on 14 November 1944 at the station of
Kvezan', Abkhazia, near the little town of Tkvarcheli. Under armed guard,
the repatriates had to walk up a steep hill. A truck followed to pick those
up who collapsed in the heat and dust. On the top of the hill they saw
a camp, surrounded by barbed wire and watchtowers. They had arrived
at 'State Filtration Camp No. 518'. Before they entered the camp, the
POWs beat up the train chief who had starved and abused them during
the travel. The camp commander was forced to intervene, arresting the
bleeding lieutenant.[29]

Camp life was harsh, but not designed to kill. D'iakov and his comrades
received military rations, minus the '100 frontline grams' of vodka. During
the day the inmates had to work in the mine and after dinner they were
interrogated by military counter-intelligence, named ominously 'Death
to Spies' (*Smert' shpionam!*—SMERSh). D'iakov's description of his main
interrogator, however, is rather positive: a friendly, 'cultured' person, before
the war a teacher of literature, he seemed to like D'iakov, a sentiment which
was mutual. The good relationship with 'his' SMERSh officer proved to

be important. Another interrogator was less well-disposed towards D'iakov and wanted to give him five years in a 'corrective labour camp' (ITL), 'so he cannot say unnecessary things' about what he had seen in Finland. His interrogator, however, cleared and released him.[30]

D'iakov's was a relatively benign experience of filtration—despite the heavy labour in what can only be called a concentration camp. He does not describe beatings or major degradations. Others do. A former officer from a deeply pro-Soviet family returned voluntarily from Germany after the war.

> We have reached the Russian zone. A few minutes after the departure of the American trucks that had brought us there we were ordered to line up. I was disagreeably surprised by the great number of armed soldiers who guarded us on all sides. At last an officer showed up and without greeting ordered us to tear off our shoulder straps in terms little suited for the ears of the women and children present.... he proceeded to tell us that we were traitors, that we had gone over to the enemy on purpose.

This was only the beginning of a long line of humiliations. Together with some other former officers he was taken to 'an unspeakably filthy empty hut'. For two days they did not get anything to eat and had to wait.

> Then two of our comrades were called out and taken away. One of them soon returned but refused to answer our questions; the other never came back. Late in the night I was summoned. The examining officer... instead of interrogating me began to heap accusations on me. Why had I let myself be captured? Why hadn't I escaped? Why had I consented to work for the Germans? Why had I failed to engage in sabotage? Why had I failed to kill any Germans while in prison? Why had I failed to do anything to liquidate any of those who joined the Vlasov army? I asked him when and to what army unit I would be directed. He smiled and said that first I would have to expiate my guilt and air out my infected ideology. At this I got mad: I who had fought bravely to the last, who had been wounded twice, whose hand had been crippled, who had experienced all the torment of captivity and forced labour, who had refused to join the Vlasov army, who had never done anything disreputable in my life—I was to be accused of treason and deprived of decorations won in battle? Was this justice? I said that I would complain to Marshal Zhukov and demand a thorough investigation. To this he replied with a torrent of profanity.

To further disgrace the former officers they were forced to wear filthy and tattered German uniforms 'that seemed to have been taken off corpses'. Then they were herded into a freight train—sixty-two persons to a car—and sent to some thirty to forty kilometres outside of Omsk, Siberia. Because he spoke German he became a translator in a concentration camp for German POWs.[31]

D'iakov escaped such involuntary travel to Siberia, but he had not yet shaken off the grip of direct state control. The filtration camp he went through was attached to a coalmine, which he could not simply leave after his release from camp, because of the wartime labour laws. 'Those who had gone through filtration could not abandon the town until they got special permission. They mingled in shabby and broken-down dormitories and in tents, while they went on working in the mines, now already as free labour.' Some tried to adjust to this situation and arranged for their wives to come and live with them—at least until they managed to leave and return home. D'iakov tried to escape the hard work in the mine altogether, because he realistically saw that it might kill him. His good relationship with his SMERSh investigator allowed him—over tea and pastries served during the final interview(!)—to negotiate his release to work above ground. Once outside the camp and working as an unskilled labourer on building sites, the ability to strike up friendships and create personal bonds remained important, as the most basic issues of everyday life required the assistance of others. D'iakov's whole property after release from filtration was what he wore plus one change of underwear. In order not to have the latter stolen from the tent he lived in, he stored it in the apartment of a skilled worker, who had become his friend.[32]

When he finally managed to get out of the worker job and into employment at the local newspaper, his stigma as a former POW stood in his way for the first time: the editor considered it risky to hire him as a journalist, so he was employed as a proof-reader instead—which meant lower pay. In a fit of anger about this situation D'iakov decided on a bold move. He went to the local MGB branch to ask the boss of the local chekists if as a former POW he could officially work as a journalist. 'But why not, if its suits you?', he remembers the answer of the smiling state security officer. 'I know you from your articles in the newspaper and, excuse me, also from other materials.' D'iakov told him about his problem and the officer pulled the telephone towards himself, called the editorial office, and told the editor that his 'proof-reader' did not pose a threat to the security of the state. Patting D'iakov on the back he dismissed a stunned man: 'My god! Good chekists (*khoroshie chekisty*) ...' This extreme case illustrates what supplications to state organs could *sometimes* accomplish—if one was lucky with the person in charge of that specific state organ. Securing the job with the newspaper also bettered his living situation: he could now move out of the tent and into a room in a communal apartment. However, all he had managed to achieve with so much social skill, risk-taking, and luck evaporated nearly overnight: the new secretary of the district party committee demanded to know why a non-party member worked in the party press—and D'iakov was dismissed in February 1947.[33]

As his barely reconstructed civilian life in Abkhaziia crumbled under him, the logical step was to return to his home region, where family and old friends promised support. The first thing he had done after his release from filtration was write to his mother, who had not heard from him in years. So in 1947 he returned to his village, jobless. He soon learnt that an old schoolfriend had come to visit his mother. D'iakov went to meet him. It turned out that his friend had a leading position in the local newspaper and was willing and able to employ his old pal as a journalist. As in the first instance, getting the job resolved the housing question as well: a hayloft in the yard of the newspaper building became his new residence in Ranenburg. His luck did not last for long and he soon lost the job in the same manner as the first one—again, his lack of party membership combined with the stigma of being a former POW induced the regional party committee to demand his dismissal 'as socially unreliable' (*kak sotsial'no nenadezhnogo*).[34]

Nothing, it seemed, could secure the employment of a former POW—neither prewar friends who could act as patrons, nor even the support of the state security organs. Local party secretaries, nervously considering the possibility of a new purge, would not tolerate any reason to be accused of lack of vigilance. However, it is also noteworthy that in both cases the authorities decided not simply to sack him (there were no legal grounds for that—having been a POW was not illegal), but to dismiss him on his 'own accord' and with excellent references.

Having lost his work (and also his home) D'iakov left his home region again, this time for Moscow. At this point, he still had not become resigned to his status as a second-class citizen. He hoped to fulfil a long-held dream and travel to the polar regions. He had an interview in the cadres administration of Northern Sea Route Department (*Glavsevmorput'*) which went well. After two weeks of waiting, however, the administrator told him that he would really like to hire him 'if it were not for that damn captivity' (*Esli by ne etot prokliatyi plen!*). He received similar answers in several newspapers. By 1948 in Moscow nobody wanted to risk employing former POWs as journalists. He returned to Ranenburg, at a loss what to do.[35]

D'iakov's experience of relative calm until 1947/8, followed by increasing problems in the late 1940s and early 1950s, is fairly typical for those POWs who had been released from filtration and returned to a civilian existence. The state first attempted to ease their reintegration through a range of legal acts. In August 1945 the Organizational Bureau of the Central Committee passed a special resolution which pointed out to local authorities that hostile attitudes against former POWs were not called for. Those repatriated, the resolution stated, 'have again received all rights of Soviet citizens and should be drawn into active participation in labour and the societal–political life'.[36] A *Pravda* article from October 1946, which summarized the rights and privileges of returnees, also emphasized that they had all citizen rights and were supposed to be included actively in the work and social-political life of the country.[37] This is, to my knowledge, the first public mention of the fact that the Orgburo of the Central Committee had decided in August 1945 to make those repatriated into full citizens.[38]

Between 1944 and 1948 the Soviet government passed sixty-seven resolutions regarding rights of repatriated citizens, including fourteen on material and legal benefits. The right of war invalids to leave their job to return home also applied to invalided POWs.[39] Certain national groups among the repatriated were also allowed to leave the enterprise they had been assigned to and return home. First, Latvian, Lithuanian, Estonian, Azerbaidzhani, Georgian, and Armenian nationals were allowed to return to their home republics in April and October 1946. On 12 June 1947 this right of return was extended to all other nationals who had been residents of these republics. Excluded were Germans and former collaborators with the Nazis.[40] A secret directive of 17 July 1945 even freed repatriated citizens for the rest of the year from customs controls at the border to the Soviet Union—a right which in theory allowed them to bring material goods back home.[41] This directive was renewed at least twice and was still in force on New Year's Day 1947, thus applying to the large bulk of citizens subjected to repatriation.[42] On paper, if not always in practice, this put them on an equal footing with demobilized soldiers returning from Germany, who had been freed from customs controls in 1945.[43] It was only consistent with the logic of legislation, then, when on 30 September 1946 nearly all privileges of the demobilization law were extended to former POWs as well.[44] The real commitment of the state to the reintegration of repatriates was also expressed in the large sums of money earmarked to this end—hundreds of millions, on average 219 rubles per returnee.[45]

From 1947, however, a colder wind started to blow into the faces of repatriated POWs. The centre stopped sending signals down the chain of command that reintegration of repatriates was a major policy aim.[46] The state security, slowly working its way through huge piles of forms filled out during filtration, started to call in returnees for renewed interrogations as early as 1946.[47] Local hostility increased, often out of fear of being accused of lack of vigilance in the next round of purging, and many lost the jobs they had been given at the war's end. One example of this changed atmosphere is the story of a certain Lysov who worked in a machine-building factory in Tula province as a hammerer (*molotoboets*). As a good worker he was promoted in October 1948 to the position of norm setter of the blacksmith's shop. In 1949 he lost his job. Asking for an explanation his boss yelled at him: 'Swine! Scoundrel! Bastard! I'll throw you out! Don't forget where you are and who you are!'[48]

V. Andreev provides another example of this pattern of the short postwar breathing space followed by renewed troubles. Born in 1915,[49] he had worked before the war in the administration of the Chuvash party apparatus. Drafted on 10 November 1941, he served as the secretary (*otsekr*) of a regimental party bureau. On 14 August 1942 his regiment was encircled with other army units during the German drive to Stalingrad. After several days of heavy fighting, the regiment dispersed and Andreev and a couple of his comrades went into hiding. After four months and four days, advancing Red Army troops reclaimed the territory. The next two weeks Andreev fought with the unit which had liberated him. Then, from 5 January until June 1943, he underwent filtration in camp 201 in Podol'sk and Liubertsy, outside of Moscow. He passed the screening, was re-enlisted into a reserve brigade and on 1 August 1943 transferred to a storm battalion (*shturmbat*). He was severely wounded on 28 September 1943 (holding the rank of captain).[50] With bones and nerves of his left hand shattered he was medically discharged. The next few months he spent in military hospitals, until he was released on 4 January 1944 to work in his final hospital until it was disbanded in 15 August 1945.[51] Before he lost his job in a purge of the Chuvash State Pedagogical Institute during the spring of 1948 he then worked as aide to its director.[52]

Andreev was not alone. When local authorities, ever suspicious of possible 'traitors' or 'spies', no longer received signals from above which could have checked such sentiments, they acted accordingly. The xenophobic hysteria surrounding the 'anti-cosmopolitanism' campaign and the professional suspiciousness of state security made things worse. As the panic about anything foreign intensified, more and more former POWs lost their jobs as teachers and as workers in finance (*finantsovye rabotniki*—tax inspectors, other *revizory*, and accountants) because they had been in German captivity. Others could not get a job in their (white-collar) profession for the same reason. By 1949 this technically illegal discrimination against former POWs had become so widespread (and their letters of complaint so numerous) that the repatriation administration felt compelled to intervene on their behalf.[53] Its Estonian branch reported in January 1949 that 'from year to year, and from month to month' the job situation of former POWs and others who had been repatriated became worse. In any cadre reduction the first to lose their jobs were repatriates. Finding a job became increasingly difficult as well, even if assisted by the organization created in late 1944 to deal with the millions of returnees—the Administration of the Plenipotentiary for Affairs of Repatriation.[54] Even a personal intervention in January of 1950 by its boss, General-Colonel F. I. Golikov, remained without practical results.[55] As a report on letters to the Presidium of the Supreme Soviet summed up the situation in May 1952:

> many repatriated former POWs ... are being retired from their work and are not accepted in other jobs, which results in a hard [material] situation and forces them to ask the central government organs for help. Instead of giving them work in their profession ministries, directors of enterprises and local [state] organs withdraw from their placement by all means ...[56]

D'iakov was not the kind of person meekly to accept unfair discrimination. Maybe because of his positive experience with the state security he again decided to mobilize a higher up authority on his behalf. He wrote a letter to Stalin but never received an answer.[57] This did not immediately stop him. On the contrary, it seems that writing letters became his main occupation after his return from Moscow. However, this resulted in the opposite of what he had hoped for. Instead of Stalin, *Pravda*, or anybody else from the heights of the political system stepping in for his defence, the letters circled back to the region, increasing the problems he already had with the local authorities.[58] Likewise, many other former POWs unsuccessfully tried to mobilize the higher levels of the state hierarchy on their behalf by writing letters. The Central Committee, the Golikov administration, the Council of Ministers, the Supreme Soviet, the Ministry of Defense, and other state organs received many such letters in the late 1940s and early 1950s.[59] Former POWs also went in person to complain about their loss of a job or the inability to find one.[60] Sometimes their complaints were heard, but as a rule central organs did not put much pressure on local institutions in order to enforce the existing legislation regarding former POWs after 1947. The repeated attempts of the repatriation administration to change this situation failed. Even personal intervention on the highest level of its chief, Golikov, remained without results, because of resistance within the central party apparatus, from the Ministry of Interior, the General Staff, as well as powerful industrial ministries and the state planning agency (Gosplan).[61]

Letters of supplication were largely doomed to failure under such conditions, and eventually D'iakov understood this. Having spent some time writing anywhere he could imagine, he realized that he would not find work in his home region and that he might get into serious trouble if he stayed too long. Thus, he decided to go underground. He left for Abkhaziia without telling anybody. Back in the periphery of the empire, D'iakov found a job as a librarian in a sanatorium. Fearing arrest, he lived there without official registration (*propiska*). Everything went well until a financial scandal in the sanatorium prompted an audit. As the commission found him working without registration by both the civilian and the military authorities, he was told to get out of there, or else. He took this advice and left Abkhaziia immediately.[62]

Illegality, or at least hiding one's past, was one important way to deal with this stigma—discrimination can be avoided by hiding that one belongs to the discriminated group. During their inquiries into the composition of the student body at Chuvash State Pedagogical Institute in 1947, the Chuvash regional party committee found that 'individual students' had concealed 'the fact that they had been POWs'. Others had gone one step further and 'studied under assumed names'.[63] Such 'masking' occurred at the workplace as well.[64] Others went further than just avoiding the stigma and created a more positive public (and maybe even private) persona by joining the Communist Youth League: 'Well, that was in 1946. You know that I had been repatriated and I had to cover up a little so I joined the Komsomol,' explained one defector interviewed by American sociologists after his escape from the Soviet Union.[65] At the extreme end of the spectrum were men who made a virtue out of the necessity

of hiding the fact that they had been POWs. They joined what might
be the most spectacular instance of conmanship in the postwar years:
the fake military-construction administration ('UVS-4', 'UVS-10', and
'UVS-1') of the equally imaginary 'colonel' (*inzhener-polkovnik*) Pavlenko.
This fictitious military organization managed to function quite profitably
for years, defrauding the authorities, until the latter finally realized in
the summer of 1952(!) that no 'administration' of this name existed.
The group attracted basically people who had to hide their 'real selves'
anyway—former POWs, escaped prisoners, former collaborators with the
Germans, former kulaks, and former Ukrainian Nationalist guerrillas.[66]

His means of existence again shattered, D'iakov left Abkhaziia and
again turned to the family as a network of reciprocal help. In 1950 he
arrived in Sarapul, a town on the Moscow–Sverdlovsk train line, where
his brother (the 'enemy of the people') lived and worked. As attempts to
find employment failed because of his stigma as a former POW, D'iakov
worked for the family: 'I became the main work force on the building
site of our own house. But I did not have an official job: they refused
me everywhere because I had been a POW.' Once house and garden
were finished D'iakov finally managed to find work he liked in the capital
of Udmurtiia, Izhevsk, as head corrector in the state publishing house,
probably because he again hid his stigma. On the side he finished the tenth
class at a night school. After graduation he returned to Sarapul, and now
managed to enter the teachers' institute, where he was on Stalin's death.
The demise of the dictator did not immediately change D'iakov's status.
He was still confined to the provinces, but graduated from the institute in
1955 and found work as a teacher in Kazakhstan. It is here that the news of
the Twentieth Party Congress reached him. The Thaw then enabled him
to go to Moscow in 1957.[67]

Was D'iakov, the man with the benign experience of filtration, the man
who was seemingly not beaten but instead treated to tea by his interrogator,
the man who escaped the labour battalions and returned to the relatively
unsupervised life of a civilian, a 'typical' prisoner of war? In one way
he certainly was not, because he returned alive to the Soviet Union.
Nearly 59 per cent of Soviet POWs did not survive the German genocidal
approach to those they considered 'sub-humans'.[68] D'iakov was lucky, in
part, because he was neither a woman nor Jewish, as the survival chances of
the former were much reduced and those of the latter close to nil. Female

soldiers were punished by the Germans for their 'unnatural' transgression into the male realm of organized violence as well as their presumed ideological contamination. They were frequently treated like 'commissars', that is, taken aside upon capture and shot. Those who survived this initial 'selection' had to endure sexual violence and other degradations, including in some cases forced sterilization.[69] If they were Jewish, they shared the fate of their male comrades, who, if their identity was established, were murdered by their capturers. We do not know the exact numbers involved, but of those Jewish soldiers who fell into German hands, only some 6 to 9 per cent survived.[70]

D'iakov was also relatively lucky because he had been captured by the Finns rather than the Germans—which massively increased his chances of survival. While under the genocidal regime of the Nazis far over half of the captives were either executed or died of malnutrition, overwork, and disease, in Finnish captivity less than a third died. Finally, he was lucky that he was not Karelian. This national minority was privileged by the Finns as a closely related nationality, which in turn made them highly suspicious to the Soviet security organs after their return to the Soviet Union.[71] As D'iakov notes, these men were locked up in a special train car marked 'Traitors to the Homeland', and secured by barbed wire and extra guards. After filtration, such former Red Army men tended to share the fate of those who had served in the ROA or in other units fighting on the side of the Germans.[72] Rank and file members and lower level officers of such outfits were, as a rule, given six-year terms in 'special settlement' in Siberia or other regions in the periphery. In many cases, their terms were renewed as they expired in 1951 or 1952. They were allowed to leave only after September 1955, when a special amnesty freed those who had collaborated with the Germans.[73] Some of the most prominent, like General Vlasov himself, were sentenced in closed court and executed in 1946 and 1947.[74]

Finally, D'iakov was relatively lucky because he had not been an officer. From the very beginning of the war, higher ranks who had 'given themselves into captivity' were treated much more harshly than rank and file soldiers, a hierarchy of penalties introduced already by the famous 'Order No. 270' of 16 August 1941.[75] Commanders and political workers who 'gave themselves over' were considered defectors, 'whose families are liable to arrest as families of deserters, who have broken the [military] oath and betrayed their country'. If recovered, these 'traitors' were to be shot on the spot (art. 1). All other soldiers were told to fight no matter what in

encirclement and to demand the same from their commanders, if necessary
by force of arms. If they were captured nevertheless, simple soldiers were
not threatened with execution; their families were to be denied state aid
and welfare payments, but not arrested (art. 2).[76]

As a result of the large number of recovered captives, the policy of
executing officers was not consistently applied during the war, as Table 5.1
makes clear. Their treatment was harsher than that of the rank and file,
though: 32 per cent of officers were sent into penal battalions as opposed
to 5 per cent of rank and file. Moreover, the table gives no data for 33 per
cent of officers—over 16,000 people—while the data add up for the lower
ranks. What happened to them? Were they all shot? We can only guess,
but it should be noted that there are no data for the number of officers
who died and it is unlikely that all survived. Moreover, we do know
that recovered officers were shot, and probably in significant numbers.
Extralegal executions were especially prominent during the first chaotic
phase of the war. The years of 1941 and 1942 were also the high-point of
death sentences by military tribunals—suggesting that many were formerly
encircled or POWs.[77]

Officers constituted about 8 per cent of the repatriated former POWs
by 1 March 1946, and just under 7 per cent by the end of the repatriation
process. This minority did not fall under the victory amnesty of 1945.[78] Of

Table 5.1. Filtration of former POWs and encircled soldiers in 'special camps' as of 1 October 1944

| | All ranks | Officers | % all ranks | % officers |
|---|---|---|---|---|
| Total in source | 354,592 | 50,444 | 100.00 | 100.00 |
| Re-enlisted into Red Army | 249,416 | 27,042 | 70.34 | 53.61 |
| Joined 'storm' battalions | 18,382 | 16,163 | 5.18 | 32.04 |
| Mobilized into industry | 30,749 | 29 | 8.67 | 0.06 |
| Drafted into guard units to secure the filtration camps | 5,924 | | 1.67 | |
| Arrested by SMERSh | 11,556 | 1,284 | 3.26 | 2.55 |
| Died | 5,347 | | 1.51 | |
| Still in 'special' camps | 51,601 | 5,657 | 14.55 | 11.21 |
| Total | 354,593 | 34,012 | 100.00 | 67.43 |
| Difference to total in source | +1 | −16,432 | | 32.57 |

Source: Iu. Arzamaskin, Zalozhniki Vtoroi mirovoi voiny: repatriatsiia sovetskikh grazhdan v 1944–1953 gg. (Moscow: Arzmaskin, 2001), 12.

fifty-seven generals who had been in German POW camps and returned to the Soviet Union, twenty-three were sentenced to death, and an additional five to between ten and twenty-five years. Two died in prison before they could be sentenced. More than half were thus 'repressed' while the rest went on serving in the army after filtration.[79] Lower ranking officers did not fare better. As the repatriation administration reported in March 1946:

> liberated officers were sent into NKVD camps and into reserve units of the Red Army for more thorough checking and establishment of categories. After the verification, those who have not been mixed up in anything were sent into the army to continue their service or were transferred to the reserve. The rest were given over to the NKVD.[80]

Of the 126,037 officers who were repatriated between 1944 and 1953, only less than 1 per cent still served in the army in 1953; 48 per cent had been demobilized into the reserve.[81] The remaining half might have been dead as, from November 1944, all officers who found themselves in filtration camps were put into highly lethal 'storm battalions'.[82] The end of the war did not change this approach in any fundamental manner. Former officers were likely to be periodically harassed by state security and often arrested as well—a continuation of the harsh treatment of officers during the war.[83]

Those who, like D'iakov, had been released home after filtration (17 per cent) and those who had been redrafted into the armed forces (50 per cent) and were thus demobilized as regular soldiers after the war (if they survived), were the fortunate groups among former POWs. Up to 17 per cent were less lucky—to say nothing of those unfortunates who did not clear filtration in the first place (see Table 5.2).

In total 334,448 'cleared' former POWs were mobilized into labour battalions at the end of the war where they joined 263,647 civilian returnees in militarized work outfits which in many ways resembled forced labour and were used in sectors of the economy which could not attract enough free workers.[84] Living conditions were, consequently, grim. Former POWs in Stalin region complained that those who were considered sick or invalids even by the labour-medical board were not released home as they should have been. 'There are cases in which repatriates do not receive medical attention but are sent to work in an easier job and die after a couple of days.' Members of a labour battalion of the repatriated in Bobruisk province who were used for logging complained about bad and irregular food and lack of bread. They ate the meat of horses killed

Table 5.2. Reconstruction of results of filtration of former POWs

|                                           | Millions | %       |
| ----------------------------------------- | -------- | ------- |
| Total recovered POWs                      | 1.8      | 100.0   |
| Into labour battalions                    | 0.3      | 16.7    |
| Given over to NKVD                        | 0.3      | 16.7    |
| Into the army (regular and penal units)   | 0.9      | 50.0    |
| Sent home                                 | 0.3      | 16.7    |
| Total                                     | 1.8      | 100.1*  |

\* - rounding error.
Note: A wide variety of numbers circulate in the literature, often mixing numbers for repatriated citizens with those for POWs (a subgroup of the former). This table summarizes an attempt to clear up this confusion. See Edele, 'A "Generation of Victors"?', 86–90.
Source: Aleksei Alekseevich Sheviakov, '"Tainy" poslevoennoi repatriatsii', Sotsiologicheskie issledovaniia, 5 (1993): 10; id., 'Repatriatsiia sovetskogo mirnogo naseleniia i voennoplennykh, okazavshikhsia v okkupatsionnykh zonakh gosudarstv antigitlerovskoi koalitsii', Naselenie Rossii v 1920–1950-e gody: Chislennost' poteri, migratsii (Moscow: In-t rossiiskoi istorii RAN, 1994), 211, 214, 215; V. Zemskov, 'Repatriatsiia sovetskikh grazhdan i ikh dal'neishaia sud'ba (1944–1956)', Sotsiologicheskie issledovaniia, 5 (1995): 11; id., 'K voprosu o repatriatsii sovetskikh grazhdan 1944–1951 gg.', Istoriia SSSR 4 (1990): 36.

by starvation (there was no fodder for them either), which also provided leather for the only available footwear. There was no bedding, a shortage of clothes, and the repatriates slept on the bare floors.[85] D'iakov escaped such potentially lethal working conditions because of his good relationship with his interrogator. Originally, he was supposed to be 'released' into mining work under militarized conditions. He managed, however, to negotiate a less arduous job above ground, which was the first step to getting away from the mining town.[86]

In August 1945, the members of labour battalions became regular cadres of the enterprises their disbanded battalions had worked for. The slightly unclear status in which they were left for the first year made directors of enterprises treat them, essentially, as forced labour. A resolution of the Council of Ministers of the Soviet Union of 30 September 1946 stressed that former POWs who had been enlisted into worker battalions and subsequently given over as regular cadres to work in industry had the same rights as other workers (art. 1).[87] The resolution was an important step in the history of the legal situation of former POWs. Not only were they now explicitly equal to other workers, they also received some of the privileges of other veterans—such as most benefits of the demobilization law or the right of war invalids to leave their enterprise in order to reunite with their families (arts. 2 and 4). Ministers as well as directors of enterprises were ordered to place former labour battalion members into a job of their profession. If there was no such job, they were to be transferred 'with their consent' to another enterprise (art. 3). This legislation still applied in 1948.[88] Nevertheless, the stringent labour laws of the postwar years did not allow those who had become regular cadres of the enterprises to leave their place of work without the permission of the director, which was seldom granted.[89] A schoolfriend of D'iakov, also a former POW, was unable to leave the mine in which he had been put to work at least until late summer of 1947, and it seems that it was only the resulting disability which released him from work in 1949.[90]

Because labour battalions were used in regions and sectors of the economy which could not attract workers by themselves, those former POWs found themselves in unpopular and hard work (such as logging or mining) in heavily destroyed or distant regions.[91] Only invalids had after 30 September 1946 the right to leave their enterprise in order to reunite with their families. Everybody else was stuck. Some took advantage of the right granted in August of 1945 to move their families to them, financed by their enterprise.

Labour battalions were also formed after the 1945 decision to disband them, or at least officials continued to refer to them as such. By March 1946 there were 774 of these outfits which included 607,095 repatriates (both former POWs and civilians).[92] In July 1946 the Council of Ministers of the Soviet Union allowed the formation of ten military–construction battalions with 1,000 men each. They were to be staffed by Estonians, Latvians, and Lithuanians of draft age who had served in the German army and had to build the *kombinat No. 7* of the Ministry of the Interior (MVD). In October 1946 another resolution delayed the demobilization of all military–construction battalions. In order to ensure 'a stable workforce' on MVD building sites, the members of these battalions were not to be reclassified as 'free labour' until their work was done. On the basis of this legislation the MVD contested in 1947 attempts by the Estonian Council of Ministers to let the Estonians from these labour battalions return home, and demanded to keep them 'to the end of the year 1948'.[93]

Those who were mobilized into regular engineering battalions which helped in the reconstruction of the country had to wait longer to escape the control of the army. In January 1949 the General Staff asked the

Golikov administration what to do with the repatriated who worked in a soon-to-be disbanded engineering battalion who had worked in the rebuilding of Dneprostroi. The administration answered that all repatriated members of the battalion were to be sent home. The travel was to be paid by the battalion, and every repatriated person should get a MVD certificate about the results of the filtration process. The battalion was disbanded completely by 10 April 1949. Of the 305 repatriated who had worked in it, 135 were sent home, while 141 signed up for construction work for three to six months (more than thirty of them had received family apartments (*semeinye kvartiry*) and the rest lived in dorms). The remaining 29 people turned out to be residents of Zaporozh'e, who found work on their own. All the repatriated received what they had earned during their time in the battalion plus compensation for unused holiday time. At least one repatriation official declared that the late demobilization of repatriated in this battalion was illegal.[94]

Others were stuck because of a Kafkaesque abstruseness of jurisdiction. Two military units in Stalin region of the Ukraine refused to release repatriated citizens who worked there. They had been given over to the units by the Ministry of Coal Mining for the reconstruction of a mine. Therefore, the army argued, they could not leave without permission of the Ministry of Coal Mining in the Western Regions. The ministry, in turn, argued that the military units in question were not under its jurisdiction, and that therefore they could not decide this question. The army did not change its position on the question and renewed its interpretation in a letter to the Golikov administration of summer 1949.[95] Their further fate is unknown.

D'iakov was not only in one of the most fortunate groups of former POWs because he avoided initial arrest during filtration and was demobilized as opposed to being put into a labour battalion. He was also fortunate in that he avoided outright clashes with the state security after 1945—there were, of course, arrests among former POWs who had been 'cleared' during filtration.[96] Arrests had already occurred in 1946 and by 1947 local MGB officials actively prevented former POWs and their relatives from getting responsible jobs such as kolkhoz chairman or head of a grain delivery station.[97] A series of resolutions of the Council of Ministers of the Soviet Union of 21 February 1948 began a new wave of repression against people deemed to be dangerous, including those who had 'anti-Soviet connections'. The generality of the formulation made the registered former POWs a logical target group.[98]

It is impossible to know how many former POWs were arrested in the postwar years for the simple reason that they had been POWs, but it is clear that this was not an uncommon experience. A 1956 report of Zhukov to the Central Committee talked of 'a large number' of such cases. We do know, for example, that in October 1947 the MVD counted 55,000 veterans (including partisans) in places of confinement (camps, colonies, prisons). In addition, there was an unstated number of veterans who had been sentenced for 'particularly dangerous crimes' (*osoboopasnye prestupleniia*). We also know that in late 1955 the MVD counted 54,176 'special settlers' who were either war participants or decorated by the state. As the Central Committee pointed out in 1956, 'the state security organs went on baselessly to bring former POWs to criminal responsibility after the war', and 'illegally repressed' many of them.[99] How many remains unclear, despite extensive archival research by several historians. One estimate holds that maybe 150,000 repatriates were arrested in 1946 and 1947.[100] If we assume (counter-factually) that this number does not include civilians as well, these would be 5 per cent of the POWs who returned since 1941. As civilians must be included, this number is likely to be lower but does not include post-1947 arrests.

Whatever the numbers, D'iakov might well have become part of this substantial minority. In 1948 he ran into one of his friends from the POW and filtration camps. They started to write each other, but suddenly the answers stopped. D'iakov learnt only decades later that the state security had become interested in this communication between former POWs, and had started to put his friend under pressure to produce 'compromising material' in order to arrest D'iakov.[101] Others had less loyal friends. I. M. Kargin, a former colonel and veteran of the Civil War, cleared filtration in Podol'sk in 1944 and began to work as a teacher in the electromechanical institute in Leningrad. In 1949 he was arrested on the basis of 'untrue compromising material' (*lozhnyi kompromat*) about his time as a POW, and sentenced to twenty-five years of camp, with subsequent suspension of civil rights for five years. After seven and a half years in the Gulag he returned to Leningrad, to a meagre civilian pension instead of a better military one.[102] The Estonian repatriation administration reported in 1949 to their Moscow superiors that 'frequent arrests among repatriated, mass-interrogations by the organs of the MGB ... complicate the agitational-propagandistic work among repatriated and do not provide the material necessary for our propaganda work'. In the same year the first secretary of the Armenian Communist Party

Arutiunov asked Stalin for permission to round up 2,500 of the 11,170 former POWs registered in the republic, and send them to 'remote regions of the Soviet Union'. Stalin consented. In 1951–2 the wave of arrests gained additional momentum. In October 1951 the MVD issued an order about the intensification of repression against former POWs and many former repatriated reported to the presidential Commission for the Rehabilitation of Victims of Political Repression (set up by Yeltsin in the 1990s) about their arrests on the basis of denunciations as German collaborators in late 1951 and early 1952. Even if they were not arrested, many former POWs were confronted with frequent harassment and interrogations by the security organs.[103]

One final reason for D'iakov's success in avoiding arrest was the experience of the unmerited arrest of his father and his own problems as a result of this injustice. This experience taught D'iakov early that no good could come from trust in the justice of the authorities, and that a person's fate was best controlled by staying below the state's radar screen, relying on family and friends instead. This was certainly a lesson many others had learnt as well. Those who had not, however, were likely to get into trouble again, particularly if they tried to make a career after the war—the higher one tried to climb in the official hierarchy, the more exposed one got. Many of those who wrote in to the Golikov administration or to the chairman of the Presidium of the Supreme Soviet N.M. Shvernik about their troubles were members of the lower to middle service class. Alim Sandovich Galiev wrote from Alma-Ata. He had managed to get an academic job after he passed filtration in June 1946. While working fulltime at the Kazakhstan Academy of Sciences he also started graduate study. In January 1947 he was both sacked from work and dismissed from the *aspirantura* 'because he had been a prisoner of war'. Similarly, Mikhail Mikhailovich Kas'ianov, a former officer who had been demobilized after the end of the war, got a job as an inspector of state expenses (*inspektor gosdokhodov*) in Frunze province. After working for one and a half years he was dismissed in March 1947 on initiative of the *raikom* who did not want to have a former POW in such a position.[104]

The fulfilment of aspirations towards higher education were severely complicated by the stigma of being a former POW, but not made completely impossible. By late September 1948 former POWs still studied in the educational institutions (*vuzy*) of the city of Voronezh.[105] D'iakov managed in 1953, still before Stalin's death, to get admitted to a teachers' institute in Sarapul. Then, in the academic years 1955/6 and 1956/7 he taught Russian language and literature in Kazakhstan before the Twentieth Party Congress opened the gates to Moscow.[106] Even before 1947 one of D'iakov's friends had failed to get admitted to study law as an extern.[107] And those who did manage to get into *vuzy* were not left in peace. In May 1948 the secretary of the Chuvash obkom reported that there were still (*do sikh por*) twenty students in the State Pedagogical Institute who were former POWs, and that the director was not paying attention to the 'littering (*zasorenie*) of the institute with elements who had been prisoners of war under the Germans'.[108]

Social mobility outside the educational system was equally problematic. The life story of one such victim of the increasing pressure on former POWs is narrated by his mother in a letter of complaint preserved in the procuracy of the RSFSR. Vasilii Sergeevich D. was born in 1927 in the village of Skorniakovo, in Voronezh province. In 1933 the family moved to Rostov-on-Don where his father had worked as a seasonal worker since 1905 on building sites. Altogether they were nine siblings. 'Despite all hardships', his mother reports, he showed interest in learning and graduated from ten-year school in 1940. During the war he was taken prisoner by the Germans, but released, and returned home to Rostov, where he was drafted by the occupation forces to work in Germany. He was repatriated in 1945 and moved with his wife to the Donbass, to the city of Makeevka, her home town. He found work in a factory and learnt the trade of electrical welder. To escape the hardships of postwar life he left Makeevka and moved with his wife to Rostov in 1948. He found work as electro welder in the Sel'mash factory. Once life became a little better he started to attend a technicum for cold metal works, still eager to learn, to become a 'specialist'. His drive to leave the working class behind is not hard to understand: he lived with his mother in a wet dugout (*zemlianka*) and owned one suit and one bed, which he shared with his wife and their child. His only luxury item was a watch (which presumably he had brought from Germany). His drive showed results: he was a model student and a model worker as well. Suddenly, on 29 September 1950, and totally unexpected for his mother, he got 'arested', as she called it, right out of the technicum. Obviously based on a couple of denunciations, he was sentenced for paragraph 58–10 of the criminal code ('anti-Soviet agitation'). His further fate is unknown.[109]

While every former POW was a possible target of discrimination and repression, the more prestige and social status connected to a position, the more likely its holder was to come under fire. Mid-level administrative posts, together with anything connected to academia, were especially vulnerable. But the practice was by no means restricted to the middle service class. Pavel Grigor'evich Oberin wrote from a kolkhoz in Krasnodarskii krai. He complained that the kolkhoz administration refused to give him work because he was a former POW. Two others who shared this stigma were even denied membership in the kolkhoz.[110] V. N. Shchipitsyn wrote from the city of Molotov to Shvernik in 1952 in an attempt to get his job in a factory back, where he had worked as a war invalid from 1946 to 1950.[111]

The Soviet leadership never officially announced a policy change towards former POWs, but stopped enforcing its own laws regarding the rights of former POWs and other repatriated sometime around 1947. While this spared many the worst, it still created, in the words of one historian, 'very big discomfort'.[112] That it was institutional practice rather than explicitly formulated policy which made life miserable for former POWs was hardly much of a consolation. As one of them complained bitterly:

> It hurts very much and is morally too hard to bear to realize that after all of this [war effort and suffering] they do not trust me and consider me nearly alien, nearly not a Soviet person.... Again a civilian, I meet on every step all possible suspicion, mistrust, and sometimes even persecution (*travlia*) and especially from people who sometimes do not even have the most elementary understanding of the front.[113]

Rehabilitation was equally silent, nearly hidden. It was also, and partially as a result of this secrecy, incomplete. Nevertheless, the mid-1950s were an important turning point for former POWs. Perversely, this shift started with the pardoning of those who had collaborated with the Germans, and were either in places of confinement or special settlement within the Soviet Union, or remained as displaced persons (DPs) abroad (decree of 17 September 1955).[114] The context for this decision was the efforts of the Soviet authorities to return displaced persons to the 'Homeland', in order to prevent their participation in the expected war of the USA against the Soviets. The internal argument was that one of the main reasons for non-return was fear of reprisals, which was supposed to be taken care of by the amnesty.[115] This first amnesty did not extend to those veterans who had been rounded up as part of the usual suspects in the late 1940s and early 1950s, if they had not been sentenced explicitly for collaboration with the Germans. In a process typical for Soviet legislation, however, the benefits of the first amnesty decree were soon applied to a wider group. The amnesty of 24 November 1955 freed all war participants—former POWs or not—from 'special settlement' (*spetsposelenie*). It did not allow them, however, to return to their home region and explicitly stated that they had no rights to their former housing.[116]

On 19 April 1956 the Presidium of the Central Committee decided to form a commission (headed by Zhukov) to investigate the fate of former POWs after the war. After a report of the commission on 4 June 1956, the Central Committee passed a resolution on 29 June 1956, which condemned the 'flagrant violations of legality' with regard to former POWs in the postwar years, and ordered the Presidium of the Supreme Soviet to deliberate about an amnesty for those sentenced for having 'given themselves over' (art. 3). The resulting resolution was passed on 20 September 1956, which freed the last of the former POWs who had been imprisoned for 'treason'.[117]

These acts amounted to a silent amnesty rather than a full rehabilitation of former POWs.[118] Nevertheless, the 1955–6 decisions did start a process of normalization, despite the suspicion, discrimination, and hostility which remained lingering under the surface. D'iakov, for one, could finally leave the periphery and make a fairly high-powered career in the capital. Later in his life he also became something of an activist for the rights and the recognition of former POWs, an activity which also explains why he wrote his memoirs: the experience of rejection after the war, of having one's wartime suffering devalued and slandered as 'treason', remained a thorn in the flesh which needed to be removed, or at least soothed in some way. Such healing became possible only with the slow dismantling of the Stalinist system of domination which started after the tyrant's death.

As for the history of veterans as a whole, then, 1947/8 rather than 1945 and 1955–6 rather than 1953 were the decisive turning points. Under Khrushchev, the topic of captivity could finally be discussed in public. After 1956, in part guided by a special section for POWs of the new veterans' organization, a range of memoirs of survivors told the story of captivity, of course in decidedly heroic terms. Even Mikhail Aleksandrovich Sholokhov—famous for such socialist realist tomes as *Quiet Flows the Don* (1928–40)—took this topic as his theme in *Fate of a Person* (*Sud'ba cheloveka*, 1956–7), a novel which had been stopped by the censor in 1946 but could now even be made into a movie by Sergei Fedorovich Bondarchuk in 1959. Two years later, the movie director and war veteran Grigorii Chukhrai

denounced Stalinist persecution of returned POWs in a slightly kinky love
story between a boozing fighter pilot and an innocent but willing schoolgirl
(*Clear Sky*, 1961).[119]

The increasingly bombastic war cult under Brezhnev had little use for
realistic depictions of captivity, even if the theme did not completely drop
out of the published sphere. Stepan Pavlovich Zlobin's novel *Missing in
Action* (*Popavshie bez vesti*) is a good illustration of this renewed freeze.
Zlobin, who had survived German captivity from 1941 to 1945, wrote the
novel straight after the war. In 1947, he sent it to the journal *Novyi mir* for
consideration. Instead of publication, the manuscript was confiscated by
the security organs and returned to the author only in 1953, after Stalin's
death. Three years later, after the silent rehabilitation of former POWs
in 1956, Zlobin returned to work on the novel, which was published in
two volumes in 1962, and became a cult book nearly overnight. In the
second half of the 1960s, however, the book disappeared from the library
shelves and was locked away in the 'closed collection', accessible only to a
minority.[120]

The theme returned with a vengeance in the period of Glasnost' and
Perestroika. In 1987 and 1988, major publications—from *belles lettres* to
newspaper articles—divulged the enormity of the numbers involved and
started a long discussion about captivity and repatriation, which kept
the Soviet and post-Soviet public excited for years to come.[121] A major
polemic was started by a long article by E. Maksimova in the government's
*Izvestiia*, on 21 August 1987, asking why former POWs were still treated
with suspicion instead of respect, and proposing a legal act restoring their
honour. The reactions of veterans, some of them published later, were
mixed: in letters to the editor as well as phone calls, some greeted the
article with enthusiasm, while others reacted with indignation to the
proposal that the stigma of captivity should be removed. While *Izvestiia*
claimed that the positive responses were more typical, the army newspaper
*Red Star* published a strong example of the opposing view. This letter
to the editor was written by two high-ranking officers, Main Marshall of
Artillery V. Tolubko and retired Lieutenant-Colonel A. Kovalenko, and
can be seen as the army's response to the government's PR campaign
finally to rehabilitate former POWs. Quoting Stalin's Order No. 227
('Not a step back!'), the authors renewed the old line that as a rule
POWs needed to be seen as traitors, unless proven not guilty. Only
those who were captured seriously wounded and unconscious and those

who mounted active resistance in captivity were exempted from this
stigma. Moreover, the authors declared the problem solved: 'Part of the
deserters, and we cannot call these people differently, were sent to diverse
fronts. They fought, redeeming their heavy guilt. Today, nobody holds
anything against them.' Indeed, the writers pointed out, they held the same
privileges as other *frontoviki*—so why did this old story, long forgotten,
have to be dragged out again? The authors reiterated the old Stalinist
line and claimed that the campaign to rehabilitate POWs missed the
point that there were two different types of captives: 'Yes, there were
those who gave themselves over, and there were those who were taken
captive—gravely wounded, without consciousness....How can we put
them next to each other?' Each former captive, they held, had to be
judged from the moral 'height' of those who lost their life in honourable
battle.[122]

If the position of the army had not been clear, *Red Star* made sure the
message came across in 'polemical letters from the editor', published on
16 January 1988 and signed by one of the 'special correspondents' of the
newspaper, Colonel V. Filatov. The letter was a Stalinist rebuttal of more
than just the POW campaign, but of the politics of history of the Perestroika
era and of Glasnost' in general. It started with the charge that those who
tried to tell the history of the Great Terror did not understand 'dialectical
time, dialectical life'. Similarly, those who wrote about the horrors of the
Afghanistan war and what these did to the psyche of individual soldiers did
not understand 'the difference between imperialist brigandage' exemplified
by the Americans in Vietnam (who had a reason to become alcoholics)
and 'international help' exemplified by the Soviet troops in Afghanistan
(who, therefore, had no reason to become alcoholics). After these opening
salvoes, Filatov trained his guns on *Izvestiia*, or rather on 'one of the
newspapers', as he put it. The suggestion that those who were captured
had actually fought for the Homeland was scandalous. 'Never, in the entire
history of our people, has anything like this happened before. It follows,
they were wrong when they said that captivity means disgrace, dishonour,
degradation? It follows, that today they are trying to prove that captivity
means gallantry and heroism?' Clearly, this was incorrect: it gave the wrong
message to young soldiers as it devalued real heroism and re-evaluated the
ultimate disgrace of captivity. Mobilizing all his outrage against rethinking
his values, quoting Vietnamese soldiers, a German general, Lev Tolstoi,
and the entire pantheon of wartime heroes—Kosmodemianskaia, Gastello,

Matrosov—Filatov declared *Izvestiia's* position both erroneous and highly dangerous.[123]

The government shot back on 5 February 1988, with an *Izvestiia* article titled 'White and Black', signed by the newspaper's 'Department for Propaganda, Law, and Morality' (*Otdel propagandy, prava i morali*). Adopting a sober tone and quoting the many letters which the newspaper had received 'already for a decade' the article took Filatov's Stalinist rant apart. The article made clear that desertion to the enemy was not the issue. The issue was how to treat people who had been taken prisoner against their will, and how to relate to these people today. The issue was, among other things, language: did people 'give themselves into captivity' or did they 'fall captive'? Could one really believe that millions had wanted to become POWs? Was it really true that there were no situations in war when captivity was the only option? The article dissected Filatov's quotations, showing that he had taken them out of context in order to mythologize and hide what had actually happened in the first phase of the war; it countered these myths with striking statistics about the mass phenomenon of captivity, particularly in 1941. The article asked for a more inclusive history, which went beyond Filatov's black and white, and which included not only victory parades and heroism, but also tragedy and loss.[124]

This article did not end the discussion, and it is unlikely that anybody changed positions in the process, largely because these views were so deeply entrenched, so passionately held, and so strongly intertwined with very fundamental ideas about ethics and justice. In the short run, the reformers did not win out, but nor did the reactionaries manage another roll-back as they had in the 1970s. Only the breakdown of the Soviet Union in 1991 removed the last brakes on rehabilitation. The line asking if one had been a POW during the war was finally removed from questionnaires (*ankety*) in 1992. Full legal recognition of former POWs as 'war participants' and their full rehabilitation was granted only in 1995.[125]

# 6

# 'Honour to the Victors!'

Worst off were the returning soldiers. Having seen life in the countries of Poland, Czechoslovakia, Rumania, Hungary and Bulgaria, they were disillusioned and rebellious. Awaiting them were bread lines, lack of clothing, high prices and a shortage of living quarters. Most of their families were dead or deported. The day of the soldier as the 'hero of the Soviet Union' was over; once again the Communists, who had taken a back seat during the war, came to the front. (Oksana Kasenkina, 1949)[1]

The demobilization of the Soviet Army was ... the most important source for the reinforcement and improvement of the composition of leading cadres in party, soviet, economic, and societal organizations. This significance of demobilization was caused not only by the return of a significant number of leading workers, but also by the fact that during the war a significant number of organizers were promoted in the Soviet Army. They developed, under army conditions, experience with organizational and political work with the masses. (V. N. Donchenko 1970)[2]

Two views of veterans' social position after the war; two very different assessments. One stresses the disappointments of victory; veterans are contrasted with 'communists' and portrayed as victims of the war, political repression, and economic hardship. The other notes that veterans made a career in the army which was prolonged after the war; here, veterans are not opposed to communists, they are the communists; veterans are not losers of postwar life, cheated of their victory, they are victors, not only in a symbolic, but also in a social sense. They moved up in the world.

Whom should we believe? The strongly anti-Soviet eyewitness, who saw the disaffected veterans after the war, but wrote her memoirs in part to establish her worthiness for political asylum in cold war America; or the Soviet historian with access to the archives, but labouring under severe ideological constraints in Brezhnev's Soviet Union? The reader of the preceding chapters might well side with Kasenkina, the anti-Soviet memoirist. This would be a good choice: for many, the return home was a bitter disappointment of the high hopes of victory—especially for those most heavily marked by the war, as war invalids and returned POWs were in their different ways.[3]

To accept this truth, however, does not force us to dismiss Donchenko's account. Indeed, many later historians—both Westerners and Russians whose anti-Stalinist credentials are beyond questioning—have followed her line. 'For many soldiers', writes Sheila Fitzpatrick, 'army service in World War II turned out to be a channel of upward mobility.' Peasants entered the urban labour force. Soldiers rose through the ranks, joined the Communist Party, and became administrators or managers after the war. The pattern of workers becoming Stalin's elite in the interwar years was now replaced by 'the appointment of veterans who had joined the party during the war to positions of civilian leadership'.[4] Similarly, Donald Filtzer writes of 'the unwillingness of demobilized peasants to return to the countryside'. Instead of going back to the 'second serfdom' of kolkhoz life, they used 'their status as veterans in order to find jobs in industry'.[5] And not only there—even the prestigious Gor'kii Literature Institute in Moscow was, according to Nikolai Mitrokhin, full of demobilized 'peasant lads' who fought as hard as they could and with all means at their disposal to stay in the capital and in their new status position (and apartments).[6]

Historians have good reason to follow what at first sight might look like Soviet propaganda: veterans did dominate the party; many of them did take over leading positions in party, government, and the economy, where their frontline manners often annoyed contemporaries; many others left the village and moved up in the world by becoming workers or even writers—a very prestigious profession in the Soviet context. Social success, however defined, is clearly part of the experience of Soviet veterans in the postwar decades. The question remains, however, how significant such success was within the collective trajectory of veterans' lives. And was it caused by the impact of the war or by broader transformations well under way before the Germans invaded in 1941?

This chapter offers some answers to these questions. It starts with a case study of a veteran who did make a career after the war, and a career which at several important junctions relied on what amounted to informal affirmative action for veterans. Rather than taking this to be *the* story, however, we need to account for at least some of the complexity of the issue of social mobility of veterans after the war. As a medievalist has warned in a different context, the historian of social mobility needs to balance instances of 'successful careerism … against those of individual social decline. The full story must also take account of gender differences', and, one might add, differences in ethnicity, generation, and social position before induction into the army as well.[7]

To start unravelling this complexity, let us look closely at the life of an individual. Irina Efremovna Bogacheva was born in 1920 in Briansk region, into what she describes in her memoirs as a 'simple peasant family'. She spent the first ten years of her life in her home village, then the family moved to Donetsk in the Donbass industrial region, where her father had found work. In a manner typical for upwardly mobile peasants, the family encouraged learning among the children and, despite severe poverty, Irina Efremovna completed the entire course of secondary education—the so-called ten-year school, which she finished with distinction.[8] Her outstanding academic results allowed her to enter university without exams, and she followed a friend to the University of Voronezh, where she enrolled in the physical-mathematical faculty. Living on a meagre stipend, she was also a serious athlete, competing in running as well as skiing events. A week before the final exam of 1941, on 22 June, the German *Wehrmacht* attacked the Soviet Union, changing her life, like the lives of millions, forever.[9]

Like most memoirists, Bogacheva remembers well what she did that day. In the morning she had won a two kilometre cross-country race, and she was in the process of planning the rest of the season with her team, when the news of the German attack broke. When she returned to her dormitory, a friend met her with the words: 'Well, Ira, what about it: will we fight?' The same day, Bogacheva volunteered as a frontline nurse.[10] She served the entire war—and survived it physically and mentally intact—to be demobilized with the first wave in July 1945. After a short visit to the completely destroyed Voronezh ('there was no place left to lay one's head'), she returned to 'the unloved Donetsk', where her family still lived, and soon found a job, despite her youth and her lack of qualifications.[11]

The reason for this quick success was simple: she was a veteran. The first time when this informal status worked to her advantage was when she entered the regional educational administration of Donetsk in search of employment. The head of the administration 'rose, saluted (I was in uniform, with decoration)'. After a short conversation he invited her to become director of her old ten-year school, despite her utter lack of training and experience. The 'practice' of war, he decided, was enough.[12] It turned out that he had romantic ambitions as well, which were frustrated by Bogacheva, who scoffed at the idea of marrying a home-front rat. The resulting conflict with her superior, together with her sense of insecurity in the job, made her resign from the post of director.

After a failed attempt to get into the Highest Party School (like many others she had joined the Communist Party at the front), she worked for two years as a teacher, but started to become increasingly restless: 'I wanted more, [I wanted] movement ahead, creative growth. I think that this feeling about the necessity to grow was not accidental. It was the result of the experience of the long years of war with their extraordinary exertion of spiritual and physical strength, will, [and] mind.' She also hated the climate of Donetsk and the lack of woods and streams. She clearly needed to leave.[13] She went on a visit to Voronezh, dropped into the department of physical education to see old friends, and was immediately invited to come along to a Mountaineers' Camp in the Caucasus (how could she have refused?). The department's chair also promised to help regarding the move to Voronezh and the next day they went together to see the rector of the university, also a *frontovik*. He suggested she should become a graduate student (*aspirant*), an idea she immediately embraced: 'Graduate school opened excellent perspectives for growth, for a future.'[14] However, the recommendation was again based merely on her wartime record—in fact, her preparation was fairly poor, due to the shortening of her university education, the long years at the front, followed by two years as a teacher.[15]

After her return from the Mountaineers' Camp, she thus started to attend university lectures in Donetsk to ready herself for graduate school. It soon became clear how poor her preparation was, so she shifted from physics to the less rigorous 'philosophy' (i.e. dogmatic Marxism-Leninism). Together with another *frontovik* she was admitted to graduate school in Voronezh in the academic year 1948/9. It was not a coincidence that those admitted were both veterans—Bogacheva's supervisor had served as well.[16] She defended her dissertation in 1952 and began to work as a lecturer in both the historical-philosophical and the physical-mathematical faculties of her university—as usual despite her rather sketchy preparation: 'The only preparation as a teacher in philosophy I had was that in my third year I led seminars in the university...I think, that these appointments showed the belief in me, largely caused by the fact that I was a frontline veteran (*frontovichka*).'[17]

Bogacheva was part of what is probably the most celebrated group of veterans: young, urban, and successful—particularly in higher education. Representations of this group abounded after the war. Tortuous novels like Iurii Trifonov's Stalin-prize winning *Students* (1950) had veterans in higher education as their main protagonists, while the satirical magazine *Krokodil* good-humouredly celebrated the way veterans were 'taking' exams with the same zeal they had formerly 'taken cities'.[18] The pages of real-life university newspapers also singled out veterans who had become top students, Komsomol and party leaders, and 'social activists' (*obshchestvenniki*). Novels of the Thaw as well as memoirs also give prominent place to the veteran–student.[19]

Such prominence in representations of the period is not completely misleading. Higher education was, indeed, one of the few fields of legislation where special privileges applied to all war participants after the war, but these advantages were rather slim and a far cry from the American GI bill.[20] They included easier access to stipends, preferred admission to preparatory courses, technicums, and institutions of higher education (*vuzy*), tuition exemption for preparatory courses and technicums (but not for *vuzy*), the right to return to one's studies after the war, and the right to take advantage of one's former status as an outstanding student (*otlichnik*) in admissions (which allowed the student to enrol without exams). All other war participants did have to take exams, but if they passed were admitted outside of the regular ranking system (*vne konkursa*).[21]

Such formal advantages were increased by informal ones. In their memoirs, veterans frequently report how their admissions were based on their wartime record, the orders and medals on their chest, rather than their usually insufficient academic preparation. 'I entered the office of... [the] dean of the history faculty of Moscow University.... He glanced at my bar of medal ribbons, pulled my application towards himself and wrote something in it. Thus I became a student of Moscow University.' Similar practices prevailed in examinations in the immediate postwar years. Vladimir Kabo, who attended the summit of Soviet tertiary education, Moscow State University, recalls the following scene: the examiner 'half-listened to my answer, ... glanced at the medal ribbons on my chest, and inquired with interest what I had won them for. Then he took my record card and wrote in it, "Excellent".'[22]

As a result of this preferential treatment, some institutions, such as the famous Gor'kii Literature Institute in Moscow, were dominated by returning servicemen,[23] but in most universities, they were a distinct if highly influential minority. Even during the years of mass-demobilization, veterans constituted only between 9 (1945/6) and 11 per cent (1946/7) of newly admitted students in higher education (*vuzy*).[24] These enrolments led to a share of veterans in the student body of between 7 and 23 per cent depending on the university.[25] In 1947, according to *Izvestiia*, one-sixth (17 per cent) of all university students were 'ex-service men and women'.[26]

Veterans were not only a minority among students, students were also a minority among veterans—around 1 per cent of demobilized soldiers by early 1947. Even among those who returned to cities (a minority, as we shall see below) only around 3 per cent became students.[27] The quantitative data we have do not allow a definitive conclusion, but it appears that the majority of veteran-students simply returned to the trajectory of their prewar lives. About half of the students who were admitted to higher educational institutions during mass-demobilization were most likely reinstatements of former students who had interrupted their education to serve in the war.[28] Of the other half, many must have been inducted from the school-bench and would have gone on to university in any case. Again, Bogacheva is a good example for this process: she had been a good student before the war and she might well have gone on to graduate school if the war had not interrupted her career. In this respect, it does not appear that the war actually changed the basic course of her life—but rather that she needed special consideration after the war because returning to her prewar track was not easy after four years at the frontline.

Within the veteran-student body also existed a distinct minority of new students, who were socially mobile, and whose mobility was connected to their wartime service. These were the 'peasant lads' dominating the Literature Institute, but other places had their share of this type as well. Mikhail Gorbachev reports that veterans of 'worker-peasant background' were admitted preferentially to Moscow State University in order to 'optimize' the social composition of the student body.[29] Veterans from more educated backgrounds felt that they had little in common with these social climbers.[30] Among non-veterans, such socio-cultural distinctions sometimes went beyond indifference and bordered on hostility. The sons and daughters of the Soviet elite frequently wrinkled their noses and made fun of these upstarts in their old uniforms, conveniently forgetting that their own parents had themselves risen from a similar background through

Stalin's revolution from above and the extraordinary cadres exchange made possible by the blood-letting of the Great Purges. As one daughter of such *vydvizhentsy* ('promotees') remembered:

> The Department of History [of Moscow State University] got a special breed of *frontoviki*: peasant boys who had become Komsomol and party functionaries in the military. The war had given them a taste of power, and now they were determined to stay in the city for the rest of their lives. Most of them visualized the same career ladder: a degree in the history of the USSR or the history of the Communist party, then a position someplace in the party apparatus. They had no interest in history; they had no burning questions. They were incapable of critical thinking. They studied to become bosses.
>
> They couldn't even write a decent love note. 'The ribbon in your hair makes you more beautiful,' a *frontovik* attempted to write to a friend of mine at a party. When he got to 'more beautiful,' the sentence misfired. He wrote '*krasivshe*,' which is folksy and, presumably, was appropriate for his sweetheart at the kolkhoz. *Krasiveye* would have been correct Russian. The note was widely circulated.[31]

Such arrogant laughter would soon turn to terror as the veterans' influence in the universities expanded far beyond their numerical strength. Returning soldiers tended to be older than the rest of the student body; they were marked by their army uniforms (which they continued to wear both for reasons of pride and for lack of alternatives), and they stuck together celebrating their 'frontline brotherhood', frequently over a bottle of vodka.[32] Younger students were impressed by their ability to hold their liquor and disturbed by their cynicism.[33]

These close-knit groups of frequently aggressive veteran-students dominated many institutions politically, despite their minority share. In Gor'kii State University demobilized soldiers were extremely visible, although they constituted under 9 per cent of those admitted in 1948.[34] The university's newspaper singled out veterans as models for other students to follow, and the party as well as the Komsomol at the university were dominated by veterans as well.[35] At Moscow State University, too, veterans took over the Komsomol and party cells.[36] This was part of a wider phenomenon within the party, which had in many ways become an organization of ex-warriors.[37] We can distinguish two groups of former soldiers in the party after 1945: those who had been communists (i.e. either full members or candidates to membership) before the war, and those who had joined during the conflict, largely at the frontline. The first group comprise the survivors of the 600,588 communists who had been in the armed forces as the war broke out and those of a total of 1,678,377 who joined the army from civilian party organizations.[38] The second group was composed of the remainder of those 3.9 million soldiers and sailors who were admitted to candidate status during the war.[39] Together, these groups might have been as strong as 4.2 million by the end of hostilities, representing as much as 72 per cent of the party.[40]

Given the numbers involved and the horrendous casualties particularly early in the war, the majority of veterans in the party must have been those who had joined at the front, i.e. were newly admitted.[41] Unpublished internal party statistics give a fairly detailed sociological breakdown of this group, showing that prewar trends in the composition of party membership were continued rather than disrupted by frontline admissions.[42] Like before the war, Russians were hugely over-represented: they comprised 58 per cent of the population in 1939 but took up 71 per cent of party admissions in the military during the war.

The overall changes in the national composition of the Communist Party throughout the war were caused to a significant degree by the influx of those admitted in the army and at the front: the over-representation of Russians increased, the under-representation of Ukrainians and Belorussians grew, the position of Georgians and Armenians was strengthened, the under-representation of Central Asians was reduced, and the share of Azeri declined.[43] Latvians were the one nationality which was not under-represented if compared to their share of the population in 1939. This is best explained by their above-average educational level. The same is true for Armenians and Georgians, whose under-representation was also comparatively small. However, this explanation does not work for the equally well-represented Moldavians, Kirgiz, Turkmen, and Kazakh, whose educational level was far below average.[44] The poor representation of Ukrainians, Azeri, and Belorussians had a political background (in addition to the educational underperformance of Azeri). Ukrainians and Belorussians were under the suspicion of being nationalists and anti-Soviet, maybe even pro-German.[45] Suspicion of nationalism and military cooperation also extended to Azeri, who had had national formations within the German army.[46]

The largest under-representation are the unspecified 'other' nationalities. Given the general anti-Semitic atmosphere of the postwar years it would

Table 6.1. Nationality breakdown of persons admitted to candidacy during the war in military party organizations compared with population

| | A<br>Admitted to military party organizations during war (%) | B<br>Population in 1939 (%) | C<br>Index of representation (A−B) |
|---|---|---|---|
| Latvians | 0.1 | 0.1 | 0.0 |
| Moldavians | 0.1 | 0.2 | −0.1 |
| Tadzhiks | 0.1 | 0.7 | −0.6 |
| Turkmen | 0.1 | 0.5 | −0.4 |
| Estonians | 0.2 | 0.1 | 0.1 |
| Kirgiz | 0.2 | 0.5 | −0.3 |
| Azeri | 0.5 | 1.3 | −0.8 |
| Uzbeks | 0.7 | 2.8 | −2.1 |
| Georgians | 0.9 | 1.3 | −0.4 |
| Armenians | 1.0 | 1.3 | −0.3 |
| Kazakhs | 1.4 | 1.8 | −0.4 |
| Belorussians | 2.4 | 3.1 | −0.7 |
| Other nationalities | 7.1 | 11.4 | −4.3 |
| Ukrainians | 14.6 | 16.5 | −1.9 |
| Russians | 70.6 | 58.4 | 12.2 |
| Total | 100.0 | 100.0 | |

Note: The data for admissions in the military refer to the period from the first quarter of 1942 to the second quarter of 1945.
Sources: Column A: Edele, 'A "Generation of Victors"?', 577–9 (app. 2); column B: Vsesoiuznaia perepis' naseleniia 1939 goda: Osnovnye itogi (Moscow: Nauka, 1992), 57–8.

make sense to assume that Jews were one of the groups who did poorly in party admissions at the front as well.[47] This assumption might be erroneous. Jews remained over-represented in the party throughout the war. In military party organizations their number rose from 23,289 in early 1941 to 100,101 in early 1945. They thus constituted 3.1 per cent of all communists in military party organizations at the end of the war.[48] While their absolute numbers dropped during demobilization, the relative number rose to 3.9 per cent by 1948.[49] This means that Jews were more likely than other nationalities to make a career in the army, as they had done before the war.[50] In the party as a whole their share dropped from 4.6 per cent in 1941 to 3.7 per cent by early 1946, but their absolute numbers still rose from 177,135 to 202,969.[51] This share, moreover, implies a massive over-representation of Jews in comparison with their proportion both in the population (1.1 per cent in 1959) and the wartime army

(1.5 per cent).[52] Whoever the under-represented 'other nationalities' were, surprisingly enough the Jews were not one of them.

One reason why Jewish soldiers did so well in admissions to the party was their above-average level of education.[53] Frontline admissions were not only skewed to particular nationalities, but also to soldiers of higher social position and (which usually coincided in the Soviet Union) higher education. Soldiers of white-collar background were more likely than anybody else to join the party at the front (42 per cent), followed by workers (35 per cent). Both these groups, who in the prewar census had made up 16 and 30 per cent of the population, respectively, were thus over-represented if compared with the population at large. Kolkhoz peasants, on the other hand, were severely under-represented: while comprising 44 per cent in the prewar census, they constituted only 23 per cent of 'young communists' (as the new recruits were called, independent of their age) admitted at the front. The prewar trends of over-representation of white-collar workers and under-representation of peasants were thus continued by frontline admissions.[54] Officers were more likely to join than other ranks, and the more specialized the branch of arms, the more party members it comprised: those with higher education were more likely to be admitted than those without.[55] Kolkhoz peasants were thus the least likely to join the Communist Party, even at the front.

But join they did. As among veteran-students after the war, kolkhozniki who signed up at the front were an important minority among new party members. For them, the war 'turned into an autobiographical point of reference and point of departure'.[56] It was this group more than any other which was transformed by the war from 'peasants into Soviets'.[57] They were unlikely to return to the village and more likely to preserve the momentum of upward mobility after the war as their often aggressive presence in higher education illustrates. If they did go back to the village, they tended to work in positions of authority as more than half of the communists in collective farms did in 1948.[58]

Demobilization coincided with a major turnover in kolkhoz chairs. In 1946, 41 per cent of them had 'a tenure of less than one year'. According to Jerry Hough, the replacements 'were usually men returning from the army'. I was unable to find aggregate data on this question for either the Soviet Union as a whole or for any of the Union republics. What is clear, though, is that women were pushed out of these positions which they had held during the war.[59] While the men were away at the front, 20 per cent of kolkhoz chairs were women.[60] By the start of 1950 their share had dropped to less than 5 per cent,[61] only to fall still further to 2.4 per cent by 1952.[62] Thus, while the majority of the population in the countryside was female by 1950, the positions of influence and power were in the hands of men.[63] This was not lost on contemporary observers: 'Why were nearly all women in leading posts replaced by men?' asked one citizen in Rostov province in 1949.[64]

Local data imply that a large share of these men were veterans. Already by January 1945, 40 per cent of the kolkhoz chairmen in Voronezh region were war invalids.[65] In Smolensk region 72 per cent of kolkhoz chairs were veterans shortly after the war.[66] By the fall of 1946 in Rostov province 51 per cent of leading cadres and specialists in state farms (sovkhozy) were veterans.[67] In Chkalovsk region by February 1946 a little less than half (48 per cent) of the positions of kolkhoz chairmen were in the hands of old soldiers,[68] and in the Ukrainian village described in detail by the later defector Fedor Belov, by 1947 'all the top posts … [had] passed into the hands of former front-line officers'.[69] In Ukraine as a whole half of those promoted to leading positions in the first half of 1946 were demobilized communists.[70]

Many veterans who got into positions of authority after the war simply returned to jobs they had held before. 'New cadres' among demobilized soldiers in Rostov region in 1945/6 were often in fact old ones who had worked in these organizations before the war and who now returned from the army.[71] One raikom secretary explained part of the heavy turnover of kolkhoz chairs in 1945 and 1946 with the circumstance that 'old experienced cadres' (starye opytnye rabotniki) had returned from the army and had taken some of these positions out of less experienced hands. As a result, 70 per cent of kolkhoz chairmen were 'comrades who have worked between four and fifteen years' in similar positions.[72] In Murmansk province 66 per cent of employed demobilized soldiers worked in their old professions at the start of 1946, while 34 per cent worked in new professions they had acquired in the Red Army.[73] In the Chuvash Autonomous Republic 37 per cent of demobilized soldiers in leading positions had worked in them before the war, while the rest were promoted (vydvinuto).[74] In Voronezh province in 1947, only 35 per cent of veterans in leading positions had not worked in similar jobs before.[75]

Data for party secretaries also indicate that the two processes—return of experienced cadres and the promotion of new ones from among the defenders of the Homeland—ran in parallel. The picture becomes especially clear if we look at the length of experience with work in responsible party positions. As Table 6.2 shows, the absolute numbers of secretaries of all experience levels grew during the years of demobilization, indicating that both prewar cadres came back *and* new cadres took over. This was made possible by the overall expansion of civilian party organizations during demobilization and the connected increase of the number of primary party positions which doubled between July 1945 and January 1949. The influx of new cadres was, indeed, significant. Three years after the beginning of mass-demobilization, those with less than three years of experience in responsible party work constituted 84 per cent of party secretaries of primary party units.[76]

Lack of experience should not be confused with youth, however. The high time for women getting pushed out of the position of party secretary was the year 1946—at the beginning of this year women had a larger share of secretary positions than their share in the party, at the start of 1947 they were, instead, under-represented.[77] Men of the first three demobilization waves were, thus, especially likely to push women out of responsible positions. This is hardly surprising: they were older (birth years 1893–1921) and often specialists (who were demobilized in the second wave) and therefore more likely than the following cohorts of younger soldiers to take over positions of authority.[78] Local data on other leading positions support this conclusion. The much quoted Belov, who was born shortly after the

Table 6.2. Party secretaries by experience in leading cadre work (index of growth of absolute numbers; 1945 = 100)

| Experience | 1 July '45 | 1 Jan. '46 | 1 Jan. '47 | 1 July '47 | 1 Jan. '48 | 1 July '48 | 1 Jan. '49 |
|---|---|---|---|---|---|---|---|
| up to 6 months | 100 | 121 | 207 | 249 | 210 | 200 | 190 |
| 6 months to 1 year | 100 | 105 | 186 | 188 | 221 | 205 | 187 |
| 1–2 years | 100 | 117 | 128 | 168 | 197 | 221 | 230 |
| 2–3 years | 100 | 115 | 129 | 135 | 148 | 186 | 217 |
| 3–5 years | 100 | 113 | 124 | 131 | 139 | 153 | 168 |
| more than 5 years | 100 | 115 | 144 | 155 | 166 | 181 | 197 |
| Total | 100 | 114 | 159 | 181 | 190 | 198 | 201 |

*Source for raw data:* RGANI f. 77, op. 1, d. 4, l. 1760b, 1770b; d. 5, l. 1740b, 1750b; d. 6, l. 810b, 820b.

revolution, was the youngest kolkhoz chairman in his district. The other veteran turned chairman in his village, Volodymyr, was a retired colonel and considerably older.[79] In Voronezh province by 1947 the average age of a leading worker was 39, and that was lowered by first secretaries of Komsomol *raikomy*, who were on average 24 years old. Other positions had considerably older staff on average: Sovkhoz directors, 44 years; MTS directors, 42 years; or Raiispolkom chairmen, 42 years.[80] The data on the age structure of party secretaries show a similar pattern: the largest numbers and the largest absolute increase were in secretaries aged 31 to 40, followed by those over 40.[81]

The first returnees immediately after war's end had much better chances than later demobilization waves to get into good positions, which proliferated in 1945. Initially, local authorities reacted to the demands of demobilized servicemen by creating new posts in such numbers that the administrative apparatus became increasingly top-heavy.[82] The trade union newspaper published many attacks on the increase of clerical and administrative staff as well as on the growing number of line managers in 1946.[83] A decree of August 1946 outlawed further increase of the administrative apparatus of Soviet, government, economic, co-operative, and societal organizations, prohibited administrative reorganizations of Ministries and departments of both Union and Republic level, and ruled that all vacant positions were to be eliminated and not restaffed.[84] Subsequently, this decree created serious problems in finding 'appropriate' work for demobilized servicemen, as the Groznyi obkom secretary reported in November:

> After the decree of the Council of Ministers of the USSR about the prohibition since 15 August to admit [anybody] to vacant administrative posts, the question of job placement (*trudoustroistvo*) of demobilized became a little bit more complicated. This especially concerned demobilized officers who had no civilian occupation, who before this [decree] could be placed into all sorts of positions (*na vsevozmozhnye dolzhnosti*) in the administrative apparatus.[85]

Something similar happened in the countryside. The decree of 19 September 1946, which toughened the kolkhoz regime after the liberality of war, complained about the 'baseless increase of administrative and management personnel'. This increase led 'in many kolkhozes' to a lack of peasants to work the fields. Instead, a large number of administrative positions were staffed with 'people who do not do anything and who

receive a larger income than in production work'.[86] The decree created
similar problems as its equivalent in the cities. By 1947, returning veterans
complained that jobs such as herdsman (*zhivotnovod*) or kolkhoz accountant
were no longer available.[87]

In order thus to not confuse the successful minority with the broad
masses, a closer look at veterans in the village is useful. The vast majority
of returning soldiers—at least 79 per cent, possibly more—were not party
members.[88] Most were not in leading positions but kolkhoz peasants, who,
after release from the army, returned to the countryside. Of those service
men and women who returned between the summer of 1945 and 1 January
1947, only 33 per cent went to cities and towns.[89] Demobilization thus did
not immediately lead to further urbanization or a shift of kolkhoz peasants
to industry, as is sometimes suggested.[90]

That peasants returned to the unloved collective farms might be surprising, but given the context, it was quite logical: the kolkhoz, however
disliked, was the only home they had. Here were their families and
the little property Stalin's revolution from above had left them. Here
were their gardens, which promised food in a heavily destroyed and
hungry country; here were, maybe, still their huts, which promised shelter. Moreover, rumour had it that the hated collectives would soon be
abolished, and propaganda told demobilized soldiers that they would get
any help they needed to re-establish their household economy.[91] As a
result of the massive return of demobilized soldiers, the countryside was
for a while 'dominated by vast networks of Red Army veterans and their
families', expecting to have gained a special status in the new postwar
village.[92]

They were quickly disabused of this illusion, and the new village of
veterans ceased to exist by the 1950s. Far from being dismantled or quietly
dropped, the kolkhoz regime was re-established along prewar lines, and
those who resisted this renewed 'enserfment' were liable to be sent to
Siberia as 'parasites' under two 1948 decrees designed by the Ukrainian
party leader and later Stalin-successor Nikita Khrushshev on the model
of old Tsarist directives.[93] Life in the Soviet village remained marked
by backbreaking labour, poverty, exploitation, and lack of control over
production, marketing, and even consumption of agricultural goods by the
tillers of the land. Once returning veterans saw the level of destruction
of the formerly occupied territories, once they realized how miserable
rural living conditions were, that in the kolkhoz they practically had

to work for nothing, and that the regime had no intention of easing the kolkhoz order, they left in overwhelming numbers, particularly after 1948.[94]

Veterans were unlikely to accept exploitation in the collective farms and looked for a more bearable existence elsewhere, some in the holiday regions such as the Black Sea coast or the Caucasus,[95] and more in the cities. Male outmigration was a continuation of prewar patterns, which were reinforced by the chaos of the postwar years (which made control of movement over the peasantry harder), and the strong sense of veterans that they had fought for a good life, not for a return to serfdom. 'We fought for Soviet power...so life would become easier and we would pay less taxes', as one of them remarked. 'But it happened the other way around and now the peasants pay more taxes than before.' The only way out was to abandon the village. 'One needs to run away,' said the same veteran, 'only slaves work in the kolkhoz.'[96]

Whether they were intelligentsia, workers, or peasants, whether they returned to their prewar professions or moved up in the world, whether they were old or new communists, or not in the party in the first place, most veterans had one thing in common—they were men. Only a minority were, like Bogacheva, women. Their number is shrouded somewhat in mystery as the available data are 'distressingly vague'.[97] According to recently published statistics, a total of 570,000 female soldiers served in the armed forces during the war, of them 80,000 officers. By 1 January 1945 only 463,503 women were on active roll.[98] One older, frequently (mis)quoted Soviet source claims (without a footnote) that 'more than' 800,000 women served in the Red Army during the war.[99] This is also the number given by other official publications in the 1970s.[100] If we take the half million (463,503) women who were in the army by 1 January 1945 as the lower limit (as it excludes those who were demobilized earlier), and the 0.8 million as the upper limit (as we do not know how many died), we arrive at a share of between 2 and 4 per cent, depending on what estimate of the number of veterans we use.[101] As a growing literature on this minority points out, frontline women faced widespread hostility after the war.[102]

However, this point is easily overstressed, as Bogacheva's example illustrates. Her career, as far as we can tell from her memoirs, seems to have been fairly uninhibited by gender discrimination. Indeed, the socio–cultural context women veterans returned to was complex and ambivalent. Prestige was

intermingled with anxieties about orderly sexual relations, self-assertiveness
was confronted with sometimes aggressive dismissal. Female veterans were
treated with respect and hostility. While some civilians got up and saluted
when Bogacheva entered the room (and subsequently fell in love with
her), others called the medal *For Battle Merit* (*Za boevye zaslugi*), if worn
by a woman, *For Sexual Merit* (*Za polovye zaslugi*).[103] Women veterans did
thus face specific problems after the war, but most of them were related to
marriage chances, family life, and the politics of sexual morality rather than
to employment and career.[104] Those which were related to the latter were
more often than not caused by their strange position in the life-cycle rather
than by gender *per se*. Such problems were not specific to women, but
shared by their male coevals as well: they were the problems of young and
proud veterans.[105] In a famous speech at a meeting with female *frontoviki*,
Politburo member and Old Bolshevik Mikhail Kalinin pointed towards this
problem:

> It is one thing to demobilize, for example, a kolkhoz peasant: he has a
> purpose—he goes [back] to an [already] prepared place where his family, his
> wife, and his children wait for him. It is a different thing to demobilize a
> 20 or 23 year old girl (*devushka*), who, as a matter of fact, fulfilled the first
> serious work of her life at the front. And she got used to this military work,
> despite all problems and dangers. Before the war the majority of girl-soldiers
> (*devushki-voiny*) were not independent. They studied and went [to the front]
> from under the wing of their mothers, grandmothers, and fathers. Here, at
> the front, they became independent. This independent life went on for three
> or four years and now it suddenly comes to an end. Therefore it is completely
> natural that 90 per cent of you are nervous about this new life and what it
> has in store for you.[106]

It is noteworthy that what the wise patriarch stressed was not a conflict
about gender expectations, but a problem with life-cycle stages—the war
had suddenly treated adolescents as grown-ups. This sudden transition
was probably more marked for many women who had been given less
autonomy as adolescents than their male coevals, but it was there for men
as well. For protected daughters, entering the armed forces could lead to
an extremely sudden jump, as in the case of one veteran whose 'mother
would not let her go to see her grandmother without an escort, saying
she was too young, and two months later she went to the front, became a
medical orderly, and fought all the way from Smolensk to Prague. When
she came back from the war she was 22.'[107]

These self-assertive and proud young warriors came back into civilian society without the necessary qualifications to go on living in the same grown-up manner. They had to take a step back into an earlier stage in the life-cycle, acquire a profession, and then move back up into the 'independent life' of grown-ups. Women veterans shared this complex problem of a disjuncture between expectations and opportunities created by their sudden jump to another stage of personal development during the war with their male coevals. The youngest cohorts of veterans (born 1923–7) had considerable problems in the adaptation to civilian life. They 'had gone to the front straight from the schoolroom without the chance to acquire any occupational experience at all. War was their profession, their only competence the capacity to wield weapons and fight.'[108]

These problems were exacerbated by the lack of open positions by the time these age groups were demobilized in 1947 and 1948 (see Table 1.1). For these reasons, young officers with high expectations were a major headache for local officials in the later stages of demobilization. The regional administration of Ivanovo province had 'considerable problems' in the spring of 1947 in finding jobs for 'cadre officers and youth, who have been drafted from the school-bench' and had no civilian profession.[109] The job placement of officers without civilian expertise was a 'tight spot' in the attempts of the Kuibyshev city Soviet to put demobilized soldiers to work in the spring of 1947.[110] In Moscow region, the job placement of this group was 'especially unsatisfactory'.[111] While for local officials this was mainly an administrative problem, for the officers themselves this was a major obstacle to rebuilding a civilian life which was 'more or less satisfactory … in a material respect', as they complained to the army newspaper *Red Star*.[112] Moreover, the experience of a severe drop in social status had a psychological dimension as well. Highly decorated veterans often resented having to go back to the school-bench or to get job training instead of getting a good position right away.[113] One veteran told me the story of her commander. Humiliated by the inability to find work he deemed appropriate he became a severe alcoholic.[114]

One important reason for adaptation problems, then, was a disjuncture between expectations aroused by the social status achieved in the army (the 'independence' Kalinin talked about) and possibilities of maintaining this status after demobilization. To some extent this must have been less of a problem for female veterans than for some of their male peers: women rarely reached high military rank in the army,[115] which made the transition to civilian life less of a fall. However, dominant gender expectations put them at a disadvantage if war service had given them the taste for certain 'male' professions.

Nurses who wanted to become surgeons were one such group. They posed enough of a problem to be addressed directly in postwar didactic fiction. A 1947 novel tells the tale of the frontline nurse Taia Daletskaia. A true *frontovichka* she returns short-haired, proud, and self-assertive, the order of the Red Star pinned to her chest. Her plans are clear-cut and ambitious: during the summer of her demobilization she would become a surgical nurse for Professor Barinov in the First Hospital of her home town. At the same time she would prepare for medical school and 'maybe she will succeed in going to Leningrad the next year ... and attend the medical institute'. From the beginning she runs into the walls of gender conventions. The head physician refuses to give her the position with Professor Barinov. Instead, she offers her work as a children's nurse. Taia protests: 'Comrade head physician ... I am a demobilized soldier. I know discipline. But this here is not the home front. Rather, it is no longer war. I cannot deal with children, and I have work experience [as a surgical nurse] (*u menia stazh*).' The head physician is not impressed and answers with a rant directed to all veterans: 'you should understand how things stand, and not simply be guided by your desires, comrades'. This greatly upsets Taia. She will get the job anyway, she grumbles. 'One does not talk like that to *frontoviki*.' And off she goes to the local government, the city executive committee, but has no luck there, either. The chairman (like the head physician, a woman) tells her that she is needed in the day nursery. Period. Her wish to work in her profession (*po spetsial'nosti*) is simply irrelevant. Taia goes on to the party district committee—again without results. And because this is a socialist realist novel and not real life, she suddenly stops being insulted by this persistent request to work in a clearly gendered, inglorious, and low-status job she does not like. She swallows her pride together with some of her ambition and starts to understand that her place is the nursery where she is needed, and not the surgeon's table where she wants to work.[116]

It is easy to imagine the resentment such attempts to put women into their 'natural place' in society must have caused real-life veterans. One medical worker, who could not get her prewar job back after demobilization because it was taken by somebody else, ran through the institutions for a year before she wrote a frustrated letter to the Supreme Soviet. 'I went on to go from the city health administration (*gorzdravotdel*) to the regional health administration, from the regional health administration to the provincial government (*oblispolkom*), I went to the director of the polyclinic [where she had worked before the war], but until now I remain without work…'[117] Others complained that nobody treated their job requests in a humane manner (*po chelovecheski*).[118] Another profession where gender roles stood in the way of postwar dreams of female veterans was that of pilot: 'after the war our regiment was released, and we all wanted to fly in civil aviation', remembers Mariia Smirnova of the 46th Night Bomber Aviation Regiment. Only a minority, however, won out in the competition with men for these positions. Of seventy-seven air-force veterans, only ten managed to get positions in civilian aviation.[119]

The story about the social mobility of veterans, thus, is far from straightforward. Some veterans did remarkably well. They left their former life in the village behind, made a career in the army, which they prolonged through higher education in the postwar years. Veterans became highly influential in the creative arts under Khrushchev, they dominated the party numerically, and they took over more than a fair share of leading positions after the war. Those who did well were an important group, no doubt, but they were by no means the majority of veterans. Whatever group we take — party members, students, or those taking over leading positions after the war — in each case these were a minority of returned soldiers: party members made up at most 21 per cent; students were a small minority of only 3 per cent even among urban demobilized soldiers (see above); and leading positions were given, depending on the region, to between 4 and 15 per cent of returnees.[120]

Whether or not we judge veterans as socially mobile depends to a large extent on how we define the term. Most often 'social mobility' means (1) the movement of individuals up or down the social hierarchy; less frequently, the term is used to describe (2) 'the grading up or down of entire social groups or classes'; finally, it can refer to (3) a change in the social hierarchy itself.[121] During the first postwar decade, social mobility in the first sense clearly occurred among veterans. Returning soldiers did move up in the world, either because they had been on this trajectory before the war already, or because what they had learnt in the army combined with the widespread respect towards those who had defended the country from German slavery opened doors which formerly had been closed. Once we move from the first to the second meaning — from the question of individual mobility to changes in the social position of the entire group—things do get more complicated.

If we talk of veterans as a social group in its own right, we cannot speak of it as socially mobile. Many of those who were successful after the war were indeed just returning to what they had done before they had joined the army (Donchenko calls this 'the return of a significant number of leading workers'). There was little official across-the-board affirmative action policy for veterans qua veterans in the immediate postwar years, which would have contributed to a general elevation of the social standing of all veterans. There was also no extraordinary cadres exchange comparable to the Stalin Revolution and the Great Terror, which would have opened up positions in sufficient numbers to lead to a takeover of power by veterans. Exceptions to this rule are the officer corps and the Communist Party, which were strongly dominated by old hands of the Second World War. However, overall the Soviet elite was not replaced by newly successful veterans. Those 'maturing during the bitter struggle of the Great Patriotic War' did not manage to get into the Central Committee (CC) until the early 1960s (2 per cent in 1961). Even as late as 1971, only 13 per cent of CC members were part of this political generation, compared with 72 per cent of the Stalinist elite which had risen to power in the context of the First Five-Year Plan and the Great Terror.[122]

Some groups of veterans also faced massive obstacles, either because of an underdeveloped welfare system (as in the case of war invalids) or because of outright discrimination and repression (as in the case of former POWs). There were also some—although minor, if compared to these massive problems—disadvantages for women, for a variety of nationalities, and for young veterans. Social mobility within the army created problems upon return when this new status did not translate into an equally elevated status as a civilian.

Reintegration into civilian life thus divided veterans from each other, establishing social hierarchies, 'fracturing' the group.[123] This should not be too surprising. Soviet veterans were a socially, culturally, and politically diverse group to begin with.[124] In this respect they resembled veterans in other times and places, who also felt that their frontline brotherhood was torn apart by the re-establishment of civilian hierarchies through demobilization.[125] Some historians of veterans, such as Antoine Prost in his classical study of French *anciens combattants* in the interwar years, even maintain that veterans do not exist unless they are conscious of their existence. They only become a social group when they organize and express an identity through public discourse.[126] Others have focused on state policies as creating a legal category which, in turn, created a social reality.[127]

Questions of organization and positive discrimination of veterans relate to social mobility in the final meaning: a special legal status defended by a strong organization can, indeed, elevate them to a new level within the social hierarchy. Social mobility in this sense did eventually occur in the Soviet Union, and indeed became much more important in the long run than whatever the aggregate of the social success of individual members of the frontline cohorts could have been. In the 1960s and 1970s, Soviet society started to accommodate veterans with a special position of respect, but also of privileged access to scarce goods and services. By the early 1980s, indeed, veterans had become a special status group in Soviet society—a radical change if we consider that they were not a group provided for in Marxist–Leninist theory. How this tectonic shift in the socio–cultural landscape came about is the topic of the final part of this study.

# PART III

## Movement

# 7
# The Struggle for Organization

In the late summer of 1946, V. Barykin, a journalist with the state news agency Sovinformbiuro, sent a letter to Andrei Aleksandrovich Zhdanov, the man in charge of the postwar cultural policies of the Communist Party.[1] The author did not write in the persona of the supplicant, but rather as a citizen, giving unsolicited policy advice to the comrades of the Central Committee.[2] He pointed to a possibility of increasing the effectiveness of propaganda both within the country and abroad. At the centre of his proposal was the creation of a veterans' organization similar to what existed elsewhere.

> It is well known that veterans' organizations exist in America, France and other countries. They organize millions of people. On 22 August TASS reported in a telegram from New York: 'The press reports that as a result of the recent, successful revolt (*miatezh*) of war veterans against the corrupt government of the city of Athens (Tennessee), the war veterans of Tennessee discuss at the moment their plan to found a political organization of veterans for the state as a whole; they also discuss reforms of the election system and the system of administration. This organization might become the origin of a third national party.' (Internal circular of TASS of 22 August, p. 73-O)

Somewhat naively, Barykin assumed that this story of veterans taking on the establishment would be likely to convince the comrades in the Central Committee that a Soviet veterans' organization would be a good idea. He saw demobilized soldiers as a progressive force, naturally aligned with the party–state, a group which could further the interests of the Soviet Union. His letter, in effect, formulated the basic programme of the Soviet veterans' movement as it would start to emerge a decade later.

> We could and should use veterans' organizations for our international propaganda for the fight against the warmongers, the unmasking of the

reactionaries who speak out against the Soviet Union, against the new democracy.

What needs to be done in this respect?

We need to found an international organization (association) of war veterans.

The Soviet war veterans should take the initiative in the foundation of such an international organization. Therefore, a society (association, organization) of veterans of the Patriotic War should be founded in the Soviet Union. The slogan, the motto of this organization should be:

'For peace in the whole world' (*Za mir vo vsem mire*).[3]

Barykin had already drafted a programme. The goal of the organization was to be the fight against warmongers, fascists, reactionaries, and other enemies of democracy. This was article 1. Articles 2 and 3, however, made the organization into more than an organ of international propaganda. Rather, it would combine this work with lobbying and welfare for Soviet veterans within the Soviet Union itself. The organization was to help veterans with everyday and material problems, organize invalids' homes and other supporting institutions, and oversee the execution of Soviet laws about work placement and welfare (*obespechenie*) of war invalids and war veterans more generally. It was to organize veterans' clubs and provide 'cultural-educational work' for them in order to fight 'unhealthy phenomena', such as former soldiers engaging in trade, drinking, or 'hooliganism'. The organization, as Barykin envisioned it, would have its own daily newspaper (called 'The Veteran of the Patriotic War'), which was to go after international enemies without and '*chinovniki* and bureaucrats' within—anybody who broke welfare legislation for veterans.[4]

In his letter to the Central Committee, Barykin formulated a vision which was widespread after the war—a vision of a strong, organized movement which would ensure the well-being of the defenders of the Homeland. As one of them put it in several letters to the famous war-hero and new Deputy Minister of Defence Georgii Konstantinovich Zhukov in 1953, veterans needed such an organization 'like air'.[5]

In Barykin's fairly sophisticated plan, this movement would legitimize domestic veterans' politics by providing the political leadership with an important service: propaganda work abroad. Like many of his comrades, he also assumed that such an organization would be regarded favourably in the Central Committee—an assumption which proved to be unfounded. In the long run, however, such resistance was partially overcome, an organized veterans' movement emerged, thrived, and eventually became a pillar of the late Soviet order. How did a group which officially was not supposed to exist manage to get institutionalized in the Soviet polity? Why, how, and to what extent did veterans in the end get the organization many of them had desired since the end of the war?

The evolution of the veterans' movement cannot be understood simply as a result of pressure from below or action from above. It required shifts in state policy to allow the actualization, legalization, formalization, and further growth of pre-existing mass desires, social relations, and organizational forms—which in turn influenced the way veterans thought, felt, and acted. The history of the veterans' movement is, thus, best understood as an interaction between socio-psychological pressures present throughout the Soviet social formation and resistant, tactical action by the political leadership. The fact that the Soviet veterans' movement was not simply an artificial state-creation but deeply rooted on an emotional and psychological but also a social level might explain why it survived the death of its host—the Union of Soviet Socialist Republics—and remained an influential political player after 1991.

Barykin seems to have been completely ignorant of the fact that the Soviet government had a long-term commitment *against* any form of veterans' organization in the Soviet Union. In rejecting the wishes of the veterans of the 'Great Patriotic War' the political leadership was repeating a policy formulated for the First World War as well as the Civil War. After the February Revolution of 1917 a variety of organizations of war invalids had emerged all over Russia and in June they had united in an All-Russian Union of Crippled Soldiers (*Vserossiiskii Soiuz uvechnykh voinov*).[6] Delegates of this association beleaguered the newly created Commissariat of Social Welfare of the RSFSR during its first months of existence in 1917.[7] Annoyed with this constant pestering of its officials, the Bolshevik leadership declared the union 'unnecessary' in August 1919. It was abolished after the end of the Civil War. The desires of disabled Bolshevik veterans of this conflict to at least get their own party cells were disappointed as well: on 7 July 1919 such special branches for veterans were outlawed by the Central Committee, and attempts to found a veterans' organization were frustrated by the political leadership in the 1920s.[8] Only a few local friendship societies of former soldiers managed to survive during the interwar years—a far cry from a Union-wide veterans' movement.[9] This prohibition of veterans' organizations was unique in the interwar period: all other belligerent nations had mass movements of veterans.[10]

The stubborn refusal of the party leadership to give in to demands for a veterans' organization was due to ideological, political, and economic reasons. Ideologically, veterans simply did not exist 'objectively' as a group with shared interests. They were not a social class in an orthodox Marxist sense, thus did not exist 'in themselves' and therefore also not 'for themselves'. Ergo, they did not need an organization which would represent their (non-existent) interests. They were, simply, Soviet citizens who at some point had served in the army. Politically, veterans could not be allowed to organize because this would challenge the organizational monopoly of the Bolshevik Party and would thus be 'counter-revolutionary'. No foci of political organization independent of the party-state could be tolerated. Finally, the economic reasons: the main role of such a movement, presumably, would be to push for and then defend special privileges of veterans—welfare provisions which the Soviet Union could not afford for a long time.[11]

The German attack in 1941 and the ensuing life and death struggle changed this line only temporarily. As more and more war invalids first trickled, then flooded back into the hinterland, the underdeveloped and understaffed local welfare organs were unable to deal with their reintegration into civilian life. Local authorities tried to ease the pressure by calling invalids' meetings, which took place in various localities by 1943. A little later, 'assistance committees' and 'groups for work with invalids' started to appear in several regions of the country. These organizations were often as much surveillance and policing agencies as they were representative organs of veterans' interests. Sometimes, however, they developed into local lobbying and welfare organs for war invalids.[12]

The spontaneous emergence of these organizations and the obvious popularity of the idea of veterans' associations did not change the general policy line, however. The party leadership reacted swiftly whenever the phenomenon of former soldiers organizing themselves was brought to its attention—which occurred frequently around the war's end. After the Party Control Commission's plenipotentiary for Kazakhstan had supported local desires for a 'Union of Invalids of the Patriotic War' in the summer of 1944, he was slapped down in no uncertain terms. His position was declared 'completely incorrect' and its 'faultiness' was 'explained to comrade Chubarov'.[13] A few months later, on 9 September 1944, a tiny, thirty-four-word note appeared in several newspapers, reporting on the creation of Committees for Officer War Invalids in several districts of Moscow.[14] The reaction to this rather innocent report indicates how alarmed the political leadership was about any kind of even semi-independent organization of veterans. The Central Committee apparatus started to review this question immediately, and—after checking with Stalin's inner circle by involving Malenkov—noted that the creation of the committees was an initiative of the Moscow Military Council, that this initiative had not been cleared with higher level authorities, and that the publication of the TASS communiqué advertising these groups to an all-Union audience had been a mistake. On 15 September 1944 the Central Committee's Secretariat declared this publication 'faulty' and warned local party organizations about the 'inappropriateness' (*netselesoobraznost'*) of such committees.[15] This was not the last time the Central Committee *apparat* had to intervene and stop the spontaneous development of an organized veterans' movement. In early 1945, a Party Control Commission inspector noted that enterprises still created illegal veterans' committees to deal with returning *frontoviki*.[16] In May 1945, the boss of *Sovinformbiuro* A. Lozovskii had to be slapped down for a proposal to create two veterans' organizations: the Council of Marshals (*Sovet Marshalov,* to be chaired by Stalin himself!) and the Society of Heroes of the Soviet Union (*Obshchestvo Geroev Sovetskogo Soiuza*)—hardly organizations prone to be disloyal.[17]

Given these precedents, it is not surprising that the leadership did not endorse Barykin's proposal to found a Soviet veterans' organization in 1946. A report to Zhdanov summarized the ideological mistakes of Barykin, who was subsequently informed that his ideas were 'far-fetched' and 'inappropriate'.[18] For one, Barykin did not understand the 'real political face' of the veterans' movement abroad. The most important US organization, the American Legion, was by no means progressive, but 'imperialist and anti-Soviet'. It encouraged the American government in an aggressive stand towards the Soviet Union and its former leader advocated a nuclear attack on Moscow. 'Individual episodes of progressive speeches by veterans' did not change this 'general picture'. The American veterans' movement had a 'clearly reactionary essence' (*reaktsionnaia sushchnost'*). The British Legion, too, was declared reactionary and full of 'petty Churchillesque ideas' (*cherchillevskie ideiki*) about an Anglo-American military alliance. In France, the veterans' movement was dominated by Pétainists and DeGaullists, and in other countries, too, they were as a rule 'reactionary'. As a result, an international organization would be reactionary, too—an undesirable outcome.[19]

On the domestic front, a veterans' organization was simply unnecessary, noted the report, as there were no special problems of veterans, and those few which did exist were taken care of by the government:

> In our country, the problem of 'work placement' of demobilized soldiers does not exist as a social problem which would be hard to resolve. The Soviet government caters through legislation to the interests of demobilized soldiers as well as war invalids. In our country the demand for labour is larger than the supply. The attempt to isolate a section of the Soviet people (those who have been in the army) from the rest (those who have not been in the army) in a separate 'society' is absolutely unnecessary.[20]

Four decades later, the political leadership had changed its tune. In his report to the Central Committee Plenum, on 27 January 1987, General Secretary Mikhail Gorbachev not only noted the recent foundation of the All-Union Organization of Veterans of War and Labour—an important advance in 'socialist self-governance of the people'—but also, in passing, explained why such an organization was necessary. Veterans were now seen as one of the 'strata' of the population (*sloi naseleniia*), which Gorbachev described as differentiated by class, gender, nation, and generation—'the working class, the kolkhoz peasantry, the intelligentsia, women and men, veterans and youth, ... nations and nationalities'.[21] A lot had changed since Stalin's time: veterans had been transformed from a complex group of several birth cohorts into a generation; they had been granted official privileges and an official status; and they had the backing of two powerful organizations. These changes were not predetermined. They did not follow (ideo)logically from the premises on which the regime was based. They were the result of political action—both of a mass character and of a backroom-politics kind. The change started after Stalin's death, in the late 1950s, and accelerated in the 1960s and 1970s, but had deep roots in the war and postwar years, when veterans emerged from the slaughter of the Soviet–German front united by a sense that they deserved special treatment from society at large.

To return to the beginnings: under Stalin, veterans' desires to organize were watched with suspicion by the political leadership. This did not change with the dictator's death. Well into the 1950s, the party line on veterans' groups remained rooted in the long tradition of denying any legitimacy or necessity to veterans' organizations under Socialism. This negative approach of the leadership did not, of course, ensure that all forms of veterans' association, all formal, semi-formal, and informal ties between veterans were severed after demobilization. Below the radar screen of the central party, the beginnings of a veterans' movement survived throughout the postwar years.

This immanent veterans' movement was integrated on several levels of formality. On the most basic level, veterans shared a sense of entitlement which made them act alike in certain situations—a phenomenon to be explored in the next chapter. Veterans also interacted with each other frequently. Their networks were strongest in the party, which had become, if not a veterans' organization, then an organization dominated numerically by war participants.[22] A second institutional ground in which veterans' networks took deep root was the army.[23] Outside these power structures, that is, in the environment where most veterans moved, informal inter-actions remained important, but here they did not constitute a 'network'. Aggregations of veterans emerged and dispersed again, forming an unstable pattern more akin to drops of mercury on a shifting surface: veterans stuck to each other when they met, but their connections were quickly disrupted by the unsettlement of postwar life—only to conglomerate again elsewhere.[24]

At times, such unstable veterans' groups solidified into temporary networks.[25] At the fringes of army and party such nuclei sometimes crystallized even further and acquired a more formal and less transitory character. On Victory Day 1945, a group of soldiers of the 53rd Guard Rifle Division—a unit which had been formed out of Moscow party members at the beginning of the war—decided to meet twice a year: on Victory Day (9 May) and on the anniversary of the division's formation (15 October). A year later, they started to call themselves the Veterans' Council of their unit. Besides their annual meetings, they gave public lectures in factories and enterprises celebrating their war experience. The group existed throughout the postwar years and claimed 700 members in 1958. Its persistence amazed and alarmed the newly formed Soviet Com-mittee of War Veterans (SKVV) when the Council came to join forces with it in 1956: 'What group is that? What kind of a Council is that? It needs to be disbanded, broken up.'[26] Instead, the organization was coopted as part of the Section of Former Frontline Soldiers and was even allowed to keep its own organizational form.[27] The new committee also demanded in 1956 that other existing 'organized groups of veterans should now discontinue their activities'. Examples of such rival organizations were a Kiev group and an association in Vladivostok. The latter was based in the Museum of the History of the War Fleet, had been founded in 1952, called itself the 'Section of Veterans of the Fight for Soviet Power in Primor'e', and existed under the jurisdiction of the Political Administration of the Pacific Fleet. 'These and similar groups of war veterans, which exist in other places, should be dissolved, and their members should integrate themselves in the local branches of the Soviet Committee of War Veterans.'[28]

Probably the biggest annoyance for the SKVV leaders was the other group they mentioned in their report, the most untypical example of a formal organization in the postwar years. It came from the Ukraine, where a local assistance committee grew into a republic-level association that managed to survive officially until 1951 and continued illegally thereafter. We know about this organization from a letter the activists of the (disbanded) organization wrote to the SKVV in 1956. According to this material, the foundation of the organization was initiated in 1944 by a group of disabled officers who worked in the Military Department of the Central Committee of the Ukrainian Communist Party. As a result of their initiative the party's city committee for Kiev founded a Committee for the Assistance of War Invalids of Officer Rank. Organizationally, it was connected with both the city military registration office and the executive committee of the city soviet. The main task of the organization was assisting the city's executive committee and military registration office in reintegrating disabled frontline soldiers into civilian life. Together with local administration and party organizations, the *aktiv* of the committee tried to improve the work of welfare administrations, and helped returning officers in the search for housing, in medical support and access to sanatoria, in receiving ration cards, and in the reintegration into the labour force.[29]

A joint decision of the Politburo of the Ukrainian Communist Party and the Ukrainian government of 14 July 1945 elevated the work of the committee to a higher level. It called for the organization of a Republican Commission for the Assistance of Invalids of the Patriotic War of officer rank under the Ukrainian Ministry of Social Welfare. Similar commissions were founded under the welfare administrations of provinces, cities, and districts. According to the statutes these commissions were to assist socially needy officers and those with many children, help in the search for housing, organize the improvement of medical assistance including sanatorium visits, organize and audit job placement, and coordinate requalification efforts for invalids. They also called for the organization of mutual aid funds of invalided officers.[30] The commissions soon widened the scope of their activity to include patronage (*shefstvo*) of industrial enterprises over invalids of the first group, provision and maintenance of vegetable gardens (*ogorodnichestvo*), distribution of heating fuel, 'cultural-educational work', and housing construction.[31] This work went on throughout the postwar years.[32]

The timing of the further history of this organization suggests that Nikita Sergeevich Khrushchev—first secretary of Ukraine from 1944 to 1946 and again from 1948 to 1949—might have been something of a patron of this organization. This hypothesis would explain why the veterans' movement was allowed to take off on an all-Union level once he was in charge of the country as a whole. Be this as it may, after Khrushchev was recalled by Stalin to Moscow in 1949, the fortunes of the organization took a turn to the worse. At the end of 1950 the Ukrainian Ministry of Social Welfare first dissolved the mutual assistance funds, and at the beginning of 1951 also the assistance commissions themselves. Attempts by the leadership of the Republican Assistance Commission Colonel Minshenko (a Hero of the Soviet Union) and Major Pustovalov to get an audience with the Minister of Social Welfare led to nothing.[33] At the moment of its dissolution, the organization counted 105,000 members.[34] The suspension of the organization was not accepted by some of its activists. A core group kept campaigning for its re-establishment,[35] refusing to terminate its work in 1951. Rather, the veterans shifted their activities elsewhere: 'In recent times we have kept liaison with the chairman of the Soviet Committee for the Defence of Peace' Nikolai Semenovich Tikhonov, who was a veteran himself.[36] The group kept annoying the SKVV at least into the mid-1960s.[37]

This organization was itself the result of the first quantum leap in the history of the Soviet veterans' movement. After Stalin's death in 1953, his successor Khrushchev—maybe because of his positive experiences with the Ukrainian prototype—finally allowed new organizations, if very cautiously at first. In the mid-1950s, assistance committees were created again, like their precursors during the war, to help with the reintegration of demobilized soldiers—this time largely officers who were demobilized *en masse* from 1953 onward. The difference was that this time they were not created on the level of enterprises, but under the military registration offices. As access to the military archive remains strongly restricted, information on these committees is scarce. We do know, however, that they were founded around 1955 by the Ministry of Defence, and that they survived to the end of the Soviet Union.[38] Better documented is the second partial reversal of postwar policy: the foundation of an all-Union veterans' organization in Moscow in autumn 1956. The archival holdings of this organization show clearly that the Soviet Committee of War Veterans (*Sovetskii komitet veteranov voiny*, SKVV) was not simply a recognition 'from above' of popular aspirations, but rather an appropriation 'from below' of an institution which was created for fundamentally different purposes.

The SKVV was explicitly not meant to be an interest group for veterans, but was founded as a *Potemkin* institution for international propaganda. It was organized because the Soviet leadership wanted to use the terrain of international veterans' politics within the World Veterans Federation (*Fédération Mondiale des Anciens Combattants*, FMAC) as an arena for cold war propaganda. This organization still awaits its historian. It was founded in 1950, has its headquarters in Paris, and today represents 170 veterans' organizations from 84 countries on five continents, with a combined total membership of around 27 million.[39] In 1952 it represented 16 million veterans,[40] a number which by 1955 had risen to 18 million.[41] In 1954 the Federation held its fifth annual assembly in Vienna. The Soviet Union staged a counter-meeting of resistance fighters from Eastern Europe and Western fellow travellers, which was duly ignored by the Austrian press.[42]

By 1956 Soviet tactics had changed. Maybe encouraged by the (on the whole) positive experience with a delegation of US veterans celebrating the tenth anniversary of the first meeting of American and Soviet troops in Torgau at the Elbe,[43] the Soviet Union tried to join the FMAC. The initiative group for the foundation of the organization was decreed into existence by the Presidium of the Central Committee of the CPSU in 1955, in the context of the festivities of the tenth anniversary of Victory Day.[44] The initiative group met on 3 May 1956 and decided that the foundational conference of the Soviet veterans' organization should be held at the beginning of June.[45] Shortly after this meeting, in May and June, the group sent two observers to the sixth general convention of the World Veterans Federation. They had a long 'business meeting' with the president and the general secretary of the FMAC regarding the admission of Soviet veterans to the Federation. Their desire to join was disappointed, but both sides agreed to create exchange programmes between the (not yet extant) Soviet and Western veterans' organizations.[46] In the end, the Soviet Union did not become a member of the Federation until 1988.[47]

It might have been this setback or other undocumented complications which delayed the organization of the conference. In any case, it did not take place as originally planned in June. In fact, the Central Committee did not decide until 31 July 1956 to create the Soviet Committee of War Veterans,[48] which was finally founded in September during the first All-Union Congress of war veterans.

The new organization was created for the express purpose of international propaganda. The leadership tried to drive this basic point home in speech after speech, and article after article: veterans already lived in the best of the existing worlds; they had no grievances of their own because everybody—veteran as well as non-veteran—was cared for and loved by the government; no interest group was therefore necessary in Socialism; the organization would engage in propaganda work both among veterans and, more importantly, abroad; it would not do anything else.[49]

At the end of the conference, the delegates unanimously acclaimed the decision to found the Soviet Committee of War Veterans as a societal organization centred in Moscow. The highest organ of the Organization of Soviet War Veterans (*Organizatsiia sovetskikh veteranov voiny*—basically a fictitious entity) should remain the all-Union conferences of veterans which were supposed to take place every four to five years. The executive organ of the 'organization' was the SKVV proper, a seventy-five-person committee, which was elected at the conference. Its presidium did the actual work between the legitimizing grand conferences. To help the presidium of the SKVV in its work, three sections were formed from among the 'socially active veterans' (*aktiv veteranskoi obshchestvennosti*): the section of former frontline soldiers of Civil War and Great Patriotic War, the section of former partisans and underground workers, and the section of former concentration camp inmates (i.e. POWs). In addition a bureau for propaganda and a bureau for international connections were formed.[50]

The organization was thus structured in a typically Soviet manner with a larger legitimizing body that had little to say in practice, a smaller 'committee' that did not meet often either, and a very small Moscow-based circle of people who did the actual work. There were no primary organizations in the localities and no regional or republic-level equivalents; there was no formal membership, either. It seemed that the main goal was accomplished—to form a Potemkin organization which could join the World Veterans Federation, without actually giving an institutional base to veterans' domestic interests.[51]

However, the organizers had not considered that they could not start a veterans' organization without veterans. The trouble started right at the beginning. During the first plenary meeting of the SKVV on the day of the founding conference, the leadership had a hard time keeping the seventy-five core members on course. Again and again they explained that the main task was international propaganda, that there would be no mass organization, that there should be local meetings of veterans, but no local membership, and that the reason why they needed local representatives in the first place was that they needed an organizational structure once foreign visitors had to be carted around the Union.[52] The stubbornness with which even the core members misunderstood the task of the organization gave the leadership a taste of things to come. The activists who started to staff the organization—in their vast majority retired career officers born before 1922[53]—simply believed that they needed to defend veterans who were not treated correctly: 'This is the sense of such an organization', as one of them put it in complete ignorance of the statutes.[54]

The tensions between the official tasks of the organization and the self-understanding of the activists as representatives of veterans exploded in a stormy meeting of the section for war invalids on 26 December 1956.[55] During this meeting, the activists (some of whom had learnt about it through rumour spread through the informal communication channels between veterans) challenged the understanding of the increasingly exasperated leadership regarding the tasks of the organization.[56]

The session was preceded by an article by the writer and *frontovik* Emmanuil Kazakevich on 'the affair of the motorized wheelchair', published in *Literary Gazette* eight days before the meeting. At the end of the article, which described in detail the poor quality of these mechanical helps for war invalids which had been produced since 1953, he suddenly addressed the new organization:

> And, last but not least, two words to the comrades from the Committee of War Veterans. The care about war invalids is your immediate affair. We have so far not heard that you have taken up this problem. I was wounded three

times during the war and there are many like me. Luckily, we got away with comparatively slight wounds. Let us not forget about those of our comrades who had to empty the cup to the bottom![57]

Understandably, these words reinforced the activists in their notion that the SKVV was a lobbying organization. At the same time, the leadership still tried to stem the tide and stick to the original task of propaganda work. At the beginning of the meeting, Aleksei Petrovich Mares'ev, the famous disabled fighter pilot who chaired the meeting, reminded everybody that the main work of the organization was international propaganda in veterans' organizations, which should be used as 'tribunes' for the fight against 'the forces of reaction, who try to start the third world war'.[58] In addition, some domestic tasks were also important: the registration of all war veterans, 'educational work' among them as well as among the 'young generation', the publication of literature about 'the mass heroism of our Soviet people', and care for war memorials and graveyards.[59] Moving away from the initial line, however, he also cautiously admitted that something could be done for war invalids, namely to 'care about them' in order to help their 'spiritual growth' (pomoch' im dukhovno rasti).[60]

> The Committee of War Veterans also bumped into (stolknulsia) such questions as the everyday conditions and work placements of our veterans. It needs to be said frankly that the Soviet Committee of War Veterans cannot be directly concerned with these questions, and will not concern itself with them. But you all understand, that we have a whole range of Soviet and governmental institutions, which are directly concerned with these questions. These are diverse ministries and departments. There are a lot of cases, where these institutions disgracefully handle inquiries of our war invalids, poorly and in a formal manner relate to our Soviet person. This is what we should fight against as a societal organization, as a social force. There are many ways to do that.[61]

However, for the 'enthusiastic individuals' who had come to the meeting equipped with Kazakevich's article this did not go far enough. Throughout the meeting, Mares'ev was confronted with activists who challenged his authority and the goals of the organization:

VOICE: May I speak?

COMRADE MARES'EV: Please.

VOICE: Why does this all happen in such a stereotypical manner? Where do these candidates come from, who nominates them? We don't need either generals nor colonels. We met here mainly with questions about our transportation—wheelchairs.

COMRADE MARES'EV: You are wrong, comrade. Do you know the statutes of our organization?

VOICE: No.

COMRADE MARES'EV: You have to understand the goals and tasks of our organization. Our basic task is public work in defence of peace (*vystuplenie v zashchitu mira*).[62]

With some difficulty, Mares'ev got his presidium elected (with votes against as well as abstentions) and again reminded the meeting that the work of the section had to move within the boundaries drawn by the statutes of the SKVV. But then the official line was immediately subverted again by one of the participants, who claimed to be able to explain the tasks to those who did not know the goals of the organization. What he said had little to do with international propaganda work, though, and a lot with running an interest group:

> Comrades, we have come together here and we see that not everybody has understood the basic tasks of this meeting. I want to say some words which will make them clear to you.
>
> I work in the professional-technical school of the Moscow city welfare administration…. The school was founded [in 1943] for the requalification of war invalids, former *frontoviki*, who because of their sickness can no longer work in their old profession. At the moment in our school study 300 students, half of them invalids of the Great Patriotic War. We train accountants, tailors, diverse mechanics for the repair of sewing-machines, typewriters and so on, among them also mechanics for the repair of television sets. These we train for two years. After these two years we are supposed to find them an internship and then work. The incorrect ways of several officials cut off the path to work for the prepared mechanics. We learnt that the Committee of war veterans had formed itself and we addressed the Committee [with our problem]. We wrote a letter to the chairman of the Committee Marshal Vasilevskii. Our question was commissioned to the comrades Mares'ev and Lukin, who helped us in this question. Thanks to the positive resolution of this question we sent our graduates into a television workshop. So here we have an example which shows the usefulness of this Committee…. we already have cases of help from this Committee. I am convinced that the Committee will also help us in the future with all difficulties [we encounter].[63]

Another speaker gave an immensely creative reading of the statutes of the SKVV. After recounting that the main task was the fight for peace and the work with international organizations, he went on to rephrase what Mares'ev had said:

> In the statutes of the Committee of War Veterans it says, that it also takes part in some tasks regarding the development of our domestic economy [i.e. it was supposed to conduct propaganda among veterans to work harder]. But that the Committee, our section of war invalids is concerned with its more narrow questions. But we should appear in this part of the economy which serves us. After all, there is a whole range of ministries and departments, which cater to us, and to say it openly, cater to us poorly. You all read on the 18th in *Literary Gazette* the article by the writer-invalid Kazakevich about the question of our transportation. And we, as a societal organization can appeal to several ministries and departments regarding the shortcomings in the help to invalids. We can also write articles in the press in the name of the section and in the name of the committee about the questions regarding our transport, and about questions of medical care and about several other urgent questions.[64]

This interpretation of the statutes put the care for invalids at the centre of the section's agenda. Not unlike Barykin in 1946, this speaker started with an acknowledgement that this was all about fighting for peace and ended on the note that the section would defend the interests of war invalids. Other participants argued for the same end in a much more confrontational manner. One comrade told Mares'ev about a letter he had written together with other war invalids to the committee. They had never received an answer, which he blamed on the general 'deception' war invalids had to endure in the past as well as in the present: 'The majority of invalids have many burning questions, about which they were many times deceived even in the press.' He then basically threatened a strike of the activists if the organization did not reconsider its priorities: 'if the presidium or the section will not pay attention to these letters [from invalids] or to other inquiries, then there will be no work'.[65]

Others also expressed their bitterness with what they saw as a betrayal:

> There were already too many meetings of all sorts and conferences of invalids, and every time they betrayed (*obmanivali*) the invalids in an impertinent and unceremonious manner. Invalids also appealed to the press, which ignored all our questions... Of course, the founding of the Committee is a necessary and good thing, but it is not an organ which can make decisions. After all, it can only raise, but not decide a question; it has no possibility to better the everyday life and the job placement of invalids. It seems to me, that our section cannot justify itself, cannot justify our hopes, because it cannot

concern itself in earnest with the questions which interest invalids most of all, and which worry them the most. What kind of a section is this, which will only engage in discussions and in the education of invalids? After all, the war and life have already educated (*vospityvat'*) us a long time ago. We are sufficiently educated already and able to educate our children and descendants.[66]

The persistence with which speakers ignored, dismissed, or argued with the actual goal of the SKVV is truly astonishing:

> Regarding education of and care about war invalids. The Committee exists for a long time already [in fact it had existed less than three months!]. Why has there still not been an investigation about the everyday life and the living conditions of invalids? And why has there still not been a report about that to the leading organs, i.e., the Moscow City Council? Why has the question of the betterment of war invalids' everyday life not been posed? That's also why there is no trust [in the leadership of the SKVV].... I hope that our section will care for war invalids and help [them] with all questions—with regard to political as well as material and everyday life needs.[67]

Many more invalids rose to express their desire to have a lobbying and welfare group for war invalids. Some of them were simply ignorant of the statutes, others ignored them, or misrepresented what they said. Some, however, understood quite well what the organization was meant to do, but did not accept this definition of its tasks and goals:

> I am glad that finally such an organization was founded in our country (*u nas*), an organization which should concern itself not only with questions of an international nature, but also with everyday problems and material well-being (*bytovoe i material'noe ustroistvo*). There are many such problems and the Committee should help us.[68]

Some even challenged outright the legitimacy of the section:

> A lot has been said here about tasks. I want to underline: what kind of a bureau will there be, out of how many people? ... We start to nominate candidates and nothing can come out of all this. Why? Because the organization of the meeting was a narrow one. The invalids were not informed about it. And that is here [in Moscow], so how will it be in the periphery? One should have been informed through the district welfare administrations or in the press about today's meeting. Why was that not made public? Because the organization of this happened haphazardly (*samotekom*). The goal of our organization is clear to us, but tell us, comrade Mares'ev, is it possible to elect from the 50 people present here a committee of all-union importance (*soiuznogo znacheniia*)? One should have organized a larger meeting, but that has not been done.[69]

At the end of the session, Mares'ev tried to calm the waves. It was not correct, he stated, that the committee ignored the material needs of veterans, or would not engage in them in a serious manner. He again cautiously stated the new line the leadership had developed as a compromise between the aspirations of the *aktiv* and the task given by the Central Committee—some lobbying would be allowed, as long as it remained strongly circumscribed:

> Yes, comrades, as a Committee we cannot have the same function as, for example, the Ministry of Social Welfare or the Ministry of Health. But I should say that a social force (*obshchestvennaia sila*) at times plays a big role, even a bigger one than another official organ.... See, the member of our inspection-commission General-Major Lukin recounted here how he went, researched the question of the [television] workshops and the question was decided positively. It's the same with housing questions. An invalid came to us and said that he lives in nightmarish conditions. We sent a member of the Committee, he saw it with his own eyes, and we decided to go with the letter in our hand to the Chairman of the Raiispolkom. The latter said that in the nearest future the request will be complied with. And our committee, as a societal organization, of course plays its big role.[70]

As this meeting showed, the leadership of the SKVV had some serious problems keeping activists focused on international propaganda. But not only the veterans' activists, who had been drafted to staff the Potemkin organization (or who had showed up uninvited), misunderstood its tasks. Rank and file veterans from all over the Union started what amounted to a letter-writing campaign. During the first months of its existence, the SKVV received 3,781 letters, followed by 6,700 in 1958, 6,300 and 4,000 in 1959 and 1960, respectively.[71] This campaign was coordinated solely by the deeply felt notion that veterans were entitled to special treatment by the community and the state they had defended; the SKVV seemed like the long-awaited organization which would defend these special entitlements and transform them into actual privileges. For these reasons, veterans wanted to join the organization and asked it for help in their local struggles for recognition.[72]

The leadership of the SKVV was thus both pushed and pulled towards taking a position of representation of and lobbying for veterans within the political system. They were pulled by the allure of a large group of people who trusted them, who appealed to them for help, and who would be grateful if such assistance was provided.[73] But they were also pushed by their own activists, without whom they could hardly run even the most minimalist version of a Potemkin organization. In order to engage in international propaganda, they needed to allow the activists to be representatives of what they considered their constituency. In return, they got their commitment and work for the 'cause of peace'. This compromising attitude could win out because it conformed to the new Khrushchevian line of mass participation in the political system. However, the driving forces behind this change of the SKVV towards a lobbying function were not caused by the new policy line.

The SKVV tried to coopt some of the veterans' activists, not least in order to divert them from more problematic forms of organization and protest. In the second half of the 1950s, war invalids staged demonstrations in Moscow in front of the Central Committee building, in front of the Ministry for Social Welfare, and close to a major invalids' hospital. They pointed out that care for war invalids was much better developed in many capitalist countries and demanded that their Socialist homeland match such privileges. Such 'wild' protests within as well as outside of the organization were fought with a mixture of state repression and 'police socialism': on the one hand, the SKVV contacted the Ministry of State Security (MGB) about the brouhaha in the first meeting of the invalids' section; on the other hand, they tried to neutralize such protest by partially taking up the concerns of veterans, particularly of war invalids.[74]

During the first decade of the SKVV's existence, a dynamic emerged which remained characteristic of the development of the veterans' movement in subsequent decades as well: local action constantly outpaced what the leadership, bound to the party line, could allow. Like Barykin in 1946, the veterans' activists who were coopted to run the Potemkin organization of Soviet veterans ten years later consistently expressed their desire to represent the interests of veterans through a strong, organized veterans' movement. Such wishes were constantly frustrated; little progress was made on the question of developing an official local infrastructure which could have rooted the organization deeper in the actual concerns of veterans in the localities. The organization's leaders were caught between a rock and a hard place—on the one hand they constantly struggled against the spontaneous development of a local infrastructure, which happened without their authorization and outside of their control; on the other hand they tried to lobby a resistant party leadership, which consistently

opposed such spontaneous developments.[75] Inspired by newspaper reports
about the formation of the SKVV in 1956, local veterans soon formed
their own groups. What was the Moscow organization to do with them?
One could, of course, tell them to disband, but there were no real means
to enforce such demands. Moreover, the local organizers were unlikely to
comply. 'That's not for you to decide, comrades', answered a representative
of the Veterans' Council of the 53rd Guard Rifle Division to a request
to disband his organization in 1958. 'You can't disband us! We are 700
people, we are connected to each other, we are Mosovites, Communists,
volunteers—remember that! You should have remembered that a long
time ago!'[76] So the SKVV's leadership adopted a wait-and-see attitude: 'We
recommend ... that they don't act underground, but inform the bureau of
their section [in Moscow], talk to the local newspaper and with the district
committee of the party, and sort out all questions there.'[77]

Some spontaneous veterans' organizations went beyond merely local
associations. The former partisan group Medvedev, for example, was
organized across four provinces. In late February 1958, the group sent its
representative, a comrade Stekhov, to the SKVV Presidium to voice the
activists' resentment about the lack of leadership from Moscow. He reported
that the 'Partisans' public' (*Partizanskaia obshchestvennost'*) of Rovensk,
Volynsk, L'vov, and Vinnitsa regions in the Ukraine had successfully lobbied
their Obkom secretaries to allow their association. Stekhov assumed that
such organizations were part of the SKVV and demanded clearer guidelines
from above.[78] Such demands started to annoy the committee's leaders:

> I have already explained our statutes on two presidium meetings, and now I
> will say it for the third time. There are international veterans' organizations.
> It is very important for our fight for peace that we work among the several
> tens of thousands of people who are organized in the two international
> organizations of veterans. And to this end, by a decision of the Central
> Committee of the Party, the Soviet Committee of War Veterans was
> founded. I should tell you that our statutes were written, so there would be
> no problems with joining an international organization. That's why several
> points were included: not because the CC of the Party thought that we
> should engage in this work, but because these points will make it easier for
> us to fulfil the important task which we have been given.[79]

In line with the compromise reached in 1956, some limited interest
group politics was permitted, as long as it was restricted to the sections
in Moscow—especially the section of war invalids. Under its energetic

chairman General Mikhail Federovich Lukin, the section functioned as something of the avant-garde of the veterans' movement between 1956 and 1961, when Lukin retired from public office.[80] However, the policy line was clear: no local organizations unless the Central Committee decided otherwise: 'It is likely that the CC will soon consider this question, as not long ago some of us had a conversation with comrade Khrushchev. It is possible that we'll get additional decisions [about this question], then we'll inform you about them. We cannot take such a decision on our own. Some people are better able to see [than us], what's necessary to be done in the country.'[81]

A couple of months later, the SKVV's leadership had received a negative answer from the Central Committee and informed the plenum of the organization accordingly. Again, the stress lay on international propaganda work, to which end local organizations and mass membership were 'inappropriate'. Such a mass organization 'is a very expensive, labour-intensive, and—most importantly—at the moment unnecessary pleasure'.[82] As before, this did not stop the activists, given their fundamentally different understanding of the organization's goals and tasks—an understanding, which had little to do with the official statutes, but a lot with the widespread hopes and desires which had been voiced already by Barykin in 1946.

Ten years later, activists like comrade Samson from Latvia put such hopes into practice. Their only concession to the official line was the naming of the local organizations. After Samson and another Latvian participant of the 1956 founding conference had returned from Moscow, they immediately set to work. They lobbied the Latvian Central Committee to allow the creation of a 'republican assistance group to the Soviet Committee of War Veterans'. The group had eleven members, three sections, and a chairman. In 1957, the group organized a conference of Latvian veterans, a meeting of 700 activists in Riga. After this conference, the Latvian CC allowed the organization of district-level 'assistance groups'. Within less than two years of the SKVV's foundation, and despite the completely clear central line against a local and regional infrastructure, Latvia had acquired a veterans' organization on both republic and lower administrative levels. The republic level 'group' next wanted to bring up the question of officially recognized mass membership. The group also wanted to be renamed according to the function it *de facto* fulfilled: 'So why should we not call this group by its real name—Republican Committee of War Veterans?'[83] By the early summer of 1958, assistance groups also existed in Uzbekistan and Krasnodarskii krai.[84]

These groups and their activists raised some fundamental questions about the organizational structure, goal, and direction of the veterans' movement, which the SKVV's leadership tried to keep unresolved as long as there was no positive decision by the Central Committee. In the 1958 plenum, the chairman of the meeting attempted to ignore the issue, but the activists did not let him get away with silence. His answer showed that the SKVV's leadership was constrained by resistance from above, but willing to try to push the issue. The Central Committee had already twice responded negatively to requests to introduce membership and build a local organizational structure. Such desires were, said the CC, 'inappropriate'. Despite this clear stance of the decision-makers, the SKVV's leadership was ready to accept the existing local organizations as an experiment worth 'studying' in order to gain better arguments for the next lobbying round in the Central Committee.[85]

This would remain a refrain in the history of the SKVV over the next decade: again and again the question of membership and local organization was raised; again and again the leadership went lobbying in the Central Committee; again and again they got the same answer—their efforts were 'inappropriate'.[86] At the same time—and that remained a constant, too—local development outpaced what was centrally allowed: 'the tendency towards the formation of new committees...is growing', as a report of late 1958 put it.[87] By that time, the city of Gor'kii had acquired its 'assistance group' and Cheliabinsk had a 'Section of Veterans of the Great Patriotic War'; in Leningrad eighteen committees of war veterans had formed on their own (stikhiino); Stalingrad had a veterans' organization, which lobbied for the introduction of membership dues;[88] Azerbaidzhan had a republic-level Committee of War Veterans; Estonia a republic-level 'assistance group'; and there were self-proclaimed 'sections' of the SKVV in the Far East. In addition to such republic or regional organizations, self-proclaimed Soviet Committees of War Veterans sprang up in factories, enterprises, military schools, and military units. In Gor'kii, for example, there was a Council of Veterans of the Volga Military Fleet which organized up to 300 people and which approached the SKVV for directions. Such groups were founded—usually in cooperation with local party organizations—either by members of the SKVV after their return from the 1956 conference, or by other veterans who took the creation of the SKVV as the start signal for the long-awaited veterans' movement. In addition, a whole range of organizations had developed below the radar screen of the Central Committee well before the foundation of the SKVV.[89] Institutionally, these groups frequently found a home in the local museum (*kraevedcheskie muzei*), the House of Officers, the local party or Komsomol committee, or the House of Political Enlightenment.[90] Sometimes a republic-level history museum fulfilled this function as well.[91]

In 1961, Semen Konstantinovich Timoshenko (1895–1970) became the third chairman of the SKVV, serving until his death in 1970.[92] Under his watch, the SKVV again tried to formalize such spontaneous organizational growth and harness the new local organizations for the purposes of the Moscow Committee. Meanwhile, the spontaneous growth of veterans' organizations had continued. A report from Timoshenko's first year in office notes organizations in Stavropol', Uralsk, Khar'kov, Ufa, Semipalatinsk, Gor'kii, Moscow, Riga, Kuibyshev, Stalinsk, Ul'ianovsk, Nizhnii Tagil, Sverdlovsk and Cheliabinsk, as well as in Bashkiriia and Tartaria.[93]

The question of local associations was one of the major points of discussion during the Fourth Plenum of the SKVV, which took place in March 1963 in Moscow. Several speakers appealed to the representatives of the Central Committee to reconsider the matter. Timoshenko reported in his concluding remarks that the presidium of the SKVV had raised the question again with the political leadership but 'we have not received a decision yet'.[94] In a presidium meeting of 12 April, A. P. Mares'ev reported on the repeated but unsuccessful attempts to push the issue.[95]

Timoshenko had taken up this cause at least from 1962, when he had drafted his frontline comrade Sergei Vavvich Bel'chenko to run the new organizational commission of the committee.[96] The actual creation of this commission, however, was delayed for another year, because the SKVV could not get approval for this initiative. By late 1963, the new commission could finally set to work. In 1964, it met every month at least fifteen times, and in some months as much as 21 times.[97] Its job was to find ways and means to create a local infrastructure, to replicate what in some regions had emerged spontaneously elsewhere, and to try to unify the chaotic organizational variety.[98]

These efforts culminated in the second quantum leap in the history of the veterans' movement. The first leap had been the institutionalization of an all-Union organization and its partial takeover by veterans' activists in 1956; the second leap was the sudden expansion of this rump organization's infrastructure and mandate in the 1960s. Like the first one, this second leap had been prepared by the persistent spontaneous efforts of veterans all over the Soviet Union, but it could only happen once the political leadership removed the brakes it had put on this spontaneity ever since 1956. This removal happened in 1965 under the new First Secretary Leonid Il'ich Brezhnev. The SKVV's leadership now managed to receive support from the Central Committee for the creation of new organizations, and changed statutes which legalized local organizations were introduced at the Second All-Union Conference of War Veterans (25 to 26 February 1965).[99]

Permission to organize this meeting had been granted during the last months of Khrushchev's watch. The precise mandate of the conference, however, was still unclear by the time Khrushchev was sacked from his position in October 1964. As a result of this leadership change, the conference was postponed for a couple of months, which gave the SKVV's representatives the chance to lobby the new leadership regarding the old question of local organizations. This time they were successful: the conference was allowed to consider the creation of a local infrastructure.[100]

The conference sent mixed messages about the future direction of organizational development. On the one hand, the changed statutes called only for 'sections' in the 'localities' (*na mestakh*).[101] On the other hand, the speakers at the conference drew a picture of an association which would be organized on all levels of Soviet political life: the city, the district, the province, and the republic.[102] This was more than just a misunderstanding of lower level activists. Timoshenko himself had come away from negotiations with the political leadership with the impression that they could put together 'sections of war veterans in Republics and hero-cities'.[103] In a meeting before the conference, the SKVV leaders informed their activists that the conference would decide on the creation of 'republican, krai, and province sections'.[104] While the spontaneous emergence, since 1956, of 'diverse councils, committees, groups' all over the Soviet Union gave some reason for concern and more orderly change was preferable, the SKVV's leadership found it unwise to ask for reorganization of groups which already existed. After the organization's recent lobbying success, the core group thought it was possible to pass regulations now and change them later—an approach which, as it turned out, was overly optimistic.[105]

On 18 March 1965 the SKVV's presidium decreed the creation of 'Sections of war veterans' of twenty-five representatives each in the cities of Leningrad, Kiev, Minsk, Tashkent, Alma-Ata, Tbilisi, Baku, Vil'nius, Kishinev, Riga, Frunze, Dushanbe, Erevan, Ashkhabad, Tallin, Volgograd, Odessa, and Sevastopol. At the same meeting, they passed the Regulations about Sections of the Soviet Committee of War Veterans in the Localities.[106] This document would remain the basic regulation governing the local infrastructure of the SKVV for the next two decades. It called for the creation of 'sections' in the localities 'where this is necessary'. The sections were supposed to work under double oversight: on the one hand, they were to function under the leadership of the SKVV; on the other hand they were to coordinate their work with 'the local Soviet and societal organizations' (*mestnye sovetskie i obshchestvennye organizatsii*). Their main tasks were said to be the fulfilment of 'missions' (*porucheniia*) of the SKVV's presidium, assistance to local organs in the propaganda of the 'battle traditions of the Soviet Armed Forces', 'education' of veterans as well as young people 'in the spirit of Soviet patriotism', assistance in the collection of material about 'the heroic fight of the Soviet people against interventionists, German-fascist occupiers and other imperialist aggressors', and 'immortalization of the memory of Soviet soldiers and partisans who perished in battles for the Soviet homeland and the memory of Soviet people who perished in Hitler's concentration camps'.[107]

The decisions of the Second Conference and the adoption of the regulations for local sections in 1965 allowed the Soviet veterans' movement to grow vigorously. The official expansion of the local infrastructure—by Victory Day 1975, the original 18 city-level sections had grown to 36;[108] by the end of the decade, the number had further grown to 43;[109] and by 1981 there were 46 sections with more than a million activists[110]—went hand in hand with the continuation of the already well established dynamic of local enthusiasm outpacing the concessions made in the centre. The approaching twentieth anniversary of victory had already led to an intensification of organizational efforts on a local level. To prepare for the festivities, party organizations in enterprises put together special commissions which, after the anniversary, demanded to become 'permanently existing committees of war veterans' which would be part of an all-Union infrastructure of the SKVV.[111]

The pronouncements of the Second Conference only intensified such local organizational efforts. Although officially only eighteen city-level 'sections' had been created, the organization of the Soviet veterans' movement soon became—and to some extent already was—considerably more diverse. Veterans' councils (*Sovety veteranov*) developed on republic, province, and district levels, as well as within factories and enterprises; in several places, the Komsomol created its own veterans' organizations, and assistance committees at the military registration offices also continued to exist. Tadzhikistan had a republic level Veterans' Council by early 1966; Belorussia a republic-level organization and corresponding organizations on province and district level; in Armenia, thirty district 'groups' existed; the Tashkent and Frunze sections functioned *de facto* as republican sections of Uzbekistan and Kirgistan, respectively. SKVV activists in the localities tried to absorb other, often pre-existing organizations into their own hierarchy of command, and in fact lower level organizations frequently asked them for guidance and advice. According to the official line, the city-level sections were to liaise with the other organizations in their city, but not give orders or control them in any way—these bodies were under the control of the organization which had created them. The tendency of veterans' activists, however, was to see these different institutions as parts of the larger veterans' movement, whose logical focus was the SKVV.[112]

Thus, much of the dynamic development of the veterans' movement remained outside of the control of the SKVV. The main difference from the years 1956 to 1965 was that the vigour and dynamism of the movement had increased. The mixed signals sent by the Second All-Soviet conference were read by veterans all over the country as clear signs to go ahead and build a strong organization which would defend the interests of war participants. Under its new general secretary, the leadership of the CPSU was for a while ready to watch and 'study' such 'experiments'.[113]

For a decade after 1965, the door was thus opened to a major change in the role of the organized veterans' movement, a change which brought it in line with the programme outlined already in the 1940s by visionaries like Barykin—the SKVV became an organization rooted in the localities which legitimized its function as a lobbying organization for war veterans with service to the regime in the arena of international veterans' politics and the cold war. At the third congress of Soviet war veterans in 1971, part of this changed role of the SKVV was institutionalized in new statutes. Like the old ones they again stressed domestic and international propaganda as the main concern of the organization. At the same time, however, the representation and furthering of the interests of veterans was now explicitly mentioned—the organization was to be active in helping to execute 'the decisions of the CPSU and the Soviet government about the increase of the material, everyday, and housing conditions of war participants, invalids, and the families of fallen soldiers'. At the same time, the organizational changes which had gone on since 1965 were *not* acknowledged as legitimate. The statutes recognized only three units of action: the SKVV in Moscow, its city-level sections, and the Councils of Veterans at unit level (*sovety veteranov-odnopolchan*).[114] Shortly thereafter, the presidium passed new regulations for sections, which went a step further. They noted that the sections 'unite the councils of war veterans in enterprises, institutions, and educational institutes, as well as the organizations of former military units of their city'.[115] Reality, of course, had long outpaced this formal structure. Veterans had long created a much more diverse and vibrant organized movement than was acknowledged in the official statutes and regulations.

Inevitably, this movement ran into conflict with the party. Indeed, between 1965 and 1975 the SKVV threatened to become a parallel power structure, which could call on the loyalty of millions of veterans. In the long run, this could not be tolerated by the political leadership, and the rather disorderly development of the veterans' movement had to be stopped eventually. The slap-back, called euphemistically a 'restructuring' (*perestroika*), came in 1976. The Central Committee resolution of 12 October 'On the further improvement of the activities of local organizations of war veterans' forcefully reminded the SKVV that its *raison d'être* was international propaganda. Following this resolution, the SKVV's organizational structure was cut to size. In several cities, district councils were abolished; in other cities, organizations not described in the statutes (*neustavnye organizatsii*) were made into city-level 'sections'. These city sections were instructed to confine their work to the city-limits (and thus not function as *de facto* province or republican organizations); the oversight over veterans' councils in enterprises, bureaucracies, or educational establishments—which in the past were frequently treated like primary organizations of the SKVV—were now explicitly put under 'direct control' (*neposredstvennoe rukovodstvo*) of the respective party organizations. The competition between veterans' organization and party organization on this level was thus ended in favour of the party cells. Similarly, conflicts with party organizations on the diverse territorial levels (republic, province, district) were also resolved in favour of the party: here, veterans' organizations were to be abolished. Finally, a smouldering conflict with the military was ended as well. Rather than claiming control over all unit-level Councils of Veterans in their respective cities, the SKVV sections could only oversee those of units which no longer existed or were deployed outside of the country.[116]

This restructuring simplified the SKVV considerably. Instead of further developing the all-Union structure which had started to evolve since 1965 and which had started to include organizations on the levels of the Union, the republic, the province, the city, and the district, as well as primary organizations both on unit and enterprise level, the SKVV now officially had only three levels: the central apparatus in Moscow, 40 city-level 'sections', and 613 'groups' or 'councils' of comrades-in-arms (*sovety veteranov-odnopolchan*) of units which no longer existed or were far away, and thus not under the control of the local military administration and party organizations.[117] By the summer of 1978, this structure had expanded a bit, with now 42 city sections and 700 councils and groups, but this was a far cry from what had existed prior to 1976.[118] The crippling results of this *perestroika* of the veterans' movement can be studied in the example of the Kiev organization (Table 7.1).

As one might expect, this restructuring did not go smoothly. Local activists dragged their feet, delaying the implementation process considerably. Originally, the reform was supposed to be finished by the summer of 1977, but the work continued throughout 1978.[119] Local activists tried to ignore the new line: 'In many cities, provinces and districts, the well-known carefulness prevails, the aspiration to preserve what existed in the past, to not destroy what was built over years, even if this today does not conform

Table 7.1. The Kiev Veterans' Organization before and after the reform

|  | Before 1976 | At end of 1977 |
| --- | --- | --- |
| Province organizations | 1 | 0 |
| District councils | 12 | 0 |
| Primary groups in enterprises, institutes, *vuzy*, state institutions | 750 | 0 |
| Councils or groups of comrades in arms (military unit level) | 32 | 42 |
| Number of veterans organized | 72,000 | More than 5,000 |

*Source*: GARF f. r-9541, op. 1, d. 1504v, l. 9.

to the demands of the Resolution of CC CPSU of 12 October 1976 and the Statutes of the Organization of Soviet War Veterans.'[120] As a result of such reluctance, Leningrad, for example, still had non-statutory organizations recognized by the city's SKVV section more than a year after the resolution. In some cities, local activists kept organizing veterans' councils in enterprises, educational institutions, or military units throughout 1977, while others kept attempting to oversee the work of such lower level organizations, which they saw as their primary units. In several cities, groups of veterans not recognized by Moscow kept on calling themselves SKVV sections or city-level veterans' councils.[121] By the end of 1978, illegal province, city, or district Councils of Veterans still existed in several regions.[122] The pressure from the base for new and more organizations also persisted, as did the confusion of activists about why they should not give in to such pressure.[123]

The reorganization did also not always mean that structures not recognized by the statutes were destroyed; rather, they were relabelled at best and decentralized at worst. District councils of veterans could, for example, be renamed into local chapters of the society 'Knowledge' (*Znanie*), or the military-educational organization DOSAAF, while representatives of these organizations as well as of councils under the jurisdiction of the army were coopted into the city section of the SKVV. Local sections could also claim to not *direct* primary organizations in enterprises or military units, but still keep 'liaison' (*sviaz'*) with them.[124] Such methods considerably softened the impact of the 1976 resolution. They allowed the words of the party line to be adhered to, while keeping the spirit and structure of the local veterans' movement relatively intact.

In addition, all kinds of veterans' organizations kept developing outside of the SKVV's mandate and without its sanction. With surprise, the organization's leaders learnt of organizations of former 'sons of regiments' (*sovety sinovei polkov*)—young boys who had been adopted by military units during the war. Similarly, non-statutory organizations like councils which united veterans who had been in German concentration camps (i.e. organizations of former POWs) existed in several cities by December 1978—more than two years after the move against the wild organizational growth.[125] Despite the non-sanctioned and non-statutory status of such organizations, a 'troupe of former prisoners [of war]' in the international department of the SKVV's Moscow apparatus 'keeps liaison with these...organizations, leads them, demands reports from them, organizes conferences and so on'.[126] Moreover, the SKVV's leadership kept instructing the locals that if they wanted to have their own city-level sections, they should first organize on their own, lobby their local party organizations, and then, if they could show that they were useful, one could see if their organization could become part of the SKVV's city-level structure.[127]

Notwithstanding such delaying tactics, the 1976 resolution had a real impact. As avenues for formal organization were closed, veterans shifted their energies to lobbying for privileges, and the years after 1978 saw the biggest growth in special regulations which made veterans into a status group.[128] Organizationally, by contrast, relatively little happened until Mikhail Sergeevich Gorbachev came to power, although under the surface the old pressures and dynamics remained in evidence.[129] With the beginnings of *perestroika* the veterans' movement became an institutionalized pillar of the political system—a new mass organization which was represented in the legislature. For Gorbachev, veterans were no longer an unreal group, but one of the 'strata' into which Soviet society was divided.[130] By 1987, the veterans' movement had thus managed to finally convince the political leadership that veterans really existed and had shared interests and a common outlook, no matter if this was prefigured in official dogma. Once this was accomplished, once the reality of the entitlement group was acknowledged and inscribed in law as a legal status, it could also be organized and represented. As far as veterans are concerned, then, Gorbachev's reforms were the logical result of a long institutional development rather than a radical break with Brezhnevism.

Gorbachev's speech to the 27th Party Congress in 1986 marked a major change in the organizational makeup of the veterans' movement. The new general secretary called for the creation of an 'all-Union societal organization of veterans of war and labour'.[131] The resulting organizational change led to a bifurcation of the veterans' movement. On the one hand, a new organization was built, which united war veterans with veterans of the home front, that is, it became an organization of the 'older generation'. At the same time, the SKVV was not disbanded, but became a semi-independent union which was officially part of the new organization but also distinct from it.

Within less than a year, Gorbachev's words were put into practice. On 25 September 1986, the Politbureau of the CC decided to found the 'All-Union Organization of Veterans of War and Labour' (*Vsesoiuznaia organizatsiia veteranov voiny i truda*), which was to unite on a voluntary basis 'working pensioners as well as veterans, who are on their well-earned retirement'. Much as the SKVV had combined international propaganda work with domestic lobbying for the interests of veterans, the new organization combined such interest politics with service to the Soviet state. The mandate of the organization included mobilization of 'this category of citizens to socially useful activity' and education of the younger generation, but also 'care (*zabota*) for the better satisfaction of their needs'.[132] The new organization was founded in December 1986 at a conference in Moscow, which passed statutes and elected the All-Union Council of War and Labour Veterans (*Vsesoiuznyi sovet veteranov voiny i truda*). Delegates to the conference came from existing veterans' councils outside the SKVV structure. After their return, they organized similar conferences on province level, which in turn created a unified organization down to the level of enterprises, which could build on the existing veterans' organizations outside of the SKVV.[133]

In sharp contrast to the Soviet Committee of War Veterans since the reform after 1976, the new organization was built—like the party—on the 'territorial-production principle'—that is, its organization followed, on the one hand, the administrative hierarchy of the country (Union, republic, province, city, district), and, on the other hand, primary organizations were based in the place of employment of the members. The SKVV was not disbanded, but became a semi-independent part of the new structure. This odd arrangement of 'statutes within statutes' defining an organization within an organization was kept because the SKVV was too established internationally to be disbanded.[134] One suspects that the political leadership did not want to strengthen this group, which in the past had proven to be difficult to control; therefore, it was subordinated to the new organization.

The SKVV activists were not too thrilled about this settlement, but it was still better than what could have happened—the complete dissolution of the old organization and its replacement by the new structure. The SKVV was initially sidelined in the process of the creation of the new association. The task of drafting the statutes fell to a working party of representatives of the Main Political Administration of the Army and the Central Council of Trade Unions. The SKVV was consulted, but initially not invited to participate in this working group. The leadership argued vigorously against the possible dissolution of the organization, pointing to their three decades of experience with both domestic and international work in the veterans' movement. Finally, they were included in the working party, which drafted statutes for the new organization in April and May 1986 and sent them to the Central Committee in June, which worked on the draft itself and sent it back to the working group in July.[135]

What the SKVV had tried to press during these negotiations was that it would be recognized as *the* organization of *war* veterans, and would therefore be the co-founder of the new organization—together with an organization which would represent the veterans of labour. This proposal, however, was dismissed and replaced by the more ambivalent arrangement, which made the SKVV both an organization in its own right, but also part and parcel of the new organization and subordinate to its executive organ.[136]

This settlement was the basis of many future conflicts. The SKVV leaders hoped that under the new organization they could finally re-establish organizational ties beyond the confines of the 1976 resolution, which still restricted them to work within particular cities.[137] The leadership of the new organization, however, had an allergic reaction to anything which could be seen as institutional imperialism by the SKVV. Even local initiatives which called themselves 'sections' got into trouble for this reason. In 1987, for example, one such 'section' was told to disband and reform itself as 'commission', that is, as an organization defined in the statutes of the new Organization of War and Labor Veterans—an order which was complied with, if grudgingly: 'we, veterans, are disciplined people ... but, this is a completely formalist approach'.[138] Existing sections of the SKVV, too, were put into a complicated situation as they were now under dual subordination, to the SKVV in Moscow and to their city-level Council of War and Labour Veterans.[139]

Despite such quibbles, the organizational change in 1986 meant that veterans were finally organized in an all-Union organization with considerable reach. The veterans' movement now paralleled the organizational structure of party and state institutions and became—together with other mass organizations—another pillar of the late Soviet order. By January 1991, at the eve of the breakdown of the Soviet Union, the new organization had more than 180 units on republic, province, and krai level, about 5,000 city or district associations, and more than 150,000 primary organizations in work collectives, as well as 29,000 in apartment blocks (*po mestu zhitel'stva*).[140]

Moreover, it was now thoroughly integrated into the political process. The constitutional reform of December 1988 had created a new Congress of People's Deputies, which in turn elected the new Supreme Soviet and its chairman, the new head of state (Gorbachev). A third of the 2,250 people's deputies were elected by societal organizations, such as the labour unions or the Komsomol.[141] One of these societal organizations was the new All-Union Council of War and Labour Veterans, which elected seventy-five deputies, that is, 10 per cent of those elected by organizations, and a bit over 3 per cent of the overall number.[142] The organization also openly and aggressively lobbied state and societal organizations on behalf of veterans and their privileges—a role which was now, at long last, officially recognized in the statutes.[143]

# 8

# Entitlement Community

We have shed blood for Soviet power, now she will also stand up for us.[1]

Throughout most of Soviet history, the vast majority of veterans were unconnected to organizations. Nevertheless, they, too, formed part of a wider popular movement. Most combat survivors were part of what I call an 'entitlement group'—a collection of individuals sharing similar claims to special treatment.[2] As time went on, this entitlement community was transformed into a status group and, ultimately, an organized unit integrated into the Soviet order. The story of this institutionalization of the consequences of war is not as straightforward as sometimes assumed. It progressed in fits and starts and had to overcome political, economic, and ideological barriers in what amounted to a thirty-year struggle for recognition. This effort was intertwined with the related one for organization which it to some extent paralleled, and which was embedded in a history of entitlements, privileges, and benefits—a conceptual triad which makes it possible to analyse the complicated interaction of shared emotions, the state's construction of status, and the economics of shortage in the actual delivery of advantages.

By entitlement, I mean a *claim* to the right to special treatment by the wider community. Such demands are distinct from their actual reciprocation by rights—an institutionalization better described by the term 'privileges'. This institutionalization is, above all, symbolic: it acknowledges that a certain category of citizens has a prerogative to scarce goods, services, and esteem more important than those of others. The extent to which such special treatment can actually be delivered depends on a variety of factors, including the availability of goods and services, the willingness of actors on all levels of society to deliver them, the nature of the administrative system, including its ability to administer distribution, as well as the power of the privileged group to push for the implementation of its privileges against the claims of competing groups. For this reason, the introduction of a third analytical term—'benefits'—is useful. It describes the actual delivery of goods, services, or esteem which are promised by privileges.[3]

In the dynamic relationship between entitlements, privileges, and bene-fits, cause and effect are sometimes hard to untangle. The strong sense of entitlement of veterans was partially a result of the wartime practice of making members of the armed forces the most valued citizens. The official promises of a special status and the delivery of some benefits during demo-bilization reinforced these sentiments, which did not suddenly disappear once privileges were cancelled in 1947 and 1948. Veterans continued to feel that they did have special rights and kept campaigning for their institution-alization. Moreover, the status accorded to soldiers during the war and to veterans from 1978 was in part the result of a reluctant yielding of the state to persistent demands of soldiers, veterans, and their families—campaigns which were driven by feelings of entitlement. Finally, the uneven and in-sufficient delivery of actual benefits further fuelled the sense of uniqueness veterans had: in order to receive what the legislation acknowledged as their right, old soldiers had to write letters, complain in person, and seek the assistance of state actors higher up in the hierarchy who could enforce the implementation of legislation in each individual case. In the process, veterans had to stress their entitlement, advertise their war record, and argue for their membership in the privileged group. This constant ritual display of belonging to the category 'war participant' could not but deepen claims to special status already held: the causal nexus between entitlements, privileges, and benefits was closed.

What we can observe, then, is a socio-cultural process which is neither intended, nor controlled by any of the participants; it is neither a simple outcome of the state's 'grand strategies' running onto the reef of mass in-dividual resistance, nor a movement 'from below' completely independent of these strategies.[4] Rather, it is a dynamic of strategic and tactical action of both state and non-state actors, which in the long run resulted in the institutionalization of a group within Soviet society which the state had never intended to create.[5]

This new social entity underwent several changes in its mode of in-tegration—both as a group in its own right (intrinsically), and as part of the larger social compound of Soviet society (extrinsically).[6] Intrinsically, the social entity started to include formally organized groups from 1956 onwards and in the late 1970s more and more veterans were drawn into the growing status group of war participants. Extrinsically, the growing influence of the SKVV linked the veterans' movement ever closer to the political system, while the rituals and discourses of the war cult anchored veterans symbolically within Soviet society at large.[7] Finally, during Perestroika, veterans became a fully fledged corporate group, with an extensive organization and direct representation within the state. The integration of veterans into the political structure and the system of privileges stratifying Soviet society fed back on the intrinsic integration of the group. For one, privileges bred further entitlements; second, the shared privileges united veterans more and more into a status group; and third, the new status bred resentment by those excluded from the new social entity of veterans. It was at this point that the entitlement community was transformed into a generation: on the one hand, as the older cohorts of veterans died, the group became more and more restricted to the frontline generation proper; on the other hand, this group was confronted more and more often with the resentment, anger, or simple dismissal of their status by younger Soviet citizens.[8]

The core of the popular movement of veterans in the Soviet Union was the notion that wartime service gave a right to postwar benefits. This idea did not suddenly emerge out of the gore, mud, and suffering of frontline experience; nor was it a result of Bolshevik ideology and its strategic implementation; nor simply one of the components of 'modernity'. Rather, the culturally mediated experience of war activated and amplified a long political tradition. The Russian state had acknowledged early on that war service was to be reciprocated with special privileges—even if many of them remained on paper only and state help for victims of war remained insufficient. Even inadequate support for veterans, however, drives home the message that discharged soldiers have an entitlement to special treatment.

Russia had a long history of such meagre welfare.[9] As elsewhere, war veterans, especially invalids, were among the first groups singled out for special state care.[10] As far back as the second half of the seventeenth century, the state provided some minimal privileges for discharged servicemen, including grants, easier access to administrative positions, and land allotments. Disabled or feeble veterans could also take advantage of a few almshouses operated by the church. Peter the Great built on this system in connection with the introduction of a standing army and lifelong service, which entitled to a range of privileges after discharge. Monasteries operated almshouses for invalids, as did the church and regional governments in Petersburg, Moscow, and Kazan. Under Catherine the Great, this system was further developed. Veterans could now settle in special 'veterans' towns' and received a salary to support their retirement. A 'high point' of government welfare was reached in the 1790s, when all veterans who had served for twenty-five years received pensions—at least on paper. In reality, the state was unable to deliver, given the rapid expansion of the army. Nevertheless, basic welfare was provided.[11]

The connection between soldiering and special status was both strengthened and complicated by the military reforms of 1874, which introduced universal military conscription. From then on, the privilege system grew, but the special status was largely confined to soldiers and their families, not to discharged servicemen. Care for the special needs of victims of military service was mostly in the hands of non-governmental, philanthropic societies until these were outlawed by the Bolsheviks.[12] The Great Reforms introduced universal conscription on the model of a modern citizens' army, including 'rights and benefits that soldiers could expect in return for military service'.[13] This implicit deal between the soldiers and the state was first skewed towards the latter—soldiers and their families lacked the means to enforce what they quickly saw as their rights. They lacked 'a solid institutional base and effective levers of political influence'. During the prolonged period of violence between the outbreak of the First World War in 1914 and the end of the Civil War in 1921, however, the scale tipped towards the soldiers' entitlement claims.[14]

The 'citizen-soldier', argues Joshua Sanborn, became the 'paragon of the political community'. In the context of the Bolshevik dictatorship, however, much of this status was expressed in material and symbolic benefits rather than in political rights.[15] Most of these privileges, moreover, were granted to soldiers who were still on active duty, not to discharged veterans. In this respect, the Bolshevik state followed what can be called the 'service principle': it rewarded active service, not past laurels.[16] This was partly in line with prewar developments, although there were some signs of this trajectory changing towards a logic of welfare during the last decade and a half of the old regime. The law of 25 June 1912 instituted pensions for invalided soldiers, if their impairment was directly caused by wounds or illnesses suffered during service. Most of the benefits of the law, however, referred to serving soldiers and their families, not to veterans.[17]

This system of privileges was further expanded after the revolution of February 1917. Lobbied massively by soldiers' wives (*soldatki*) and the new councils of soldiers' deputies, the Petrograd Soviet approved more and more aid to servicemen's families. Much of this system was dismantled once the Bolsheviks took power, but was replaced during the Civil War of 1918 to 1921 by privileges for the families of Red Army soldiers, who became major beneficiaries of the new regime's redistribution efforts.[18] Thus, the general system of reciprocity between military service and privileges which had developed since 1874 remained intact over the 1917 divide. In fact, the deal between the citizen-soldier and the revolutionary state became the centre of 'militarized socialism', where Red Army soldiers served the Bolshevik leadership in return for special status and rewards, rather than political rights.[19]

What remained consistent over the 1917 divide, too, was the greater attention to privileges for serving soldiers and their families than to the claims of discharged veterans. While special provisions for the former increased massively during Dual Power between February and October 1917, both sources of authority—the Provisional Government and the Petrograd Soviet—'paid little attention to veterans' pensions'. Despite lobbying by soldiers' wives, 'no legislative activity was reported'.[20] During the few months of its ill-fated existence, the Provisional Government never got beyond declaring help for war invalids a central task of the state.[21] In fact, assistance to veterans decreased during the revolutionary upheaval. Imperial Army veterans and their families received no aid during demobilization in April to October 1918—despite 'at times violent protest'. Pensions were restricted to poor war invalids, while under the 1912 regulations eligibility to pensions had been independent of social and economic position. Discharged soldiers of the new Red Army also received a pension only if they had been incapacitated through wounds or illness. However, every demobilized Red Army soldier had a right to a land allotment.[22]

After victory in the Civil War, the Red Army was demobilized under conditions of mass unemployment and economic crisis.[23] Between 1921 and 1924, a total of 4.7 million Red Army soldiers re-entered civilian life. Local government and party organs were expected to care for their reintegration by organizing festive meetings of the returnees, making sure their housing was sorted out, their everyday needs met, and their employment secured.

Those who returned to the countryside were supposed to get 'complete help in the establishment and strengthening of [their] peasant [household] economy'. Special committees were founded locally to deal with the returning servicemen and help their families. Demobilized soldiers were seen as a pool of possible 'red specialists', who were to be trained in special courses and then become cadres in the countryside; tuition for preparatory courses to enter tertiary education (*vuzy*) was also waived to allow mobility of those who had defended Soviet power.[24] War invalids got additional privileges, as policy-makers linked poor care for war invalids with low army morale.[25] Despite such connections between welfare and warfare, social and medical care for victims of war remained painfully underdeveloped in the interwar years. Soon, financial considerations won out and pensions declined to all but those who were institutionalized in invalids' homes and co-operatives.[26]

By the time of the German attack in the summer of 1941, then, Soviet society was marked by a deeply entrenched social compact between soldiering and special status. The Soviet Union also partook to a lesser degree in the long-standing idea of rewarding discharged servicemen for their past war service—a tradition which in Europe goes back at least as far as Roman Antiquity.[27] Special postwar—and post-service—rewards for former soldiers, however, were not institutionalized to the same extent as the reciprocal relation between the soldier and the state. Quite limited benefits awaited only those veterans who had lost limbs or health, while the vast majority of demobilized personnel was expected to reintegrate smoothly into civilian life. Future privileges were to be earned through ongoing service to the Soviet state, rather than ascribed as a fixed status earned at the front.

During the war and its immediate aftermath, this service class of soldiers was transformed into an entitlement community whose members expected ongoing rewards for their wartime deeds. The enormity of the frontline soldiers' sacrifice rendered during the war implied for many an ongoing debt of the wider community to its defenders. Such feelings were further fuelled by the state's response to entitlement claims of veterans and their families during and after the war, which for a while seemed to indicate that a special status had in fact been achieved: step by step, Soviet legislation ascribed special privileges to more and more subcategories of veterans (war invalids, demobilized soldiers under the 1945 law, former POWs), until more or less all veterans were covered under a system of minimal privileges.[28] Official promises for special treatment during demobilization further entrenched veterans' feelings of entitlement.[29] It seemed for a while that participants in the Great Patriotic War had become a Soviet *soslovie*—an estate-like status group—not unlike the ascribed classes of the interwar years.[30]

The state's acknowledgement of veterans' feelings of entitlements, however, stopped abruptly at the end of 1947. Many of the privileges for veterans—such as a lump sum paid upon demobilization, access to housing construction loans and building materials, or a job equal or higher to prewar occupation—were inscribed in the demobilization law of 23 June 1945 and therefore only temporary in the first place. Once veterans were reintegrated into civilian life and labour, their special status ended and they were transformed into regular civilians. Moreover, once it had become clear that mass-demobilization had happened without any major threat to political stability, the men born in 1925 who were discharged in the final wave of demobilization in 1948 no longer received even these limited advantages—with the exception of a one-off payment.[31]

This downgrading of the final wave of demobilization was in line with the general termination of special rewards for wartime service, which had emerged during 1947. Policy-makers increasingly realized the costs of veterans' privileges and—as it had become clear that no new Decembrist movement was in the making—followed the economic arguments for their abolition.[32] In the case of the confiscation of most privileges connected to high decorations this logic is particularly well documented.[33]

The process which led to this major policy change started, innocently enough, as a review of procedures to deliver the benefits promised to decorated war heroes. During the war, many new orders and medals had been created to recognize outstanding frontline service. The more prestigious ones came with a wide variety of privileges—larger housing, tax exempt monthly payments, an annual free round trip by train, free tram transport in cities, income tax exemptions, pension benefits, etc.[34] Most of these benefits were handed out on the basis of coupons which the decorated soldiers received in little booklets containing a supply for five years. As the first big wave of wartime heroes—decorated in 1941 and 1942—had used up their coupons in 1947, the state was confronted with a massive administrative problem: how to handle the renewal of more than 300,000 coupon booklets—ten times more than the Department for Registration of Decorations of the Supreme Soviet had processed the previous year. The Department had neither enough staff to deal with such a workload, nor all the information it needed to check the legitimacy of all requests. The Ministry of Defence, whose cooperation was essential in the process, was unable to help, because all its resources were tied up in exchanging temporary certificates for decorations into permanent ones.[35] Indeed, the system of administration of benefits was thoroughly outdated. It had been set up at a time when only 22,000 decorated citizens existed, but after the war over 12 million decorations adorned the chests of around 5.6 million Soviets.[36]

Searching for a solution to this problem, the procedures for the administration of benefits for decorated wartime heroes came under scrutiny.[37] In the context of this review, the bureaucrats became aware of the massive cost of the benefits programme. One administrator calculated that the simple process of filling out the coupons, handing them to a cashier in a bank, receiving the money in return, cost 125,000 workdays per year—and this was a conservative estimate, which did not include the rest of the work necessary to operate the benefits system.[38] By April 1947, the bureaucrats started to discuss how much the privileges cost the state. Summing up transfer payments, the cost of free tickets, the tax benefits, and the reduced housing rent the Department for Registration of Decorations put the cost at 3,455.9 million rubles a year.[39]

By August the discussion had shifted from streamlining the administration of benefits to cancelling the privileges altogether as too expensive—a decision which was finally taken formally on 10 September 1947.[40] Veterans frequently refused to believe that their privileges—which they thought they had earned in blood—had in fact been abolished. The Department for Registration of Decorations was bombarded with requests for clarification from veterans to such a degree that it had to print cards with answers to the most frequent questions. All the bureaucrats had to do was tick one out of five standard answers and send off the card.[41] Once the reality of the abolition had sunk in, veterans started to lobby for the reinstatement of the old system.[42] This was not without risks, as long as comrade Stalin was alive. Those who voiced their discontent too aggressively were handled by the security services and disappeared behind barbed wire for 'anti-Soviet agitation'.[43] Lacking an organization to defend their interests and thus the ability to consistently pressure the regime, veterans lost this battle with the bureaucrats.

Welfare for war invalids was cut following the same economic logic. The overarching goal of Soviet legislation was reintegration of the maximum number of invalids into the labour force at minimal cost. During the war, the incentives to work were increased by allowing war invalids of group III to receive their full pension independent of their income (while work 'evaders' were punished by pension cuts). After October 1948, employment guaranteed as a rule only a reduced pension, which was adjusted downward according to income: pension plus salary were not to exceed the pre-disability income and only 50 per cent of the pension was guaranteed. Refusal to work by a group III war invalid was punished by cancellation of pension payments.[44]

The abolition of most privileges of veterans in 1947 and 1948 was primarily caused by economic considerations, but politics and ideology played a part as well. As long as Stalin was alive, the Soviet state in fact refused to institutionalize the social consequences of war. Veterans were not to be acknowledged as a new status group in Soviet society—they were not a class, after all, but merely citizens who at some point had served in the army. Quickly, official propaganda made it clear that the war had not changed anything. In fact, it had demonstrated that the Stalin Revolution had been the correct path to Socialism; victory was increasingly assigned to the genius of the leader. In the context of global confrontation with the United States and the devastating destruction of the country, the industrial revolution of the 1930s had to be repeated—a process which did not need a new privileged group of old soldiers resting on their wartime laurels.[45] To drive home this point on a symbolic level, the leadership decided in late 1947 to make Victory Day into a regular working day.[46] At around the same time, a new wave of repression engulfed former POWs who—if released from 'filtration'—had been granted a short breather after 1945.[47] Clearly, the postwar honeymoon was over.

The history of veterans thus follows the general periodization of the history of postwar society—1947/48 was a turning point in many respects: rationing was abolished and a currency reform attempted to bring wartime inflation under control in late 1947; the wartime lapses in the collective farm regime were countered, in 1948, with a campaign against 'shirkers' and 'parasites' who were now threatened with deportation; internal discussions about legalizing the *de facto* existing trade finally failed at about the same time.[48] Overall, the regime tried to rebuild the kind of society it had engineered in the 1930s. The turn for the worse in veterans' affairs falls into this pattern of Stalin's state re-establishing a semblance of the prewar order. The privileges for veterans were—like rationing or laxities in the collective farms—holdovers from the emergency situation of war and were abolished once this seemed possible.

For veterans, the results of the return to prewar normalcy proved to be long-lasting. By 1948 they had been 'unmade' as a unified category of state policy. Most had lost their special legal status, while an entire subgroup (former prisoners of war) were victims of outright discrimination. Only war invalids remained as a group with very limited and utterly insufficient privileges. This situation did not change fundamentally until the 1970s.[49] The only major legal change under Khrushchev was the silent amnesty of POWs during the 1950s.[50] Other reform attempts did not change the status of veterans fundamentally. The 1956 pension law in many ways unified the ad-hoc legislation for war invalids, and increased the pension for those of them who had been regular draftees.[51] It did not, however, alter the fundamentals of the pension system for victims of war, which continued to disadvantage war invalids from the youngest generation.[52]

Similarly, non-public discussions about reintroducing payments for decorations did not go anywhere. The driving force behind this attempt to restore some of the privileges was Georgii Zhukov, then Minister of Defence. On 14 July 1955 he sent a proposal to the Central Committee which asked for the reinstatement of money payments for major battle decorations. Zhukov estimated the cost of this reintroduction of the payments alone at 271.2 million rubles.[53] Not surprisingly, therefore, Zhukov was asked to come up with ways to finance this legal change. He did this in a letter to the Central Committee at the end of April 1956 by, first, revising the total sum necessary down to 200 million rubles, and, second, by proposing to cut costs amounting to 260 million rubles elsewhere in the defence budget.[54] The Central Committee was still not content—probably because diverting funds away from paying for active service rather than past laurels was not seen as a good idea—and Zhukov had to again argue his case in a final report to the Central Committee on 7 August 1956. He stressed that the sum necessary would not exceed 200 million, and this time estimated much higher possible cost cuts of 340 million.[55] In the end, no resolution was reached. Under Khrushchev's chairmanship, the CC Presidium decided on 9 August 1956 to 'postpone the decision' of this question. Zhukov, who attended the meeting, had lost another battle for the status of war veterans in the postwar Soviet Union.[56]

Very little changed from then on, although the question of privileges for high decorations was raised by citizens again and again, particularly in context of the increasing cult of the Second World War in the 1960s: 'I think it is time that the privileges for decorated defenders of the Homeland were re-established, even if only in regard to [free] train travel', wrote one veteran in 1965 to the Central Committee.[57] Between 1955–6 and the late 1970s, the major legal changes concerned war invalids only.[58] In 1965, in connection with the take-off of the war cult under First Secretary Leonid Brezhnev, veterans got 'their' holiday back. From then on, as between 1945 and 1947, Victory Day was a non-working holiday.[59] In the same year, the material privileges of war invalids were increased.[60] In celebration of the fiftieth anniversary of the October Revolution, Heroes of the Soviet Union and Knights of the Order of Honour received some additional privileges.[61] None of this changed the basic fact that since 1948 veterans had not been treated as a unified group in legal terms. Rather, there was one group with growing (if still meagre) privileges (war invalids), while basically all other veterans remained without them, despite the bombastic war cult.

The organizational shift in the 1950s described in Chapter 7 was, thus, not accompanied by a re-establishment of a privileged position for veterans. However, the unmaking of the status group of veterans in and after 1947 did not spell the end of the entitlement community of combat survivors. Despite its totalitarian aspirations and its relatively modern means of social engineering, the Soviet state could not make and unmake social groups at will. Once a social unit was integrated on such a deep psychological level as the entitlement community of veterans, the state's resistance to its members' claims to special status could only prevent the institutionalization of such feelings; it could not erase them.

Veterans' entitlement claims always outpaced officially granted rights. Veterans had never been content with the meagre privileges they officially received. Even during the comparatively 'fat' years of 1945 to 1947 ('fat', of course, only in terms of legal privileges, not in absolute benefits), veterans were liable to invent rights which in fact did not exist. The most persistent and popular one was a misreading of the one-month regulation in the demobilization law. While the law ruled that local authorities were to give veterans work within a month of their arrival (a directive connected to prescriptions regarding pension rights), this was popularly read as an entitlement to one month of vacation for the returning soldiers.[62]

Veterans frequently managed to convince local authorities of the existence of this imaginary right to a holiday. The secretary of the party's

district committee of Arkhangel'sk, B. Nikolaev, for example, proudly
reported to Malenkov in November 1945 that many demobilized soldiers
immediately started to work 'like Stakhanovites' after their return 'without
using their month-long holiday'.[63] The secretary of Kurgan region's party
committee tried to excuse the 8,814 veterans who were not working under
his jurisdiction by mid-January 1946 with the fact that 'a large part of
them are still using the holiday which the law gives them a right to'.[64]
Many returning heroes, reported the Sverdlovsk region's party secretary,
'don't even take their lawful holiday', while others refused to start working even 'after they have taken their lawful month-long holiday'.[65] The
practice of granting such recreational leave was so widespread that even
a plenipotentiary of the Party Control Commission did not criticize this
practice itself, but only its excesses. Even party members, the KPK's man in
Arkhangel'sk province reported in late 1945, did not go back to work after
relaxing for a month.[66] Some veterans tried to stretch the interpretation of
the demobilization law even further and demanded one and a half or two
months off.[67]

Another imaginary right veterans convinced each other—and sometimes
local authorities—of having was the return of housing for dekulakized
peasants. In the second half of 1945 more and more reports reached the
centre that sons of kulaks demanded their housing back in reciprocation
for their war service. Even more disturbing to Moscow bureaucrats was
the fact that these 'class enemies' sometimes managed to convince local
authorities that they had indeed earned the right to their old houses
back.[68] One demobilized major wrote from Moscow to the army's *Red
Star* newspaper regarding another privilege he had invented after reading
the British propaganda journal *Britanskii soiuznik*. He referred to a piece
written by the author J. B. Priestley about demobilization in Britain:
'In particular, he wrote that they [the British veterans] receive an order
for buying (or for receiving free of charge) a civilian suit.' Since no
country cared so much about its veterans as the Soviet Union, as *Pravda*
constantly claimed, he logically concluded that if the exploited veteran
in capitalist Britain got a suit, he should get one as well. 'Please explain
to me if our Soviet demobilized officers have a right to receive an order
to buy civilian clothes? And how is such a right implemented (if it
exists)?' Whether he convinced anybody of his right to smart dress remains
unknown.

Many veterans fought with bitter determination for privileges they felt they had earned in blood. What gave them, in their view, a right to expect special status after the war was that they had performed the ultimate service for the community. They had risked their health and their lives to defend it. They had put their bodies between the enemy and the community, and were frequently maimed in the process. For this sacrifice, the community owed them—or so they thought. 'I gave half of my life, its best years, to the army,' wrote Boris Mikhailovich Andreev from the city of Chkalov to *Red Star* in 1946.

In twenty years of service I travelled around all of our Union. I served in the North and in the South, in the centre and in the Urals....I participated in the Great Patriotic War. I have several government awards. And now, because of the cutting back of the army (*po sokrashcheniiu shtata*) I proved to be superfluous.[69]

'I ask for your help with registration in the city of Leningrad', wrote another veteran to the Supreme Soviet. 'Please take into account my long military service, where I served in the Red Baltic Fleet from 1938 to 1945. During all this time I participated without interruption in battles against the German invaders. I was four times wounded and in 1945 I was demobilized because of a wound.'[70]

This reference to injuries was common.[71] If defending the community already entitled to special treatment, having not only risked, but actually sacrificed one's own body made this claim even stronger. In letters to the Supreme Soviet in which they asked for cancellation of loan debt, war invalids used this notion to argue for their cause. They referred to themselves as war invalids (in the singular: '*Ia iavliaius' invalidom Otechestvennoi voiny*...'), detailed their wounds and mutilations, and asked for cancellation of loans. 'I ask for an order so they give me a discount (*skidka*) on the loan without repayment, or a discount at least of 50 per cent, because I am an invalid of the Patriotic War.' They also mentioned their inability to work, their general misery, and the lack of family support, but the important point here is that they consistently stressed their war service and assumed that wounds suffered as a result entitled them to be treated in a special manner, obviously without being aware of the extent that this was (or was not) in accord with legislation. 'During the execution of a battle task I received a severe wound: I lost my left hand, lost my eye-sight by 100 per cent and injured my right hand—one finger is missing. Therefore I ask to cancel my debt.'[72]

The entitlement based on shed blood, on wounded and mutilated bodies, was only the extreme case of the sense of reciprocity of war service and postwar treatment, which is expressed in many individual as well as collective letters:

> We think that the Government came to meet us half way with the decision to organize preparatory departments [in institutions of higher education], and that this decision remains on paper only, by guilt of several organizations…
>
> One hundred demobilized ask for your help to take up our studies again, which were interrupted for service in the army during the Patriotic War.[73]

In August 1951 Aleksandr Apolinar'evich T., accused of 'anti-Soviet agitation', tried a final defence. He appealed to the Omsk regional court to take into account that he was a war participant (*uchastnik voiny*) and a group II invalid. He hoped that this would get him a lighter sentence.[74] Others imagined that the war service should be reciprocated with the abolition of the collective farms ('My husband Aleksei fought in vain in this war. He thought that after the war the kolkhozes would be destroyed, but this did not happen.'[75]), or that wartime service and devotion to the officer corps translated into a right to remain an officer, even if one's services were no longer needed ('I have earned the right to further service in the cadres of the army').[76]

Veterans reacted with indignation if the collectivity they had fought for did not hold up its side of what they saw as a fair deal. One demobilized soldier wrote that he returned home 'with victory' into his severely destroyed home region. After some futile running through the institutions he finally went to the chairman of the regional executive committee. 'For the time being,' the chairman answered philosophically, 'it is still warm under the clouds.' Annoyed, the veteran wrote a letter to the chairman of the Supreme Soviet. Speaking beautiful Bolshevik he clearly formulated the claim to a reciprocal relationship between war service and postwar treatment:

> During the war I did not answer like that, dear comrade Chairman of the Supreme Soviet. I went ahead with victory, confident in the reputation (*slava*) of dear Stalin. I put up the banner of victory over Berlin. At the moment it follows that I did not [even] win (*zavoeval*) for myself wood to rebuild the house which the bastards (*gady*) have burnt down. And here I

am, a victorious warrior (*voin-pobeditel'*), and I am supposed to build myself a semi-pit dwelling and live in the ground.[77]

The father of a demobilized soldier who had come back too late to get into an educational institution for the ongoing academic year reported his son's reaction in a letter asking for intervention from above:

> He says: I gave four years to the Homeland (*Rodina*), I defended the Homeland, and only for formal reasons I can't be a student. And others who did not know the front, or work, and who have worse grades, can be students.[78]

Similarly, the attempts to retighten the kolkhoz order[79] could be challenged by veterans on the basis that they had fought for the Homeland. During the general assembly in a kolkhoz in Novosibirsk, which was convened in 1948 to discuss violations of the statutes, a veteran got up and declared:

> I fought. I defended the Homeland. I lost a leg. Now I have two milk-cows. I live in hard material circumstances. I have seven children. And they now tell me to sell the second cow [to the state]. I think this is incorrect. It should have been warned earlier that one should not have two cows. Now I will not give [them] the second cow.[80]

A verb frequently used to express notions of entitlement was *zasluzhivat'*/ *zasluzhit'*. It translates as 'to deserve, to merit, to win, to earn' but literally means to have acquired through service (*sluzhba* (n.), *sluzhit'* (v.)). The typical formulation is 'Did I really not earn' (*neuzheli ia ne zasluzhil*) material help, a motorized wheelchair, a right to this or the other advantage, job, suit, house, resident permit, holiday, etc.[81]

This widespread notion was not only expressed in letters asking for special treatment. It was also expressed in frustrated comments about postwar life, as recorded in procuracy materials and reports on the mood of the population. 'Now, how much did we fight, we fought and fought so well for the good life that I am about to starve to death. Under our Soviet power there will be no good life and it is useless to wait for it.'[82] Another veteran also expressed his dismay at the non-fulfilment of the deal by the community (or so a witness claimed): 'he said, that he fought and now they don't even register him [to live in a city], that they had sentenced him illegally ... that now in case of war he would take up arms not against the enemy but against the other side'.[83] Another grumpy veteran complained in 1951: 'After the war they promised us a good life, but in reality they increased taxes and life became worse and worse all the time. And for what we fought we don't know ourselves.'[84] Confronted with the hardships of postwar life, veterans often felt cheated:

> While we were drinking at D.'s apartment Nestor Ivanovich said to me: 'Now you see three of your sons died at the front for Soviet power, but Soviet power does not pay you anything for them, now is this fair (spravedlivo). [He turned to two other veterans in the room:] Now we fought for Soviet power, that life would become easier, and that one would pay less taxes, but it turned out just the other way around, now the peasants pay more taxes than before.'[85]

In 1946 the director of a regional trading centre was reported saying: 'Life becomes more beautiful, more cheerful. They increased my salary by 60 rubles, and took away 600. We fought to the end. We won. Fight in China, feed Yugoslavia and Finland, but die of hunger yourself.' The secretary of the party organization of a fish factory was reported uttering: 'Now, well, we survived. This is what is called care about the material needs of working people in the Fourth Stalinist Five-Year Plan.... There will be riots, uprisings, and the workers say: "What did we fight for?" '[86] Changes in bread norms also led to expressions of anger based on the notion of reciprocity between war service and postwar treatment:

> A war invalid went to the store No. 18 [in Vologda] and as the salesman gave him 1.4 kilograms of bread, he asked: 'Why so little?' The salesman answered: 'That's how much you get according to the new norms.' The customer swore, threw the bread to the ground and said: 'Is that what I fought for? They did not kill me at the front, so now they want to starve not only me to death but also my family.'[87]

Sometimes, veterans also tried to use what they perceived as their entitlement to special treatment in order to help loved ones. Veterans living in Moscow often appealed to the authorities on behalf of their kin who had a previous conviction and could therefore not live in the capital. To quote one example, a letter to the Supreme Soviet from a citizen residing in Moscow region: 'I am a participant of the Patriotic War and write to you with a supplication regarding my brother...'[88]

Veterans imagined the community was indebted to them in various ways. Often it was 'the state' (gosudarstvo), the 'Homeland' (Rodina), or 'Soviet power' (Sovetskaia vlast'). In other cases it was 'the people' (narod) who owed the veteran, and 'the people' and 'Soviet power' could be interchangeable:

> I ask the Supreme Soviet, considering that I honourably gave away half of my life to the Soviet people and to Soviet power, became a cripple (*kaleka*), [therefore] I ask the Soviet people to free me at least of 60–70 per cent of the loan repayments. With this application I turn through you to the Soviet people, whose call [to arms] I followed and whom I served with devotion and honour until being crippled (*do iskalecheniia*). And therefore the Soviet people should not deny my request.[89]

In other cases the community which owed them were simply those around them, those whom they had defended more concretely. Nikolai Ivanovich T., a veteran in his mid-twenties, lived in 1947–8 in a kolkhoz in Moscow region. He refused to work and made a living by stealing and selling coal from the railroads. He spent his days and evenings shooting dogs in the village, playing the accordion, and agitating among other veterans: 'Let the kolkhozniki work for us. We are not required to work.'[90] In Voronezh province veterans also refused to work in the village, apparently for the same reason: 'women get up at kolkhoz meetings and criticize the men. They say: How long will you make a nuisance of yourself? You were in the war, we worked at the kolkhoz, and now [that you are back] nothing has changed.'[91]

Personal campaigns for recognition of entitlement were not isolated instances of particularly odd characters. They were, rather, a mass phenomenon in postwar Soviet society and are the most tangible evidence for the existence of the entitlement community. At certain moments, veterans' mass reactions formed the necessary context for major policy shifts. The first time this happened was in 1956, when the response of veterans both inside and outside of the new organization pushed the leadership towards acknowledgement of domestic representation of veterans' interests.[92] The SKVV became a major new avenue for entitlement claims of veterans, which were fuelled further by the war cult of the 1960s and 1970s. War invalids approached their section 'with all possible types of questions' in 1963.[93] Before the 23rd Party Congress in 1966, veterans from all over the Soviet Union came with their supplications and letters of complaint to the SKVV. They asked for help in editing these before they submitted them to the congress—only to be told quite often that their 'pretensions' were 'unfounded'.[94] Veterans also addressed republic-level Veterans' Soviets as long as those existed,[95] but the Moscow-based SKVV became one of the major clearing houses for veterans' claims. Between 1973 and 1976–7 the number of letters to the SKVV nearly doubled. On average, the SKVV received about 25,500 letters per annum during this period. In addition, 6,700 to 7,500 veterans crowded the corridors on Gogolevskii Boulevard every year. Such supplicants often had to wait for four or more hours with thirty or forty other veterans in a small space in front of the SKVV's headquarters.[96] And the numbers did not diminish. In 1977, the committee received about 30,000 letters and talked to 6,000 supplicants who came in person.[97] The Moscow section alone worked every day to get through the 15,000 or so letters they received that year. They struggled to find out which of the entitlement claims were 'justified' (*spravedlivyi*), and which were not.[98]

Once organizational growth was allowed, the efforts to build a strong association absorbed much of the energies of the most active members of the entitlement community. This should not be too surprising: privileges were, after all, only in part material phenomena. As important was the symbolic aspect—a special status acknowledged war service, the suffering and trauma of the long and bloody years of fighting for the community. An organization, too, acknowledged a special status and provided symbolic rewards for war sacrifices—not least the possibility of talking about the heroic period of one's life. Both the struggle for organization and the fight for privileges were expressions of veterans' desire for recognition.

As further organizational growth was stopped in 1976, the campaign for gratitude shifted back to the field of privileges—this time with a vengeance. The context for this renewed push for acknowledgement of wartime service was the discussion surrounding the new constitution. Once a draft had been published, the government invited citizens throughout 1977 to comment on it.[99] Veterans responded enthusiastically, suggesting that all kinds of privileges be written into the basic law and that 'respect' (*uvazhenie*) and 'care' (*zabota*) towards them become a central goal of social policy. S. P. Berezkin from Smolensk, for example, urged the inclusion of the following sentence: 'Citizens of the Soviet Union, who have participated in battles for the defence of the Homeland, have a right to privileged medical treatment', while I. V. Ponomarenko from the village of Trilesi in Kiev province proposed making 'care for war participants and war invalids the responsibility of all leaders of organizations and institutions, the duty of [each] citizen of the Soviet Union'.[100] Others suggested institutionalizing 'special care and attention' to veterans in the constitution; lowering the retirement age for war invalids, increasing their pensions, giving them privileged fares on public transport and exempting group III invalids from income tax; lowering the retirement age and increasing pensions to war veterans more generally and giving them privileged access to housing; granting retired soldiers who had served twenty-five years or longer the right to a single apartment; reinstating the privileges for major battle decorations and making those part of the constitution; giving war veterans the right to use public transport in cities free of charge; and even creating special sections for war veterans in cemeteries. More generally, letter writers asked to 'make provisions in the constitution for rights and privileges of participants and invalids of the Great Patriotic War', or to simply declare 'respect towards war veterans and care for them the moral duty of all of our [state] organs and each citizen'.[101] One letter writer proposed the following addendum to the basic law:

> Respect towards veterans of the historical battles, the care about them—this is the law of our life. It is the law for the organs of [state] power as well as for every citizen. The Soviet people will never forget a single drop of blood shed by Soviet people for the Homeland, for its freedom and happiness.[102]

The political leadership studied these propositions with interest. Just before the new constitution was ratified on 7 October 1977, Brezhnev answered in public, in a speech to the Supreme Soviet on 4 October. He praised the 'discussion involving the whole people' (*vsenarodnoe obsuzhdenie*), listed which of the 'about 400,000 propositions' were integrated into the constitution, and then moved on to those which could not be taken into account. It was in this context that veterans' privileges came up, as part of those proposals which were 'psychologically understandable ... and correct in themselves' but could not become part of the constitution, as the basic law only included 'basic, principal provisions'. However, they could still become part of the general legislation outside of the constitution itself:

> In our view, propositions about the further betterment of the living conditions of veterans of the Great Patriotic War ... merit attention. The party and the Soviet government, who display constant care about participants of the Great Patriotic War, have already done quite a bit in this respect. Could one not find additional means to give a couple of more privileges to those who defended the freedom and independence of our Homeland in the hardest of all wars? It seems to me, that this is possible.   (Prolonged applause).[103]

It is hard to decide if this public announcement of the possibility of 'a couple more privileges' is an expression of populism of Brezhnev, or an attempt to increase popular pressure in order to push through legislation against considerable resistance within the political system. Maybe Brezhnev was also carried away by the dynamic of the war cult he himself had instituted as a new basis for legitimation since his inauguration into office.[104]

Whatever the motives, the result of the 1977 promise was another massive letter-writing campaign by veterans. The SKVV's Commission for Affairs of War invalids received 'a large amount of letters' regarding privileges, which they forwarded to the 'appropriate organs' in order to increase the pressure on the government to implement the promise.[105] Newspapers received letters from veterans interested to know 'when any kind of legal acts will be passed about the privileges of veterans of the Great Patriotic War'. Such letter writers also challenged Brezhnev's line that the Soviet state 'already does quite a bit for veterans'. In fact, one of them groused, 'there are absolutely no such privileges'.[106] In May 1978, lecturers of the Department of Propaganda of the Central Committee were asked 888 times by their audiences when the promised new privileges would finally be delivered;[107] in the same month, *Pravda* received 884 letters asking the same question, followed by another 604 such letters in June, and—prompted by the first anniversary of the promise—another 153 in October.[108] Lecturers of the Department of Propaganda also remained on the spot, with audiences still asking the same question in October 1978.[109]

The veterans' organization, too, lobbied strenuously. The SKVV, led by its Moscow section, worked out proposals for new privileges and presented them to the State Planning Agency (Gosplan).[110] The planners were wary of the proposal—it cost too much and potentially distracted from more pressing international problems. As SKVV chairman Pavel Ivanovich Batov explained in December 1977 to his organization's plenum:

> I have to say that this is not an easy question and not a cheap question [either].... We still need money. First of all, we have to ensure the power of our state. Once that is accomplished we will deal with our domestic problems. There is reason to believe that towards the 60th anniversary of the Armed Forces a part of the measures, which were prepared [by us], come before the government organs and will partially be realized. Again, this depends on the possibilities and on the state budget for 1978.[111]

Nevertheless, things moved slowly. The most obvious date to announce new privileges for veterans—the sixtieth anniversary of the creation of the Red Army (February 1978)—went by without such an announcement. By June 1978, after negotiations between Gosplan, SKVV, and various ministries, a compromise was reached and the draft legislation was forwarded to the Council of Ministers for decision.[112]

In 1977 and 1978, then, the entitlement community of veterans fought and won its third major campaign. After mass individual response to the SKVV's establishment in 1956 had pushed it towards domestic represent-ation and after enthusiastic response on the local level had prompted the creation of a local infrastructure, now the question of legal status was put on the agenda and signed into law. On 10 November 1978, the Coun-cil of Ministers and the Central Committee passed landmark decree no. 907, which made 'participants of the Great Patriotic War' eligible for a half-price round trip to any destination in the Soviet Union once a year, interest-free loans for the construction of individual houses, annual holiday at whatever time they pleased and the right to an additional two weeks of unpaid leave, if they so desired. Veterans also had the right to use the polyclinic of their workplace after retirement, were to get preferential ac-cess to travel passes to sanatoria, to gardening co-operatives, and to private telephones.[113]

It seemed, thus, that veterans had finally been made into a status group. The social consequences of war—the emergence of a new entity within Soviet society—were finally acknowledged, the entitlement community integrated into the Soviet system. Many of those subject to the new legislation greeted this development with satisfaction. While some still griped that the resolution provided 'practically no material privileges',[114] the general tone of letters to *Pravda* and *Izvestiia* in December 1978 changed from the demanding to the positive: 'Many veterans thank the party and the government for the measures regarding the further betterment of their material and everyday situation.'[115] However, soon disillusionment set in. More and more veterans were told that the resolution did, in fact, not apply to them. The reason for this were technicalities hidden in paragraph two of resolution no. 907, which defined who was a 'war participant' (*uchastnik voiny*) in the understanding of the resolution. The two key terms were 'draftees' (*voennosluzhashchie*) and 'field army' (*deistvuiushchaia armiia*).[116]

Anybody who was officially a 'civilian' employee of the army (*volnon-aemnyi*) was excluded from the legislation—independent of how close they had been to the front. In addition, only people who had served in the 'field army' were 'war participants' in the understanding of the new resolution. Who was and who was not part of this 'field army' depended on a list of units which a 1956 resolution of the General Staff had defined in connection with the pension reform of 1956. This list excluded many veterans who had received the veterans' medal 'For Victory over Germany' of 1945 as well as various anniversary medals (Twenty, Twenty-Five, Thirty Years of Victory).[117]

Veterans who were thus excluded from the celebrated new legislation were outraged. 'How could that be', wrote one of them to Brezhnev, 'I was at the Western Front, the Northwestern, Briansk, Don, Stalingrad, Central, Second Ukrainian, Third Belorussian, and First Belorussian fronts.... and I, it turns out, am not a war participant?'[118] 'Why do the privileges ... not apply to all war participants?' asked others.[119] 'Why are *volnonaemnye* not considered participants of the Great Patriotic War?' 'Why do the privileges for participants of the Great Patriotic War not apply to participants in the war with Japan in 1945?'[120] Other groups of veterans such as railway personnel also wrote in, demanding to know why they were excluded from the privileged group.[121]

Over the next decade, such continued pressure from the entitlement community led to a dual process—the expansion of the categories of citizens included in the privileged group and a growth of privileges for those already in the group as well. Both processes followed the logic of similarity: while veterans excluded from the group argued that they were fundamentally similar to other war veterans and should thus be included in the group, others argued about similarity of entitlements they desired to already existing privileges. The first process is particularly well documented in the case of war correspondents—one of the groups of *volnonaemnye* who were excluded from the new status category of 'war participants'.[122] Their concerted lobbying effort in 1980 spearheaded the inclusion of *volnonaemnye* into the new status group on 27 February 1981.[123] Other groups followed, as Table 8.1 demonstrates. During the same period, privileges ascribed to veterans were extended. Already on 25 August 1979, the interest-free loans were widened from individual housing construction to houses built by co-operatives as well as to loans which had been granted before November 1978.[124] On 1 May 1980, further benefits, including privileged access to housing and a 50 per cent income tax reduction were added to those instituted in 1978.[125] In the 1980s and 1990s, main anniversaries of Victory

Table 8.1. Process of widening group of persons privileged as 'war participants'

| Year | Group | Legal act |
|---|---|---|
| 1981 | Draftees who had worked in staff organizations but spent at least one month on commission to the front | Resol. of Central Committee & Council of Ministers, 27 Feb. 1981, No. 219 |
| 1985 | Workers in factories in Leningrad during Blockade | Resol. of Central Committee & Council of Ministers, 14 May 1985, No. 416 |
| 1988 | Subset of privileges applied to decorated soldiers who served in the hinterland as well as to home-front workers | Resol. of Council of Ministers, 12 May 1988, No. 621 |
| 1988 | Minors who had suffered as concentration camp inmates in German camps during the war | Resol. of Council of Ministers, 6 Oct. 1989, No. 825 |
| 1995 | Former POWs | Decree of President of Russian Federation, 24 Jan. 1995 |
| 1995 | All veterans who had received Victory over Germany medal in 1945, independent of where they served | Federal Law on Veterans, 12 Jan. 1995 |

Source: T. V. Chertoritskaia, Dorogie moi veterany: Iz istorii razrabotki i priniatiia zakonodatel'stva o veteranakh (St Petersburg: Glagol', 1995), 43–6, 48–9; SP SSSR 16 (1985): st. 73, p. 287; 33 (1989): st. 152, pp. 813–14; Velikaia Otechestvennaia Voina 1941–1945, iv. Narod i voina (Moscow: Nauka, 1999), 194. The original version of the Federal Law on Veterans is published in Sobranie zakonodatel'stva Rossiiskoi Federatsii, 3 (16 Jan. 1995): st. 168, pp. 355–79; see esp. paragraph 1.z.

Day were celebrated by handing out further privileges (pension increases, better access to medical care, loans, free use of public transport etc.).[126] The list could go on.

By the 1980s, then, veterans had been transformed from a rather weakly integrated entitlement community into a corporate group within Soviet society. They now had their own organizations, legally defined privileges, and a clear identity as rescuers of the fatherland, which was propagated in the official cult of the war and celebrated every year in the 'veterans' holiday' of Victory Day. New decorations were handed out to veterans decades after the war, leaving virtually nobody without metal on the chest.[127] Hardly a public ritual took place without the participation of medal-covered former soldiers.[128] Finally, in 1988, the new All-Union Council of War and Labour Veterans became one of the 'societal organizations' which sent representatives to the new Congress of People's Deputies.[129] Veterans had become an officially recognized pillar of Soviet society.

This institutionalization was reinforced by the re-establishment of front-line ties that had been dormant for decades. From the 1960s onwards, official veterans' meetings re-established connections lost in the upheaval of postwar life.[130] Such reunions triggered private follow-ups. The frontline friends Nikolai Borodulin and Vladimir Dudchenko met for the first time after the war in 1977 during the opening of a war monument. They decided to meet again and in late 1978 Borodulin travelled to Dudchenko's village.[131] Veterans also used Soviet media to try and re-establish front-line ties. In October 1978 A. Novikova sent a photo to *Pravda*. As she explained in the accompanying text, the snapshot showed herself and her two frontline friends Aleksandra Aleksandrova and Antonina Tikhonenko before demobilization in 1945. They had not seen each other since then, and Novikova asked the other two to get in touch.[132] Three weeks later the newspaper published the enthusiastic response of Aleksandra Fedorovna Martynova, née Aleksandrova: 'Now I firmly believe that our dream will come true and we, who did such a hard frontline travel together, from Moscow to Berlin, will [finally] meet.'[133] As veterans re-established their frontline ties in the context of the unfolding cult of the war and their own growing privileges, the communication between them increased substantially.

They were further pushed together by generational dynamics, as their numbers decreased steadily, leaving only the youngest alive. By war's end, veterans had been differentiated into three generations—the largest group were those born in 1905–22, who had been established as adults before the war. They were flanked on either side by two substantial minorities—the wartime generation (born 1923–7) and those who had fought in previous wars as well (the 'double veterans', born 1890–1904).[134] As time went on, the two older cohorts started to disappear and the entitlement community became more and more coterminous with the frontline generation. In 1979, men 75 years or older (who could have been double veterans) constituted only 1.7 per cent of the male population. By contrast, men 50 to 54 years of age (closest to the frontline generation) made up 6 per cent.[135] Two decades later, the oldest wartime cohort had all but disappeared, while the wartime generation dominated the survivors of the draft cohorts of the Second World War.[136]

This cohort came into conflict with younger Soviet citizens who had no immediate war memory of their own. Members of what an anthropologist has called 'the last Soviet generation'[137] were frequently irritated by the high symbolic status of veterans and their privileges within a context of material scarcity. Younger Soviet citizens frequently resented the constant war stories of those they derisively called the *vovy* (from 'VOV', the Russian acronym for 'Great Patriotic War').[138] Veterans' privileges, now thoroughly endorsed by the state, were challenged in everyday life, in those central sites of Soviet public life: the queue (*ochered'*) and public transport.

Veterans complained that students did not jump up once a bemedalled veteran entered a bus or tram; instead of giving up their seat respectfully, these youngsters simply ignored their elders. The invalid's right to jump the queue in the factory's polyclinic could be challenged by 'a girl' (*devushka*) who reasoned that this old man had time to wait, while she had just received permission to leave work for a short while and needed to hurry back. In a store, similar attempts to go straight up to the counter rather than wait like everybody else in line (a privilege which, depending on local arrangements, was granted to war invalids or to veterans more generally) could lead to angry hisses and 'undesirable conversations' from those without such special access.[139] One veteran reported in 1985 that if one jumped the queue, this 'immediately' led to 'panic, unfriendly mood—that's how they relate to war veterans'. He suggested that a way out would be a further increase in privileges—instead of jumping the queue, veterans should have their own section in the store.[140] Another veteran, a war invalid, who jumped a queue for milk in 1988 was told off by those waiting: 'How sick we are of those invalids. They are everywhere!' Such feelings were caused, he believed, by the thoughtlessness of the young generation: 'In this line stood largely people of the postwar generation, who have seen the war only in the movies.'[141]

The resentment against veterans' privileges was not always a consequence of a lack of social memory. Rather, many Soviet citizens felt that they, too, had done their share of suffering for victory. The daughter of a fallen soldier might, for example, have to wait to get ice-cream for her son (who was, after all, the nephew of a *frontovik*), while a veteran who had survived the war jumped the queue to get ice-cream for his own nephew.[142] It did not help that some veterans used their ability to jump the queue to obtain deficit goods for friends and acquaintances, or to sell them on the black market.[143] A thoughtful minority understood the connection between special status and resentment very well and started to feel uneasy about the entire culture of privilege. One N. Boiko publicly announced that he was 'ashamed' to be a veteran, ashamed of the behaviour 'of the majority of our brothers'.

Writing to the veterans' weekly in 1988, he asked, rhetorically: 'Who are we—a foreign people? Did we defend a foreign country? Do you think it was easy for that old woman to lose her husband and her sons, and live alone all her life, crying about the dead? ... Didn't the whole country, after all, fight? So why do we, frontline soldiers, get such privileges?'[144]

In the frequent conflicts over their special status, the state was now consistently on the side of the veterans. How far this could go can be illustrated by the amazing campaign against Nikolai Afanas'evich Zatsarnyi. His unfriendly but rather innocent challenge to a war invalid's special privilege to jump a queue led not only to censure by the omnipresent older woman in the queue, but also to public shaming in three big articles in *Izvestiia*, mobbing on the job, and finally a lawsuit.

It all started in a typical Soviet manner. Nikolai Afanas'evich had been waiting in line for three hours just to renew a prescription for an allergy. He finally had made it to the front of the slowly moving queue—and along came, of course, one of those *vovy* who went straight to the door. 'Stand in line', Zatsarnyi angrily told him. 'I'm an invalid of the Great Patriotic war', the old man replied. 'We know such invalids,' retorted Zatsarnyi. 'Why don't you show your certificate.' The exchange was cut short by a nurse letting the invalid (who was apparently known already) into the doctor's office. That Zatsarnyi would be accosted by an elderly lady telling him that he should be ashamed (*Kak vam ne stydno*) might be predictable.[145] What Zatsarnyi did probably not expect, however, was that he would be made the object of a mini-campaign. The old lady did not stop with telling him off in the queue. She went to denounce him to *Izvestiia*, who took up the case, investigated it, and published no less than three large articles on Zatsarnyi's misdeed.[146]

As a result of the public shaming, Zatsarnyi was mobbed out of his job and the state prosecutor opened a case against him. The charge was 'public insult of an invalid of the Patriotic War' (*publichnoe oskorblenie invalida Velikoi Otechestvennoi voiny*). By the time of the trial, the story as told by *Izvestiia* had changed markedly. Now the war invalid showed Zatsarnyi his certificate from the start, while the offender supposedly physically obstructed the entrance to the doctor's office and insulted the invalid. The judge was not troubled by such inconsistencies and sentenced him to community service (*ispravitel'nye raboty*) for three months and cut his salary by 20 per cent. That the judge was a war veteran himself might have contributed to this outcome. By the late 1970s, veterans were not only aligned with the state, in many instances they now *were* the state.[147] This alignment might explain some of the real hostility veterans experienced during Perestroika: 'You Victor!' sneered teenage thugs as they physically abused a veteran in a park in the final years of the Soviet Union, 'If you hadn't won, we would now be drinking Bavarian beer...'[148]

Several processes thus contributed to the increasing cohesion of the new social entity of veterans in the final decade of the Soviet Union: organization and integration into the political system, re-establishment of wartime ties and the thickening of communication which came with it, the increasingly high symbolic as well as legal status, and the continuing crystallization of the status group into a generation in conflict with younger cohorts of Soviet citizens. In this generational conflict, the resentment of outsiders tended to bring veterans even closer together. But resentment played a role in the group integration not only because of the jealousy of outsiders, it was also the flip-side of status in a situation of scarcity of the goods and services promised by privileges. The consistent gap between the symbolic position of veterans and their actual material status—or, to use the language of this chapter, the gap between privileges and benefits—was a constant irritation. The fact, for example, that a war veteran could get a car quicker than others did not mean that he got the car—there were too many veterans and too few cars.[149] And cars and other luxury goods were not the only examples where privileges outpaced the available benefits.

Even privileged citizens suffered from the Soviet economy of scarcity. Let us take telephones, for example, which had been promised by the 1978 legislation. In the city of Kalinin, three war invalids—V. Zharov, P. Efstaf'ev, and P. Shtuko—fought from 1981 to get private telephones installed. They were told again and again that it would happen 'next year'. In 1988, when the three of them wrote a letter to the editor of the journal *Veterans*, they were still without phone connections.[150] They were not alone: in the same year about 800,000 veterans were waiting for the installation of a private phone in the Soviet Union.[151] The problem of 'telephonization' of veterans persisted: by the twenty-first century, the problem was still not solved, though it was much smaller. During 2000 more than 36,000 war invalids and more than 15,000 war veterans received telephones and the veterans' organization planned, optimistically, that this problem would be solved by the end of 2002.[152]

Housing is another example. In 1988, only 2.1 per cent of the families of veterans who were on the waiting list for housing improvement in the RSFSR, actually received such a benefit. In 1990 and 1991 the corresponding numbers were 1.8 and 1.4 per cent.[153] During Perestroika, a despondent veteran wrote to the weekly of the veterans' organization. He had returned in 1946 from the war in which he had fought from the beginning and which saw him wounded seriously several times. His village was in ruins, burnt down by Hitler's soldiers. The only building material he could obtain was a bunch of poles. He used them to build a makeshift hut in which he and his wife lived for the next forty years—winter as well as summer. In the 1980s, a war invalid, he went on a march through the institutions reminiscent of the immediate postwar years: he asked his former place of employment for help finding a better home; he went on to ask his local rural council, then the regional council, finally the province council. In the end, the couple in their seventies received money—to renovate their house on their own. 'They built houses with all conveniences in our village. So I thought: I fought honourably, my wife and I worked all our lives, now we are old and sick ... Who needs us now? Who can help us?' This letter was written in 1988.[154]

The breakdown of the Soviet Union was thus by no means a major discontinuity in terms of veterans' privileges, as some observers claim—veterans were not awash in benefits before and suddenly deprived of them after 1991, even if the 'transition' increased the state's problems in delivering the promised benefits.[155] Housing is a case in point. Both the absolute number of families of veterans whose housing improved and their share among those on the waiting list decreased dramatically. One year after the breakdown of the Soviet Union, only 29 per cent of the number of families received housing improvement, compared to 1988. Interestingly, too, the waiting lists must have been purged, as the decline in the relative numbers is much less dramatic.[156] It is easy to overstate this breakdown of state aid, though. Most old soldiers did not receive the special treatment promised by law before the breakdown of the Soviet Union; and most did not receive any thereafter. The effects of the breakdown were insignificant in the aggregate. After all, in 1988, 97.9 per cent of those on the waiting list had *not* received housing—as compared to 99 per cent in 1992.[157] The Soviet Union had never been able to deliver the 'relatively impressive benefits' which were inscribed in its legislation, a problem which during Perestroika was also debated in public.[158] Despite such discussions, the state continued after 1991 to promise more than it could deliver. In fact, the 1995 law 'On Veterans' was subject to a similar gap between privileges and actual benefits, despite the strong lobbying effort of the veterans' organization to implement these promises.[159]

What did change dramatically after 1991, however, is the tone of published sources. The politics of resentment, which before Perestroika were restricted to conversations and unpublishable letters, were now articulated in public. The weekly newspaper *Veteran*, the organ of the All-Union Organization of Veterans (founded by Gorbachev in 1986), suddenly excluded from the establishment, adopted this tone wholeheartedly.[160] But resentment seeped also into more mainstream media, for example, *Izvestiia*. To give just one more example: one veteran couple, after finally receiving their telephone in 1997, demanded that the phone company take over their enormous bill, which they were unable to pay ('someone' had called overseas three times a day). They based this request on their status as decorated war heroes and invalids.[161]

There are, thus, some marked continuities in the history of Soviet veterans as a social group and as part of Soviet society between the war and the end of the Soviet Union. Entitlement—the one most important factor uniting veterans across all generational, political, gender, social, and ethnic divisions—consistently outpaced the privileges provided by the state. Throughout, the state provided either no or rather limited privileges, but celebrated them as extraordinary and without parallel anywhere else in the world. Entitlements, however, were hard to satisfy in the first place, as they proved remarkably flexible: any privilege granted bred resentment in those subgroups of veterans who did not receive it and any privilege granted also implied a whole range of other possible privileges, which then became subject to entitlement claims. The second major continuity in this history was the continuous gap between privileges granted on paper and benefits delivered in practice. The connected practical aspects of obtaining actual benefits within a highly bureaucratized economy of scarcity also reinforced entitlement claims. From conversations between veterans in the ante-room or the queue, to the constant display of one's worthiness of support—much about this process contributed to the elasticity of entitlement claims.

The grandiose state discourse about the Great Patriotic War, too, played its role. If Victory over Hitler's Germany was the major claim of the Soviet state to legitimacy and international standing, why were those who had actually done the fighting and winning not elevated to a privileged caste within this society? The closed nature of the Soviet political system made public discussion of the costs of a privilege system, and the finite nature of state finances, difficult. Finally, the enormity of wartime experience, the real trauma—both physical and psychological—which Soviet soldiers were exposed to, called for recognition which could never be satisfied by any of the symbolic or material benefits provided by the state. The persistence and pliability of entitlement claims by war veterans is, thus, on one level also an expression of the slow healing process of the deep scars left by the war on the European Eastern Front.

# Afterword

Organizations typically unite only a fraction of the surviving combatants of a given country. In post-Second World War Germany, for example, only between 10 and 35 per cent of veterans were organized.[1] Such poor participation rates were not unique to the vanquished. Victor nations did not show a larger percentage, either. The American Legion organized maybe 25 per cent of those who had fought in the First World War and the survivors of other wars followed a similar pattern. As the American Historical Association noted in 1946, 'no veterans' organization ... has ever represented a majority of the servicemen who fought a given war'.[2] The Soviet Union was no exception in this regard. If anything, the Soviet Committee of War Veterans (SKVV) organized a smaller share than usual, as formal membership never became an option under the Soviet order. The organization's functionaries were, consequently, a tiny minority among veterans. As late as 1985, for example, under 7 per cent of the veterans living in Rostov-on-Don were organized in the various veterans' associations.[3] To equate this minority with the veterans' movement, however, would confuse the part with the whole. As in the case of many other popular movements, Soviet veterans were organized in dynamic circles of decreasing commitment and lessening organizational connectedness. The functionaries within the SKVV and the few other organizations were surrounded by veterans' activists who, while not officially organized, could be mobilized to work for the association.

Functionaries tended to be men, retired career military men, as a rule from the older cohorts, and frequently party members. This profile is well embodied by the chairmen of the SKVV, who into the 1980s were career officers from the generation I call the 'double veterans' (born between 1890 and 1904). When the middle generation took over in the 1980s, the leadership still remained in the hands of highly decorated career military men.[4] The majority of the delegates to both the First and the Second All-Union Conference of War Veterans, held in 1956 and 1965 respectively, came from the same group as the SKVV's leaders—they were men, high-ranking career officers from the older cohorts, often with Civil War experience.[5] Similarly, nearly 19 per cent of the functionaries of the SKVV's local chapters in 1965 were retired generals, while 58 per cent were retired officers. A little under 5 per cent were women.[6]

The functionaries were surrounded by what the Soviets called the *aktiv*—a group who would from time to time perform certain tasks for the organization without being officially part of its structure. In 1966 the Volgograd section of the SKVV had twenty-five functionaries, but counted more than 300 people who they could call upon to work for and with the section. Among those activists, 'more than 100 participate continuously and actively in [our] work'.[7] This was still a minority among combat survivors, however. By 1985, the SKVV claimed that in some cities between 17 and 25 per cent of the veterans were part of the *aktiv* of the movement.[8] A year later, one presidium member estimated the total share of activists surrounding the SKVV's structure as 'not more than 10 percent of the total'.[9] By 1989, maybe 30 per cent of veterans were part of the inner circles of the movement. Only a few of these activists were very strongly committed and engaged on a more or less daily basis. Only 1 or 2 per cent of veterans, for example, were active propagandists by 1989.[10] In early 1994, just over 60,000 people subscribed to the newspaper of the new organization of war and labour veterans,[11] at a time when 3.6 million veterans were counted on the territory of the former Soviet Union and 2.4 million in Russia.[12] Before the organized movement took off in the 1970s and 1980s, the share of veterans in the inner circles was much smaller—there were many more veterans and a much less extensive organizational structure. Nevertheless, the activists were not the final circle of the movement. The third ring was formed by a wider field of people who in certain situations saw themselves as veterans, wrote letters, and went in person to complain about injustices or insults to their 'honour'.[13] The Soviets referred to this wider group as *veteranskaia obshchestvennost'*—a term which might be translated as 'veterans' public'.

The share of these three categories (functionaries, activists, and the wider *veteranskaia obshchestvennost'*) among veterans as a whole increased through the triple processes of growth of veterans' organizations, institutionalization of the cult of the Second World War, and decline of the total number of veterans through death—a tendency which can be reconstructed only approximately as the available data are far from satisfactory.[14] The veterans' organization talked about 20.1 million war participants by the end of the war.[15] This number seems to exclude some categories of personnel who had served in the armed forces during the war. Based on official numbers of service in the armed forces and wartime losses, my own estimate is significantly higher—25.3 million by 1945.[16] In either case, the figures decreased massively—by 1978, the SKVV estimated the number of veterans of the Great Patriotic War at 9 million, a year later, the same organization spoke of 8 million, including Civil War veterans; by 1990, Second World War veterans had decreased to between 5 and 6 million; and by 1994, only 3.6 million were counted on the territory of the former Soviet Union. Russia had 2.6 million war participants in 1994, 2.4 million in 1995, and a decade later, on Victory Day 2004, only a bit over one million were still alive in the Russian Federation.[17] Within this declining number a larger and larger share became drawn into the circles of the movement surrounding the growing organization until—after the breakdown of the Soviet Union—the successor organization of the SKVV managed to expand its influence enough to organize nearly as many old soldiers as were still alive at the beginning of the new century: about one million.[18] The entitlement community of veterans had metamorphosed into a corporate group tied into the institutional structure of the surrounding society, internally united by a strong organization, well-defined legal privileges, a strong sense of self.

During most of the postwar period, thus, the majority of survivors of the war were outside of the organized movement—but still part of a unified phenomenon. It is one of the central findings of this study that veterans were a social entity which existed in interaction with, but relatively independent from, organization and legislation. Veterans came back from the war with a strong sense that, as victors over Nazi Germany and as saviours of their home towns and villages, their families and communities, their people and the Soviet regime—and of civilization itself—they had a right to special treatment by all those they had defended. As long as they still posed a security threat, as long as they were still armed and organized in functional military units, the regime made sure to cater to this sense of entitlement, to promise assistance and advancement, and to deliver at least part of it. Once the threat was over, once veterans had become isolated

from their comrades-in-arms, once they had become civilians again, the
cost of such policies quickly outweighed the benefits. From 1948 onwards,
veterans were no longer acknowledged as a legal category worthy of state
subsidies. Attempts at organization—unless they stayed below the radar
screen—were also frustrated and declared 'inappropriate' by the political
leadership.

This lack of state support failed to convince veterans that they really were
unworthy of a special position and a good life. The continued existence
of former soldiers as an entitlement group during the first postwar decade
belies the notion of historians that veterans only exist if either organized or
constructed by legislation. True, they did not form a social class, whether
in the sense proposed by Karl Marx or in the meaning of Max Weber. The
decentralized nature of the reintegration process, its reliance on family,
friends, and other social institutions outside of the state, and the lack of a
consistent affirmative action policy, ensured that social difference quickly
re-established itself into what was already a much more diverse group than
the notion of the 'frontline brotherhood' implied. Veterans were not, as a
group, elevated to a new position after the war and individual success only
contributed to the fracturing of that sense of community which had ruled in
the demobilization trains of 1945, 1946, and 1947. Even war invalids—the
one group with at least some state support after 1948—were torn apart by
the reintegration into civilian life.

Nevertheless, veterans continued—mostly as individuals but sometimes
also as groups—to ask for special treatment based on their wartime record.
Even if the state often denied such demands, they formed part of the
normal environment of postwar life. Once organization was cautiously
allowed from 1956 onwards, these pent-up energies were released and the
veterans' movement constantly blossomed far beyond the limits of what was
allowed. It was held in check, to be sure, but the most determined attempt
to stop the disorderly growth—the 1976 reorganization—only diverted
the energies of veterans elsewhere. From then on, the old demand for
special privileges was voiced louder and louder. Eventually, in 1978, it was
signed into law and subsequently grew to encompass both more people and
more advantages. Under Gorbachev, the process reached somewhat of a
climax in the new organization as well as its representation in the Supreme
Soviet. Alas, at the very moment when the consequences of war were
finally acknowledged as legitimate by the state, the very regime which had
waged the war, and denied veterans so much for so long, collapsed in 1991.

The emergence of the entitlement community and its transformation into a status group can be understood in three contexts—the impact of war on modern society in general, the *moyenne durée* of Russian history, and the logic of social stratification in an authoritarian, state-centred social formation. It has become a commonplace in the literature on 'war and society' to state that the impact of war varies according to the makeup of the polity in question. While a detailed comparative history of veterans remains to be written, it is clear enough that different nations react to returning servicemen in different ways—but react they must. Mass mobilization of citizen soldiers, ideological indoctrination in order to steel their resolve, and the trauma of total war leave many legacies, and veterans are one of them. From this perspective, then, the Soviet case can be seen as one variant of an international pattern of social change during the epoch of mass societies and total war.[19]

This pattern played itself out in particular ways in Russia, which had entered military modernity with the army reform of 1874 and had engaged in warfare in 1904–5, and from 1914 onwards. As a result, during the final years of its existence, the Tsarist state had started to accommodate the veterans produced in these wars. The emergence of former soldiers as a specifically privileged group had started under the Old Regime but was then slowed down by the ideological preoccupation of the Bolsheviks with class struggle. It took the slow metamorphosis of the revolutionary regime into a post-revolutionary welfare state for the history of veterans' benefits to return to the track it seemed to be on before 1914—the accommodation of veterans as a specific status group.[20]

It is tempting to see the Second World War as the great transformation of one type of society into the other. However, while the war did have consequences—the entitlement community among them—the way the postwar settlement took shape was specific to the social formation which had emerged between 1914 and 1939—a society centred around a large state apparatus claiming control over the economy and most aspects of everyday life as well.[21] In this society, the dominant factor of social stratification was status rather than economic position. Status could be earned either by achievement, that is, by service to the revolution and the Soviet state, or by ascription, that is, by membership in a group imagined to be a priori allied with the regime (such as 'the working class' in the interwar period). The enormity of service rendered at the fronts of the Great Patriotic War implied for many that such a special status had been earned, that veterans had become such an ascribed status group. Within the Soviet economic order, where the state allocated resources to deserving sections of the population, this argument made sense to many—both veterans and non-veterans. It took a while until political, ideological, and economic barriers were overcome and this notion was realized, but that it was in the long run appears quite logical in retrospect.[22]

Given the increasing integration of veterans into a corporate group and an organized movement, and this movement in turn into the political system and the political process itself, it comes as no surprise that veterans' activists were shocked by the breakup of the Soviet Union.[23] However, the movement was already too well established to go under with the political system it had evolved in. After a period of renaming and partial splitting (along both the new state and the older organizational lines), the veterans' movement prolonged its vigorous representation of veterans' interests. In order to keep the movement together despite the breakup of the territorial state, the All-Union Organization of War and Labour Veterans renamed itself as Coordinating Council of the Commonwealth (Union) of Veterans' Organizations of the Independent States in December 1991.[24] More important than this attempt to ignore the breakdown of the Union would become the Russian successor, the All-Russian Council of Veterans, founded in late November 1991,[25] replacing the All-Russian Council of War and Labour Veterans, which had been founded along with the Union-level organization in 1986.[26]

The SKVV's leaders, in turn, tried to make the best out of the situation. Following their long-time desire to build their own organization into a full network, they used the breakup of the Soviet Union to pass new statutes, which called for the creation of organizations in the localities—a step which led to protests from the rival organization.[27] In March 1992, the SKVV held a new conference, in which it recreated itself as the Russian Committee of War Veterans (*Rossiiskii Komitet Veteranov Voiny*)—the successor of the SKVV on the level of the Russian Federation. The RKVV immediately set out to solidify its structure on the lower levels. By June 1993, the RKVV had created organizations in sixty-four out of seventy-nine territorial-administrative units of the Russian Federation.[28] The breakdown of the Soviet Union thus finally removed the brake which had constantly blocked this development. Finally, the renamed SKVV could build an organizational structure beyond Moscow and the major cities. Now, it added organizations in those republics which were still part of the Russian

Federation, but also on province and krai level, and all the way down to primary organizations in workplaces and housing collectives.[29]

But the RKVV could no longer claim a monopoly over *frontoviki*. After 1991, a whole new variety of veterans' organizations sprang up. By the end of the century, in Moscow alone they filled two pages of the phone book.[30] Despite the generally resentful tone in their official publications, they remained influential players in the political process. In 1993, for example, representatives of three veterans' organizations participated in the conference which was to work out the new constitution for the Russian Federation.[31] Their consistent lobbying pushed through major legislation in 1995,[32] and more recently, a vigorous campaign has slowed the implementation of major welfare reforms.[33] The entrenched special privileges of war veterans, in fact, functioned as a major deterrent to a necessary overhaul of a pension and welfare system which constantly outpaces available state budgets. The 1995 Law on Veterans continues their special position in the system of social provisions.[34] Moreover, veterans of the Great Patriotic War remain 'the veterans' in the Russian context, with better and more extensive benefits than the survivors of Afghanistan or Chechnya. In both the 1995 Law and its reformed 2006 version, the maybe one million remaining survivors of 1941–5 retained 'their previous preferred position and super-level of welfare', writes a Russian specialist on military law.[35] In cultural production, too, this remains 'the quintessential war' which 'has yet to be supplanted' by those newer and more ambiguous conflicts.[36] Most soldiers of the Second World War might be dead, but the consequences of this war live on.

# Notes

## INTRODUCTION

1. Boris Urlanis, *Bilanz der Kriege: Die Menschenverluste Europas vom 17. Jahrhundert bis zur Gegenwart*, tr. Gerhard Hartmann (Berlin: VEB Deutscher Verlag der Wissenschaften, 1965), 367.
2. Eric Hobsbawm, *The Age of Extremes: A History of the World, 1914–1991* (New York: Vintage Books, 1996).
3. A classic interpretation of this period remains Sheila Fitzpatrick, *The Russian Revolution*, 2nd edn. (Oxford and New York: Oxford University Press, 1994). On the minority who made the Stalin Revolution see Lynne Viola, *The Best Sons of the Fatherland: Workers in the Vanguard of Soviet Collectivization* (New York and Oxford: Oxford University Press, 1987). On the participation of ordinary people in the ideological and practical project of Stalinism see Jochen Hellbeck, *Revolution on my Mind: Writing a Diary under Stalin* (Cambridge, Mass, and London: Harvard University Press, 2006).
4. On Stalinism as a revolutionary regime see Robert C. Tucker, 'Stalinism as Revolution from Above', in Tucker (ed.), *Stalinism: Essays in Historical Interpretation* (New York: W. W. Norton & Co., 1977), 77–108; Sheila Fitzpatrick (ed.), *Cultural Revolution in Russia, 1928–1931* (Bloomington, Ind.: Indiana University Press, 1978); Robert Service, *Stalin: A Biography* (Cambridge, Mass.: Harvard University Press, 2005). On the mass scale of the Great Purges see also Paul Hagenloh, ' "Socially Harmful Elements" and the Great Terror', in Sheila Fitzpatrick (ed.), *Stalinism: New Directions* (London and New York: Routledge, 2000), 286–308.
5. Moshe Lewin, 'The Social Background of Stalinism', in his *The Making of the Soviet System: Essays in the Social History of Interwar Russia*, 2nd edn. (New York: New Press, 1994), 258–85; for the term: p. 265.
6. On popular opinion in urban Russia before the war see Sarah Davies, *Popular Opinion in Stalin's Russia: Terror, Propaganda, and Dissent, 1934–1941* (Cambridge: Cambridge University Press, 1997). On peasant resentment and resistance see Sheila Fitzpatrick, *Stalin's Peasants: Resistance and Survival in the Russian Village after Collectivization* (New York and Oxford: Oxford University Press, 1994); and Lynne Viola, *Peasant Rebels under Stalin: Collectivization and the Culture of Peasant Resistance* (New York and Oxford: Oxford University Press, 1996). On the equivalent processes among workers see

Donald A. Filtzer, *Soviet Workers and Stalinist Industrialization: The Formation of Modern Soviet Production Relations 1928–1941* (Armonk, NY: M. E. Sharpe, 1986); and Jeffrey J. Rossman, *Worker Resistance under Stalin: Class and Revolution on the Shop Floor* (Cambridge, Mass., and London: Harvard University Press, 2005). On a different group of outcasts see Golfo Alexopoulos, *Stalin's Outcasts: Aliens, Citizens, and the Soviet State, 1926–1936* (Ithaca, NY: Cornell University Press, 2003).

7. Sheila Fitzpatrick, 'War and Society in Soviet Context: Soviet Labor before, during, and after World War II', *International Labor and Working-Class History*, 35 (Spring 1989): 37–52.

8. For a sophisticated and non-reductive analysis of Soviet totalitarianism see Raymond A. Bauer, Alex Inkeles, and Clyde Kluckhohn, *How the Soviet System Works: Cultural, Psychological, and Social Themes* (Cambridge, Mass.: Harvard University Press, 1956); Alex Inkeles and Raymond Bauer, *The Soviet Citizen: Daily Life in a Totalitarian Society* (Cambridge, Mass.: Harvard University Press, 1961).

9. Janos Kornai, *The Economics of Shortage*, 2 vols. (Amsterdam: North-Holland Publishing Co., 1980); Alena Ledeneva, *Russia's Economy of Favours: Blat, Networking and Informal Exchange* (Cambridge: Cambridge University Press, 1998); Elena Osokina, *Za fasadom 'Stalinskogo izobiliia': Raspredelenie i rynok v snabzhenii naseleniia v gody industrializatsii 1927–1941* (Moscow: Rosspen, 1999); id., *Our Daily Bread: Socialist Distribution and the Art of Survival in Stalin's Russia, 1927–1941*, tr. Kate Transchel and Greta Bucher (Armonk, NY, and London: M. E. Sharpe, 2001); Sheila Fitzpatrick, *Everyday Stalinism: Ordinary Life in Extraordinary Times. Soviet Russia in the 1930s* (New York and Oxford: Oxford University Press, 1999), 40–66; Julie Hessler, *A Social History of Soviet Trade: Trade Policy, Retail Practices, and Consumption, 1917–1953* (Princeton and Oxford: Princeton University Press, 2004); and Jean-Paul Depretto, 'Stratification without Class', *Kritika: Explorations in Russian and Eurasian History*, 8/2 (2007): 375–88.

10. Richard Stites (ed.), *Culture and Entertainment in Wartime Russia* (Bloomington and Indianapolis: Indiana University Press, 1995).

11. The best introduction remains David M. Glantz and Jonathan House, *When Titans Clashed: How the Red Army Stopped Hitler* (Lawrence, Kan.: University Press of Kansas, 1995). On the Soviet home front see John Barber and Mark Harrison, *The Soviet Home Front, 1941–1945: A Social and Economic History of the USSR in World War II* (London and New York: Longman, 1991). On the occupied territories see Karel C. Berkhoff, *Harvest of Despair: Life and Death in Ukraine under Nazi Rule* (Cambridge and London: Belknap Press of Harvard University Press, 2004). For an overview of the large literature on the German conduct of war see Rolf-Dieter Müller and Gerd R. Ueberschär, *Hitlers Krieg im Osten 1941–1945: Ein Forschungsbericht* (Darmstadt: Wissenschaftliche Buchgesellschaft, 2000).

12. G. F. Krivosheev and M. F. Filimoshin, 'Poteri vooruzhennykh sil SSSR v Velikoi Otechestvennoi voine', in V. B. Zhiromskaia (ed.), *Naselenie Rossii v xx veke. Istoricheskie ocherki*, ii. *1940–1959* (Moscow: Rosspen, 2001), 25. Partisan numbers are notoriously hard to establish. The Central Staff of the Partisan Movement registered as few as 69,705 active fighters in June 1942 and as many as 138,889 in early 1944. Kenneth Slepyan, *Stalin's Guerrillas: Soviet Partisans in World War II* (Lawrence, Kan.: University Press of Kansas, 2006), 51.

13. On the experience of ordinary soldiers see Catherine Merridale, *Ivan's War: Life and Death in the Red Army, 1939–1945* (New York: Metropolitan Books, 2006); on irregulars see Slepyan, *Stalin's Guerrillas*.

14. Michael Ellman and S. Maksudov, 'Soviet Deaths in the Great Patriotic War: A Note', *Europe–Asia Studies*, 46/4 (1994): 671–80.

15. G. F. Krivosheev, *Soviet Casualties and Combat Losses in the Twentieth Century* (London: Greenhill Books, 1997), 92.

16. A. A. Friedrich, 'Veterans', *Encyclopaedia of the Social Sciences* (New York: Macmillan Co., 1935), 243–47.

17. Gerhard L. Weinberg, *A World at Arms: A Global History of World War II* (New York and Cambridge: Cambridge University Press, 1994), 894.

18. V. A. Pron'ko, 'Voina, narod, pobeda: vzgliad skvoz' gody', in V. A. Zolotarev et al. (eds.), *Velikaia Otechestvennaia voina 1941–1945*, iv *Narod i voina* (Moscow: Nauka, 1999), 294.

19. Elena Zubkova, *Russia after the War: Hopes, Illusions, and Disappointments, 1945–1957*, tr. Hugh Ragsdale (Armonk, NY, and London: M. E. Sharpe, 1998); Kees Boterbloem, *Life and Death under Stalin: Kalinin Province* (Montreal: McGill-Queens Press, 1999); Julie Hessler, 'A Postwar Perestroika? Toward a History of Private Trade Enterprise in the USSR', *Slavic Review*, 57/3 (1998): 516–42; Donald Filtzer, *Soviet Workers and Late Stalinism: Labour and the Restoration of the Stalinist System after World War II* (Cambridge: Cambridge University Press, 2002); Mark Edele, 'More than just Stalinists: The Political Sentiments of Victors 1945–1953', in Juliane Fürst (ed.), *Late Stalinist Russia: Society between Reconstruction and Reinvention* (London and New York: Routledge, 2006), 167–91.

20. Nina Tumarkin, *The Living and the Dead: The Rise and Fall of the Cult of World War II in Russia* (New York: Basic Books, 1994); Bernd Bonwetsch, ' "Ich habe an einem völlig anderen Krieg teilgenommen": Die Erinnerung an den "Großen Vaterländischen Krieg" in der Sowjetunion', in Helmut Berding, Klaus Heller, and Winfried Speitkamp (eds.), *Krieg und Erinnerung. Fallstudien zum 19. und 20. Jahrhundert* (Göttingen: Vandenhoeck & Ruprecht, 2000), 145–68; Amir Weiner, *Making Sense of War: The Second World War and the Fate of the Bolshevik Revolution* (Princeton and Oxford: Princeton University Press, 2000); Beate Fieseler, *Die Invaliden des 'Grossen Vaterländischen Krieges'*

*der Soujetunion: Eine politische Sozialgeschichte 1941–1991*, Habilitationsschrift (Ruhr-Universität Bochum, 2003), 456–68; Lisa A. Kirschenbaum, *The Legacy of the Siege of Leningrad, 1941–1995: Myth, Memories, and Monuments* (Cambridge and New York: Cambridge University Press, 2006); Denise J. Youngblood, *Russian War Films: On the Cinema Front, 1914–2005* (Lawrence, Kan.: University Press of Kansas, 2007).

21. Tumarkin, *The Living and the Dead*, 100, 134. 'War-Hero-in-Chief' is Denise Youngblood's term. See her, *Russian War Films*, 95.

22. Amir Weiner, 'The Making of a Dominant Myth: The Second World War and the Construction of Political Identities within the Soviet Polity', *Russian Review*, 55 (1996); id., *Making Sense of War*, 20–1, 49–70.

23. Petr Pavlenko, *Schast'e: Roman* (Moscow: Pravda, 1947).

24. Nikolai Mitrokhin, *Russkaia Partiia: Dvizhenie russkikh natsionalistov v SSSR 1953–1985* (Moscow: Novoe literaturnoe obozrenie, 2003), 141–68; Peter Vail' and Aleksandr Genis, *60-e: Mir sovetskogo cheloveka*, 3rd edn. (Moscow: Novoe literaturnoe obozrenie, 2001), 88–96.

25. On Nekrasov see Wolfgang Kasack, *Lexikon der russischen Literatur des 20. Jahrhunderts: Vom Beginn des Jahrhunderts bis zum Ende der Sowjetära*, 2nd edn. (Munich: Sagner, 1992), 817–19; L. I. Lazarev, 'Nekrasov Viktor Platonovich', in P. A. Nikolaev (ed.), *Russkie pisateli 20 veka: Biograficheskii slovar'* (Moscow: Bol'shaia Rossiiskaia Entsiklopediia, 2000), 492–3.

26. Viktor Nekrasov, 'V rodnom gorode', *Izbrannye proizvedeniia: Povesti, rasskazy, putevye zametki* (Moscow: Khudozhestvennaia literatura, 1962), 248–470; first published: *Novyi mir*, 10 (Oct. 1954), 3–65; 11 (Nov. 1954), 97–178; Iurii Bondarev, *Tishina: Roman* (Moscow: Sovetskii pisatel', 1962), first published: *Novyi mir*, 3 (Mar. 1962), 3–43; 4 (Apr. 1962), 64–135; 5 (May 1962), 43–92.

27. Grigorii Chukhrai, *Ballada o soldate* (Mosfil'm, 1959); *Chistoe nebo* (Mosfil'm, 1961).

28. Tumarkin, *The Living and the Dead*, 110–13; Lars Karl, 'Von Helden und Menschen: Der Zweite Weltkrieg im sowjetischen Spielfilm (1941–1965)', *Osteuropa*, 1 (2002): 67–82; Youngblood, *Russian War Films*, 107–41.

29. Wolfgang Kasack, *Deutsche Literatur des 20. Jahrhunderts in russischen Übersetzungen: Historischer Überblick. Bibliographie 1945–1990* (Mainz: Liber Verlag, 1991), 12–15, 54, 57, 58, 60, 62, 65, 67, 82, 83, 92, 94, 96, 98, 102, 105, 111, 118, 122, 123, 128, 132; and A. A. Surkov (ed.), *Kratkaia literaturnaia entsiklopediia*, 9 vols., vi (Moscow: Sovetskaia entsiklopediia, 1971), 247–50, esp. 249. Many thanks to June Farris for bibliographical help regarding this question.

30. Iurii Idashkin, 'No esli zadumat'sia …', *Oktiabr'*, 9 (1962): 212–13; V. Gusarov, 'Uspekh ili neudacha', *Zvezda*, 9 (1962): 209–11.

31. Tumarkin, *The Living and the Dead*, 110–13.

32. Fieseler, *Die Invaliden des 'Grossen Vaterländischen Krieges'*, 458–9.

33. Youngblood, *Russian War Films*, esp. ch. 7.

34. 'Religion of war' is Russian film critic Aleksandr Shpagin's term. Quoted by Youngblood, *Russian War Films*, 231–2.

35. Weiner, *Making Sense of War*.

36. KGB chairman V. Semichastnyi to Central Committee (11 May 1965), No. 1025-s, Rossiiskii gosudarstvennyi arkhiv noveishei istorii (hereafter: RGANI) f. 5, op. 30, d. 462, l. 38–43 [unsigned report from Leningrad, 12 May 1965]; d. 462, l. 45; report by head of sector for letters in the General Department of the CC B. Nikolaev on letters in connection with the anniversary celebrations (22 May 1965) RGANI f. 5, op. 30, d. 462, l. 59–64.

37. L. I. Brezhnev, *Leninskim kursom: Rechi i stat'i*, i (Moscow: Politicheskaia literatura, 1970), 118–55; for Stalin: 124, 130.

38. V. S. Nechaev, 'Sila veteranakh—v edinenii', *Veteran*, 31 (320) (Oct. 1994), 1; and GARF f. r-9541, op. 1, d. 1505, l. 176; Mark Edele, 'Soviet Veterans as an Entitlement Group, 1945–1955', *Slavic Review*, 65/1 (2006): 120, table 2. For an overview of different estimates of the population after the war see id., 'A "Generation of Victors?" Soviet Second World War Veterans from Demobilization to Organization 1941–1956' (Ph.D. diss., University of Chicago, 2004), 581 (app. 3).

39. Beate Fieseler, 'The Bitter Legacy of the "Great Patriotic War": Red Army Disabled Soldiers under Late Stalinism', in Juliane Fürst (ed.), *Late Stalinist Russia: Society between Reconstruction and Reinvention* (London and New York: Routledge, 2006), 46–61.

40. Edele, 'More than just Stalinists: The Political Sentiments of Victors 1945–1953', 167–91.

41. A good introduction is Pavel Polian, *Deportiert nach Hause: Sowjetische Kriegsgefangene im 'Dritten Reich' und ihre Repatriierung* (Munich and Vienna: Oldenbourg, 2001). For more literature on POWs see the notes in Ch. 5.

42. See Chs. 7 and 8.

43. Deborah Cohen, *The War Come Home: Disabled Veterans in Britain and Germany, 1914–1939* (Berkeley, Los Angeles, and London: University of California Press, 2001).

44. Theda Skocpol, 'The G.I. Bill and U.S. Social Policy, Past and Future', in Ellen F. Paul, Fred D. Miller, and Jeffrey Paul (eds.), *The Welfare State* (Cambridge: Cambridge University Press, 1997), 95–115; and Michael J. Bennett, *When Dreams Came True: The G.I. Bill and the Making of Modern America* (Washington, DC: Brassey's, 2000).

45. Cf. Elena Zubkova, *Russia after the War: Hopes, Illusions, and Disappointments, 1945–1957*, tr. Hugh Ragsdale (Armonk, NY, and London, 1998), 24–5.

46. Cf. Michael Geyer, 'Ein Vorbote des Wohlfahrtsstaates: Die Kriegsopferversorgung in Frankreich, Deutschland und Großbritannien nach dem Ersten Weltkrieg', *Geschichte und Gesellschaft*, 9 (1983): 230–77.

47. Antoine Prost, *Les Anciens Combattants et la société française: 1914–1939*, 3 vols. (Paris: Presses de la Fondation nationale des sciences politiques, 1977).

48. Prost, *Les Anciens Combattants*, i. *Histoire*, 2.

49. The term 'imagined community' is, of course, Benedict Anderson's. See his *Imagined Communities: Reflections on the Origins and Spread of Nationalism*. rev. edn. (London and New York: Verso, 1991).

50. Edele, 'Soviet Veterans as an Entitlement Group', 111–37.

51. Karl Mannheim, 'The Problem of Generations', in Paul Kecskemeti (ed.), *Essays in the Sociology of Knowledge* (London: Routledge & Kegan Paul, 1964), 276–320.

52. For the complications of generational analysis even in this case see the very subtle discussion in Robert Wohl, *The Generation of 1914* (Cambridge, Mass.: Harvard University Press, 1979), esp. 203–37.

53. E. S. Seniavskaia, *1941–1945: Frontovoe pokolenie. Istoriko-psikhologicheskoe issledovanie* (Moscow: RAN institut Rossiiskoi istorii, 1995); Catherine Merridale, *Ivan's War*.

54. G. F. Krivosheev, 'Poteri vooruzhennykh sil SSSR', *Liudskie poteri SSSR v period vtoroi mirovoi voiny. Sbornik statei*, ed. Rostislav Evdokimov (St Petersburg: Blits, 1995), 78.

55. Merridale, *Ivan's War*, 338.

56. Some historians even count four. See V. F. Zima, *Mentalitet narodov Rossii v voine 1941–1945 godov* (Moscow: RAN institut Rossiiskoi istorii, 2000), 22.

57. Zubkova, *Russia After the War*, 23.

58. Viktor Platonovich Nekrasov, 'V rodnom gorode', 284–5.

59. Cf. Zubkova, *Russia After the War*, 23; Seniavskaia, *1941–1945*, 32 and *passim*.

60. See e.g. the voluminous reports on demobilization to the CC administration for control of party organs (*Upravlenie po proverke partorganov*) in 1945 and 1946: Rossiiskii gosudarstvennyi arkhiv sotsial'no-politicheskoi istorii (RGASPI) f. 17, op. 122, d. 102 (1945, 274 pp.); d. 145 (Jan. to Mar. 1946; 196 pages); d. 146 (Jan.–July 1946, 208 pp.).

61. See Ch. 6.

62. This generation, i.e. men born between 1890 and 1904, was mobilized in Aug. 1941. Seniavskaia, *1941–1945*, 77.

63. Cf. Boris Potapovich Pavlov (ed.), *Veterany v stroiu* (Moscow: Voenizdat, 1981), 13–14, 19–21; Iosif Prut, *Nepoddaiushchiisia o mnogikh drugikh i koe-chto o sebe* (Moscow: Vagrius, 2000), 25 (quotation) and *passim*.

64. On Lieutenants' prose see Vail' and Genis, *60-e. Mir Sovetskogo cheloveka*, 91–2, 94–6. Victory posters typically depict young, beaming veterans,

frequently with battle decorations on their chests. See e.g. V. Ivanov, 'Ty vernul nam zhizn'' (1943); id., 'Tak ono i budet' (1945); A. Kokorekin, 'Voinu-pobediteliu—vsenarodnaia liubov'' (1944); L. Golovanov, 'Krasnoi Armii—slava!' (1946). All reprinted in G. Demosfenova et al. (eds.), Sovetskii politicheskii plakat (Moscow: Iskustvo,1962), 371, 372, 374, 382.

65. The two main statistical reconstructions are Evgenii Mikhailovich Andreev et al., Naselenie Sovetskogo Soiuza: 1922–1991 (Moscow: Nauka, 1993); and V. S. Gel'fand, Naselenie SSSR za 50 let (1941–1990): Statisticheskii sbornik (Perm': Izd-vo Permskogo universiteta, 1992). They need to be used carefully. For one, these data are statistical reconstructions on the basis of the prewar censuses of 1937 and 1939, the postwar census of 1959, some incomplete postwar demographic data, and a lot of computation and conjecture. Secondly, the cohorts of these reconstructions refer to all males presumed alive after the war, which leads to two sources of inaccuracy: it ignores the minority of women among veterans, and it includes men who did not serve in the armed forces during the war. As inaccurate as they may be, these data are one of the few statistical orientations we have.

66. Edele, 'Soviet Veterans as an Entitlement Group', 117 (with footnotes guiding to the relevant literature).

67. Decree of Presidium of Supreme Soviet of 25 September 1945, Vedomosti Verkhovnogo Soveta SSSR, no. 69 (3 Oct. 1945), 1.

68. See Ch. 1.

69. V. N. Donchenko, 'Demobilizatsiia Sovetskoi armii i reshenie problem kadrov v pervye poslevoennye gody', Istoriia SSSR, 3 (1970): 96–106, here 98.

70. 'New social entity' (novyi sotsium) is Elena Zubkova's term. See her Poslevoennoe sovetskoe obshchestvo: Politika i povsednevnost' 1945–1953 (Moscow: Rosspen, 2000), 28–36.

71. For a framework to think about the Soviet state as part of society see Mark Edele, 'Soviet Society, Social Structure, and Everyday Life: Major Frameworks Reconsidered', Kritika: Explorations in Russian and Eurasian History, 8/2 (2007): 349–73.

72. Stephen Lovell, 'Soviet Russia's Older Generations', in Lovell (ed.), Generations in Twentieth-Century Europe (Houndsmills, Basingstoke: Palgrave Macmillan, 2007), 205–26; here 221.

73. Cf. Lovell, 'Soviet Russia's Older Generations', 214–23.

74. Sheila Fitzpatrick, 'Ascribing Class: The Construction of Social Identity in Soviet Russia', Journal of Modern History, 65 (1993): 745–70; Terry Martin, 'Modernization or Neo-Traditionalism? Ascribed Nationality and Soviet Primordialism', in Sheila Fitzpatrick (ed.), Stalinism: New Directions (London and New York: Routledge, 2000), 348–67.

75. On the service principle and service classes in Russian history see V. O. Kliuchevskii, Russkaia istoriia: polnyi kurs lektsii, 3 vols. (Rostov-on-Don:

Feniks, 2000); Richard Hellie, 'The Structure of Modern Russian History: Toward a Dynamic Model', *Russian History*, 4/1 (1977): 1–22.

76. Jeffrey Brooks, *Thank You Comrade Stalin! Soviet Public Culture from Revolution to Cold War* (Princeton: Princeton University Press, 2000).

77. Cf. Vera S. Dunham, *In Stalin's Time: Middleclass Values in Soviet Fiction*, enlarged and updated edn. (Durham, NC, and London: Duke University Press, 1990).

78. P. Batov, 'Sovetskie veterany voiny v bor'be za mir', *Voenno-istoricheskii zhurnal*, 6 (1979): 71–5, here 75.

79. For the creation of status groups as a result of the implementation of Bolshevik ideology see Fitzpatrick, 'Ascribing Class: The Construction of Social Identity in Soviet Russia'. See also the expanded discussion in id., *Tear Off the Masks! Identity and Imposture in Twentieth-Century Russia* (Princeton and Oxford: Princeton University Press, 2005), chs. 2–4.

80. Roger Pethybridge, *The Social Prelude to Stalinism* (London and Basingstoke: Macmillan, 1974), 73–131; Sheila Fitzpatrick, 'The Civil War as a Formative Experience', in Abbott Gleason, Peter Kenez, and Richard Stites (eds.), *Bolshevik Culture: Experience and Order in the Russian Revolution* (Bloomington: Indiana University Press, 1985); Peter Holquist, *Making War, Forging Revolution: Russia's Continuum of Crisis, 1914–1921* (Cambridge, Mass., and London: Harvard University Press, 2002).

81. Joshua A. Sanborn, *Drafting the Russian Nation: Military Conscription, Total War, and Mass Politics, 1905–1925* (DeKalb, Ill.: Northern Illinois University Press, 2003).

82. Melissa K. Stockdale, 'United in Gratitude: Honoring Soldiers and Defining the Nation in Russia's Great War', *Kritika. Explorations in Russian and Eurasian History*, 7/3 (2006): 459–85.

83. Mark von Hagen, *Soldiers in the Proletarian Dictatorship: The Red Army and the Soviet Socialist State, 1917–1930* (Ithaca, NY, and London: Cornell University Press, 1990).

84. E. S. Seniavskaia, *Psikhologiia voiny v xx veke: Istoricheskii opyt Rossii* (Moscow: Rosspen, 1999), 3–4.

## CHAPTER I

1. 'Leningrad gotovitsia k vstreche demobilizovannykh voinov', *Krasnaia zvezda*, 6 July 1945, p. 3.

2. For an account of demobilization as a well-controlled process see V. N. Donchenko, 'Demobilizatsiia Sovetskoi Armii i reshenie problem kadrov v pervye poslevoennye gody', *Istoriia SSSR*, 3 (1970): 96–106; for an account stressing the agency of the demobilized soldiers over controls see Sheila Fitzpatrick, 'Postwar Soviet Society: The "Return to Normalcy",

1945–1953', in Susan J. Linz (ed.), *The Impact of World War II on the Soviet Union* (Totowa, NJ: Rowman & Allanhead, 1985), 129–56, esp. 135–6. For a recent archive-based account see Catherine Merridale, *Ivan's War: Life and Death in the Red Army, 1939–1945* (New York: Metropolitan Books, 2006), 336–71.

3. G. F. Krivosheev and M. F. Filimoshin, 'Poteri vooruzhennykh sil SSSR v Velikoi Otechestvennoi voine', *Naselenie Rossii v XX veke. Istoricheskie ocherki*, ii. *1940–1959* (Moscow: Rosspen, 2001), 26; and G. F. Krivosheev, *Soviet Casualties and Combat Losses in the Twentieth Century* (London: Greenhill Books, 1997), 92.

4. Krivosheev, *Soviet Casualties*, 91.

5. See the discussion in Mark Edele, 'A "Generation of Victors?" Soviet Second World War Veterans from Demobilization to Organization 1941–1956', (Ph.D. diss., University of Chicago, 2004), 69–71.

6. Historians generally agree that the total number of demobilized soldiers between the end of 1945 and somewhere in 1948 was roughly 8.5 million, often without citing a primary source. It appears that this number goes back to a speech given by Khrushchev, in which he noted that by May 1945 the armed forces contained 11.365 million people and 'towards 1948' (*k 1948 godu*) the number had fallen thanks to demobilization to 2.874 million (*Pravda*, 15 Jan. 1960, pp. 1–5, here 3). The difference of roughly 8.5 million cannot be equal to the number of demobilized soldiers. Many more must have been demobilized during 1945 and the end of 1948 because during this time new recruits were drafted into the army and the 1948 number must include these draftees.

7. See Ch. 5.

8. F. Bykov to Malenkov, Rossiiskii gosudarstvennyi arkhiv sotsial'no-politi-cheskoi istorii (RGASPI)f. 17, op. 122, d. 44, l. 4–5.

9. Such demobilization happened according to individual petitions by enterprises. It was systematized in SNK resolution of 13 Sept. 1945, no. 2346-605s. Gosudarstvennyi Arkhiv Rossiiskoi Federatsii (hereafter: GARF) f. r-5446, op. 47a, d. 3705, l. 83–81. On the return of specialists see e.g. N. Shvernik to N. A. Voznesenskii (12 Dec. 1945), GARF f. r-9517, op. 1, d. 52, l. 38. For individual examples see RGASPI f. 17, op. 125, d. 397.

10. Grigorii Chukhrai, *Moia voina* (Moscow: Algoritm, 2001), 296–7.

11. B. Volin to Malenkov (11 Sept. 1945), RGASPI f. 17, op. 125, d. 310, l. 36–9.

12. I. Kuz'min to Malenkov on reception of and help for demobilized soldiers in the countryside (22 Aug. 1945) RGASPI f. 17, op. 122, d. 102, l. 138–42, here 140.

13. Peter Pirogov, *Why I Escaped: The Story of Peter Pirogov* (New York: Duell, Sloan & Pearce, 1950), 235.

14. V. V. Kovanov, *Prizvanie* (Moscow: Politicheskaia literatura, 1970), 245–6. Thanks to Chris Burton for bringing this memoir to my attention.

15. 'Vsenarodnaia zabota o demobilizovannykh voinakh', *Krasnaia zvezda*, 10 July 1945, p. 1.

16. e.g. *Krasnaia zvezda*, 18 July 1945, p. 3; 6 July 1945, p. 3; 20 July 1945, p.1; 8 July 1945, p.1; 20 July 1945, p. 22 July 1945, p. 3; 27 July 1945, p. 1. *Bloknot agitatora Krasnoi armii*, 21 (June 1945), 27–30.

17. KPK plenipotentiary for Uzbekistan to Malenkov, report about implementation of demobilization law, 24 Aug. 1945g., RGASPI f. 17, op. 122, d. 102, l. 96–104, here 96–7.

18. See the photo in *Krasnaia zvezda*, 25 July 1945, p. 1; and Merridale, *Ivan's War*, 356.

19. Mikhail Tanich, *Igrala muzyka v sadu* ... (Moscow: Vagrius, 2000), 253–4.

20. L. Beriia to Molotov, Malenkov, Bulganin, Antonov (27 Oct. 1945) GARF f. r-9401, op. 2, d. 104, l. 283–4.

21. Head of NKVD of Kalinin oblast' Pavlov to L. P Beriia (10 Nov. 1945) [forwarded to Molotov], GARF f. r-9401, op. 2, d. 105, l. 3–4.

22. Head of main administration of the militia within the NKVD Galkin to Beria (12 Dec. 1945), GARF f. r-9401, op. 2, d. 105, l. 367–8.

23. I. Kuz'min to Malenkov, report on reception of demobilized soldiers and help in re-establishment in everyday life in countryside, 22 Aug. 1945, RGASPI f. 17, op. 122, d. 102, l. 138–42, here 140.

24. Short report on letters received by *Red Star* in July 1946, RGASPI f. 17, op. 125, d. 429, l. 138–62, here 157.

25. Ibid.

26. Komi Obkom Sekretary Ignatov on execution of CC resolution of 25 Aug. 1945 on help to demobilized soldiers, 30 Oct. 1945, RGASPI f. 17, op. 122, d. 102, l. 193–200, here 197.

27. Telegram of Iakutsk obkom secretary Maslennikov to Malenkov, 11 Oct. 1945, RGASPI f. 17, op. 122, d. 102, l. 126–7, here 126.

28. Telegram of Iakutsk obkom secretary Maslennikov to Malenkov, 20 Nov. 1945, RGASPI f. 17, op. 122, d. 102, l. 245.

29. Iakutsk obkom secretary Maslennikov to Malenkov, report on executen of CC resolution of 25 Aug. 1945, 31 Jan. 1946, RGASPI f. 17, op. 122, d. 145, l. 132–5, here 133.

30. Telegram of Tiumen obkom secretary Chubarov to Malenkov, 13 Nov. 1945, RGASPI f. 17, op. 122, d. 102, l. 216.

31. Astakhov to Malenkv (16 Nov. 1945), RGASPI f. 17, op. 122, d. 102, l. 217.

32. Head of dept of organization and instruction in the CC Shamberg to Malenkov, 4 Dec. 1945, RGASPI f. 17, op. 122, d. 102, l. 218.

33. Svetlana Alexiyevich, *War's Unwomanly Face*, tr. Keith Hammond and Lyudmila Lezhneva (Moscow: Progress Publishers, 1988), 19.

34. Report to Stalin, Molotov, Mikoian on returning soldiers and repatriates selling things in Polish border towns, 10 July 1945, GARF f. r-9401, op. 2, d. 97, l. 323.

35. See draft of Council of Ministers Resolution of June 1949, GARF f. r-9401, op. 2, d. 235, l. 245–6.

36. KPK plenipotentiary for Uzbekistan V. Tatarintsev to Malenkov, 21 Oct. 1945, RGASPI f. 17, op. 122, 102, l. 143–4, here 143.

37. RGASPI f. 17, op. 122, 102, l. 143.

38. Chukhrai, *Moia voina*, 297.

39. Tanich, *Igrala muzyka v sadu*, 253–4.

40. Quoted in RGASPI f. 17, op. 125, d. 316, l. 96.

41. KPK plenipotentiary for Uzbekistan V. Tatarintsev to Malenkov, 21 Oct. 1945, RGASPI f. 17, op. 122, 102, l. 143–4, here 144; Julie Hessler, *A Social History of Soviet Trade: Trade Policy, Retail Practices, and Consumption, 1917–1953* (Princeton and Oxford: Princeton University Press, 2004), 249.

42. KPK plenipotantiary for Kazakhstan V. Kanareikin to Malenkov, on problems with reception and work placement of demobilized soldiers, 21 Sept. 1945, RGASPI f. 17, op. 122, d. 102, l. 110–11.

43. Krivosheev and Filimoshin, 'Poteri vooruzhennykh sil', 26.

44. See the discussion of the available (and inconclusive) statistical evidence in Edele, 'A "Generation of Victors"?', 56–7.

45. Jan T. Gross, *Revolution from Abroad: The Soviet Conquest of Poland's Western Ukraine and Western Belorussia*, expanded edn. (Princeton and Oxford: Princeton University Press, 2002), 29–50; see also Pirogov, *Why I Escaped*, 225.

46. Manfred Zeidler, *Kriegsende im Osten: Die Rote Armee und die Besetzung Deutschlands östlich von Oder und Neisse 1944/45* (Munich: R. Oldenburg Vlg., 1996), 135–67; Naimark, *The Russians in Germany*, 69–140, 145; Pirogov, *Why I Escaped*, 209–28; and E. Sherstianoi, 'Germaniia i nemtsy v pis'makh krasnoarmeitsev vesnoi 1945 g.', *Novaia i noveishaia istoriia*, 2 (2002): 137–51, here 144–5.

47. Sherstianoi, 'Germaniia i nemtsy v pis'makh krasnoarmeitsev vesnoi 1945 g.', 144.

48. KPK plenipotentiary for Uzbekistan V. Tatarintsev to Malenkov, 21 Oct. 1945, RGASPI f. 17, op. 122, 102, l. 144.

49. Deputy state prosecutor for Turkmenistan, report on results of checking of handling of military parcels, 28 Aug. 1945, GARF f. r-8131, op. 22, d. 93, l. 62–3.

50. Tanich, *Igrala muzyka v sadu*, 253.

51. A. S. Iakushevskii, 'Protivnik', in V. A. Zolotarev *et al.* (eds.), *Velikaia Otechestvennaia voina 1941–1945*, iv. *Narod i voina* (Moscow: Nauka, 1999), 241–80, here 271–2. See also Bernd Bonwetsch, 'Sowjetunion: Triumph im

Elend', in Ulrich Herbert and Axel Schildt (eds.), *Kriegsende in Europa: Vom Beginn des deutschen Machtzerfalls bis zur Stabilisierung der Nachkriegsordnung 1944–1948* (Essen: Klartext, 1998), 52–88, here 87.

52. R. G. Pikhoia, *Sovetskii Soiuz: Istoriia vlasti 1945–1991*, 2nd edn. (Novosibirsk: Sibirskii khronograf, 2000; orig. 1998), 41. On Zhukov see also Albert Axell, *Marshal Zhukov: The Man Who Beat Hitler* (London: Longman, 2003), 160.

53. Report of work of KPK party collegium between June 1939 and 1946, RGANI f. 6, op. 6, d. 3, here 57–8.

54. KPK plenipotentiary for Uzbekistan V. Tatarintsev to Malenkov, 21 Oct. 1945, RGASPI f. 17, op. 122, 102, l. 143–4, here 143.

55. Pirogov, *Why I Escaped*, 217.

56. KPK plenipotentiary for Uzbekistan V. Tatarintsev to Malenkov, 21 Oct. 1945, RGASPI f. 17, op. 122, 102, l. 143–4, here 144. See also report of Vladimir obkom secretary Pal'tsev to Malenkov on execution of CC Orgburo resolution of 25 Aug. 1945, 17 Nov. 1945, RGASPI f. 17, op. 122, d. 102, l. 232–7; here 233; and Groznyi obkom secretary Chepliakov to Malenkov on the same issue, 25 Oct. 1945, RGASPI f. 17, op. 122, d. 102, l. 133–70b, here 137.

57. Tanich, *Igrala muzyka v sadu*, 29.

58. Tsentr Dokumentatsii 'Narodnyi arkhiv', Kollektsiia 'moia zhizn'', fonodokumenty no. 227: Sakhonenko Tatiana Sergeevna [Kamenskaia]. Interv'iu. O zhizni v Moskve v 1940e gg (7.6.93 Moskva). Transcript: Panfilova Pavla Borisovicha, 'Kursovaia rabota. Nauchnaia publikatsiia. Interv'iu studenta IV kursa IAI RGGU Pafilova s Sokhanenko Tat'ianoi Sergeevnoi (urozhdennoi Kamenskoi) ob istorii svoei sem'i—Serovykh, Novikovykh, Kamenskikh.' Rossiiskoi Gosudarstvennoi Istoriko-arkhivnyi institut, 1993, p. 22; and Sherstianoi, 'Germaniia i nemtsy v pis'makh krasnoarmeitsev vesnoi 1945 g.', 145.

59. Seniavskaia, *1941–1945*, 91–2.

60. *Bloknot Agitatora vooruzhennykh sil*, 7 (1947): 12–19, here 14.

61. Zakon (23 June 1945) 'O demobilizatsii starshikh vozrastov lichnogo sostava Deistvuiushchei armii', *Vedomosti Verkhovnogo Soveta SSSR*, 36 (30 June 1945), p. 1.

62. The demobilization law of 23 June 1945, which defined these benefits, was published again and again, e.g. in *Vedomosti Verkhovnogo Soveta SSSR*, 36 (30 June 1945), p. 1; *Krasnaia zvezda*, 24 June 1945, p. 1; *Pravda*, 24 June 1945, p. 1; *Izvestiia*, 24 June 1945, p. 1; *Bloknot agitatora krasnoi armii*, 18 (June 1945): 25–7; and Glavnaia voennaia prokuratura Vooruzhennykh Sil SSSR (ed.), *Pamiatka demobilizovannym riadovym i serzhantam Krasnoi Armii*, 2nd enlarged edn. (Moscow: Voennoe Izdatel'stvo, 1946), 3–5. In addition, many articles appeared summarizing the law.

63. *Krasnaia zvezda*, 10 July 1945, p. 1.

64. *Krasnaia zvezda*, 13 July 1945, p. 3.

65. Cf. Jeffrey Brooks, *Thank You, Comrade Stalin! Soviet Public Culture from Revolution to Cold War* (Princeton: Princeton University Press, 2000), 199, 201.
66. *Bloknot agitatora Krasnoi armii*, 18 (June 1945): 28–33, here 31–2.
67. *Krasnaia zvezda*, 17 July 1945, p. 3.
68. For some examples see *Pravda*, 23 Dec. 1946, p. 2; 11 Jan. 1947, p. 3; 21 Oct. 1947, p. 2; 17 July 1946, p. 2; 14 Oct. 1947, p. 2; *Pravda*, 8 Jan. 1947, p. 3.
69. *Bloknot agitatora*, 20 (1945): 41–8, here 47.
70. *Bloknot agitatora Krasnoi armii*, 21 (June 1945): 1–6, here 5.
71. *Krasnaia zvezda*, 4 July 1945, p. 1.
72. *Krasnaia zvezda*, 17 July 1945, p. 3.
73. For a critique of the poor work of one of them see *Krasnaia zvezda*, 5 June 1945, p. 3.
74. See the KPK reports on reviews of local efforts contained in RGASPI f. 17, op. 122, d. 102.
75. *Bloknot agitatora Krasnoi armii*, 1 (Jan. 1945): 31–3, here 31. Chukhrai's *Ballada o soldate* also includes a scene where frontline papers go up in smoke.
76. *Bloknot agitatora Krasnoi armii*, 30 (Oct. 1945): 25–6.
77. *Bloknot agitatora vooruzhennykh sil*, 30 (1947): 27–31, here 28.

CHAPTER 2

1. Cf. Elena Zubkova, *Russia After the War: Hopes, Illusions, and Disappointments, 1945–1957*, tr. Hugh Ragsdale (Armonk, NY, and London: M. E. Sharpe, 1998).
2. Mark Edele, 'More than just Stalinists: The Political Sentiments of Victors 1945–1953', in Juliane Fürst (ed.), *Late Stalinist Russia: Society between Reconstruction and Reinvention* (London and New York: Routledge, 2006), 169.
3. Leonard Schapiro, *The Communist Party of the Soviet Union* (New York: Vintage Books, 1964), 511; Zukoba, *Russia after the War*, 60–2; and Jean Lévesque, ' "Part-Time Peasants": Labour Discipline, Collective Farm Life, and the Fate of Soviet Socialized Agriculture after the Second World War, 1945–1953', (Ph.D. diss., University of Toronto, 2003), 52.
4. Zubkova, *Russia After the War*, chs. 6–10, 12, 13; Robert Service, *Stalin: A Biography* (Cambridge, Mass.: Harvard University Press, 2005), 485–500; Julie Hessler, 'A Postwar Perestoika? Toward a History of Private Trade Enterprise in the USSR', *Slavic Review*, 57/3 (1998): 516–42; O. M. Verbitskaia, *Rossiiskoe krest'ianstvo:Oot Stalina k Khrushchevu* (Moscow: Nauka, 1992); and Lévesque, 'Part-Time Peasants'.
5. Service, *Stalin*, 498.
6. On everyday life in the 1930s see Sheila Fitzpatrick. *Everyday Stalinism: Ordinary Life in Extraordinary Times. Soviet Russia in the 1930s* (New York and Oxford: Oxford University Press, 1999); on the return to Stalinist normalcy

see Sheila Fitzpatrick, 'Postwar Soviet Society: The "Return to Normalcy",
1945–1953', in Susan J. Linz (ed.), *The Impact of World War II on the Soviet
Union* (Totowa, NJ: Rowman & Allanhead, 1985), 129–56.

7. For a comparison of the situation in the rest of Europe see Greta Bucher,
*Women, the Bureaucracy and Daily Life in Postwar Moscow, 1945–1953* (Boulder,
Colo.: East European Monographs, 2006), 3–6. On the famine see V. F.
Zima, *Golod v SSSR 1946–1947 godov: Proiskhozhdenie i posledstviia* (Moscow:
Institut Rossiiskoi istorii RAN, 1996); Michael Ellman, 'The 1947 Soviet
Famine and the Entitlement Approach to Famines', *Cambridge Journal of
Economics*, 24/5 (2000): 603–30; and Zubkova, *Russia After the War*, ch. 4.
On the ruling circle after the war see Yoram Gorlizki and Oleg Khlevniuk,
*Cold Peace: Stalin and the Soviet Ruling Circle, 1945–1953* (Oxford and New
York: Oxford University Press, 2004).

8. On written supplications see Sheila Fitzpatrick, 'Supplicants and Citizens:
Public Letter-Writing in Soviet Russia in the 1930s', *Slavic Review*, 55/1
(1996): 78–105; 'Petitions and Denunciations in Russian and Soviet History',
*Russian History/Histoire Russe*, 24/1–2 (1997): 1–9. On personal petitioning
see her 'The World of Ostap Bender: Soviet Confidence Men in the Stalin
Period', *Slavic Review*, 61/3 (2002): esp. 547. One of the first authors to
systematically discuss letter writing as a systemic feature of the Soviet system
was Alex Inkeles, *Public Opinion in Soviet Russia: A Study in Mass Persuasion*
(Cambridge, Mass.: Harvard University Press, 1967), 109–203, 207–15.

9. Archive of Social Organizations of Voronezh Region (TsDOOSO) f. 4,
op. 31, d. 728, l. 10.

10. Report on work of state prosecutor's office of Kazakhstan, 15 Nov. 1945,
GARF f. r-8131, op. 22, d. 97, l. 172–88, here 172, 178.

11. Handwritten letter to State prosecutor of SU (10 July 1945), GARF f. r-8131,
op. 22, d. 5, l. 213–213ob: here 213.

12. GARF f. r-8131, op. 22, d. 5, l. 214, 216.

13. Savel'ev, report on letters from Ukraine, 18 June 1946, GARF f. r-7523,
op. 55, d. 10, l. 78–89, here 87.

14. Report of KPK plenipotentiary for Chuvash republic, A. Nekipelov on
problems with reacting to complaints (11 Apr. 1946), RGASPI f. 17, op. 122,
d. 148, l. 12–14, here l. 14.

15. RGASPI 17-125-616, l. 69–70.

16. State prosecutor for Azerbaidzhan on implementation of demobilization law,
August 1945, GARF f. r-8131, op. 22, d. 97, l. 2–4, here l. 4.

17. KPK plenipotentiary of Kalinin oblast reporting on problems with reacting to
complaints, 18 Apr. 1946, RGASPI f. 17, op. 122, d. 148, l. 28–35, here 28–9.

18. Report on work of social welfare organs of RSFSR on work with war
invalids (28 Jan. 1950), GARF f. r-5451, op. 29, d. 457, l. 182–97, here 195.

19. KPK plenipotentiary of Kalinin oblast reporting on problems with reacting to
complaints, 18 Apr. 1946, RGASPI f. 17, op. 122, d. 148, l. 28–35, here 31.

20. Report of Savel'ev on work of the office with complaints, 16 Feb. 1948, GARF f. r-7523, op. 55, d. 14, l. 122–47, here 132.

21. Report of Savel'ev on work of the office with complaints, 12 Jan. 1948, GARF f. r-7523, op. 55, d. 24, l. 2–33, here 9–10.

22. RGASPI f. 17, op. 122, d. 148, l. 32–4.

23. See the reports of the letter department of the newspaper GARF f. r-8131, op. 22, d. 5, l. 187–9,; 170–3, 266–8.

24. Fitzpatrick, 'World of Ostap Bender', 548–50.

25. Ibid. 549.

26. Ibid. 549–50.

27. See the data on personal supplications to Office of Presidium of Supreme Soviet in 1946: GARF f. r-7523, op. 55, d. 12, l. 3, 9, 15, 25, 30, 34, 44 (summarized in table 3.5 in Edele, 'A "Generation of Victors"?', 204).

28. GARF f. r-7523, op. 55, d. 14, l. 47–8 (from a report about the work of the office, 1947).

29. The material about this affair is collected in one file of the procuracy, titled 'Protest na otkaz zaveduiushchego Mosgorono o vosstanovlenii demobilizo-vannogo uchitel'ia Ozerova na rabote v shkole no. 4, st. Bykovo Leninskoi zhel. dor' (1–29 Mar. 1946), GARF f. r-8131, op. 23, d. 187.

30. SNK resolution of 28 July 1941, no. 1902, GARF f. r-5446, op. 1, d. 195, l. 60; published e.g. in *SP SSSR* 17 (1940). For the corresponding rights of demobilized see art. 7 of the demobilization law (23 June 1945), *Vedomosti Verkhovnogo Soveta SSSR*, no. 36 (30 June 1945), p. 1.

31. GARF f. r-8131, op. 23, d. 187, l. 1–6; for the letter itself: l. 1–2.

32. Ibid., l. 7.

33. Ibid., l. 8.

34. Kirovgradsk Gorkom Secretary Privalov to Head of Military Dept of Sverd-lovsk obkom (10 Oct. 1945), TsDOOSO f. 4, op. 31, d. 728, l. 73; and Gorkom Sekretary I. Matuzkov to Head of Military Dept of Sverdlovsk obkom Baskov (13 Dec. 1945), TsDOOSO f. 4, op. 31, d. 705, l. 198.

35. Gorkom Sekretary Nikitinskikh to Sverdlovsk obkom secretary Andrianov (Aug. 1945), TsDOOSO f. 4, op. 31, d. 704, l. 205.

36. Neviansk Raikom Secretary Igumnov to Sverdlovsk Obkom secretary Andri-anov (1945), TsDOOSO f. 4, 31, d. 704, l. 196; Head of Military Department Suetnikov to Sverdlovsk obkom secretary A. P. Panin, 'Spravka k spets-soobshcheniiu Upravleniia NKGB po Sverdlovskoi oblasti 'O zhalobakh invalidov Otechestvennoi voiny po materialam voennoi tsenzury' (8 Aug. 1945), TsDOOSO f. 4, op. 31, d. 704, l. 180–1.

37. e.g.: GARF f. r-9541, op. 1, d. 49, l. 13; GARF f. r-7523, op. 55, d. 10, l. 86; GARF f. r-9541, op. 1, d. 40, l. 29.

38. Report of KPK plenipotentiary for Chuvash republic, A. Nekipelov on problems with reacting to complaints, 11 Apr. 1946, RGASPI f. 17, op. 122, d. 148, l. 12–14, here 13.

39. RGASPI f. 17, op. 122, d. 148, l. 13.

40. On the centrality of flea markets during and after the war see Julie Hessler, *A Social History of Soviet Trade: Trade Policy, Retail Practices, and Consumption, 1917–1953* (Princeton and Oxford: Princeton University Press, 2004), ch. 6.

41. KPK plenipotentiary for Kostroma oblast', reporting on problems with reacting to complaints, 30 May 1946, RGASPI f. 17, op. 122, d. 148, l. 41–50, here 43–4.

42. State prosecutor of Moscow oblast' reporting on work regarding execution of demobilization law, 21 Aug. 1945, GARF f. r-8131, op, 22, d. 97, l. 267–71, here 268. This process already started during the war, on the basis of the legislation giving soldiers entitlements to their prewar housing space. For the work of the procuracy on this question see e.g. GARF f. r-8131, op. 20, d. 1, which holds cases for 1942 and 1943.

43. Deistvitel'nyi Gosudarstvennyi Sovetnik Iustitsii K. Gorshenin to State prosecutor of the Soviet Union Rudenko, 2 June 1945, GARF f. r-8131, op. 21, d. 5, l. 2.

44. See the case described by KPK plenipotentiary for Voroshilovgrad oblast', 13 Nov. 1946, RGASPI f. 17, op. 122, d. 148, l. 127–8.

45. For the description of the case see the answer of Abkhazian State Prosecutor Mamuliia to the telegram of the Soviet state prosecutor Gorshenin inquiring about the case (23 Aug. 1945), GARF f. r-8131, op. 22, d. 5, l. 197–8; for further details see also the original letter of complaint of Turkiia to the military procuracy of his naval base, ibid. l. 191, 191ob.

46. GARF f. r-8131, op. 22, d. 5, l. 192, 193, 196. As a result of the affair the acting chairman of the gorispolkom of Sukhumi Gokhokidze lost his job. See GARF f. r-8131, op. 22, d. 5, l. 203.

47. See the case described in Savel'ev's report on complaints from Belorussia, July 1948, GARF f. r-7523, op. 55, d. 20, l. 1–17, here 8.

48. Report of Ashkhabad state prosecutor Fateev, 2 Nov. 1945, GARF f. r-8131, op. 22, d. 93, l. 6–11, here 11.

49. Nekrasov, 'V rodnom gorode', 323–4.

50. Savel'ev reporting on complaints, 22 Feb. 1950, GARF f. r-7523, op. 55, d. 39, l. 12–21.

51. See e.g. the cases mentioned in the report of the Tula obkom secretary N. Chmutov to Malenkov (12 Nov. 1945), RGASPI f. 17, op. 122, d. 102, ll. 210–13, here: 210ob.

52. Hessler, *A Social History of Soviet Trade*, 271; and Ettore Vanni, *Io, Comunista in Russia* (Bologna, Cappelli Editore, 1949), 130–2. For privileges associated with decorations see Ch. 8.

53. Report to Patolichev (25 May 1946), RGASPI f. 17, op., 122, d. 192, l. 1.

54. Excerpt from protocol 574 of Gor'kii obkom meeting, of 18 Aug.1947, RGASPI f. 17, op. 122, d. 292, l. 6–60b.

55. Report on illegal acquisition of party card, 14 Aug. 1947, RGASPI f. 17, d. 122, l. 292, l. 8–80b, here 80b.

56. RGANI f. 77, op. 1, d. 3, l. 45–8, 125–8, 205–8; d.4, l. 45–8, 140–3; d. 5, l. 46–9, 139–42; d. 6, l. 46–9, 143–9; d. 7, l. 46–9, 142–5; d. 8, l. 46–9, 150–3. These data are summarized in chart 3.4 in Edele, 'A "Generation of Victors"?', 225.

57. Iudin to A. Suslov, 29 Aug. 1947, RGASPI f. 17, op. 122, d. 292, l. 11–12, here 12.

58. G. Borkov to Zhdanov and Kuznetsov (n.d.), RGASPI f. 17, op. 122, d. 292, l. 13–14, here 13.

59. See Paul Fussel, *Wartime: Understanding and Behavior in the Second World War* (New York and Oxford: Oxford University Press, 1989), esp. 79–95.

60. Handwritten letter to Prokuror SSSR (10 July 1945), GARF f. r-8131, op. 22, d. 5, l. 2130b.

61. On frontline nostalgia see Zubkova, *Russia After the War*, 28. The connection between red tape and frontline nostalgia is suggested by Viktor Platonovich Nekrasov, 'V rodnom gorode', in *Izbrannye proizvedeniia: Povesti, rasskazy, putevye zametki* (Moscow: Khudozhestvennaia literatura, 1962; orig. 1954), 248–470, here 323–6.

62. P. Savel'ev, Head of the office of Chairman of Presidium of Supreme Soviet, report on letters of complaint, July 1948, GARF f. 7523, op. 55, d. 20, l. 1–17, here 12.

63. Edele, 'More than just Stalinists', 180.

## CHAPTER 3

1. Mark Edele, 'Soviet Society, Social Structure, and Everyday Life: Major Frameworks Reconsidered', *Kritika: Explorations in Russian and Eurasian History*, 8/2 (2007): 349–73.

2. Raw data from report on work with demobilized soldiers in Moscow by 20 Nov. 1945, reprinted in *Moskva poslevoennaia 1945–1947: Arkhivnye dokumenty i materialy* (Moscow: Mosgorarkhiv, 2000), 321.

3. Greta Bucher, *Women, the Bureaucracy and Daily Life in Postwar Moscow, 1945–1953* (Boulder, Colo.: East European Monographs, 2006).

4. The pioneer of using Soviet novels as sources for unintended information about Soviet life was Vera Dunham. See her seminal *In Stalin's Time: Middleclass Values in Soviet Fiction*, enlarged and updated edn. (Durham, NC, and London: Duke University Press, 1990).

5. Savel'ev on petitions regarding debt from housing loans granted to war invalids and others, 14 Aug. 1946, GARF f. r-7523-55-10, l. 120–9, here 121.

6. Ibid., l. 122.

7. Ibid.

8. Ibid., l. 123.

9. Ibid., l. 124.

10. Savel'ev to Shvernik on complaints regarding ration cards received by office of chairman of Presidium of Supreme Soviet, 19 Nov. 1946, GARF f. r-7523, op. 55, d. 10, l. 131–46, here 140.

11. Ibid.

12. Bucher, *Women*, 118.

13. The archival record is full of examples of horrible living conditions. For one of them, see the report of the KPK plenipotentiary for Saratov region, on work with war invalids (29 Sept. 1945), reprinted in E. Iu. Zubkova et al. (eds.), *Sovetskaia zhizn' 1945–1953* (Moscow: Rosspen, 2003), 311–14, here 312.

14. KPK plenipotentiary for Uzbekistan Tatarintsev on execution of demobilization law, 24 Aug. 1945, RGASPI f. 17, op. 122, d. 102, l. 96–104, here 98.

15. P. Savel'ev, report on complaints from Ukraine, 18 June 1946, GARF f. r-7523, op. 55, d. 10, l. 78–89, here 87.

16. Chukhrai, *Moe kino*, 7.

17. KPK plenipotentiary for Tatar Republic, on everyday help and reintegration into production of demobilized soldiers, 11 Aug. 1945, RGASPI f. 17, op. 122, d. 102, l. 71–5, here 74.

18. See the case described in P. Savel'ev's information on petitions regarding debt on house-building loans to war invalids and families of fallen soldiers, 14 Aug. 1946, GARF f. r-7523, op. 55, d. 10, l. 120–9, here 121.

19. For a general and theoretical discussion of the importance of practices of reciprocal exchange and networking see Alena V. Ledeneva, *Russia's Economy of Favours: Blat, Networking and Informal Exchange* (New York and Cambridge: Cambridge University Press, 1998). For a discussion of reciprocal exchange circles (*blat*) in Stalinism see Sheila Fitzpatrick, 'Blat in Stalin's Time', in Stephen Lovell, Alena Ledeneva, and Andrei Rogachevskii (eds.), *Bribery and Blat in Russia: Negotiating Reciprocity from the Middle Ages to the 1990s* (New York: St Martin's Press, 2000), 166–82.

20. See e.g. the description of E. V. Gutnova's postwar circle of friends in her memoir *Perezhitoe* (Moscow: Rosspen, 2001), 249–53.

21. Zubkova, *Russia After the War*, 27–8.

22. Mikhail Tanich, *Igrala muzyka v sadu …* (Moscow: Vagrius, 2000), 8–9.

23. Iosif Prut, *Nepoddaiushchiisia o mnogikh drugikh i koe-chto o sebe* (Moscow: Vagrius, 2000), 312–15.

24. Personal communication with E.D., Moscow, 27 Sept. 2001. The informant kept contact with a wartime friend, but this did not entail more than writing or calling at Victory Day, since they lived in different parts of the Soviet Union.

25. See Ch. 7.

26. A. M. Samsonov, 'Iz istorii veteranov voiny (fragmenty)', *Istoriia SSSR* 2 (1985): 53−79, here: 54−5.

27. Tanich, *Igrala muzyka*, 257−8.

28. For more on veterans' networks see Ch. 7.

29. Aleksandr Gorodnitskii, *I zhit' eshche nadezhde ...* (Moscow: Vagrius, 2001), 82.

30. Vladimir Kabo, *The Road to Australia: Memoirs* (Canberra: Aboriginal Studies Press, 1998), 115−41.

31. See Mark Edele, 'More than just Stalinists: The Political Sentiments of Victors 1945−1953', in Juliane Fürst (ed.), *Late Stalinist Russia: Society between Reconstruction and Reinvention* (London and New York: Routledge, 2006), 167−91.

32. Chukhrai e.g. might have never become a movie director without the patronage of Mikhail Romm. Romm was a veteran of the Civil War, which might explain some of his support for the *frontovik* Chukhrai. More importantly, however, Romm was a major patron of promising young movie directors. On Romm's role in Chukhrai's career see Chukhrai, *Moe kino*, 35−54, esp. 49; on Romm as a commander of the Civil War, but not of the Second World War, ibid. 43; for a portrait of Romm as a patron, ibid. 33−54, 97−100.

33. Sheila Fitzpatrick, 'Intelligentsia and Power: Client−Patron Relations in Stalin's Russia', in Manfred Hildermeier (ed.), *Stalinismus vor dem zweiten Weltkrieg Neue Wege der Forschung* (Munich: R. Oldenbourg Verlag, 1998), 35−53.

34. See Boris Galin, 'Ocherki nashikh dnei: V odnom naselennom punkte (Rasskaz propagandista)', *Novyi mir,* 24/11 (1947): 135−217.

35. Tanich, *Igrala muzyka*, 103.

36. Quoted in Zubkova, *Russia After the War*, 28.

37. Nekrasov, 'V rodnom gorode', 248−470. For the initial meeting and drinking bout, ibid. 258−63.

38. On the formerly occupied territories see Amir Weiner, *Making Sense of War: The Second World War and the Fate of the Bolshevik Revolution* (Princeton and Oxford: Princeton University Press, 2000), 123−4 (quoting Nekrasov, *V rodnom gorode*). For Moscow see Bondaryev, Silence: A Novel, tr. Elisaveta Fen, Boston and Cambridge: Riverside Press, 1966, 115−16, 120.

39. See Ch. 6.

40. Zdenek Mlynarzh, *Moroz udaril iz Kremlia* (Moscow: Respublika, 1992), 18−19.

41. See also Beate Fieseler, *Die Invaliden des 'Grossen Vaterländischen Krieges' der Sowjetunion: Eine politische Sozialgeschichte 1941−1991*, Habilitationsschrift (Ruhr-Universität Bochum, 2003), 297−318.

42. See Ch. 4.

43. Julie Hessler, *A Social History of Soviet Trade* (Princeton and Oxford: Princeton University Press, 2004); James R. Millar, 'The Little Deal: Brezhnev's

Contribution to Acquisitive Socialism', *Slavic Review*, 44/4 (1985): 694−706;
A. Katsenelinboigen, 'Coloured Markets in the Soviet Union', *Soviet Studies*,
29/1 (1977): 62−85.

44. Cf. Elena Osokina, *Our Daily Bread: Socialist Distribution and the Art of Survival
in Stalin's Russia, 1927−1941*, tr. Kate Transchel and Greta Bucher (Armonk,
NY and London: M. E. Sharpe, 2001).

45. Cf. Gausner, *Vot my i doma…*, *Zvezda*, 11 (1947) 27−31.

46. Bondaryev, *Silence*, 16−17, 22−9.

47. Iurii Bondarev, *Tishina: Roman* (Moscow: Sovetskii pisatel', 1962), 18. Fen's
translation of this section is imprecise. See Bondaryev, *Silence*, 22.

48. Vera Dunham, 'Images of the Disabled, Especially the War Wounded, in
Soviet Literature', in William O. McCagg and Lewis Siegelbaum (eds.), *The
Disabled in the Soviet Union: Past and Present, Theory and Practice* (Pittburgh: University of Pittsburgh Press, 1989), 160-3; Tumarkin, *The Living and the Dead*,
98−9; Fieseler, *Die Invaliden des 'Grossen Vaterländischen Krieges'*, 316−17.

49. For examples see the report of Vladimir obkom secretary Pal'tsev on work
placement of demobilized soldiers, 17 Nov. 1945, RGASPI f. 17, op. 122,
d. 102, l. 232−7, here 233; Groznyi obkom secretary to Patolichev (5 Nov.
1946), RGASPI f. 17, op. 122, d. 147, l. 135−41, here 136; and Velikoluksk
obkom secretary Boikachev to Patolichev (9 Oct. 1946), RGASPI f. 17,
op. 122, d. 147, l. 142−6, here 143.

50. Krasnodar Kraiispolkom Chairman Bessonov to Chairman of Russian Council of Ministers Rodionov, 3 Apr. 1947, GARF f. A-259, op. 6, d. 4477,
l. 44−6, here 45−6.

51. See e.g. Upolnomochennyi KPK pri TsK VKP(b) po Ul'ianovskoi oblasti
Mironov to Malenkov: 'Spravka o rabote partiinykh organizatsii Ul'ianovskoi
oblasti s kommunistami, demobilizovannymi iz Krasnoi Armii' (2 May 1946),
RGASPI f. 17, op. 122, d. 146, l. 178−86, here 185.

52. Jeffrey W. Jones, ' "In my Opinion This is All Fraud!": Concrete, Culture,
and Class in the "Reconstruction" of Rostov-on-the-Don, 1943−1948'
(Ph.D. diss., University of North Carolina, 2000), 114.

53. Groznyi obkom secretary to Patolichev, 5. Nov. 1946, RGASPI f. 17,
op. 122, d. 147, l. 135−41, here 137; Report on work placement and help
in reintegration of demobilized soldiers in Penza oblast, 5 Apr. 1947, GARF
f. A-259, op. 6, d. 4477, l. 27−9, here 28.

54. In Groznyi oblast' in 1946 demobilized drivers refused to work in other
professions, although all the available jobs as drivers were already taken,
RGASPI f. 17, op. 122, d. 147, l. 135−41, here 136. All the drivers of
the newspaper *Vechernaia Moskva* were veterans in 1950, as editor G. A.
Meshcheriakov reported to Moscow Gorkom secretary I. I. Rumiantsev in
1950, RGASPI f. 17, op. 132, d. 296, l. 193−236, here 200.

55. Report to Stalin, Beriia, and Kuznetsov on the arrest of the demobilized
officer, 7 Dec. 1946, GARF f. r-9401, op. 2, d. 139, l. 466.

56. Minister of Interior S. Kruglov to Stalin, Molotov, Beriia, Voznesenskii (5 Apr. 1947), GARF f. r-9401, op. 2, d. 169, l. 213–17, here 214.

57. I would not have been able to write much of this section without the generous help of Nikolai Mitrokhin and Sonia Timofeeva. They pointed me to most of the published sources and gave me an excerpt from their unpublished database on Russian Orthodox Church leaders. For an earlier version of the database see N. Mitrokhin and S. Timofeeva, *Episkopy i eparkhii Russkoi Pravoslavnoi Tserkvi po sostoianiiu na 1 oktiabria 1997 g.* (Moscow: Panorama, 1997).

58. For an introductory survey see Philip Walters, 'A Survey of Soviet Religious Policy', in Sabrina Petra Ramet (ed.), *Religious Policy in the Soviet Union* (Cambridge and New York: Cambridge University Press, 1993), 3–30.

59. Ibid. 16–17.

60. Tatiana A. Chumachenko, *Church and State in Soviet Russia: Russian Orthodoxy from World War II to the Khrushchev Years*, tr. Edward E. Roslof (Armonk, NY, and London: M. E. Sharpe, 2002); Elena Zubkova, *Poslevoennoe sovetskoe obshchestvo: Politika i povsednevnost' 1945–1953* (Moscow: Rosspen, 2000), 102–10; Zubkova, *Russia After the War*, 68–73; Daniel Peris, ' "God is Now on our Side": The Religious Revival on Unoccupied Soviet Territory during World War II', *Kritika: Explorations in Russian and Eurasian History*, 1/1 (2000): 97–118. The extent to which the revival of church activity was a revival of religiosity or simply religiosity coming out of the underground is still subject to debate. See Karel C. Berkhoff, 'Was there a Religious Revival in Soviet Ukraine under the Nazi Regime?', *Slavonic and East European Review*, 78/3 (2000): 536–67.

61. Number of applications to open churches in Moscow oblast': 1944: 910; 1945: 363; 1946: 279; 1947: 255; 1948: 121. RGASPI f. 17, op 132, d. 6, l. 84–95, here 86.

62. For Muslim clergy collecting money and things and distributing them to war orphans and war invalids see RGASPI f. 17, op. 125, d. 405, l. 95. For Jewish communities taking care of invalids and orphans, ibid., l. 101.

63. Information from dept for checking of party organs, 19 July 1946, GARF f. 17, op. 88, d. 697, l. 8–14, here 8–9.

64. Zubkova, *Russia After the War*, 71.

65. Report of chairman of Council for Affairs of the Russian Orthodox Church Karpov on results of work for 1946, RGASPI f. 17, op. 125, d. 407, l. 2–42, here 7.

66. Report of Council for Affairs of Russian Orthodox Church, accompanying letter dated 19 Nov. 1949, RGASPI f. 17, op. 132, d. 111, l. 200–8, here 204.

67. Karpov to Stalin, Molotov, Beriia, Voroshilov, Zhdanov, Kuznetsov, Patolichev: information on the state of the Russian Orthodox Church, 27 Aug. 1946, RGASPI f. 17, op. 125, d. 407, l. 60–75, here 67.

68. Boris Nikolaevich Kandidov, report on the current state at the 'church front', n.d.; accompanying letter is dated 21 July 1945, RGASPI f. 17, op. 125, d. 313, l. 53–149, here 65.

69. Head of the department of organization and instruction of Grodenskii obkom in Belorussia to his obkom secretary P. Z. Kalinin, report on religious activities of party candidates and members, June 1946, RGASPI f. 17, op. 88, d. 721, l. 2–5, here 3.

70. Report from Mordvin obkom on activization of work of church leaders, RGASPI f. 17, op. 88, d. 317, l. 12–14, here 13.

71. Chairman of Council for Affairs of the Russian Orthodox Church Karpov to G. F. Aleksandrov in the Central Committee (30 Aug. 1945), RGASPI f. 17, op. 125, d. 313, l. 155–70, here 169.

72. RGASPI f. 17, op. 125, d. 593, l. 32–3.

73. On religiosity among veterans in the party cf. Weiner, *Making Sense of War*, 69 and 70 n. 78.

74. Report from a Belorussian obkom on religious activities of party candidates and party members, June 1946, RGASPI f. 17, op. 88, d. 721, l. 2–5, here 4.

75. Peris, 'God is Now on our Side', 115.

76. Memoirs of Archpriest A. Medvedskii as quoted in Chumachenko, *Church and State in Soviet Russia*, 195 n. 4.

77. Nearly 81% of the *tserkovnyi aktiv* was male. Karpov to M. A. Suslov, 12 Feb. 1949, RGASPI f. 17, op. 132, d. 111, l. 5–15, here 15.

78. Ibid. 11–12.

79. Report by Karpov on parish priests, undated, sometime in 1952 or early 1953, RGASPI f. 17, op. 132, d. 295, l. 198–209, here 198.

80. Andrei Pecherskii, 'Ia shel s evangeliem i ne boialsia…', *Rus' derzhavnaia*, 7–9 (19) (1995): 16–19; Mikhail Berzhba, 'Serzhant Pavlov ne ukhodil v monastyr'', *Trud* 7, 9 November 2001, p. 9.

81. Chumachenko, *Church and State in Soviet Russia*, 73.

82. Antonina Shapavalova, 'Ko dniu Sovetskoi Armii', *Zhurnal Moskovskoi Patriarkhii*, 2 (1947): 16–19, here 18–19; Vladimir Stepanov (Rusak), *Svidetel'stvo obvineniia*, 3 vols., ii (Moscow: Russkoe knigoizdatel'skoe tovarishchestvo, 1993), 152–3.

83. Karpov on composition of Russian Orthodox Church as of 1 Jan. 1948, 6 July 1948, RGASPI f. 17, op. 132, d. 7, l. 2–6, here 5.

84. Karpov to L. A. Slepov, 20 Nov. 1948, RGASPI f. 17, op. 132, d. 6, l. 184.

85. See e.g. the information on new priests in 1947–8, undated, RGASPI f. 17, op. 132, d. 6, l. 186–94; and Stepanov (Rusak), *Svidetel'stvo obvineniia*, ii. 155–6.

86. Chumachenko, *Church and State in Soviet Russia*, 67.

87. Maria Petrovna Kucherova (Seregina), 'Biografiia ieromonakha Petra (Seregina)', http://students.soros.karelia.ru/~kucherov/biograph.html (accessed early 2004).

88. Nikolai Mitrokhin: Interview with Vasilii Ivanovich Afonin, unpublished (Mar. 1997).

89. For the lack of change in the repressive policy towards non-orthodox 'sects' see Zubkova, *Russia After the War*, 215 n. 1.

90. Karpov reporting to Stalin, Molotov, Beriia, Voroshilov, Zhdanov, Kuznetsov, Patolichev on composition of Russian Orthodox Church, 27 Aug. 1946, RGASPI f. 17, op. 125, d. 407, l. 60–75, here 65.

91. Report on the increased activity of religious cults, 2 Aug. 1946, RGASPI f. 17, op. 122, d. 188, l. 2–6, here 4; and the information sheet of the Department for the checking of party organs, 17 July 1946, RGASPI f. 17, op. 88, d. 697, l. 1–7, here 2.

92. Voronezh obkom secretary V. Tishchenko to the deputy head of the department for the checking of party organs in the Central Committee V. M. Andrianov, 31 July 1946, RGASPI f. 17, op. 122, d. 131, l. 183–6.

93. *Pravda* correspondent M. Burdenkov on problems in the fight with religious influence in the party organization of Voroshilovgrad, n.d., sometime in 1952, RGASPI f. 17, op. 132, d. 295, l. 25–8, here 26.

94. The Ioannites were a branch of the amalgam of groups known as the Khlysts or 'Flagellants'. They are named after the famous Orthodox heretic Ioann of Kronstadt (1829–1908). After the October Revolution the Ioannites identified the new regime as the rule of Antichrist. In 1938 a Ioannite group in Tver was 'unmasked' and arrested. Ioannite literature was still circulating in the early 1960s. See Walter Kolarz, *Religion in the Soviet Union* (New York: St Martin's Press, 1961), 363–5.

95. GARF f. A-461, op. 1, d. 1196, l. 24–6.

96. GARF f. A-461, op. 1, d. 1196, l. 24, 30, 42–3.

97. On the role of women in postwar society see Bucher, *Women*.

98. Anna Krylova, ' "Healers of Wounded Souls": the Crisis of Private Life in Soviet Literature, 1944–46', *Journal of Modern History* (June 2001): 307–31.

99. See e.g. the description of the couple in Grigorii Baklanov, *Zhizn', podarennaia dvazhdy* (Moscow: Vagrius, 1999), 88–91.

100. Office adviser N. Kazakevich, report on results of investigation of the material and everyday situation of war invalid V. S. Uteknov, 20 May 1949, GARF f. r-7523, op. 55, d. 29, l. 67–9, here 68.

101. Consultant Shmakov to Chairman Shvernik, 12 Apr. 1951, GARF f. r-7523, op. 55, d. 45, l. 3–6, here 4.

102. See e.g. the stenographic report of the meeting of the Collegium of the Soviet Ministry of Health on the results of distribution of young doctors who had graduated in 1947, 18 Nov. 1947, GARF f. r-8009, op. 1, d. 621, l. 18–76, here 33, 35. Wives of still serving soldiers were also considered 'immobile', ibid., l. 21–2. See also Chris Burton, 'Medical Welfare during Late Stalinism: A Study of Doctors and the Soviet Health System, 1945–53', 193, 197.

103. See example in Baklanov, *Zhizn'*, 88. On the anti-parasites campaign see Ch. 4.

104. P. Savel'ev on complaints of women searching for fathers of their children who refused to pay alimony, 3 Apr. 1947, GARF f. r-7523, op. 55, d. 13, l. 27–58, here 29.

105. GARF f. r-7523, op. 55, d. 13, l. 37.

106. State Prosecutor D. Gorshenin to Chairman of Presidium of Supreme Soviet N. M. Shvernik, 25 Sept. 1947, GARF f. r-7523, op. 36, d. 333, l. 49–59.

107. See Fitzpatrick, *Everyday Stalinism*, 143–7, and *Tear Off the Masks!*, ch. 12. On scarcity of men and the effects of the family law of 1944 see Bucher, *Women*, 15, 18, 180–1, and *passim*; and Mie Nakachi, 'N. S. Khrushchev and the 1944 Soviet Family Law: Politics, Reproduction, and Language', *East European Politics and Societies,* 20/1 (2006): 40–68. The quotation in parentheses is from Vladimir Gusarov, *Moi papa ubil Mikhoelsa* (Frankfurt a. M.: Possev, 1978), 105.

108. P. Savel'ev on complaints of women searching for fathers of their children who refused to pay alimony, 8 July 1947, GARF f. r-7523, op. 55, d. 13, l. 59–74, here 62.

109. Zhanna Gausner, 'Vot my i doma…', *Zvezda*, 11 (1947): 4–106, here 11.

110. Most prominently Boris Polevoi's 1947 *Story about a Real Person (Povest' o nastoiashchem cheloveke*, 1947), and Petr Pavlenko's 1947 novel *Happiness (Schast'e)*. Newspapers also provided positive role models. See Krylova, 'Healers of Wounded Souls', 316.

111. Dunham, 'Images of the Disabled', 161; Krylova, 'Healers of Wounded Souls', 322. For two famous representations see Chukhrai's 1959 movie *Ballada o soldate*; and Petr Pavlenko's 1947 *Happiness: A Novel*, tr. J. Fineberg (Moscow: Foreign Languages Publishing House, 1950), 78. Cf. also Denise J. Youngblood, *Russian War Films; On the Cinema Front, 1914–2005* (Lawrence, Kan.: University Press of Kansas, 2007), 79. Memoirs also mention this phenomenon. See e.g. Nikolai Fedorovich D'iakov, *Mechenye: Dokumental'nye zapiski byvshego soldata*, ed. Nikolai Mitrokhin, *Dokumenty po istorii dvizheniia inakomysliashchikh* (Moscow: Informatsionno-ekspertnaia gruppa 'PANORAMA', 1999), 83; or Grigorii Baklanov, *Zhizn', podarennaia dvazhdy* (Moscow: Vagrius, 1999), 90.

112. For examples see D'iakov, *Mechenye*, 43; or Merridale, *Ivan's War*, 241.

113. GARF f. r-7523, op. 55, d. 13, l. 69.

114. Report on work of party collegium of KPK between June 1939 and 1946, RGANI f. 6, op. 6, d. 3, here l. 59.

115. Barbara Alpern Engel, 'The Womanly Face of War. Soviet Women Remember World War II', in Nicole Ann Dombrowski (ed.), *Women and War in the Twentieth Century: Enlisted with or without Consent* (New York and London: Garland Publishing, 1999), 146, 150–1.

116. See also Conze and Fieseler, 'Soviet Women as Comrades-in-Arms', 225–7; Peter Jahn (ed.), *Masha + Nina + Katjuscha: Frauen in der Roten*

*Armee 1941–1945 Zhenshchiny-voennosluzhashchie* (Berlin: Deutsch-Russisches Museum Berlin-Karlshorst, 2002).

117. 'Sovetskie zhenshchiny v bor'be za svobodu i nezavisimost' sotsialisticheskoi rodiny', *Bloknot agitatora*, 6 (1945): 6–7.

118. Kapitan M. Maksimov, 'Polk proshchaetsia s boevymi druz'iami', *Krasnaia zvezda*, 15 July 1945, p. 3.

119. 'Voiny protivovozdushnoi oborony vozvratilis' v rodnoi Leningrad', *Krasnaia zezda*, 17 July 1945, p. 1.

120. Z. Burina, 'Samootverzhennyi trud sovetskikh zhenshchin', *Bloknot agitatora Vooruzhennykh sil*, 5 (1947): 30.

121. See e.g. David Belkin, 'Al'bom o komsomole nashego universiteta', *Za Stalinskuiu nauku: Organ partbiuro, rektorata, komiteta VLKSM, profkoma i mestkoma Gor'kovskogo gosuniversiteta* (9 October 1948), 2.

122. N. S. Khrushchev, 'On the Cult of Personality and its Consequences', in G. H. Rigby (ed.), *The Stalin Dictatorship: Khrushchev's 'Secret Speech' and Other Documents* (Sydney: Sydney University Press, 1968), 23–89, here 61.

123. Denise J. Youngblood, *Russian War Films: On the Cinema Front, 1914–2005* (Lawrence, Kan.: University Press of Kansas, 2007), 146, 148–9, 150, 165–6, 167, 168, 179–80, 190, 224.

124. See e.g. Leonid Lench, 'V pidzhake', *Krokodil*, 30 (20 September 1945): 6.

125. For the entire conversation: Svetlana Alexiyevich, *War's Unwomanly Face*, tr. Keith Hammond and Lyudmila Lezhneva, Moscow: Progress Publishers, 1988, 62–5. She started her research in 1978 (ibid. 91). The original book appeared in 1985.

126. Ibid. 64–5.

127. Petr Pavlenko, *Schast'e. Roman* (Moscow: Pravda, 1947).

128. Nekrasov, 'V rodnom gorode', 291–4, 307–8 (quotation), 371.

129. Gausner, 'Vot my i doma ...', 8, 56.

130. I. E. Bogacheva, *Dorogi zhizni. Vospominaniia i razmyshleniia voennoi medsestry.* Voronezh: Voronezhskii gosudarstvennyi universitet, 2000, 54. She later married a veteran from her regiment: ibid. 57.

131. Aleksiyevich, *War's Unwomanly Face*, 161.

132. Ibid. 244–5.

133. Ibid. 70.

134. David M. Glantz, *Colossus Reborn: The Red Army at War, 1941–1943* (Lawrence, Kan.: University Press of Kansas, 2005), 551.

135. Bogacheva, *Dorogi zhizni*, 46.

136. Alexiyevich, *War's Unwomanly Face*, 19.

137. Ibid. 79, 89, 244.

138. Bogacheva, *Dorogi zhizni*, 45.

139. Ol'ga Dzhigurda, 'Teplokhod "Kakhetiia": Zapiski voennogo vracha', *Znamia*, 1 (1948): 3–86, here 21–4. On the implications of the name *Vetrova* cf. Dunham, *In Stalin's Time*, 118.

140. Quoted in Zubkova, *Poslevoennoe sovetskoe obshchestvo*, 31.

141. Chief military prosecutor N. Afanas'ev to Supreme Soviet, 24 Dec. 1945, GARF f. r-7523, op. 16, d. 400, l. 36.

142. Head of the dept for organization and instruction of Vladimir obkom, information on suicides in Stavrovskii raion, 31 Jan. 1946, RGASPI f. 17, op. 122, d. 131, l. 15–17, here 15.

143. Review file in connection with post-Stalinist amnesty, GARF f. A-461, op. 1, d. 1501, *passim*.

144. There are—of course—positive counter examples. For one such story of a lifelong romance between two war invalids, who met after the war was over, see *Pravda*, 16 Nov. 1978, p. 6.

145. Alexiyevich, *War's Unwomanly Face*, 80.

146. Cf. the letter of a female war invalid to Voroshilov, quoted in Zubkova, *Poslevoennoe sovetskoe obshchestvo*, 30–1. See also Alexiyevich, *War's Unwomanly Face*, 20–1, 87, 89, 92, 121, 147–8, 208–10.

## CHAPTER 4

1. GARF f. r-5451, op. 29, d. 711, l. 68–9, here 68.

2. Viktor Platonovich Nekrasov, 'V rodnom gorode', in *Izbrannye proizvedeniia. Povesti, rasskazy, putevye zametki* (Moscow: Khudozhestvennaia literatura, 1962; orig. 1954), 248–470, here 284–5.

3. Elena Zubkova, *Poslevoennoe sovetskoe obshchestvo: Politika i povsednevnost' 1945–1953* (Moscow: Rosspen, 2000), 29–31; Beate Fieseler *Die Invaliden des 'Grossen Vaterländischen Krieges' der Sowjetunion: Eine Politische Sozialgeschichte 1941–1991*, Habilitationsschrift (Ruhr-Universität Bochum, 2003), 86–7; Mark Edele, 'Soviet Veterans as an Entitlement Group, 1945–1955', *Slavic Review*. 65/1 (2006): 118–19. On medical welfare and prostetic appliances see Christopher Burton, 'Medical Welfare during Late Stalinism: A Study of Doctors and the Soviet Health System, 1945–53', (Ph.D. diss., University of Chicago, 2000); and Beate Fieseler, 'Stimmen aus dem gesellschaftlichen Abseits: Die sowjetischen Kriegsinvaliden im "Tauwetter" der fünfziger Jahre', *Osteuropa*, 52/7 (2002): 945–62.

4. G. F. Krivosheev, *Soviet Casualties and Combat Losses in the Twentieth Century* (London: Greenhill Books, 1997), 92. Archival reports mention 2 million in 1945 and 2.8 million in early 1946. RGASPI f. 17, op. 117, d. 511, l. 107; Catherine Merridale, *Ivan's War: Life and Death in the Red Army, 1939–1945* (New York: Metropolitan Books, 2006), 363.

5. Fieseler *Die Invaliden des 'Grossen Vaterländischen Krieges'*, 101–39; Burton, 'Medical Welfare', 265–80.

6. Fieseler, *Die Invaliden des 'Grossen Vaterländischen Krieges'*, 118–19; Merridale, *Ivan's War*, 268–70, and 'The Collective Mind: Trauma and

Shell-Shock in Twentieth-Century Russia', *Journal of Contemporary History*, 35/1 (2000): 39–55; and Benjamin Zajicek, 'Psychiatry and Mental Illness in the Soviet Union, 1941–1953', Ph.D. in progress, University of Chicago.

7. Burton, 'Medical Welfare', 268; Alan Barenberg, ' "For a United, Clear Pension Law": Legislating and Debating Soviet Pensions 1956–1965', MA thesis (University of Chicago, 2000), 7.

8. Burton, 'Medical Welfare', 264–80.

9. Data from Russian Commissariat for Social Welfare, as of 1 Aug. 1945, GARF f. r-5446, op. 47a, d. 5267, l. 1.

10. For a selection of documents which give a good sense of the type of material available in the archives, see E. Iu. Zubkova *et al.* (eds.), *Sovetskaia zhizn' 1945–1953* (Moscow: Rosspen, 2003), 308–25.

11. RGASPI f. 17, op. 122, d. 100, l. 38; Zubkova, *Russia After the War*, 24. See Burton, 'Medical Welfare', 279. Depending on the severity of the condition the re-evaluations of the group of invalidity was required every six months or every year; ibid. 267.

12. Pavel Stiller, *Sozialpolitik in der UdSSR 1950–80: Eine Analyse der quantitativen und qualitativen Zusammenhänge* (Baden-Baden: Nomos Verlagsgesellschaft, 1983), 132.

13. Information on the result of the checking of social welfare organs in the RSFSR, regarding their work with war invalids and others, 28 Jan. 1950, GARF f. r-5451, op. 29, d. 457, l. 182–97, here 190.

14. See Fieseler, *Die Invaliden des 'Grossen Vaterländischen Krieges'*, 146–59.

15. Max Weber, *Wirtschaft und Gesellschaft: Grundriss der verstehenden Soziologie*, 5th rev. edn. (Tübingen: J. C. B. Mohr [Paul Siebeck], 1990), 177–80 (part 1, ch. 4); Elena Osokina, *Za fasadom 'Stalinskogo izobiliia': Raspredelenie i rynok v snabzhenii naseleniia v gody industrializatsii 1927–1941* (Moscow: Rosspen, 1999), and *Our Daily Bread: Socialist Distribution and the Art of Survival in Stalin's Russia, 1927–1941*, tr. Kate Transchel and Greta Bucher (Armonk, NY, and London: M. E. Sharpe, 2001); Fitzpatrick, *Everyday Stalinism*, 40–66; and Jean-Paul Depretto, 'Stratification without Class', *Kritika: Explorations in Russian and Eurasian History*, 8/2 (2007): 375–88.

16. See Ch. 7 and A. F. Zavgorodnii, *Deiatel'nost' gosudarstvennykh organov i obshchestvenno-politicheskikh organizatsii po sotsial'noi zashchite voennosluzhash-chikh Krasnoi Armii i ikh semei v mezhvoennyi period (1921–iiun' 1941 gg)* (St Petersburg: Nestor, 2001), 128–39.

17. Mark Edele, 'A "Generation of Victors?" Soviet Second World War Veterans from Demobilization to Organization 1941–1956', (Ph.D. diss., University of Chicago, 2004), 134–43; and id. 'Soviet Veterans as an Entitlement Group', 123–4.

18. See Ch. 8.

19. Glazunov, *L'goty uchastnikam voiny*, 5–6.

20. Alan Barenberg, ' "For a United, Clear Pension Law". See also the internal Central Committee report on popular reactions to the draft law (17 May 1956), RGANI f. 5, op. 31, d. 62, l. 28–31, esp. l. 31.

21. Decrees of the Presidium of the Supreme Soviet of 27 Dec. 1959 and 31 Dec. 1964 as quoted by Glazunov, *L'goty uchastnikam voiny*, 6; no quotation of exact legal act for the 1 May 1965 change.

22. Russian Council of Ministers Resolutions of 6 Feb. 1962, no. 143, and of 2 Dec. 1964, no. 1498, both in *Sotsial'noe obespechenie v SSSR: Sbornik normativnykh aktov* (Moscow: Iuridicheskaia literatura, 1986), 596, 597.

23. Council of Ministers Resolution of 6 Mar. 1965, no. 140, *SP SSSR* (1965): st. 22 (pp. 45–7).

24. Glazunov, *L'goty uchastnikam voiny*, 6–7; *Sotsial'noe obespechenie v SSSR*, 477; *SP SSSR* 11 (1975): st. 59 (pp. 203–5).

25. For an overview of the major legislation between 1978 and 1990 see M. V. Filippova, *L'goty dlia uchastnikov Velikoi Otechestvennoi voiny* (Leningrad: Lenizdat, 1991), 108–9.

26. Law of 30 Nov. 1978, *SP SSSR* 27 (1978): st. 165 (pp. 542–4).

27. Russian Council of Ministers Resolution of 20 Mar. 1979, No. 153, *SP RSFSR* (1979): 11, st. 67 (pp. 195–7), here p. 196.

28. *SP SSSR* 12 (1981): st. 71 (pp. 315–26).

29. SNK Resolution of 5 June 1941, No. 1474, *SP SSSR* 15 (1941): st. 282 (pp. 467–73).

30. SNK Resolution of 16 July 1940, No. 1269, *SP SSSR* 19 (1940): st. 465 (pp. 641–4). For its continued relevance see Glazunov, *L'goty uchastnikam voiny*, 5; SNK Resolution of 12 Nov. 1940, No. 2291, *SP SSSR* 30 (1940): st. 729 (p. 1006). Pensions were lower for third group invalids if they earned more than 200 rubles in urban jobs or 100 rubles in agriculture and generally a pension was lower if a person was 'connected to agriculture'. For brevity's sake these complications are ignored in this discussion, which concentrates on the general rules as they applied in the immediate postwar period to the urban section of war invalids who had not been professional soldiers.

31. Abdurakhman Avtorkhanov, 'A Brief History of the Komsomol', in *Soviet Youth: Twelve Komsomol Histories* (Munich: Institute for the Study of the USSR, 1959), 18. Avtorkhanov must be drawing on the reports of other defectors here as he had left the Soviet Union in 1943. See *Biograficheskii Entsiklopedicheskii Slovar'* (Moscow: Bolshaia Rossiiskaia entsiklopediia, 2000), 10.

32. V. P. Popov, *Ekonomicheskaia politika Sovetskogo gosudarstva: 1946–1953 gg.* (Tambov: Izd-vo Tamb. gos. tekhn. un-ta, 2000), 59.

33. Ibid. 58.

34. SNK Resolution of 28 Jan. 1946, *Material'noe obespechenie pri invalidnosti, starosti, za vyslugu let i po sluchaiu poteri kormil'tsa*, ed. R. R. Kats (Moscow: Izd-vo Ministerstva sotsial'nogo obespecheniia RSFSR, 1948), 102.

35. Popov, *Ekonomicheskaia politika*, 59.

36. Rudolf Becker, *Sowjetische Lohnpolitik zwischen Ideologie und Wirtschaftsgesetz* (Berlin: Duncker & Humblot, 1965), 47.

37. Elena Zubkova, *Russia After the War: Hopes, Illusions, and Disappointments, 1945–1957*, tr. Hugh Ragsdale (Armonk, NY, and London: 1998), 24.

38. Popov, *Ekonomicheskaia politika*, 59.

39. Data compiled by *upravlenie delami* of the Council of Ministers of the Soviet Union on the basis of reports of Union Republic Council of Ministers. These numbers refer to those disabled who received pensions from the civilian welfare administrations, as opposed to former career military who were taken care of by the Ministry of Defence. GARF f. r-5446, op. 48a, d. 3742, l. 101.

40. Popov, *Ekonomicheskaia politika*, 59.

41. Fieseler, *Die Invaliden des 'Grossen Vaterländischen Krieges'*, 288–94.

42. Ibid. 295, 297.

43. Report on composition of *internaty* and rest homes for war invalids in Saratov region, undated (sometime in 1946), GARF. f. A-259, op. 6, d. 3397, l. 94–100, here 96–7.

44. For a similar assessment see Fieseler's detailed discussion, *Die Invaliden des 'Grossen Vaterländischen Krieges'*, 297–318.

45. List of *profshkoly-internaty* of the Russian Commissariat of Social Welfare, as of 1 Jan. 1946, GARF f. A-413, op. 1, d. 687a, l. 41–4.

46. Information on professional training of war invalids, as of 1 May 1946, GARF f. A-413, op. 1, d. 687a, l. 30–8, here 31.

47. Russian Council of Ministers Resolution of 6 Feb. 1948, GARF f. A-259, op. 1, d. 201, l. 111–17, here 112.

48. See e.g. R. R. Kats (ed.), *Material'noe obespechenie pri invalidnosti, starosti, za vyslugu let i po sluchaiu poteri kormil'tsa* (Moscow: Izd-vo Ministerstva sotsial'nogo obespecheniia RSFSR, 1948), 516–19, here 516.

49. For examples of this view see Danukin, 'Trudoustroistvo invalidov—vid sotsial'nogo obespecheniia', 118–25; Report to a meeting of senior bureaucrats in city welfare institutions, 25 Oct. 1945, GARF f. A-413, op. 1, d. 650, l. 33–54, here 33.

50. Report on the work of social welfare organs in Moldaviia, n.d., late 1950, GARF f. r-5451, op. 29, d. 457, l. 156–81, here 162; stenographic report of the meeting regarding the work of *Sovety Sodeistviia*, 29 Sept. 1944, GARF f. r-5451, op. 29, d. 128, l. 4–100b, here 5.

51. See e.g. the report of the Sverdlovsk gorkom secretary Kozlov to obkom secretary V. M. Andrianov, 17 Aug. 1945, and Gorkom secretary Nikinskikh to Andrianov, Aug. 1945, TsDOOSO f. 4, op. 31, d. 704, l. 192, 205.

52. GARF f. r-5446, op. 48a, d. 3742, l. 102.

53. According to a report on Belorussia in 1950 and 1951, the local social welfare administrations frequently did not know 'who was placed, when, and where to work; who exactly works where and what at the moment, how much he

earns'. In many cases the *raisobesy* did not even know 'does the pensioner work or not'. This was the case even for invalids of the third group, for whom the size of the pension depended on income. GARF f. r-5451, op. 29, d. 457, l. 13–60, here 52..

54. For examples see TsDOOSO f. 4, op. 31, d. 704, l. 197, 198, 205.

55. KPK plenipotentiary for Cheliabinsk oblast Evdokimov to Malenkov, report on work placement and everyday help for war invalids, 11 Jan. 1945, RGASPI f. 17, op. 122, d. 100, l. 21–8, here 25.

56. SNK (Council of Minsters) Resolutions of 19 Feb. 1944, no. 182; 9 Mar. 1946, no. 6; 15 Mar. 1948, no. 783; 24 Feb. 1949, no. 807; GARF f. r-5446, op. 1, d. 224, l. 145–9; *Sbornik zakonov, ukazov, postanovlenii, reshenii i rasporiazhenii 1946* (Leningrad: Lenizdat, 1947), 308–11; GARF f. r-9396, op. 1, d. 171, l. 347–8; GARF f. r-9396, op. 1, d. 273, l. 70–4.

57. Report on work of Ivanovo oblast department for social welfare for the year of the Great Patriotic War, GARF f. A-413, op. 1, d. 592, l. 16–17, here 17.

58. Vladimir obkom secretary Pal'tsev to Malenkov, report on execution of CC Orgburo resolution of 25 Aug. 1945, 17 Nov. 1945, RGASPI f. 17, op. 122, d. 102, l. 232–7, here 233.

59. Tula obkom secretary N. Chmutov, report on help to war invalids and families of soldiers, 1945, RGASPI f. 17, op. 88, d. 440, l. 10–150b, here 130b.

60. For an example see GARF f. 17, op. 122, d. 100, l. 38. This was a strategy also followed by other veterans. One demobilized soldier and his wife e.g. both refused to work an official job. Instead she worked as a private seamstress, he as a private shoemaker. The only problem turned out to be the lack of a ration card for the woman. See the report of the deputy head of the military department of the Sverdlovsk obkom, reacting to an NKGB investigation of complaints of demobilized soldiers, Nov. 1945, TsDOOSO f. 4, op. 31, d. 705, l. 74–7, here 76.

61. Art. 9 of the SNK resolution of 16 July 1940, No. 1269, *SP SSSR* 19 (1940): st. 465 (pp. 641–4).

62. GARF f. A-413, op. 1, d. 2370, l. 57. The Ministry of Social Welfare thus proposed to introduce a minimum income for those invalids, in order to keep them from suffering under the new legislation. However, the Ministry of Finance of the Soviet Union saw 'no grounds' for such a change in a letter from 2 Feb. 1953. GARF f. A-413, op. 1, d. 2370, l. 57–58, 62.

63. RGASPI f. 17, op. 122, d. 100, l. 26.

64. I am indebted to Charles Hachten for making this point.

65. RGASPI f. 17, op. 122, d. 100, l. 25.

66. Julie Hessler, *A Social History of Soviet Trade: Trade Policy, Retail Practices, and Consumption, 1917–1953* (Princeton and Oxford: Princeton University Press, 2004), 285.

67. Short report on letters received by *Krasnaia zvezda* in July 1946, RGASPI f. 17, op. 125, d. 429, l. 138–62, here 154.

68. Vera Dunham, 'Images of the Disabled, Especially the War Wounded, in Soviet Literature', in William O. McCagg and Lewis Siegelbaum (eds.), *The Disabled in the Soviet Union: Past and Present, Theory and Practice*. Pittsburgh: University of Pittsburgh Press, 1989, 161; Hubertus F. Jahn, *Fromme Pilger, artige Arme und streunende Gauner. Zur Geschichte von Bettelei, Armut und sozialer Imagination in Russland*, Habilitationsschrift (University of Erlangen, 1998).

69. On this subculture and their interaction with the office of the Supreme Soviet see Savel'ev report to to K. E. Voroshilov on changes in procedure regarding monetary help, 16 Nov. 1953, GARF f. r-7523, op. 55, d. 55, l. 7–12, here 8–9.

70. Oksana Kasenkina, *Leap to Freedom* (London: Hurst & Blackett, 1949), 95–6.

71. See Nina Tumarkin, *The Living and the Dead: The Rise and Fall of the Cult of World War II in Russia* (New York: Basic Books, 1994), 98.

72. See letter to Zhdanov of 23 July 1947 and Resolution of CC Secretariat regarding this letter, 22 Aug. 1947. In Zubkova *et al.*, *Sovetskaia zhizn' 1945–1953*, 36–7.

73. Michel Gordey, *Visa to Moscow*, tr. K. Woods (New York: Alfred A. Knopf, 1952), 31.

74. Fieseler, *Die Invaliden des 'Grossen Vaterländischen Krieges'*, 305.

75. Ibid. 315–17; Sheila Fitzpatrick, 'Social Parasites: How Tramps, Idle Youth, and Busy Entrepreneurs Impeded the Soviet March to Communism', *Cahiers du Monde russe*, 47/1–2 (2006): 381, 397. On the fate of POWs see Ch. 5.

76. KPK plenipotentiary for Bashkiriia M. Zakharov to Malenkov, report on work placement and help to war invalids, 13 Jan. 1945, RGASPI f. 17, op. 122, d. 100, l. 2–12, here l. 4.

77. Report of KPK plenipotentiary for Ivanovo region on work placement and help for war invalids, 17 Jan. 1945, RGASPI f. 17, op. 122, d. 100, l. 32–42, here 38.

78. Half-annual report of department of social welfare in Oktiabr'skii raion in Sverdlovsk, 5 July 1944, TsDOOSO f. 154, op. 1, d. 569, l. 11–140b, here 110b.

79. In Jan. 1945 the militia of Sverdlovsk oblast' questioned 35 and arrested 28 members of such a group. The main organizing principle was nationality—they were all Tatars, some of them war invalids, as the instructor of the cadres administration of the Sverdlovsk obkom reported, TsDOOSO f. 4, op. 31, d. 704, l. 22.

80. In Sept. 1945 such a gang was arrested in Tambov region. This group was largely a family enterprise headed by a deserter and a war invalid. Commissar for the Interior L. Beriia to Molotov (SNK SSSR), Malenkov (CC), A. I. Mikoian (SNK SSSR), 1945, GARF f. r-9401, op. 2, d. 104, l. 52–7, here 53.

81. Report of Minister of Interior S. Kruglov to Stalin, Molotov, Beria, and Voznesenskii (31 Jan. 1947), GARF f. r-9401, op. 2, d. 186, l. 250–3, here 251.

82. KPK plenipotentiary for Bashkiriia, M. Zakharov to Malenkov, on work
    placement and help to war invalids, 13 Jan. 1945, RGASPI f. 17, op. 122,
    d. 100, l. 2–12, here 9.
83. KPK plenipotentiary for Novosibirsk I. Kuznetsov to Malenkov, on execu-
    tion of resolutions regarding the treatment of war invalids in the towns of
    Novosibirsk oblast, 18 Jan. 1945, RGASPI f. 17, op. 122, d. 100, l. 111–16,
    here 115.
84. P. Charles Hachten, 'Property Relations and the Economic Organization of
    Soviet Russia, 1941–1948', (PhD diss., University of Chicago, 2005), 393,
    395–6.
85. *Moskva poslevoennaia 1945–1947: Arkhivnye dokumenty i materialy* (Moscow:
    Mosgorarkhiv, 2000), 462.
86. Hachten, 'Property Relations', 396.
87. Soviet Committee of War Veterans, stenographic report of meeting of the
    *aktiv* of the invalids' section, 26 Dec. 1956, GARF f. r-9541, op. 1, d. 49,
    l. 16–17.
88. Report on the work placement and everyday integration of war invalids in
    Bashkiria, 13 Jan. 1945, RGASPI f. 17, op. 122, d. 100, l. 2–12; here 6;
    Report to A. N. Kosygin on implementation of SNK resolution of 10 July
    1945, No. 406, 24 Nov. 1945, GARF f. A-413, op. 1, d. 651, l. 7–18, here
    9; KPK plenipotentiary for Altai region Komarov, report to Malenkov on
    work placement and everyday help to war invalids, 17 Jan. 1945, RGASPI
    f. 17, op. 122, d. 100, l. 92–101, here 95; KPK controller Romanov and
    senior inspector of Russian Commissariat of Social Welfare Trakhtenberg to
    Malenkov, n.d., at the end of Sept. 1945, RGASPI f. 17, op. 122, d. 100,
    l. 268–73, here 270.
89. KPK plenipotentiary for Sverdlovsk oblast to KPK Chairman A. A. Andreev,
    report on problems in work with war invalids, 9 Feb. 1945, TsDOOSO f. 4,
    op. 31, d. 738, l. 10–22, here 11.
90. Report to a meeting of senior bureaucrats in city welfare institutions, 25 Oct.
    1945, GARF f. A-413, op. 1, d. 650, l. 33–54, here 43.
91. Report to N. G. Zhukov on work of local party and Soviet organizations
    with regard to demobilized soldiers in Sverdlovsk oblast, 5 Nov. 1945,
    TsDOOSO f. 4, op. 31, d. 714, l. 414–26, here 419.
92. On tuberculosis see e.g. Grigorii Chukhrai, *Moe kino* (Moscow: Algoritm,
    2002), 199–201. P. Savel'ev to N. M. Shvernik on work with complaints,
    16 Feb. 1948, GARF f. r-7523, op. 55, d. 14, l. 122–47, here 142; KPK
    plenipotentiary for Gor'kii oblast Krylov to Malenkov, 12 Mar. 1946,
    RGASPI f. 17, op. 122, d. 146, l. 139–46, here 142. For reopening wounds
    see e.g. Savel'ev to Shvernik, report on complaints from Belorussia, July 1948,
    GARF f. r-7523, op. 55, d. 20, l. 1–17, here 12. Report of the director of
    inter-regional courses for leading cadres, accompanying letter dated 20 Aug.
    1946, GARF f. A-259, op. 6a, d. 23, l. 2–10, here 9; and Annual report of

Kishinev State University on 1947–8 academic year, GARF f. r-9396, op. 2, d. 128, l. 17–18.

93. Inspector Valiev to head of dept for social welfare of war invalids in the Russian Commissariat of Social Welfare, V. A. Aralov, 1945, GARF f. A-413, op. 1, d. 652, l. 7.

94. Chukhrai, *Moe Kino*, 28, 34–35. For Romm's role ibid. 35–54.

95. Dunham, 'Images of the Disabled', 153.

96. Burton, 'Medical Welfare', 272–3; Report of Kirov Obkom secretary V. Luk'ianov to Malenkov on execution of CC resolution of 25 Aug. 1945, 1 Feb. 1946, RGASPI f. 17, op. 122, d. 145, l. 79–91, here 89. Also: RGASPI f. 17, op. 122, d. 100, l. 38.

97. Report on work placement of war invalids as of 1 Sept. 1945, GARF f. A-413, op. 1, d. 649, l. 6–60b.

98. Report to a meeting of senior bureaucrats in city welfare institutions, 25 October 1945, GARF f. A-413, op. 1, d. 650, l. 33–54, here 34.

99. This is a synchronic application of what Alec Nove has called the 'law of equal cheating'. See Alec Nove, *The Soviet Economic System* (London: George Allen & Unwin, 1977), 352; and his clarification in *Soviet Studies*, 38/4 (1986): 634.

100. Liudmilla Alexeyeva and Paul Goldberg, *The Thaw Generation. Coming of Age in the Post-Stalin Era* (Boston: Little, Brown, & Co., 1990), 29–31.

101. 'Effectivity of work placement of invalids of the Patriotic War' (Feb. 1945) GARf f. A-413, op. 1, d. 649, l. 72–4, here 73.

102. e.g. a decision of the SNK RSFSR told the welfare administration of Sverdlovsk oblast' to organize requalification courses for 600 war invalids of group I and II. While (as always) there were severe problems in the execution of this order, it excluded group III invalids from re-education from the start. See the report of the KPK plenipotentiary for Sverdlovsk region, 9 Feb. 1945, TsDOOSO f. 4, op. 31, d. 738, l. 10–22, here 12.

103. RGASPI f. 17, op. 122, d. 100, l. 34.

104. Report to a meeting of senior bureaucrats in city welfare institutions, 25 Oct. 1945, GARF f. A-413, op. 1, d. 650, l. 33–54, here 43.

105. Report on work of Ivanovo oblast department for social welfare for the year of the Great Patriotic War, GARF f. A-413, op. 1, d. 592, here l. 160b. The sample was taken from working war invalids and thus was already biased towards those who found work in the first place. The 4,310 invalids represented 35% of all working war invalids in the region.

106. See Bernice Madison, 'Programs for the Disabled in the USSR', in McCagg and Siegelbaum (eds.), *The Disabled in the Soviet Union*, 185–8; and Fieseler, *Die Invalides des 'Grossen Vaterländischen Krieges'*, 164, 472–5.

107. See Edele, 'A "Generation of Victors"?', 155–71.

108. R. Malinovskii to N. S. Khrushchev (13 Mar. 1959), RGANI f. 5, op. 30, d. 289, l. 16–24, here 22.

109. Cf. Fieseler, *Die Invaliden des 'Grossen Vaterländischen Krieges'*, 456–78. On the growth of general material well-being under Brezhnev see Stephen Kotkin,

*Armageddon Averted: The Soviet Collapse, 1970–2000* (New York and Oxford: Oxford University Press, 2001).

CHAPTER 5

1. Christian Streit, *Keine Kameraden: Die Wehrmacht und die sowjetischen Kriegsgefangenen 1941–1945*, new edn. (Bonn: Dietz, 1997), 402 n. 77; see also p. 236.
2. *Pravda*, 11 Nov. 1944, p. 2.
3. Beate Fieseler, *Die Invaliden des 'Grossen Vaterländischen Krieges' der Sowjetunion: Eine politische Sozialgeschichte 1941–1991*, Habilitationsschrift (Ruhr-Universität Bochum, 2003), 156.
4. Report by Central Committee commission about the situation of former POWs (headed by G. K. Zhukov), 4 July 1956, repr. in A. Iu. Artizov et al. (eds.), *Reabilitatsiia: Kak eto bylo. Fevral' 1956—nachalo 80-kh godov* (Moscow: Demokratiia, 2003), 114. On enforced repatriation see Mark Elliott's classic: *Pawns of Yalta: Soviet Refugees and America's Role in their Repatriation* (Urbana, Ill.: University of Illinois Press, 1982).
5. We do not know how many of those recovered during the war survived. G. F. Krivosheev and M. F. Filimoshin, 'Poteri vooruzhennykh sil SSSR v Velikoi Otechestvennoi voine', in V. B. Zhiromskaia (ed.), *Naselenie Rossii v xx veke: Istoricheskie ocherki. ii. 1940–1959* (Moscow: Rosspen, 2001), 27.
6. This is an upper limit, assuming the maximum number of 2.8 million surviving POWs, and the smaller number for war veterans (20.1 million).
7. A good introduction to the literature up to the mid-1990s is Jörg Osterloh, *Sowjetische Kriegsgefangene 1941–1945 im Spiegel nationaler und internationaler Untersuchungen. Forschungsüberblick und Bibliographie*, 2nd rev. edn. (Dresden: Hannah-Arendt-Institut für Totalitarismusforschung e.V. an der TU Dresden, 1996).
8. On the development of the system of filtration camps see Mark Edele, 'A "Generation of Victors?"': Soviet Second World War Veterans from Demobilization to Organization 1941–1956', Ph.D. diss. (University of Chicago, 2004), 76–9.
9. On these formations see S. I. Drobiazko, *Pod znamenami vraga: Antisovetskie formirovaniia v sostave germanskikh vooruzhennykh sil 1941–1945* (Moscow: Eksmo, 2005).
10. On death and survival in the POW camps see Aron Shneer, *Plen: Sovetskie voennoplennye v Germanii, 1941–1945* (Moscow and Jerusalem: Mosty kultury, Gesharim, 2005).
11. This representation ultimately goes back to Aleksandr Solzhenitsyn's important treatment in *The Gulag Archipelago 1918–1956: An Experiment in Literary Investigation I–II* (New York: Harper & Row, 1973), 237–51, esp. 243–51. It is repeated in later accounts, e.g. Martin Malia, *The Soviet Tragedy: A History of Socialism in Russia, 1917–1991* (New York: Free Press, 1994), 287; or Iurii I.

Stetsovskii, *Istoriia sovetskikh repressii*, i (Moscow: Tasis, 1997), 93. A recent, very detailed and archive-based study also belongs to this tradition: Ulrike Goeken-Haidl, *Der Weg zurück: Die Repatriierung soujetischer Zwangsarbeiter und Kriegsgefangener während und nach dem Zweiten Weltkrieg* (Essen: Klartext Verlag, 2006).

12. Varlam Shalamov, 'Major Pugachev's Last Battle', in his *Kolyma Tales* (New York and London: W. W. Norton, 1982), 89–103; Andrea Graziosi, 'The Great Strikes of 1953 in Soviet Labor Camps in the Accounts of Their Participants: A Review', *Cahiers du monde russe et sovietique*, 33 (1992): 419–46; and Steven A. Barnes, ' "In a Manner Befitting Soviet Citizens": An Uprising in the Post-Stalin Gulag', *Slavic Review*, 64/4 (2005): 823–50.

13. Vladimir Naumov and Leonid Reshin, 'Repression gegen sowjetische Kriegsgefangene und zivile Repatrianten in der UdSSR 1941–1956', in Konstantin Kikishkin, Klaus-Dieter Müller, and Günther Wagenlehner (eds.), *Die Tragödie der Gefangenschaft in Deutschland und in der Soujetunion 1941–1956* (Cologne and Weimar: Böhlau Verlag, 1998), 339.

14. For the number in the 'special contingent' see Goeken-Haidl, *Der Weg zurück*, 547.

15. See Donald Filtzer, *Soviet Workers and Late Stalinism: Labour and the Restoration of the Stalinist System after World War II* (Cambridge: Cambridge University Press, 2002).

16. Important starting points for such a history are the studies by Viktor Zemskov, V. P. Naumov, and Pavel Polian, listed in the Bibliography.

17. See (slightly misleadingly) V. P. Naumov, 'Sud'ba voennoplennykh i de-portirovannykh grazhdan SSSR: Materialy komissii po reabilitatsii zhertv politicheskikh repressii', *Novaia i noveishaia istoriia*, 2 (1996): 102–3; and (more precisely) Naumov and Reshin, 'Repression', 346. Elliot (*Pawns of Yalta*, 210) mentions similar regulations for Odessa, Khar'kov, and Minsk.

18. On the regulations of the 1940 passport law see Marc Elie, 'Les Politiques à l'égard des libérés du Goulag: Amnistiés et réhabilités dans la région de Novosibirsk, 1953–1960', *Cahiers du Monde russe*, 47/1–2 (2006): 327–48, here 339; on the centrality of Gulag returnees in Soviet society see Golfo Alexopoulos, 'Amnesty 1945: The Revolving Door of Stalin's Gulag', *Slavic Review*, 64/2 (2005): 274–306.

19. Naumov and Reshin, 'Repression', 345, 347–8. See also Naumov, 'Sud'ba voennoplennykh', 103–4; Fedor Belov, *The History of a Soviet Collective Farm* (New York: Praeger, 1955), 68; Elliot, *Pawns of Yalta*, 209–10.

20. Viktor Zemskov, 'K voprosu o repatriatsii sovetskikh grazhdan 1944–1951 gg', *Istoriia SSSR* 4 (1990): 26–41, here 40; Naumov, 'Sud'ba voenno-plennykh', 104–5; Pavel Polian, *Deportiert nach Hause: Soujetische Kriegsgefan-gene im 'Dritten Reich' und ihre Repatriierung* (Munich and Vienna: R. Oldenbourg Verlag, 2001), 187; Elliot, *Pawns of Yalta*, 210.

21. Nikolai Fedorovich D'iakov, *Mechenye: Dokumental'nye zapiski byvshego soldata*, ed. Nikolai Mitrokhin, *Dokumenty po istorii dvizheniia inakomysli-ashchikh* (Moscow: Informatsionno-ekspertnaia gruppa 'PANORAMA', 1999). If not noted otherwise, the following biographical sketch is based on the short summary biography, ibid. 255–7.

22. Report on completion of repatriation from Finland and Sweden (7 Nov. 1944), GARF f. r-9401, op. 2 s.ch., d. 67, l. 300.

23. D'iakov, *Mechenye*, 256.

24. Ibid. 6.

25. See Ch. 1.

26. D'iakov, *Mechenye*, 36–7.

27. Ibid. 6–7, 36.

28. Ibid. 36.

29. Ibid. 38–9.

30. Ibid. 40–2, 49.

31. David J. Dallin and Boris I. Nicolaevsky, *Forced Labor in Soviet Russia* (New Haven: Yale University Press, 1947), 286–9.

32. D'iakov, *Mechenye*, 45–6, 48, 55.

33. Ibid. 60–7. There are other examples of repatriated getting jobs with the help of the state security. See Polian, *Deportiert nach Hause*, 181.

34. D'iakov, *Mechenye*, 55–6, 118, 124–6, 130.

35. Ibid. 140.

36. Quoted in Zemskov, 'K voprosu', 39; and O. M. Verbitskaia, 'Liudskie poteri v gody Velikoi Otechestvennoi voiny: Territoriia i naselenie posle voiny', in *Naselenie Rossii v XX veke: Istoricheskie ocherki*, ii. *1940–1959 gg.* (Moscow: Rosspen, 2001), 158.

37. *Pravda*, 26 Oct. 1946, p. 2.

38. See Golikov to Zhdanov (9 June 1947), RGASPI f. 17, op. 122, d. 212, l. 42–3.

39. Zemskov, 'K voprosu o repatriatsii', 38–9.

40. Council of Ministers Directive (12 June 1947) no. 7240rs, GARF f. r-5446, op. 49a, d. 62, l. 7. For an intervention by Golikov which was part of the process of widening the application to all nationals see Golikov to Molotov (14 May 1947, forwarded to MVD on 5 June 1947; osobaia papka Molotova) GARF f. r-9401, op. 2 s.ch, d. 172, l. 322. For the positive answer of MVD chef Kruglov to Molotov (5 June 1947) ibid., l. 324.

41. SNK Directive (17 July 1945) no. 10866-rs, GARF f. r-5446, op. 47a, d. 346, l. 4.

42. Council of Ministers Directive (2 Feb. 1946) no. 1308-rs and Rasporiazhenie SM SSSR (10 July 1946) no. 8533rs, GARF f. r-5446, op. 48a, d. 49, l. 1–3. In practice, the camp authorities frequently plundered the repatriates. Polian, *Deportiert nach Hause*, 162.

43. Resolution of GOKO of 14 June 1945, no. 9054s as quoted in GARF f. r-9402, op. 2, d. 235, l. 246.

44. The only exception was the one-time money payments institutionalized in article 6. See Council of Ministers Resolution (30 Sept. 1946), no. 2220, GARF f. r-5446, op. 1, d. 285, l. 240–1.

45. Goeken-Haidl, *Der Weg zurück*, 525.

46. Significantly, a reprint in a legal collection of 1948 of the order of the Ministry of Social Welfare of the Russian Federation, which passed the 30 Sept. 1946 resolution down the line of command, omitted articles 2 (application of the demobilization law) and 3 (work according to profession). See *Material'noe obespechenie pri invalidnosti, starosti, za vyslugu let i po sluchaiu poteri kormil'tsa*, ed. R. R. Kats (Moscow: Izd-vo Ministerstva sotsial'nogo obespecheniia RSFSR, 1948), 316.

47. Goeken-Haidl, *Der Weg zurück*, 462–8.

48. Naumov, 'Sud'ba voennoplennykh', 105.

49. RGASPI f. 17, op. 132, d. 61, l. 11.

50. For his rank at the moment of his wounding: 'Spravka of ranenii' (4 Jan. 1944), RGASPI f. 17, op. 132, d. 61, l. 12.

51. V. Andreev to K. Kharitonov, report on time he spent on enemy territory (1948), RGASPI f. 17, op. 132, d. 61, l. 10–100b.

52. V. Kharitonov (the institute's director) to Central Committee of the Bolshevik Party (8 June 1948), RGASPI f. 17, op. 132, d. 61, l. 8.

53. GARF f. r-9526, op. 1-s.ch., d. 617, l. 161.

54. Report of the head of the repatriation administration of the republic of Estonia to the Golikov administration (31 Jan. 1949), GARF f. r-9526 s ch, op. 1 s ch, d. 617, l. 24–5. On the creation, structure, and work of the administration see Polian, *Deportiert nach Hause*, 52–3, 56–80.

55. Naumov, 'Sud'ba voennoplennykh', 105–6.

56. GARF f. r-7523, op. 55, d. 49, l. 8.

57. D'iakov, *Mechenye*, 139–40, 256.

58. Ibid. 140.

59. Polian, *Deportiert nach Hause*, 187; report of head of the office of chairman of Supreme Soviet P. Savel'ev to Shvernik (20 May 1952), GARF f. r-7523, op. 55, d. 49, l. 1–8; materials regarding the projected CC resolution on the situation for former POWs, sent by Zhukov to the CC commission (11 May 1956) in *Georgii Zhukov: Stenogramma oktiabr'skogo (1957g.) plenuma TsK KPSS i drugie dokumenty*, ed. A. N. Iakovlev, Rossiia XX vek. Dokumenty (Moscow: Mezhdunarodnyi fond 'demokratiia', 2001), 126–30, here 128.

60. GARF f. r-7523, op. 55, d. 49, l. 2 for people who come to the *lichnyi priem* of Shvernik.

61. Edele, 'A "Generation of Victors"?', 171–6.

62. D'iakov, *Mechenye*, 140, 143, 152.

63. RGASPI f. 17, op. 132, d. 61, l. 3.

64. RGASPI f. 17, op. 122, d. 212, l. 42–3. Pozdniak to Zhanov (15 July 1947), ibid., l. 44.

65. Alex Inkeles and Raymond Bauer, *The Soviet Citizen: Daily Life in a Totalitarian Society* (Cambridge, Mass.: Harvard University Press, 1961), 289.
66. *Istochnik*, 4 (1996): 130–5. For the composition of the organization, ibid. 133.
67. D'iakov, *Mechenye*, 154–5, 168, 176, 180–5, 190, 256.
68. Streit, *Keine Kameraden*, 10. The numbers are still in dispute, largely because German and Soviet data diverge significantly. See e.g. Shneer, *Plen*, 95–6.
69. Shneer, *Plen*, 311–34.
70. The exact numbers are unknown. Estimates range from 55,000 to 85,000 POWs of Jewish nationality. Only 4,762 returned to the Soviet Union and maybe a couple of hundred remained in the West. The rest had been killed. Ibid. 407, 506.
71. Ibid. 229.
72. Iu. Arzamaskin, *Zalozhniki Vtoroi mirovoi voiny: Repatriatsiia sovestkikh grazhdan v 1944–1953 gg.* (Moscow: Rossiiskaia istoricheskaia voenno-politicheskaia biblioteka, 2001), 107–44.
73. Ibid. 142–3. The 17 Sept. 1955 decree is reprinted in A. Artizov, Iu. Sigachev, and V. Khlopov (eds.), Rossiia XX Vek. Dokumenty. *Reabilitatsiia: kak eto bylo. Dokumenty Prezidiuma TsK KPSS i drugie materialy. Mart 1953–fevral' 1956* (Moscow: Mezhdunarodnyi fond 'demokratiia', 2000), 259–60.
74. Arzamaskin, *Zalozhniki*, 139.
75. *Voenno-istoricheskii zhurnal*, 9 (1988): 26–8. Note that this was not really a turning point in the legal situation of POWs. Already the Criminal Code of 1926 defined 'giving oneself over to the enemy' as treason if it was not caused by the 'battle situation'. See L. G. Ivashov and A. S. Emelin, 'Nravstvennye i pravovye problemy plena v Otechestvennoi istorii', *Voenno-istoricheskii zhurnal*, 1 (1992): 45–6.
76. Further legislation ruled that grown-up members of the families of those POWs who were sentenced to death should be deported for five years. Ivashov and Emelin, 'Nravstvennye', 47–8.
77. Naumov and Reshin, 'Repression', 339. For examples for shootings see Dallin and Nicolaevsky, *Forced Labor*, 284, 287; and the report on the work of the Party Control Commission between 1939 and 1946, RGANI f. 6, op. 6, d. 3, l. 55. British reports mentioned execution commandoes waiting for repatriated POWs in 1945. See Polian, *Deportiert nach Hause*, 94.
78. Zemskov, 'K voprosu o repatriatsii sovetskikh grazhdan', 34–6; *Georgii Zhukov: Stenogramma*, 126.
79. Verbitskaia, 'Liudskie poteri', 159.
80. Zemskov, 'K voprosu o repatriatsii', 36.
81. Arzamaskin, *Zalozhniki*, 55–6.
82. Zhukov commission report on situation of former POWs (4 June 1956), *Reabilitatsiia* (see n. 4 above), 115.
83. Verbitskaia, 'Liudskie poteri', 159–60; Zemskov, 'Angst vor der Rückkehr: Die Repatriierung sowjetischer Staatsbürger und ihr weiteres Schicksal

(1944–1956)', in Haus der Geschichte der Bundesrepublik Deutschland (ed.), *Kriegsgefangene: Voennoplennye. Sowjetische Kriegsgefangene in Deutschland. Deutsche Kriegsgefangene in der Sowjetunion* (Düsseldorf: Droste, 1995), 157–62, here 162.

84. Zemskov, 'K voprosu o repatriatsii sovetskikh grazhdan', 36.

85. Report on letters by former POWs, GARF f. r-7523, op. 55, d. 10, l. 17–32, here 27.

86. D'iakov, *Mechenye*, 48.

87. Council of Ministers Resolution (30 Sept. 1946), No. 2220, GARF f. r-5446, op. 1, d. 285, l. 240–1.

88. GARF f. r-9526-s ch, op. 1-s ch, d. 617, l. 16–17.

89. On the continued enforcement of the stringent labor laws introduced between 1940 and 1943 during the postwar period see Sheila Fitzpatrick, 'Postwar Soviet Society: The "Return to Normalcy", 1945–1953', in Susan J. Linz (ed.), *The Impact of World War II on the Soviet Union* (Totowa, NJ: Rowman & Allanhead, 1985), 141; and Filtzer, *Soviet Workers and Late Stalinism*, 8–9, 158–67.

90. D'iakov, *Mechenye*, 115–16, 119.

91. Naumov, 'Sud'ba voennoplennykh', 103; *Georgii Zhukov. Stenogramma*, 128; Arzamaskin, *Zalozhniki*, 55 n. 156.

92. Filtzer, *Soviet Workers and Late Stalinism*, 24. The file he quotes (RGASPI f. 17, op. 121, d. 545) is part of the *Tekhsekretariat* of the Central Committee, which has been reclassified since Filtzer saw it.

93. Kruglov to Molotov (Osobaia papka Molotova, 12 Oct. 1947), GARF f. r-9401, op. 2 s. ch., d. 172, l. 335–6.

94. Correspondence of Golikov-admistration: GARF f. r-9526 s ch, op. 1 s ch, d. 617, l. 113, 115, 120, 166.

95. GARF f. r-9526 s ch, op. 1 s ch, d. 617, l. 166, l. 182–3.

96. Cf. Elliot, *Pawns of Yalta*, 210; Naumov and Reshin, 'Repression', 353–4.

97. Belov, *History of a Soviet Collective Farm*, 69; Goeken-Haidl, *Der Weg zurück*, 519, 462–8.

98. Naumov and Reshin, 'Repression', 351–2.

99. V. K. Luzherenko, 'Plen: Tragediia millionov', in V. A. Zolotarev and G. N. Sevost'ianov (eds.), *Velikaia Otechestvennaia voina 1941–1945: Voenno-istoricheskie ocherki. V chetyrekh knigakh, iv. Narod i voina* (Moscow: Nauka, 1999), 193; *Reabilitatsiia: Kak eto bylo. Fevral' 1956–nachalo 80-kh godov*, 115; Minister of Interior S. Kruglov to Molotov (23 Oct. 1947), GARF f. r-9401, op. 2 s.ch., d. 174, l. 43–44, here: 43; *Reabilitatsiia: kak eto bylo. Dokumenty Prezidiuma TsK KPSS i drugie materialy. Mart 1953–fevral' 1956*, 278; CC and Council of Ministers Resolution (29 June 1956), no. 898-490s, *Voenno-istoricheskii zhurnal*, 8 (1991): 32.

100. Goeken-Haidl, *Der Weg zurück*, 519.

101. D'iakov, *Mechenye*, 130–2.

102. Ibid. 210.

103. Report of the head of the repatriation administration of the republic of Estonia to the Golikov administration (31 Jan. 1949), GARF f. r-9526 s ch, op. 1 s ch, d. 617, l. 24; Naumov, 'Sud'ba voennoplennykh', 101, 105, 107. Naumov and Reshin, 'Repression', 355.

104. RGASPI f. 17, op. 122, d. 212, l. 42–3; for other examples see Naumov, 'Sud'ba voennoplennykh', 105.

105. Voronezh obkom secretary for propaganda and agitation I. Strakhov to head of the sector for vuzy in the dept of propaganda of the Central Committee V. D. Kul'bakin (24 Sept. 1948), RGASPI f. 17, op. 132, d. 74, l. 4–13, here 6.

106. D'iakov, *Mechenye*, 255–7.

107. Ibid. 116.

108. I. Charikov to A. A. Kuznetsov (5 May 1948), RGASPI f. 17, op. 132, d. 61, l. 1–4, here 2–3.

109. Complaint of the mother of the arrested man, to Voroshilov, 16 Nov. 1953, probably dictated to her grandson, GARF f. A-461, op. 1, d. 1171, l. 2–4.

110. Golikov to Zhdanov (9 June 1947), RGASPI f. 17, op. 122, d. 212, l. 43. Similar refusals to accept former POWs into collective farms had been reported in July 1945. Naumov and Reshin, 'Repression', 353.

111. GARF f. r-7523, op. 55, d. 49, l. 3–4.

112. Verbitskaia, 'Liudskie poteri', 161.

113. Letter to Shvernik (before 20 May 1952), GARF f. r-7523, op. 55, d. 49, l. 4.

114. Repr. in *Reabilitatsiia: kak eto bylo. Dokumenty Prezidiuma TsK KPSS i drugie materialy. Mart 1953–fevral' 1956*, 259–60.

115. Ibid. 406 n. 54.

116. Ibid. 286–7.

117. *Reabilitatsiia: Kak eto bylo. Fevral' 1956–nachalo 80-kh godov*, 73, 114–18, 129–32; Resolution of Presidium of Supreme Soviet (20 Sept. 1956), *Sbornik zakonov SSSR i ukazov Prezidiuma Verkhovnogo Soveta SSSR 1938–1961g.* (Moscow: Izvestiia, 1961), 857.

118. Beate Fieseler, 'Innenpolitik der Nachkriegszeit 1945–1953', in Stefan Plaggenborg (ed.), *Handbuch der Geschichte Russlands*, v. *1945–1991: Vom Ende des Zweiten Weltkriegs bis zum Zusammenbruch der Sowjetunion. 1. Halbband* (Stuttgart: Anton Hiersemann, 2002), 48.

119. Shneer, *Plen*, 94; Wolfgang Kasack, *Lexikon der russischen Literatur des 20. Jahrhunderts: Vom Beginn des Jahrhunderts bis zum Ende der Sowjetära*, 2nd rev. edn. (Munich: Verlag Otto Sagner, 1992), 1201–3; P. A. Nikolaev (ed.), *Russkie pisateli 20 veka: Biograficheskii slovar'* (Moscow: Bol'shaia Rossiiskaia Entsiklopediia, 2000), 779–82; *Biograficheskii entsiklopedicheskii slovar'* (Moscow: Bolshaia Rossiiskaia entsiklopediia, 2000), 87; Denise J. Youngblood, *Russian War Films: On the Cinema Front, 1914–2005* (Lawrence, Kan.: University Press of Kansas, 2007), 121–3; Grigorii Chukhrai, *Chistoe nebo* (Mosfil'm, 1961).

120. Shneer, *Plen*, 94–5; *Russkie pisateli 20 veka*, 288–9; Kasack, *Lexikon*, 1462–3.
121. Shneer, *Plen*, 95. On the academic discussion see Osterloh, *Sowjetische Kriegsgefangene*; Elena Rzhevskaia, 'Zhiv, Bratok?', *Novyi mir*, 5 (1987): 3–11.
122. *Izvestiia*, 21 Aug. 1987, p. 3; 29 Aug. 1987, p. 3; 5 Sept. 1987, p. 3; 11 Sept. 1987, p. 6; *Krasnaia zvezda*, 5 Sept. 1987, p. 6.
123. *Krasnaia zvezda*, 16 Jan. 1988, pp. 3–4.
124. *Izvestiia*, 5 Feb. 1988, p. 3.
125. Decree of the President of the Russian Federation (24 Jan. 1995) as quoted by Luzherenko, 'Plen: Tragediia millionov', 193–4; Naumov, 'Sud'ba voen-noplennykh', 101, 108–10.

## CHAPTER 6

1. Oksana Kasenkina, *Leap to Freedom* (London: Hurst & Blackett, 1949), 95.
2. V. N. Donchenko, 'Demobilizatsiia Sovetskoi armii i reshenie problem kadrov v pervye poslevoennye gody', *Istoriia SSSR* 3 (1970): 102.
3. Mark Edele, 'More than just Stalinists: The Political Sentiments of Victors 1945–1953', in Juliane Fürst (ed.), *Late Stalinist Russia: Society between Reconstruction and Reinvention* (London and New York: Routledge, 2006), 167–91.
4. Sheila Fitzpatrick, 'Postwar Soviet Society: The "Return to Normalcy", 1945–1953', in Susan J. Linz (ed.), *The Impact of World War II on the Soviet Union* (Totowa, NJ: Rowman & Allanhead, 1985), 136–7, and *Education and Social Mobility in the Soviet Union 1921–1934* (Cambridge: Cambridge University Press, 2002).
5. Donald Filtzer, *Soviet Workers and Late Stalinism: Labour and the Restoration of the Stalinist System after World War II* (Cambridge: Cambridge University Press, 2002), 30.
6. Nikolai Mitrokhin, *Russkaia partiia: Dvizhenie russkikh natsionalistov v SSSR 1953–1985* (Moscow: Novoe literaturnoe obozrenie, 2003), 152–7, quotation 155.
7. Philippa C. Maddern, 'Social Mobility', in Rosemary Horrox and W. Mark Ormrod (eds.), *A Social History of England 1200–1500* (Cambridge and New York: Oxford University Press, 2006), 114.
8. I. E. Bogacheva, *Dorogi zhizni: Vospominaniia i razmyshleniia voennoi medsestry* (Voronezh: Voronezhskii gosudarstvennyi universitet, 2000), 2–4.
9. Ibid. 6–10; quotation 10.
10. Ibid. 11–12.
11. Ibid. 51, 53.
12. Ibid. 53–4.
13. Ibid. 54–5.
14. Ibid. 55–6.
15. Ibid. 56.

16. Ibid. 58–9.
17. Ibid. 62–3.
18. Iurii Trifonov, 'Studenty. Povest'', *Novyi mir*, 10 (1950): 56–175; 11 (1950): 49–82. 'Tortuous novel' is Vera Dunham's precise term, *In Stalin's Time: Middleclass Values in Soviet Fiction*, enlarged edn. (Durham, NC, and London: Duke University Press, 1990), 45. The novel won the Stalin Prize, Third Class, for 1950. See Wolfgang Kasack, *Lexikon der russischen Literatur des 20. Jahrhunderts: Vom Beginn des Jahrhunderts bis zum Ende der Sowjetära*, 2nd edn. (Munich: Sagner, 1992), 1324. *Krokodil*, 26/7 (10 Mar. 1947), 6.
19. e.g. Viktor Platonovich Nekrasov, 'V rodnom gorode', *Izbrannye proizvedeniia: Povesti, rasskazy, putevye zametki* (Moscow: Khudozhestvennaia literatura, 1962; 1954), 248–470; Iurii Bondarev, *Tishina: Roman* (Moscow: Sovetskii pisatel', 1962).
20. Sheila Fitzpatrick, 'Social Mobility in the Late Stalin Period: Recruitment into the Intelligentsia and Access to Higher Education, 1945–1953', unpublished paper (1978), 12.
21. M. I. Movshovich (ed.), *Vysshaia shkola: Osnovnye postanovleniia, prikazy i instruktsii*, 2nd edn. (Moscow: Sovetskaia nauka, 1948), 558; *Pamiatka demobilizovannym riadovym i serzhantam Krasnoi Armii*, 2nd enlarged edn. (Moscow: Voennoe Izdatel'stvo, 1946), 55–6.
22. Vladimir Kabo, *The Road to Australia: Memoirs* (Canberra: Aboriginal Studies Press, 1998), 88, 92–3.
23. Mitrokhin, *Russkaia partiia*, 152–7.
24. Kaftanov, *Sovetskoe studenchestvo*, 4–5 (1946): 14; *Kul'turnoe stroitel'stvo SSSR* (1956): 212–13, both as quoted in Fitzpatrick, 'Social Mobility in the Late Stalin Period', 12; GARF f. r-9396, op. 1, d. 118, l. 265–8, here 265; and Edele, 'A "Generation of Victors"?', 309, table 4.14.
25. See the data on veterans in universities between 1944/5 and 1950/1 in Edele, 'A "Generation of Victors"?' 268, table 4.1.
26. 4 July 1947, as quoted in *Soviet Youth: Some Achievements and Problems. Excerpts from the Soviet Press*, ed. Dorothea L. Meek (London: Routledge & Kegan, 1957), 143.
27. See the data for eleven regions of the Soviet Union, table 4.11 in Edele, 'A "Generation of Victors"?', 300; and the data for urban demobilized for the entire Soviet Union by 1 Jan. 1947, ibid. 583 (app. 5).
28. See discussion of the data, ibid. 288–90.
29. Mikhail Gorbachev, *Zhizn' i reformy*, 2 vols., i (Moscow: Novosti, 1995), 59.
30. Kabo, *Road to Australia*, 90–1.
31. Liudmilla Alexeyeva, and Paul Goldberg, *The Thaw Generation: Coming of Age in the Post-Stalin Era* (Boston: Little, Brown, & Co., 1990), 30–1.
32. Raissa Gorbacheva, *'Ia nadeius' ...'* (Moscow: Novosti, 1991), 62–5.
33. Zdenek Mlynarzh, *Moroz udaril iz Kremlia* (Moscow: Respublika, 1992), 18–19.

34. I. Griaznov, 'O novom prieme studentov', *Za Stalinskuiu nauku: Organ partbiuro, rektorata, komiteta VLKSM, profkoma i mestkoma Gor'kovskogo gosuniversiteta*, 4 Sept. 1948, p. 1.
35. See the articles in *Za Stalinskuiu nauku*, 30 June 1948, p. 1; 27 May 1948, p. 2; 30 June 1948, p. 2; 20 May 1948, p. 1; 22 Feb. 1950, p. 1; 30 June 1950, p. 1; 7 Nov. 1950, p. 2; 1 May 1951, p. 2.
36. Alexeyeva and Goldberg, *Thaw Generation*, 29–55; and Gorbachev, *Zhizn' i reformy*, i. 66–7.
37. T. H. Rigby, *Communist Party Membership in the USSR 1917–1967* (Princeton: Princeton University Press, 1968), chs. 7, 8, 11.
38. Report on number of communists in civilian and military party organizations, 1 July 1941 to 1 Sept. 1943, RGASPI f. 17, op. 122, d. 56, l. 50; Report on number of communists mobilized into Red Army during the war, RGANI f. 77, op. 1, d. 4, l. 132–4.
39. For data on party admissions in military party organizations from the third quarter of 1941 to the first quarter of 1945 see RGANI f. 77, op. 1, d. 3. ll. 520b, 530b, 1300b, 1310b, 1320b, 1330b, 2100b, 2110b, 2120b, 2130b; d.4, ll. 500b, 510b, 520b, 530b. These data are summarized in Edele, 'A "Generation of Victors"?', 575–80 (app. 2). See also the discussion of divergent numbers in Mark Edele, 'Soviet Veterans as an Entitlement Group, 1945–1955', *Slavic Review*, 65/1 (2006): 119 nn. 38 and 39.
40. Edele, 'Soviet Veterans as an Entitlement Group', 119.
41. On 1 Jan. 1946, 56% of all full members in civilian organizations had joined the party during the war, 44% before. Among candidates to membership the majority position of wartime communists was even more striking: 96% of all candidates in the party as a whole had been admitted between 1941 and 1945. In civilian and military party organizations the respective shares were 94 and 99%. RGANI f. 77, op. 1, d. 4, l. 169, 172, 173.
42. RGANI f. 77, op. 1, dd. 3–4, summarized in Edele, 'A "Generation of Victors"?', 575–80 (app. 2).
43. Rigby, *Communist Party Membership*, 376.
44. For the average educational level of the entire Soviet population in 1939 see *Vsesoiuznaia perepis' naseleniia 1939goda: Osnovnye itogi*, 49; for the data for the nationalities (also in 1939) see *Itogi vsesoiuznoi perepisi naseleniia 1959 goda: SSSR (svodnyi tom)* (Moscow: Gosstatizdat, 1962), 234–5.
45. On Ukraine see Karel C. Berkhoff, *Harvest of Despair: Life and Death in Ukraine under Nazi Rule* (Cambridge and London: Belknap Press of Harvard University Press, 2004); and Amir Weiner, *Making Sense of War: The Second World War and the Fate of the Bolshevik Revolution* (Princeton and Oxford: Princeton University Press, 2000).
46. On Azeri 'legions' within the German army during the war see Joachim Hoffmann, *Die Ostlegionen 1941–1943: Turkotataren, Kaukasier und Wolgafinnen im deutschen Heer* (Freiburg: Rombach, 1976). An Azerbaijan Infantry Battalion

689 took part in the bloody liquidation of the Warsaw uprising. Joanna K. M. Hanson, *The Civilian Population and the Warsaw Uprising of 1944* (Cambridge: Cambridge University Press, 1982), 84–5.

47. G. V. Kostyrchenko, *Tainaia politika Stalina: Vlast' i antisemitizm* (Moscow: Mezhdunarodnye otnosheniia, 2001).

48. RGANI f. 77, op. 1, d. 2, l. 1140b; d. 3, l. 2350b; d. 4, l. 53.

49. RGANI f. 77, op. 1, d. 5, l. 147, 1710b.

50. Mordechai Altshuler, 'A Note on Jews in the Red Army on the Eve of the Second World War', *Jews and Jewish Topics in the Soviet Union and Eastern Europe*, 18 (2002): 37–9, here 39.

51. RGANI f. 77, op. 1, d. 4, l. 170.

52. Mordechai Altshuler, 'Antisemitism in Ukraine toward the End of the Second World War', *Jews in Eastern Europe*, 3 (Winter 1993): 40–81, here 49–50 n. 49. During the war 0.5 million Jews served among the 34.5 million regular troops. See Aron Shneer, *Plen. Sovetskie voennoplennye v Germanii, 1941–1945* (Moscow and Jerusalem: Mosty kultury, Gesharim, 2005), 340; and G. F. Krivosheev and M. F. Filimoshin, 'Poteri vooruzhennykh sil SSSR v Velikoi Otechestvennoi voine', in V. B. Zhiromskaia (ed.), *Naselenie Rossii v xx veke: Istoricheskie ocherki*, ii. *1940–1959* (Moscow: Rosspen, 2001), 25. See also Weiner, *Making Sense of War*, 217. On the continuing strong Jewish representation in the party see also Rigby, *Communist Party Membership*, 373–4, 383–8, who concludes that the long-term trend was one of reduction of the over-representation without undoing the over-representation.

53. Yuri Slezkine, *The Jewish Century* (Princeton: Princeton University Press, 2004), 222–3; Shneer, *Plen*, 341.

54. Cyntia S. Kaplan, 'The Impact of World War II on the Party', in Susan J. Linz (ed.), *The Impact of World War II on the Soviet Union* (Totowa, NJ: Rowman & Allanhead, 1985), 159–60; Edele, 'A "Generation of Victors"?', 292–3.

55. Edele, 'A "Generation of Victors"?', 293–4; Rigby, *Communist Party Membership*, 253; John Erickson, *The Road to Berlin: Stalin's War with Germany*, ii (New Haven and London: Yale University Press, 1983), 401; G. G. Morekhina, *Partiinoe stroitel'stvo v period Velikoi Otechestvennoi voiny Sovetskogo Soiuza 1941–1945* (Moscow: Politicheskaia literatura, 1986), 372–3.

56. Weiner, *Making Sense of War*, 20–1.

57. Sheila Fitzpatrick, *Stalin's Peasants: Resistance and Survival in the Russian Village After Collectivization* (New York and Oxford: Oxford University Press, 1994), 314.

58. Leonard Schapiro, *The Communist Party of the Soviet Union* (New York: Vintage Books, 1964), 523.

59. Jerry F. Hough, 'The Changing Nature of the Kolkhoz Chairman', in James R. Millar (ed.), *The Soviet Rural Community* (Urbana, Ill.: University of Illinois Press, 1971), 103–20, here 106; Lévesque, ' "Part-Time Peasants":

Labour Discipline, Collective Farm Life, and the Fate of Soviet Socialized Agriculture after the Second World War, 1945–1953', Ph.D. diss. (University of Toronto, 2003), 269. On the wider phenomenon of women losing jobs to veterans see Greta Bucher, *Women, the Bureaucracy and Daily Life in Postwar Moscow, 1945–1953* (Boulder, Colo.: East European Monographs, 2006), 17, 66, 68–9.

60. Lévesque, 'Part-Time Peasants', 236.
61. Stenographic report of meeting of local cadre workers of Ministry of Agriculture, 23–5 Nov. 1950, Russian State Economic Archive (RGAE) f. 7486, op. 18, d. 1076, l. 28.
62. Lévesque, 'Part-Time Peasants', 268. This trend is less pronounced for other jobs which allowed a slightly better living to be made on the kolkhoz; 38% of agricultural specialists with higher education, and 44.4% of agronomists and livestock specialists (*zootekhniki*) were women (RGAE f. 7486, op. 18, d. 1076, l. 29).
63. Fedor Belov, *The History of a Soviet Collective Farm* (New York: Praeger, 1955), 45, 107–9; RGAE f. 1562, op. 324, d. 3068, l. 6 (these archival data were collected by Jean Lévesque, who generously made them available to me).
64. List of questions posed to lecturers and agitators of party organizations (accompanying letter dated 27 Apr. 1949), RGASPI f. 17, op. 132, d. 114, l. 64–71a; here 64.
65. Tsentr Dokumentatsii Noveishei Istorii Voronezhskoi oblasti (hereafter TsDNI VO) f. 3, op. 1, d. 6580, l. 4.
66. Lévesque, 'Part-Time Peasants', 274.
67. Stenographic report of meeting on cadres questions in the Ministry of Agriculture, 2 Oct. 1946, RGAE f. 7486, op. 18, d. 910, l. 121.
68. Report of Chkalovsk obkom on work with demobilized soldiers, war invalids, and families of fallen soldiers and families of soldiers, 14 Feb. 1946, RGASPI f. 17, op. 122, d. 145, l. 173–7, here 174.
69. Belov, *History of a Soviet Collective Farm*, 26. See also Weiner, *Making Sense of War*, 315.
70. N. N. Maslov, 'Kommunisticheskaia partiia v poslevoennyi period', in Iu. P. Sviridenko A. I. Zeveleva, and V. V. Shelokhaeva (eds.), *Politicheskie partii Rossii: Istoriia i sovremennost'. Uchebnik dlia istoricheskikh i gumanitarnykh fakul'tetov vysshikh uchebnykh zavedenii* (Moscow: Rosspen, 2000), 477–99, here 481.
71. Report on the execution of CC resolution of 27 June 1945 on the work of Rostov obkom, 28 Feb. 1946, RGASPI f. 17, op. 122, d. 132, l. 3–32, here 31.
72. Report on the work of Sal'skii raikom, Rostov oblast', not after 8 July 1946, RGASPI f. 17, op. 122, d. 132, l. 116–26, here 124.
73. Report on execution of CC resolution of 25 Aug. 1945 on the work of local party and soviet organs regarding work with demobilized soldiers in

Murmansk oblast', 31 Jan. 1946, RGASPI f. 17, op. 122, d. 145, l. 95–960b, here 950b.

74. Report on work of local organs in Chuvash Autonomous Republic with regard to demobilized soldiers, 11 Feb.1946, RGASPI f. 17, op. 122, d. 145, l. 158–160ob; here 158ob.

75. Velko to Tishchenko, 'Spravka', TsDNI VO f. 3, op. 1, d. 550, l. 6, 13.

76. Raw data for 1 July 1948: RGANI f. 77, op. 1, d. 6, l. 810b. See also Kaplan, 'Impact of World War II on the Party', 167–8, 170.

77. RGANI f. 77, op. 1, d. 21, l. 21; d. 4, l. 177; d. 5, l. 82, l. 175; d. 6, l. 82, l. 183; d. 7, l. 83, l. 179; d. 8, l. 90; l. 84. Charted in Edele, 'A "Generation of Victors"?', 276, chart 4.2.

78. On the demobilization waves see Ch. 1.

79. Belov, History of a Soviet Collective Farm, pp. vii, 26, 202.

80. Velko to Tishchenko: 'Spravka', TsDNI VO f. 3, op. 1, d. 550, here 10–11.

81. See Edele, 'A "Generation of Victors"?', 284, chart 4.5.

82. Cf. Bucher, Women, 71, 82.

83. Filtzer, Soviet Workers, 21.

84. Council of Ministers resolution of 13 Aug. 1946, No. 1751, GARF f. r-5446, op. 1, d. 282, l. 180–1.

85. Groznyi obkom secretary to Patolichev, 5 Nov. 1946, RGASPI f. 17, op. 122, d. 147, l. 135–41, here 135.

86. Joint resolution of Council of Ministers and Central Committee, 19 Sept. 1946, Resheniia partii i pravitel'stva po khoziaistvennym voprosam, iii. 1941–1952 gody (Moscow: Politicheskaia literatura, 1968), 336–41, here 336.

87. Report of Savel'ev to Shvernik, GARF f. r-7523, op. 55, d. 13, l. 153–4.

88. This lower limiting case is based on the higher estimate for veterans in the army (4.2 million) and the lower estimate for the number of veterans alive after the war (20.1 million rather than 25.3 million). See Edele, 'A "Generation of Victors"?', 271.

89. GARF f. r. 9517, op. 1, d. 56, l. 1.

90. Historians usually follow Fitzpatrick's classical, pre-archival treatment, which was based on the impressions of defectors and the incomplete statistics provided by Soviet scholarship. See her two articles 'Postwar Soviet Society: The Return to "Normalcy"', 136, and 'War and Society in Soviet Context: Soviet Labor before, during, and after World War II', International Labor and Working-Class History, 35 (Spring 1989): 45, 51.

91. See Zubkova, Russia After the War, 59–67. On propaganda during demobilization see Ch. 1.

92. Weiner, Making Sense of War, 331.

93. On the postwar countryside see O. M. Verbitskaia, Rossiiskoe krest'ianstvo: Ot Stalina k Khrushchevu (Moscow: Nauka, 1992); and Jean Lévesque, 'Part-Time Peasants', and his 'Exile and Discipline: The June 1948 Campaign Against Collective Farm Shirkers', The Carl Beck Papers in Russian and East European Studies, 1708 (2006).

94. Verbitskaia, *Rossiiskoe krestianstvo*, 81, 83. For a detailed discussion of this process, see Edele, 'A "Generation of Victors"?', 312–35.
95. GARF f. A-259, op. 6, d. 4474, l. 45; RGASPI f. 17, op. 122, d. 189, l. 95–6.
96. GARF f. A-461, op. 1, d. 1128, l. 7, 9.
97. Anne Eliot Griesse and Richard Stites, 'Russia: Revolution and War', in Nancy Loring Goldman (ed.), *Female Soldiers: Combatants or Noncombatants? Historical and Contemporary Perspectives* (Westport, Conn.: Greenwood Press, 1982), 73.
98. G. F. Krivosheev, 'Poteri vooruzhennykh sil SSSR', *Liudskie poteri SSSR v period Vtoroi Mirovoi voiny. Sbornik statei* (St Petersburg: Blits, 1995), 74, 79; and G. F. Krivosheev and M. F. Filimoshin, 'Poteri vooruzhennykh sil SSSR v Velikoi Otechestvennoi voine', in Zhiromskaia (ed.), *Naselenie Rossii v XX veke*, ii. 25.
99. V. S. Murmantseva, *Zhenshchiny v soldatskikh shineliakh* (Moscow: Voennoe izd-vo, 1971), 9.
100. e.g. V. Nikolaeva-Tereshkova, 'Zhenskii voporos v sovremennoi obshchestvennoi zhizni', *Pravda*, 4 Mar. 1975, p. 2. For yet a different set of numbers, which imply that the 0.8 million exclude some important categories see 'Zhenshchiny SSSR', *Velikaia Otechestvennaia voina 1941–1945: Entsiklopediia* (Moscow: Sovetskaia entsiklopediia, 1985), 269–70.
101. Krivosheev and Filimoshin, 'Poteri vooruzhennykh', 32.
102. See Ch. 3.
103. Beate Fieseler, 'Der Krieg der Frauen: Die ungeschriebene Geschichte', in Deutsch-Russisches Museum Berlin-Karlshorst (ed.), *Mascha + Nina + Katjuscha: Frauen in der Roten Armee 1941–1945/Zhenshchiny-voennosluzhashchie* (Berlin: Ch. Links Verlag, 2002), 17.
104. See Ch. 3.
105. The rules for female volunteers stipulated that women had to be unmarried, childless, and without dependants. They were also supposed to have finished ten-year school. Of course, during the emergency of war, these rules were not always followed. See Andrea Moll-Sawatzki, 'Freiwillig an die Front? Junge Frauen zwischen Motivation und Mobilisierung', in *Masha + Nina + Katjuscha*, 21–7, esp. 22.
106. 'Vystuplenie tovarishcha M. I. Kalinina na vstreche s devushkami-voinami, demobilizuemymi iz Krasnoi Armii i Voenno-Morskogo Flota, v TsK VLKSM 26 iiulia 1945 goda', *Bloknot Agitatora Krasnoi Armii*, 21 (June 1945): 1–6, here 2.
107. Svetlana Alexiyevich, *War's Unwomanly Face*, tr. Keith Hammond and Lyudmila Lezhneva (Moscow: Progress Publishers, 1988), 11.
108. Elena Zubkova, *Russia after the War*, 23. See also Nekrasov, 'V rodnom gorode', 332; and Aleksiyevich, *War's Unwomanly Face*, 89.
109. Report on work placement of demobilized soldiers, Ivanovo oblast', 19 Apr. 1947, GARF f. A-259, op. 6, d. 4478, l. 101–3, here 103.

110. Report on work placement and material assistance to demobilized soldiers, city of Kuibyshev, 4 Apr. 1947, GARF f. A-259, op. 6, d. 4477, l. 30–1, here 31.

111. Decision of executive committee of Moscow regional Soviet on work placement of demobilized soldiers, 4 Apr. 1947, GARF f. A-259,op. 6, d. 4477, l. 16–18, here 16.

112. Short description of letters to the editor of *Red Star* in July 1946, RGASPI f. 17, op. 125, d. 429, l. 138–62, here 139.

113. See the case of the Hero of the Soviet Union described in a KPK report, 27 Nov. 1946, TsDOOSO f. 4, op. 31, d. 791, l. 364–7.

114. Personal correspondence with E. D., Moscow, 27 Sept. 2001.

115. Susanne Conze and Beate Fieseler, 'Soviet Women as Comrades-in-Arms: A Blind Spot in the History of the War', in Robert W. Thurston and Bernd Bonwetsch (eds.), *The People's War: Responses to World War II in the Soviet Union* (Urbana and Chicago: University of Illinois Press, 2000), 213. This conclusion is based on impressionistic evidence and has not yet been studied in any depth.

116. Zhanna Gausner, 'Vot my i doma…', *Zvezda*, 11 (1947): 4–106, here 6, 16–21.

117. Report of head of office of chairman of Presidium of Supreme Soviet on applications of demobilized soldiers for help in work placement, May 1947, GARF f. r-7523, op. 55, d. 13, l. 154.

118. Correspondence between military department of Sverdlovsk obkom to a raikom secretary, 1945, TsDOOSO f. 4, op. 31, d. 705, l. 195.

119. Reina Pennington, *Wings, Women, and War: Soviet Airwomen in World War II Combat* (Lawrence, Kan.: University Press of Kansas, 2001), 144, 148.

120. See Edele, 'A "Generation of Victors"?', 307, table 4.13.

121. For meanings 1 and 2 see Harmut Kaelble, 'Social Mobility', in Peter N. Stearns (ed.), *Encyclopedia of European Social History from 1350 to 2000*, iii (Detroit and New York: Charles Scribner's Sons, 2001), 19.

122. John D. Nagle, 'A New Look at the Soviet Elite: A Generational Model of the Soviet System', *Journal of Political and Military Sociology*, 3/1 (1975): 1–13, esp. 4–9.

123. Zubkova, *Russia After the War*, 24–45.

124. Edele, 'Soviet Veterans as an Entitlement Group', 113–21; id., 'More than just Stalinists'.

125. Erich Maria Remarque, *The Road Back* (New York: Fawcett Books, 1998).

126. Antoine Prost, *Les Anciens Combattants et la société française: 1914–1939* in *Histoire* (Paris: Presses de la Fondation nationale des sciences politiques, 1977), 2.

127. e.g. Michael J. Bennett, *When Dreams Came True: The G.I. Bill and the Making of Modern America* (Washington, DC: Brassey's, 2000); or David Englander, 'Soldiers and Social Reform in the First and Second World Wars', *Historical Research: The Bulletin of the Institute of Historical Research*, 67 (1994): 318–26.

CHAPTER 7

1. Barykin to Zhdanov (26 Aug. 1946), RGASPI f. 17, op. 125, d. 391, l. 70–3. I am indebted to Timothy Johnston, Oxford, for bringing this document to my attention.
2. Cf. Sheila Fitzpatrick, 'Supplicants and Citizens: Public Letter-Writing in Soviet Russia in the 1930s', *Slavic Review*, 55/1 (1996): 78–105, esp. 103–5.
3. RGASPI f. 17, op. 125, d. 391, l. 70.
4. RGASPI f. 17, op. 125, d. 391, l. 71.
5. Minutes of meeting of the Section of Frontline Soldiers at the SKVV, 20 Dec. 1956, GARF f. r-9541, op. 1. d. 40, l. 28.
6. Emily E. Pyle, 'Village Social Relations and the Reception of Soldiers' Family Aid Policies in Russia, 1912–1921', Ph.D. diss. (University of Chicago, 1997), 306–7, 310; Beate Fieseler, *Die Invaliden des 'Grossen Vaterländischen Krieges' der Sowjetunion: Eine politische Sozialgeschichte 1941–1991*, Habilitationsschrift (Ruhr-Universität Bochum, 2003), 20.
7. Bernice Q. Madison, *Social Welfare in the Soviet Union* (Stanford, Calif.: Stanford University Press, 1968), 81; A. S. Turgaev (ed.), *Vysshie organy gosudarstvennoi vlasti i upravleniia Rossii, IX-XX vv.: Spravochnik* (St Petersburg: Izd-vo 'Obrazovanie–Kul'tura, 2000), 309–10.
8. Fieseler, *Die Invaliden des 'Grossen Vaterländischen Krieges'*, 24, 37.
9. See Edele, 'A "Generation of Victors?" ', 518–19.
10. Sheila Fitzpatrick, 'The Legacy of the Civil War', in William Rosenberg *et al.* (eds.), *Party, State, and Society in the Russian Civil War: Explorations in Social History* (Bloomington and Indianapolis: Indiana University Press, 1989), 385–98, here 393.
11. Cf. Fieseler, *Die Invaliden des 'Grossen Vaterländischen Krieges'*, 37. See Ch. 8 below for a detailed discussion of the history of veterans' privileges.
12. Mark Edele, 'Soviet Veterans as an Entitlement Group, 1945–1955', *Slavic Review*, 65/1 (2006): 122, and 'A "Generation of Victors?" ', 520–30; and Fieseler, *Die Invaliden des 'Grossen Vaterländischen Krieges'*, 263–6.
13. Deputy head of the Central Committee's Dept for Organization and Instruction, Ratner to Malenkov (1 Aug. 1944), RGASPI, f. 17, op. 122, d. 71, l. 145.
14. 'Komitety ofitserov-invalidov Otechestvennoi voiny', *Krasnaia zvezda*, 9 Sept. 1944, p. 2; *Moskovskii bolshevik*, 9 Sept. 1944, p. 1; *Krasnyi flot*, 9 Sept. 944, p. 3. This episode was first reported by Fieseler, *Die Invaliden des 'Grossen Vaterländischen Krieges'*, 353–4.
15. See decision no. 46g. of 15 Sept. 1944, RGASPI f. 17, op. 116, d. 172, l. 10; and the materials to this decision, RGASPI f. 17, op. 117, d. 444, l. 21–260b.
16. KPK Plenipotentiary for Novosibirsk oblast' I. Kuznetsov reporting to Malenkov on implementation of resolutions regarding work placement and assistance to war invalids (18 Jan. 1945), RGASPI f. 17, op. 122, d. 100, l. 115.

17. Elena Zubkova, *Poslevoennoe sovetskoe obshchestvo: Politika i povsednevnost'*
    *1945–1953*, (Moscow: Rosspen, 2000), 37.
18. G. Aleksandrov to A. A. Zhdanov, 'About comrade Barykin's letter',
    RGASPI f. 17, op. 125, d. 391, l. 74–6, here esp. 74.
19. Ibid. 74–5.
20. Ibid. 75.
21. 'O perestroike i kadrovoi politike partii: Doklad General'nogo sekretaria TsK
    KPSS M. S. Gorbacheva na Plenume TsK KPSS 27 ianvaria 1987 goda',
    *Pravda*, 28 Jan. 1987, pp. 1–5, here 2, 3.
22. See Chs. 3 and 6.
23. Roman Kolkowicz, *The Soviet Military and the Communist Party* (Princeton:
    Princeton University Press, 1967), 224–81.
24. Edele, 'Soviet Veterans as an Entitlement Group', 130–1.
25. See Ch. 3.
26. Shorthand report of Second Plenum of SKVV, Moscow, 29–30 July 1958,
    GARF f. r-9541, op. 1, d. 179, l. 83–4.
27. Report of Chairman of the SKVV's revision commission A. Cherepanov on
    the composition of the organization in the localities, 31 Dec. 1958, GARF
    f. r-9541, op. 1, d. 182, l. 213–17, here 214.
28. GARF f. r-9541, op. 1, d. 19, l. 5.
29. Supporting materials to letter to CC CPSU on the question of society of
    former frontline soldiers, GARF f. r-9541, op. 1, d. 2, l. 2–10, here 2.
30. No. 1097 quoted in supporting materials to letter to CC CPSU, l. 2–3.
31. Ibid., l. 3–4.
32. Ibid., l. 5–7.
33. Ibid., l. 7.
34. Ibid., l. 7–8.
35. Letter from party members and pensioners of the Ministry of Defence of the
    Soviet Union Kadnikov, Pustovalov, Pas'ko, Shenker, Muliavko, Faiburd,
    Galishin, Chevpilov, and Zuev to Chairman of Revision Commission of
    CC CPSU P. G. Moskatov; and additional materials on the history of the
    organization (1956), GARF f. r-9541, op. 1, d. 2, l. 1–10.
36. Handwritten letter from USSR Organizational bureau of the society of
    former frontline soldiers, Kiev, to General Gundorov (n.d.), GARF f. r-9541,
    op. 1, d. 17, l. 24. *Kto byl kto v Velikoi Otechestvennoi voine 1941–1945: Liudi.*
    *Sobytiia. Fakty: Spravochnik*, 2nd ed. (Moscow: Respublika, 2000), 248.
37. See e.g. the draft statutes of the society of former frontline soldiers (1958),
    GARF f. r-9541, op. 1, d. 282; and letter from P. G. Titarneko to the
    Chairman of the SKVV S. K. Timoshenko (received by SKVV on 2 June
    1965), GARF f. r-9541, op. 1, d. 991, l. 1–2.
38. See Shorthand report of Second All-Union Conference of War Veterans,
    25 Feb. 1965, GARF f. r-9541, op. 1, d. 898, l. 64. See also Protocol of
    meeting of Presidium of Section of former frontline soldiers, 21 June 1965,

GARF f. r-9541, op. 1, d. 984, l. 130; and see Edele, 'A "Generation of Victors"?', 519–20.

39. 'Présentation de la FMAC', http://www.wvf-fmac.org/francais/presentation. htm (accessed April 2006).

40. 'Veterans of World Open London Talks', *New York Times*, 9 Dec. 1952, p. 18.

41. 'World Veterans Convene', *New York Times*, 8 July 1955, p. 5.

42. John MacCormac, 'World Veterans Gather in Vienna. Clock Red Bid to Share Stage, Back Austria Pact Aim and Honor Gold Coast Leader', *New York Times*, 28 Nov. 1954, p. 3.

43. See G. Zhukov and A. Zheltov to CC CPSU (24 May 1955), RGANI f. 5, op. 30, d. 118, l. 28–31.

44. See Boris Potapovich Pavlov (ed.), *Veterany v stroiu* (Moscow: Voen-izdat, 1981), 18; and the notes of Zhukov and Zheltov on the meeting with US veterans (23 Apr. 1956), *Georgii Zhukov: Stenogramma oktiabr'skogo (1957g.) plenuma TsK KPSS i drugie dokumenty*, Rossiia XX vek. Dokumenty, ed. A. N. Iakovlev (Moscow: Mezhdunarodnyi fond 'demokratiia', 2001), 71.

45. Handwritten protocol of meeting of initiative group for the foundation of the Soviet Committee of War Veterans (SKVV), 3 May 1956, GARF f. r-9541, op. 1, d. 1, l. 1, 4.

46. S. Borzenko, 'Net sil'nee uz tovarishchestva', *Literaturnaia gazeta*, 117 (2 Oct. 1956): 2. For the resistance of American veterans' organizations to a Soviet membership see 'Veterans Fight Bid for Link to Soviet', *New York Times*, 2 June 1956, p. 6.

47. F. Purcell, WVF Sekretariat, personal communication (email), 22 May 2006.

48. Beate Fieseler, 'Stimmen aus dem gesellschaftlichen Abseits: Die sowjet-ischen Kriegsinvaliden im "Tauwetter" der fünfziger Jahre', *Osteuropa*, 52/7 (2002): 947.

49. TASS report on First All-Union Conference of War Veterans, GARF f. r-9541, op. 1, d. 15, l. 1–2; *Pravda*, 30 Sept. 1956, p. 4; shorthand report of First All-Union Conference, GARF f. r-9541, op. 1, d. 3, l. 25.

50. Boris Potapovich Pavlov (ed.), *Veterany v stroiu* (Moscow: Voenizdat, 1981), 18–19.

51. In case there was still any ambiguity left, presidium member S. Borzenko drove home the point again in a newspaper article: 'Net sil'nee uz to-varishchestva', *Literaturnaia gazeta*, 117 (2 Oct. 1956): 2.

52. See shorthand report of SKVV plenum meeting (29 Sept. 1956) GARF f. r-9541, op. 1, d. 14.

53. See Edele, 'A "Generation of Victors"?', 515–17; Rossiiskii komitet veter-anov voiny i voennoi sluzhby (ed.), *Nam—45!* (Moscow: Mezhdunarodnyi ob" edinennyi biograficheski tsentr, 2001), 15.

54. Protocol of meeting of the section of former frontline soliders (20 Dec. 1956), GARF f. r-9541, op. 1, d. 40, l. 29.

55. See Fieseler, *Die Invaliden des 'Grossen Vaterländischen Krieges'*, 386–97.

56. Shorthand report of meeting of section of invalids (26 Dec. 1956, Moscow), GARF f. r-9541, op. 11, d. 49; Fieseler, *Die Invaliden des 'Grossen Vaterländischen Krieges'*, 386–93.

57. Em. Kazakevich, 'Delo o motokoliaske', *Literaturnaia gazeta*, 150 (18 Dec. 1956): 2.

58. Shorthand report of meeting of section of invalids (26 Dec. 1956, Moscow), l. 4.

59. Ibid., l. 5.

60. Ibid., l. 5–6.

61. Ibid., l. 7.

62. Ibid., l. 8.

63. Ibid., l. 11–12.

64. Ibid., l. 14.

65. Ibid., l. 16.

66. Ibid., l. 23.

67. Ibid., l. 17.

68. Ibid., l. 21.

69. Ibid., l. 22.

70. Ibid., l. 24–5.

71. Fieseler, *Die Invaliden des 'Grossen Vaterländischen Krieges'*, 410.

72. Short explanatory note on structure and work of the SKVV (1956), GARF f. r-9541, op. 1, d. 19, l. 5, 7; shorthand report of meeting of activists of the section of invalids (26 Dec. 1956, Moscow), GARF f. r-9541, op. 1, d. 49, l. 7.

73. Cf. Sheila Fitzpatrick, 'Intelligentsia and Power: Client–Patron Relations in Stalin's Russia', in Manfred Hildermeier (ed.), *Stalinismus vor dem zweiten Weltkrieg: Neue Wege der Forschung* (Munich: R. Oldenbourg Verlag, 1998), 35–53.

74. Shorthand report of meeting of SKVV Presidium, 20 Jan. 1958, GARF f. r- 9541, op. 1, d. 181, ll. 85, 93–4, 111; and Fieseler, *Die Invaliden des 'Grossen Vaterländischen Krieges'*, 402–3.

75. Fieseler, *Die Invaliden des 'Grossen Vaterländischen Krieges'*, 380, 399.

76. Shorthand report of second plenum of SKVV (29–30 July 1958), GARF f. r-9541, op. 1, d. 179, l. 5.

77. Shorthand report of SKVV Presidium meeting (20 Jan. 1958), GARF f. r-9541, op. 1, d. 181, l. 61.

78. Shorthand report of SKVV Presidium meeting (25 Feb. 1958), GARF f. r-9541, op. 1, d. 181, l. 144–6.

79. Ibid., l. 206–7.

80. Beate Fieseler, 'Stimmen aus dem gesellschaftlichen Abseits. Die sowjetrussischen Kriegsinvaliden im "Tauwetter" der fünfziger Jahre', *Osteuropa*, 52/7 (2002): 945–62, and, *Die Invaliden des 'Grossen Vaterländischen Krieges'*, 386–455.

81. Shorthand report of SKVV Presidium meeting (25 Feb. 1958), GARF f. r-9541, op. 1, d. 181, l. 207–8, quotation 208.

82. Shorthand report of second plenum of SKVV (29–30 July 1958), GARF f. r-9541, op. 1, d. 179, here l. 10.

83. Ibid., l. 34–7.

84. Ibid., l. 49, 57, 60.

85. Ibid., l. 101.

86. See e.g. protocol of SKVV Presidium meeting (11 Dec. 1958), GARF f. r-9541, op. 1, d. 182, 208–12; and the report of the Chairman of the SKVV's revision commission A. Cherepanov on the composition of the organization in the localities (31 Dec. 1958), GARF f. r-9541, op. 1, d. 182, l. 213–17, esp. 217.

87. Report of the Chairman of the SKVV's revision commission (31 Dec. 1958), l. 214.

88. See e.g. protocol of SKVV Presidium meeting (11 Dec. 1958), l. 208, 209; and the short report on the work of the Cheliabinsk section of the SKVV (1 June 1959), GARF f. r-9541, op. 1, d. 503, l. 1–5, esp. 1.

89. Report of A. Cherepanov (31 Dec. 1958), GARF f. r-9541, op. 1, d. 182, l. 213–17.

90. Information on the organization of veterans in the localities (7 Mar. 1961), GARF f. r-9541, op. 1, d. 512, l. 1.

91. See GARF f. r-9541, op. 1, d. 992, l. 1–2.

92. On the organization's chairmen, see *Nam—45!*, 6–14.

93. Information on the organization of veterans in the localities (7 March 1961), l. 1–4.

94. Shorthand report of fourth SKVV Plenum, 29 Mar. 1963, GARF f. r-9541, op. 1, d. 706, l. 10–11, 14, 15, 18, 78, 104, 135.

95. Shorthand report of SKVV Presidium meeting of 12 Apr. 1963, ibid. l. 4.

96. *Nam—45!* 24.

97. Overview of meetings of organisational commission in 1964, GARF f. r-9541, op. 1, d. 894, l. 13.

98. *Nam—45!* 24–6.

99. See the shorthand reports for both days: GARF f. r-9541, op. 1, d. 898–9.

100. See shorthand report of *aktiv* meeting, 8 Feb. 1965, GARF f. 5–9541, op. 1, d. 907, l. 2–3, 7–9.

101. *Ustav organizatsii Sovetskikh veteranov voiny* (Moscow: SKVV, 1966), 6.

102. See the shorthand reports of the Second All-Union Conference of War Veterans, 25 to 26 Feb. 1965, GARF f. r-9541, op. 1, d. 898, l. 42–3, 112; d. 899, l. 17, 60.

103. Shorthand report of SKVV Presidium meeting, 4 Feb. 1965, GARF f. r-9541, op. 1, d. 906, l. 4–5.

104. Shorthand report of *aktiv* meeting, 8 Feb. 1965, GARF f. r-9541, op. 1, d. 907, l. 13.
105. Shorthand report of SKVV Presidium meeting, 18 Mar. 1965, GARF f. r-9541, op. 1, d. 906, l. 27–9.
106. Resolution of SKVV Presidium on local sections (18 Mar. 1965), GARF f. r-9541, op. 1, d. 906, l. 38.
107. Statutes of SKVV sections in the localities (18 Mar. 1965), GARF f. r-9541, op. 1, d. 906, l. 39.
108. Boris Potapovich Pavlov (ed.), *Veterany v stroiu* (Moscow: Voenizdat, 1981), 25–6.
109. P. Batov, 'Sovetskie veterany voiny v bor'be za mir', *Voenno-istoricheskii zhurnal*, 6 (1979): 71.
110. Pavlov, *Veterany v stroiu*, 26–7. The number of sections then remained stable until 1986: GARF f. r-9541, op. 1, d. 1681, l. 37.
111. GARF f. r-9541, op. 1, d. 991, l. 3–4, 9.
112. Shorthand report of seminar with chairmen of Sections of War Veterans of republics and hero-cities, 21 Jan. 1966, GARF f. r-9541, op. 1, d. 996, l. 3–6, 7, 15, 20–1, 28, 37–8, 48, 50.
113. Ibid., l. 24.
114. Pavlov, *Veterany v stroiu*, 23–5, quotation 25.
115. Statutes on SKVV Sections, passed by Bureau of SKVV Presidium on 18 Aug. 1972, GARF f. r-9541, op. 1, d. 1393, l. 1–3, here l. 1.
116. Shorthand report of SKVV plenum of 23 Dec. 1977, GARF f. r-9541, op. 1, d. 1484, l. 6, 9, 28–9; Shorthand report of meeting of secretaries of SKVV sections, 20 June 1978, GARF f. r-9541, op. 1, d. 1518, l. 27–9.
117. Shorthand report of SKVV plenum of 23 Dec. 1977, GARF f. r-9541, op. 1, d. 1484, l. 29, 30–1.
118. Shorthand report of meeting of secretaries of SKVV sections, 20 June 1978, GARF f. r-9541, op. 1, d. 1518, l. 29.
119. Shorthand report of meeting of SKVV secretaries, 20 June 1978, GARF f. r-9541, op. 1, d. 1518, l. 30.
120. Report of deputy chairman of SKVV V. Moskovskii to Chairman I. Batov (early 1978), GARF f. r-9541, op. 1, d. 1506, l. 9.
121. Shorthand report of SKVV plenum of 23 Dec. 1977, GARF f. r-9541, op. 1, d. 1484, l. 30; Report of deputy chairman of SKVV V. Moskovskii to Chairman I. Batov (early 1978), GARF f. r-9541, op. 1, d. 1506, l. 10–11.
122. Shorthand report of III SKVV Plenum, 19 Dec. 1978, GARF f. r-9541, op. 1, d. 1505, l. 61.
123. Shorthand report of meeting of secretaries of SKVV sections, 20 June 1978, GARF f. r-9541, op. 1, d. 1518, l. 42.

124. Shorthand report of SKVV Presidium meeting, 15 Mar. 1978, GARF f. r-9541, op. 1, d. 1507, l. 62–3 and 67–8.

125. Shorthand report of III SKVV Plenum, 19 Dec. 1978, GARF f. r-9541, op. 1, d. 1505, l. 60–1.

126. Protocol no. 9 of meeting of Bureau of the SKVV Presidium, 30 Nov. 1978, GARF f. r-9541, op. 1, d. 1506, l. 126.

127. Shorthand report of SKVV plenum of 23 Dec. 1977, GARF f. r-9541, op. 1, d. 1484, l. 135–6.

128. See Ch. 8.

129. See e.g. the shorthand report of a seminar of section secretaries held on 26 to 27 Sept. 1985, GARF f. r-9541, op. 1, d. 1654.

130. 'O perestroike i kadrovoi politike partii: Doklad General'nogo sekretaria TsK KPSS M. S. Gorbacheva na Plenume TsK KPSS 27 ianvaria 1987 goda', *Pravda*, 28 Jan. 1987, pp. 1–5, here 3.

131. Gorbachev's speech on 25 Feb. 1986, repr. in *Materialy XXVII s'' ezda Kommunisticheskoi partii Sovetskogo Soiuza* (Moscow: Politizdat, 1986), 52.

132. 'V Politbiuro TsK KPSS', *Pravda*, 27 Sept. 1986, p. 1.

133. M. Ia. Kolpakov and Ia. I. Borisov (eds.), *Veterany ne vykhodiat v otstavku: Istoriia Omskoi oblastnoi organizatsii veteranov* (Omsk: Knizhnoe izdatel'stvo, 1998), 71–3, 76, 78; *Nam—45!* 27.

134. Shorthand report of SKVV Presidium meeting, 24 Nov. 1986, GARF f. r-9541, op. 1, d. 1681, l. 22–3, 27, 29, 34; K. Mazurov, 'Na rubezhakh perestroiki', *Veteran*, 3 (1988): 3; *Ustav Vsesoiuznoi organizatsii veteranov voiny i truda: Rezoliutsiia uchreditel'noi konferentsii Vsesoiuznoi organizatsii veteranov voiny i truda* (Moscow: Vsesoiuznyi sovet veteranov voiny i truda, 1987).

135. Shorthand report of meeting of SKVV Presidium, 31 July 1986, GARF f. r-9541, op. 1, d. 1680, l. 11, 107–10.

136. Ibid. l. 111–13, 116.

137. Ibid. l. 115.

138. O. Mukhin, 'V ugodu formalizmu?', *Veteran*, 7 (1988): 4.

139. K. Kalashnikov, 'O meste sektsii v novykh usloviiakh raboty', *Veteran voiny*. *Biulleten' SKVV*, 2 (1987): 47–9, here 48.

140. A. Pozdniakov, 'Vystoim', *Veteran*, 52/208 (1991): 2.

141. Helmut Altrichter, 'Kongreß der Volksdeputierten', *Historisches Lexikon der Sowjetunion. 1917/22 bis 1991*, ed. Hans-Joachim Torke (Munich: C. H. Beck, 1993), 157–8.

142. 'V Tsentral'noi izbiratel'noi komissii po vyboram narodnykh deputatov SSSR', *Izvestiia*, 28 Dec. 1988, p. 1.

143. P. Kravchenko, 'Ustav: prava i obiazannosti. Sovet vnosit predlozhenie', *Veteran*, 11 (1988): 3.

CHAPTER 8

1. Zhanna Gausner, 'Vot my i doma ...', *Zvezda*, 11 (1947): 19.
2. Mark Edele, 'Soviet Veterans as an Entitlement Group, 1945–1955', *Slavic Review*, 65/1 (2006): 111–37.
3. This terminology is inspired by Max Weber's discussion of status groups (*Stände*) and Sheila Fitzpatrick's notion of 'ascribed classes'. Max Weber, *Wirtschaft und Gesellschaft. Grundriss der verstehenden Soziologie. Studienausgabe*. 5th rev. edn. (Tübingen: J. C. B. Mohr [Paul Siebeck], 1990), 179–80 (part I, ch. 4, §3); Sheila Fitzpatrick, 'Ascribing Class: The Construction of Social Identity in Soviet Russia', *Journal of Modern History*, 65 (1993): 745–70.
4. See Stephen Kotkin, *Magnetic Mountain: Stalinism as a Civilization* (Berkeley, Calif.: University of California Press, 1995); Sheila Fitzpatrick, *Stalin's Peasants: Resistance and Survival in the Russian Village after Collectivization* (New York and Oxford: Oxford University Press, 1994).
5. For a conceptual discussion of state and non-state units of integration and social action see Mark Edele, 'Soviet Society, Social Structure, and Everyday Life: Major Frameworks Reconsidered', *Kritika: Explorations in Russian and Eurasian History*, 8/2 (2007): 349–73.
6. Cf. Werner S. Landecker, 'Integration and Group Structure: An Area of Research', *Social Forces*, 30/4 (1952): 394–400, and 'Types of Integration and their Measurement', *American Journal of Sociology*, 56/4 (1951): 332–40. The term 'social entity' to describe veterans is borrowed from Elena Zubkova, who writes of the 'new social entity' (*novyi sotsium*) of veterans. See her *Poslevoennoe sovetskoe obshchestvo: Politika i povsednevnost' 1945–1953* (Moscow: Rosspen, 2000), 28–37.
7. On the cult of the war see Introduction.
8. For the different generations of veterans see Introduction. On the transformation of the status group of veterans into a status group of 'the older generation' see Stephen Lovell, 'Soviet Russia's Older Generations', in Lovell (ed.), *Generations in Twentieth-Century Europe* (Houndsmills, Basingstoke: Palgrave Macmillan, 2007), 205–26.
9. Cf. Bernice Q. Madison, *Social Welfare in the Soviet Union* (Stanford, Calif.: Stanford University Press, 1968), 6, 9, 11, 21, 56.
10. Cf. Beate Fieseler, *Die Invaliden des 'Grossen Vaterländischen Krieges' der Sowjetunion: Eine Politische Sozialgeschichte 1941–1991*, Habilitationsschrift, Ruhr-Universität Bochum, 2003, 14; Theda Skocpol, *Protecting Soldiers and Mothers: The Political Origins of Social Policy in the United States* (Cambridge, Mass.: Belknap, 1992).
11. Elise Kimerling Wirtschafter, 'Social Misfits: Veterans and Soldiers' Families in Servile Russia', *Journal of Military History*, 59/2 (1995), 219–21.
12. Fieseler, *Die Invaliden des 'Grossen Vaterländischen Krieges'*, 16, 21.

13. Joshua Sanborn, *Drafting the Russian Nation: Military Conscription, Total War, and Mass Politics 1905–1925* (DeKalb, Ill.: Northern Illinois University Press, 2003), 5.

14. Ibid. 20.

15. Ibid. 49–50.

16. On the service principle and service classes in Russian history see V. O. Kliuchevskii, *Russkaia istoriia: Polnyi kurs lektsii.* 3 vols. (Rostov-on-Don: Feniks, 2000); Richard Hellie, 'The Structure of Modern Russian History: Toward a Dynamic Model', *Russian History,* 4/1 (1977): 1–22.

17. Emily E. Pyle, 'Village Social Relations and the Reception of Soldiers' Family Aid Policies in Russia, 1912–1921', Ph.D. diss. (University of Chicago, 1997), 105–75; Fieseler, *Die Invaliden des 'Grossen Vaterländischen Krieges',* 4–5, 18.

18. Pyle, 'Village Social Relations', 284–349.

19. Mark von Hagen, *Soldiers in the Proletarian Dictatorship: The Red Army and the Soviet Socialist State, 1917–1930* (Ithaca, NY, and London: Cornell University Press, 1990), 331.

20. Pyle, 'Village Social Relations', 300.

21. Fieseler, *Die Invaliden des 'Grossen Vaterländischen Krieges',* 19–20.

22. Pyle, 'Village Social Relations', 305, 311, 326, 328–9; Fieseler, *Die Invaliden des 'Grossen Vaterländischen Krieges',* 18.

23. Bruce Lincoln, *Red Victory: A History of the Russian Civil War* (New York: Simon & Schuster, 1989), 466–7.

24. A. F. Zavgorodnii, *Deiatel'nost' gosudarstvennykh organov i obshchestvenno-politicheskikh organizatsii po sotsial'noi zashchite voennosluzhashchikh Krasnoi Armii i ikh semei v mezhvoennyi period (1921–iiun' 1941 gg)* (St Petersburg: Nestor, 2001), 111–12, 114, 120–22.

25. Zavgorodnii, *Deiatel'nost' gosudarstvennykh organov,* 128; Fieseler, *Die Invaliden des 'Grossen Vaterländischen Krieges',* 38.

26. Fieseler, *Die Invaliden des 'Grossen Vaterländischen Krieges',* 21–50.

27. P. A. Brunt, 'The Army and the Land in the Roman Revolution', *The Fall of the Roman Republic and Related Essays* (New York: Oxford University Press, 1988), 240–75; and Stefan Link, *Konzepte der Privilegierung römischer Veteranen* (Stuttgart: F. Steiner, 1989).

28. I have described this process of convergence of different legislations elsewhere. See Edele, 'Soviet Veterans as an Entitlement Group', 122–5. For a detailed discussion of the legislation and its implementation see also my 'A "Generation of Victors"?', 108–83.

29. See Ch. 1.

30. Cf. Fitzpatrick, 'Ascribing Class'.

31. See Ch. 1, Table 1.1, and Edele, 'Soviet Veterans as an Entitlement Group', 124–5.

32. On the fear of 'Decembrist' tendencies among demobilized veterans see E. S. Seniavskaia, *1941–1945: Frontovoe pokolenie. Istoriko-psikhologicheskoe*

*issledovanie* (Moscow: RAN institut Rossiiskoi istorii, 1995), 91–2. On political sentiments of veterans see also Mark Edele, 'More than just Stalinists: The Political Sentiments of Victors 1945–1953', in Juliane Fürst (ed.), *Late Stalinist Russia. Society between Reconstruction and Reinvention* (London and New York: Routledge, 2006), 167–91.

33. Much of the correspondence regarding this question throughout 1947 is contained in two files in the fond of the Supreme Soviet. See GARF f. r-7523, op. 39, dd. 335 and 327.

34. For details see Edele, 'A "Generation of Victors"', 127–32.

35. Report of Head of Dept for Registration of Decorations L. Pavlov to Secretariat of Supreme Soviet of Soviet Union, 4 Mar. 1947, GARF f. r-7523, op. 39, d. 327, l. 105–6.

36. Unsigned and undated report from Department of Registration of Decorations, 1947, GARF f. r-7523, op. 39, d. 335, l. 46; explanatory note to draft of cancellation bill, between 20 and 27 Aug. 1947, GARF f. r-7523, op. 39, d. 335, l. 113–16, here 113.

37. Report of L. Pavlov to Secretariat of Supreme Soviet, 11 Mar. 1947, GARF f. r-7523, op. 39, d. 335, l. 12–15; Secretary of Presidium of Supreme Soviet A. Gorkin to Minister of Finance A. S. Sverev, Apr. 1947, GARF f. r-7523, op. 39, d. 335, l. 36–7.

38. Unsigned and undated report from Dept for Registration of Decorations, 1947, GARF f. r-7523, op. 39, d. 335, l. 47.

39. Report of Head of Dept for Registration of Decorations L. Pavlov, 23 Apr. 1947, GARF f. r-9541, op. 39, d. 335, l. 47.

40. Explanatory note to draft of cancellation bill, between 20 and 27 Aug. 1947, GARF f. r-7523, op. 39, d. 335, l. 113–16; Decree of Presidium of Supreme Soviet of Soviet Union of 10 Sept. 1947, published in *Pravda*, 22 Nov. 1947, p. 1. For more details on the legislation see Edele, 'Soviet Veterans as an Entitlement Group', 125–6.

41. For an example of such a postcard see GARF f. r-7523, op. 42, d. 64, l. 14.

42. See the collective letter to Stalin and Shvernik from the workers of several Moscow enterprises, 1949, repr. in E. Iu. Zubkova *et al.* (eds.), *Sovetskaia Zhizn' 1945–1953* (Moscow: Rosspen, 2003), 329–32.

43. See the case file in GARF f. A-641, op. 1, d. 125.

44. See Edele, 'A "Generation of Victors"', 136–7.

45. Cf. Nina Tumarkin, *The Living and the Dead: The Rise and Fall of the Cult of World War II in Russia* (New York: Basic Books, 1994), 95–105; Jeffrey Brooks, *Thank You, Comrade Stalin! Soviet Public Culture from Revolution to Cold War* (Princeton: Princeton University Press, 2000), 195–232.

46. 'V prezidiume Verkhovnogo Soveta SSSR', *Pravda*, 24 Dec. 1947, p. 1. For more details see Edele, 'Soviet Veterans as an Entitlement Group', 126 n. 75.

47. See Ch. 5 and Edele, 'Soviet Veterans as an Entitlement Group', 127–9.

48. Elena Zubkova, *Russia After the War: Hopes, Illusions, and Disappointments, 1945–1957*, tr. Hugh Ragsdale (Armonk, NY, and London: M. E. Sharpe, 1998); Jean Lévesque. 'Exile and Discipline: The June 1948 Campaign Against Collective Farm Shirkers', *The Carl Beck Papers in Russian and East European Studies,* 1708 (2006); Jeffrey W. Jones, ' "In my Opinion This is All Fraud!"': Concrete, Culture, and Class in the "Reconstruction" of Rostov-on-the-Don, 1943–1948', Ph.D. diss. (University of North Carolina, 2000); Julie Hessler, 'A Postwar Perestoika? Toward a History of Private Trade Enterprise in the USSR', *Slavic Review,* 57/3 (1998): 516–42.

49. Fieseler, *Die Invaliden des 'Grossen Vaterländischen Krieges'*, 101–357, 468–78.

50. See Ch. 5.

51. A. D. Glazunov, *L'goty uchastnikam voiny* (Moscow: Iuridicheskaia literatura, 1981), 5–6.

52. See Ch. 4.

53. V. Naumov (ed.), *Georgii Zhukov: Stenogramma Oktiabr'skogo (1957g.) plenuma TsK KPSS i drugie dokumenty* (Moscow: Demokratiia, 2001), 34–5.

54. Ibid. 71–3.

55. Ibid. 103–4.

56. Ibid. 649 n. 33.

57. Report of the Sector for Letters of the Central Commmittee on letters received in connection with the celebrations of twentieth anniversary of victory, 22 May 1965, RGANI f. 5, op. 30, d. 462, l. 62.

58. See Ch. 4.

59. Decree of Presidium of Supreme Soviet, 26 Apr. 1965, *Sbornik zakonov SSSR i ukazov Prezidiuma Verkhovnogo Soveta SSSR 1938–1975: V chetyrekh tomakh,* iii (Moscow: Izvestiia Sovetov Deputatov Trudiashchikhsia SSSR, 1975), 54.

60. Council of Ministers of Soviet Union, resolution of 6 Mar. 1965, no. 140, as quoted in Glazunov, *L'goty uchastnikam voiny,* 6.

61. Decree of Presidium of Supreme Soviet, 6 Sept. 1967, as quoted in resolution of VTsSPS, 14 Sept. 1967, *Sotsial'noe obespechenie v SSSR: Sbornik normativnykh aktov* (Moscow: Iuridicheskaia literatura, 1986), p. 477.

62. Report of Deputy Chairman of Council of Ministers of Udmurt Autonomous Republic on work placement and welfare to demobilized soldiers by 1 Mar. 1947, GARF f. A-259, op. 6, d. 4477, l. 67; Report of Groznyi obkom secretary Chepliakov to Malenkov (25 Oct. 1945), RGASPI f. 17, op. 122, d. 102, l. 137.

63. RGASPI f, 17, op. 122, d. 102, l. 219–22, here 220.

64. Report to Malenkov (26 Jan. 1946) RGASPI f. 17, op. 122, d. 145, l. 41–8, here 44.

65. TsDOOSO f. 4, op. 31, d. 784, l. 201, 205. See also the communication between the boss of the military section of the Sverdlovsk obkom and the secretary of Kirovgrad gorkom (22 Oct. 1945), TsDOOSO f. 4, op. 31, d. 728, l. 73.

66. Report of KPK plenipotentiary in Arkhangel'sk oblast Kleimenov to Malenkov about *trudoustroistvo* of demobilized (autumn 1945), RGASPI f. 17, op. 122, d. 102, l. 119–22.

67. Report of Iakutsk Obkom secretary G. Maslennikov to Malenkov (31 Jan. 1946) RGASPI f. 17, op. 122, d. 145, l. 132–5, here 133.

68. See the report on this question by P. Savel'ev, the head of reception room of the Chairman of the Presidium of the Supreme Soviet, 23 May 1946, GARF f. r-7523, op. 55, d. 10, l. 34–62.

69. Report on letters to *Krasnaia zvezda* in July 1946, RGASPI f. 17, op. 125, d. 429, l. 158.

70. P. Savel'ev to N. M. Shvernik, report on supplications and complaints, 1946, GARF f. r7523, op. 55, d. 10, l. 149.

71. On shed blood, wounds, and amnesty see also Golfo Alexopoulos, 'Amnesty Tales', paper presented at AAASS National Convention in Denver, Colorado, 9–12 Nov. 2000.

72. See Savel'ev's report on supplications to Chairman of Presidium of Supreme Soviet on loan repayments by war invalids and families of fallen soldiers (14 Aug. 1946), GARF f. r-7523, op. 55, d. 10, l. 120–9. Savel'ev pointed out that there was a resolution of the Council of People's Deputies of 21 June 1945 (no. 1826) which actually listed war invalids as one of the groups whose debt could be cancelled. However, none of the letter writers mentioned in the report was aware of this legislation. Judging from the content of the letters, they wrote not because they knew they had a legal right to a 'discount', but because they assumed that their wartime sacrifice entitled them to special treatment.

73. GARF f. r-7523, op. 55, d. 10, l. 142.

74. See the case file in GARF f. A-461, op. 1, d. 1119, l. 23. The court did not share his sense of entitlement. On 25 Aug. 1951 he was sentenced to ten years of imprisonment. Ibid., l. 4.

75. Information of Dept of Party Information of the Administration for Checking of Party Organs in the Central Committee, 15 Jan. 1947, RGASPI f. 17, op. 88, d. 810, l. 100.

76. Report by head of the sector of letters in the General Dept of the Central Committee on letters from officers who had been released from the army, Nov. 1955, RGANI f. 5, op. 30, d. 135, l. 76. I am indebted to Paul Stronski for bringing this document to my attention.

77. P. Savel'ev to N. M. Shvernik and A. F. Gorkin, October 1947, GARF f. r-7523, op. 55, d. 13, l. 201–2.

78. Handwritten letter of Tenilin to Iakovlev, 8 Oct. 1946, GARF f. r-9396, op. 1, d. 2, l. 72. The bureaucrats in charge of higher education did not follow this argument. One could not change the rules because of 'one late high-school graduate', and Tenilin should try to get into a preparatory course to study for the next academic year. Typed letter of A. Blagonravov to t. Balezin; cc-ed to Tenilin (18 Oct. 1946), ibid. l. 73.

79. See Jean Lévesque, '"Part-Time Peasants": Labour Discipline, Collect-ive Farm Life, and the Fate of Soviet Socialized Agriculture after the Second World War, 1945–1953', Ph.D. diss. (University of Toronto, 2003), esp. 45–118.
80. V. Butin (Novosibirsk Obkom of the Party) to I. I. Pozdniak (Adminstration for Checking of Party Organs in the Central Committee), information on political moods of population in Novosibirsk oblast', 29 May 1948, RGASPI f. 17, op. 122, d. 306, l. 28.
81. For some examples see the following reports on letters: GARF f. r-7523, op. 55, d. 11, l. 229 (18 Sept. 1946); RGANI f. 5, op. 30, d. 186, l. 31–32 (21 May 1956); RGANI f. 5, op. 30 d, 135, l. 76 (Nov. 1955).
82. Case file on anti-Soviet agitation, GARF f. A-461-1-1867, l. 4.
83. Protest note in case file on anti-Soviet agitation, 12 Oct. 1954, GARF f. A-461, op. 1, d. 1062, l. 9.
84. Case file on anti-Soviet agitation, GARF f. A-461, op. 1, d. 1863, l. 4.
85. Assistant state prosecutor of Orlov oblast', resolution on letter of complaint, part of case file on anti-Soviet agitation, 18 May 1953, GARF f. A-461, op. 1, d. 1128, l. 5–10, here 9.
86. I. Tsvetkov and N. Orekhov (Administration of propaganda in CC) to Aleksandrov, information on 'explanatory' work regarding price changes and salary increases, 5 Oct. 1946, RGASPI f. 17, op. 125, d. 425, l. 39–40.
87. Pozdniak (administration for checking of party organs in Central Committee) to CC secretary Patolichev, report on moods and utterances of the population regarding the CC and SM resolution of 2 Oct. 1946, RGASPI f. 17, op. 122, d. 188, l. 12–13.
88. P. Savel'ev to N. M. Shvernik, report on supplications and complaints, 1946, GARF f. r-7523, op. 55, d. 10, l. 150.
89. See Savel'ev's report on supplications to Chairman of Presidium of Supreme Soviet on loan repayments by war invalids and families of fallen soldiers, (14 Aug. 1946), GARF f. r-7523, op. 55, d. 10, l. 122.
90. V. Butin (dept for organization and instruction of Novosibirsk obkom) to I. I. Pozdniak (administration for checking of party organs of Central Committee), information on political moods of kolkhozniki regarding the decree of the Presidium of the Supreme Soviet of 2 June 1948, dated 21 June 1948, RGASPI f. 17, op. 122, d. 306, l. 32–7, here 34. The dog-shooting accordion player was deported as a 'parasite' in 1948.
91. Shorthand report of 38th plenum of Voronezh party obkom, 12–13 Mar. 1947, TsDNI VO f. 3, op. 4, d. 2, l. 19.
92. See Ch. 7.
93. Shorthand report of SKVV Presidium meeting, 25 Jan. 1963, GARF f. r-9541, op. 1, d. 798, l. 29.
94. Report to *Krasnaia zvezda*, 24 Nov. 1966, GARF f. r-9541, op. 1, d. 1002, l. 12.

95. See e.g. Shorthand report of seminar of section chairs, 21 Jan. 1966, GARF f. r-9541, op. 1, d. 996, l. 25.
96. Information on results of work with letters and supplicants in the SKVV, Apr. 1978, GARF f. r-9541, op. 1, d. 1506, l. 34–6.
97. Shorthand report of SKVV Plenum, 23 Dec. 1977, GARF f. r-9541, op. 1, d. 1484, l. 26.
98. Ibid., l. 41.
99. This episode still awaits its historian. See the material collected in the Central Committee files RGANI f. 5, op. 73, dd. 89–169.
100. Report of *Krasnaia zvezda* to Central Committee about propositions to change the draft constitution, 1 July 1977, RGANI f. 5, op. 73, d. 122, l. 20.
101. Reports of *Krasnaia zvezda* to Central Committee about propositions to change the draft constitution, June to Sept. 1977, RGANI f. 5, op. 73, d. 122, ll. 31, 36, 46, 47, 53, 56, 57, 71.
102. Ibid., l. 74.
103. Address of comrade L. I. Brezhnev at the meeting of the Supreme Soviet of the Soviet Union, 4 Oct. 1977, *Izvestiia*, 5 Oct. 1977, pp. 2–3.
104. On the war cult see Introduction.
105. Shorthand report of meeting of SKVV section secretaries, 20 June 1978, GARF f. r-9541, op. 1, d. 1518, l. 86.
106. Report of letters dept of *Trud* about letters received in Apr. 1978, RGANI f. 5, op. 75, d. 250, l. 50. Report on letters received in Oct. 1978, RGANI f. 5, op. 75, d. 257, l. 8.
107. Head of Dept of Propaganda, E. Tiazhel'nikov to Central Committee, 6 June 1978, RGANI f. 5, op. 75, d. 251, l. 2.
108. Reports to Central Committee on letters to *Pravda* in May, June, and Oct. 1978, RGANI f. 5, op. 75, d. 246, l. 5, 24, 42. *Izvestiia* received similar letters, as did *Agitator*. See reports on letters received in Oct. 1978, RGANI f. 5, op. 75, d. 257, l. 35, 51.
109. Report to Central Committee, 4 Nov. 1978, RGANI f. 5, op. 75, d. 257, l. 4.
110. Shorthand report of SKVV Plenum, 23 Dec. 1977, GARF f. r-9541, op. 1, d. 1484, l. 25. For the Moscow section's role see *Nam—45!* 21.
111. Shorthand report of SKVV Plenum, 23 Dec. 1977, GARF f. r-9541, op. 1, d. 1484, l., l. 132.
112. Shorthand report of meeting of SKVV section secretaries, 20 June 1978, GARF f. r-9541, op. 1, d. 1518, l. 25.
113. 'On measures to further betterment of the material and everyday conditions of participants of the Great Patriotic War', resolution of CC and Council of Ministers, no. 907, 10 Nov. 1978, *Sobranie postanovlenii i rasporiazhenii pravitel'stva SSSR* (hereafter *SP SSSR*), 27 (1978): st. 164, pp. 540–2.
114. Report to Central Committee on letters to *Agitator* in Dec. 1978, RGANI f. 5, op. 75, d. 260, l. 53.

115. Reports to Central Committee on letters to *Pravda* and *Izvestiia* in Dec. 1978, RGANI f. 5, op. 75, d. 246, l. 47; d. 260, l. 22.

116. The resolution also included partisans of the Great Patriotic War and MVD and KGB personnel under certain conditions—two groups I ignore here in order to not needlessly complicate the discussion.

117. Tat'iana Vladimirovna Chertoritskaia, *Dorogie moi veterany: Iz istorii razrabotki i priniatiia zakonodatel'stva o veteranakh* (St Petersburg: Glagol', 1995), 13–15, 21–5, 45–6.

118. Letter to Brezhnev, 17 Nov. 1980, RGANI f. 5, op. 77, d. 143, l. 7.

119. Report to Central Committee on letters to *Sovetskaia Rossiia* in Dec. 1978, RGANI f. 5, op. 75, d. 260, l. 56.

120. Report to Central Committee on letters to *Sel'skaia zhizn'* in Feb. 1979, RGANI f. 5, op. 76, d. 188, l. 58.

121. Report to Central Committee on letters to *Pravda* in Mar. 1979, RGANI f. 5, op. 76, d. 213, l. 99.

122. RGANI f. 5, op. 77, d. 143.

123. Central Committee and Council of Ministers Resolution nos. 2119 and 220, 27 Feb. 1981, *SP SSSR* 12 (1981): st. 70, pp. 314–15; and Chertoritskaia, *Dorogie moi veterany*, 46. For the lobbying of the war correspondents see RGANI f. 5, op 77, d. 143.

124. *SP SSSR* 24 (1979): st. 155, p. 562.

125. Central Committee and Council of Ministers resolution of 21 Feb. 1980, no. 175, *SP SSSR* 9 (1980): st. 62, pp. 194–5.

126. e.g. Central Committee and Council of Ministers Resolution of 26 July 1984, no. 812, *SP SSSR* 9 (1985): st. 34, pp. 139–143; Council of Ministers Resolution of 14 Apr. 1990, no. 375, *SP SSSR* 11 (1990): st. 64, pp. 255–8.

127. Cf. Bernd Bonwetsch, '"Ich habe an einem völlig anderen Krieg teilge-nommen": Die Erinnerung an den "Großen Vaterländischen Krieg" in der Sowjetunion', in Helmut Berding et al. (eds.), *Krieg und Erinnerung: Fallstudien zum 19. und 20. Jahrhundert* (Göttingen: Vandenhoeck & Ruprecht, 2000), 156–7.

128. Christel Lane, *The Rites of Rulers: Ritual in Industrial Society. The Soviet Case* (Cambridge: Cambridge University Press, 1981), esp. 90–1, 101, 104, 143–53.

129. See Ch. 7.

130. See e.g. A. M. Samsonov, 'Iz istorii veteranov voiny (fragmenty)', *Istoriia SSSR* 2 (1985): 54–5; and Mikhail Tanich, *Igrala muzyka v sadu ...* (Moscow: Vagrius, 2000), 257–8.

131. E. Mikulina, 'Vstretilis' v Deimanovke: Sudby liudskie', *Pravda*, 16 Nov. 1978, p. 6.

132. A. Novikova, 'Otzovites, podrugi!', *Pravda*, 21 Oct. 1978, p. 3.

133. A. Martynova, 'Nas bylo piatero', *Pravda*, 10 Nov. 1978, p. 3.

134. Edele, 'Soviet Veterans as an Entitlement Group', 113–16.

135. *Itogi Vsesoiuznoi perepisi naseleniia 1979 goda*, ii. *Pol, vozrast' i sostoianie v brake naseleniia SSSR, soiuznykh i avtonomnykh respublik, kraev i oblastei. Chast' 1. Statisticheskii sbornik* (Moscow: Goskomstat, 1989), 32.

136. The published census statistics do not allow a clear analysis as the numbers are given in five-year increments and of course do not count veterans, but only men of certain birth cohorts. The 2002 census for the first time gives figures on individual birth years. According to these data, men of the frontline generation (born 1923–7) comprised 0.7% of the male population, while the middle generation (born 1905 to 1922) made up only 0.3% and the generation of double veterans had all but disappeared (0.01%). See *Itogi vserossiiskoi perepisi naseleniia 2002 goda (v 14 tomakh)*, ii. *Vozrastno-polovoi sostav i sostoianie v brake* (Moscow: Statistika Rossii, 2004), 6–8.

137. Alexei Yurchak, *Everything was Forever, Until It was No More: The Last Soviet Generation* (Princeton and Oxford: Princeton University Press, 2006).

138. On the generational dynamics see Tumarkin, *Living andDead*, 194–5.

139. G. Gusakov, 'Neterpimost'', *Izvestiia*, 7 Sept. 1979, p. 6; D. Novoplianskii, 'Riadom—veteran: Chitaia pochtu', *Pravda*, 7 Feb. 1982, p. 3.

140. Shorthand report of seminar of SKVV section secretaries, 27 Sept. 1985, GARF f. r-9541, op. 1, d. 1654, l. 218. Such ideas were in fact realized in special stores for veterans. As early as 1978, the Baku section of the SKVV operated 15 special stores for veterans only. See Shorthand report of meeting of SKVV secretaries, 20 June 1978, GARF f. r-9541, op. 1, d. 1518, l. 43.

141. M. Zastol'skii, 'V chem by provinilis?' [letter to the editor], *Veteran*, 7 (1988): 6.

142. G. Kirina, 'I v etom—tozhe sol'!', *Veteran*, 10 (1988): 5.

143. O. Mukhin, 'V ugodu formalizmu?', *Veteran*, 7 (1988): 4.

144. N. Boiko, 'Ne za l'goty shli pod puli…' [letter to the editor], *Veteran*, 9 (1988): 9.

145. G. Gukasov, 'Obida', *Izvestiia*, 19 July 1979, p. 6.

146. Ibid.; Gukasov, 'Neterpimost'', *Izvestiia*, 7 Sept. 1979, p. 6; and Gukasov, 'Tsena zlogo slova', *Izvestiia*, 26 Oct. 1979, p. 6.

147. Gukasov, 'Tsena zlogo slova'.

148. Quoted in Fieseler, *Die Invaliden des 'Grossen Vaterländischen Krieges'*, 481.

149. A. Kiselev, 'Skol'ko zhe zhdat'?', *Veteran*, 10 (1988): 6.

150. 'Pis'mo v redaktsiiu: Gde zhe spravedlivost'?', *Veteran*, 1 (1988): 6.

151. K. Mazurov, 'Na rubezhakh perestroiki', *Veteran*, 3 (1988): 3.

152. *Nam—45!* 32.

153. CIS Committee for Statistics and International Center for Human Values, Moscow (ed.), *The Statistical Handbook of Social and Economic Indicators for the Former Soviet Union* (New York: Norman Ross Publishing, 1996), 193.

154. G. Aksenov, 'Kto pomozhet invalidu?' [letter to the editor], *Veteran*, 2 (1988): 6.

155. Cf. Ethel Dunn, 'Disabled Russian War Veterans: Surviving the Collapse of the Soviet Union', in David. A. Gerber (ed.), *Disabled Veterans in History* (Ann Arbor: University of Michigan Press, 2000), 251–70.
156. *Statistical Handbook of Social and Economic Indicators*, 193.
157. Ibid.
158. See e.g. *Izvestiia*, 2 Aug. 1989, pp. 1, 3 as quoted in *The Current Digest of the Soviet Press*, 41/37 (1989): 16. See also Andrea Chandler, *Shocking Mother Russia: Democratization, Social Rights, and Pension Reform in Russia, 1990–2001* (Toronto: University of Toronto Press, 2004), 29 and *passim*. 'Relative impressive benefits' is Dunn's term, See 'Disabled Russian War Veterans', 254.
159. V. G. Aminov, *Veterany vsegda v stroiu: Ob istorii i opyte raboty Izhevskoi gorodskoi veteranskoi organizatsii* (Izhevsk: Udmurtskii universitet, 2000), 30.
160. *Veteran* existed since 1988. It started as a supplement to the union newspaper *Trud*, and from 1990 appeared as a stand-alone publication.
161. Quoted by Dunn as evidence that 'the law on telephones is ignored'. 'Disabled Russian War Veterans', 256.

### AFTERWORD

1. Thomas Kühne, 'Zwischen Vernichtungskrieg und Freizeitgesellschaft—die Veteranenkultur in der Bundesrepublik (1945–1995)', in Klaus Naumann (ed.), *Nachkrieg in Deutschland* (Hamburg: Hamburger Klaus Naumann Edition 2001), 95.
2. American Historical Association, *Why Do Veterans Organize?* (Washington, DC: War Department, 1946), 27.
3. Shorthand report of seminar of secretaries of SKVV, 26–7 Sept. 1985, GARF f. r-9541, op. 1, d. 1654, l. 91.
4. See Rossiiskii komitet veteranov voiny i voennoi sluzhby (ed.), *Nam—45!* (Moscow: Mezhdunarodnyi ob" edinennyi biograficheski tsentr, 2001), 6–14; Martin McCauley, *Who's Who in Russia since 1900* (London and New York: Routledge, 1997), 206–7, 216; *Kto byl kto v Velikoi:Otechestvennoi voine 1941–1945. Liudi. Sobytiia. Fakty. Spravochnik* (Moscow: Respublika, 2000), 247–8, 35–6; and Mark Edele, 'Soviet Veterans as an Entitlement Group, 1945–1955', *Slavic Review*, 65/1 (2006): 113–15.
5. Analysis of the surviving 695 questionnaires of delegates (representing about 87% of the delegates) preserved in GARF f. r-9541, op. 1, d. 7 to d. 13. See also Mark Edele, 'A "Generation of Victors?" Soviet Second World War Veterans from Demobilization to Organization 1941–1956', Ph.D. diss. (University of Chicago, 2004), 350 n. 32, 515–17; Shorthand report of Second All-Union Conference of War Veterans, 26 Feb. 1965, GARF f. r-9541, op. 1, d. 899, l. 8–9.

6. Shorthand report of SKVV Presidium meeting, 12 Nov. 1965, GARF f. r-9541, op. 1, d. 906, l. 119–20.

7. S. Bel'chenko to S. K. Timoshenko, 16 Nov. 1966, GARF f. r-9541, op. 1, d. 1064, l. 3.

8. Shorthand report of seminar of secretaries of SKVV, 26–7 Sept. 1985, GARF f. r-9541, op. 1, d. 1654, l. 26–7.

9. Shorthand report of SKVV Presidium meeting, 24 Nov. 1986, GARF f. r-9541, op. 1, d. 1681, l. 23.

10. A. Nikonov, 'Ucheba aktiva', *Veteran*, 44/96 (1989): 3.

11. 'Slovo k chitatel'iu', *Veteran*, 1/290 (Jan. 1994): 1.

12. Victor Stepanovich Nechaev, 'Sila veteranakh—v edinenii', *Veteran*, 31/320 (Oct. 1994): 1 (data for Soviet Union in 1994); *Sotsial'noe obespechenie*, 1 (1995): 27 (data for Russia in 1995).

13. See Ch. 2.

14. Even by the late 1970s, the veterans' organization only had estimates rather than hard numbers available. GARF f. r-9541, op. 1, d. 1505, l. 176.

15. Victor Stepanovich Nechaev, 'Sila Veteranakh—v edinenii', *Veteran*, 31/320 (Oct. 1994): 1.

16. See Edele, 'A "Generation of Victors?" ', 96, table 1.9.

17. Shorthand report of III SKVV Plenum, 19 Dec. 1978, GARF f. r-9541, op. 1, d. 1505, l. 41; Shorthand report of IV Plenum of SKVV, 19 Sept. 1979, GARF f. r-9541, op. 1, d. 1520, l. 118; Beate Fieseler, *Die Invaliden des 'Grossen Vaterländischen Krieges' der Sowjetunion: Eine politische Sozialgeschichte 1941–1991*, Habilitationsschrift (Ruhr-Universität Bochum, 2003), 469; *Vo imia odnopolchan—frontovikov* (Moscow: Vitiaz'-Bratishka, 2001), 9; Victor Stepanovich Nechaev, 'Sila Veteranakh—v edinenii', *Veteran*, 31/320 (Oct. 1994): 1; Ethel Dunn, 'Disabled Russian War Veterans: Surviving the Collapse of the Soviet Union', in David. A. Gerber (ed.), *Disabled Veterans in History* (Ann Arbor: University of Michigan Press, 2000), 252; *Sotsial'noe obespechenie*, 1 (1995): 27; 'Russia Honors its Soldiers Past and Present Ahead of V Day', *Johnson's Russia List*, 7169, 6 May 2003, http://www.dci.org/russia/johnson/7169-9.cfm (accessed 2004).

18. Rossiiskii komitet veteranov voiny i voennoi sluzhby (ed.), *Nam—45!* (Moscow: Mezhdunarodnyi ob" edinennyi biograficheski tsentr, 2001), 19.

19. Important starting points for such a comparative history are Michael Geyer, 'Ein Vorbote des Wohlfahrtsstaates: Die Kriegsopferversorgung in Frankreich, Deutschland und Großbritannien nach dem Ersten Weltkrieg', *Geschichte und Gesellschaft*, 9 (1983): 230–77; and Deborah Cohen, *The War Come Home. Disabled Veterans in Britain and Germany, 1914–1939* (Berkeley, Calif.: University of California Press, 2001).

20. The history of the Soviet welfare state remains to be written. For beginnings see Bernice Q. Madison, *Social Welfare in the Soviet Union* (Stanford,

Calif.: Stanford University Press, 1968); Andrea Chandler, *Shocking Mother Russia: Democratization, Social Rights, and Pension Reform in Russia, 1990–2001* (Toronto: University of Toronto Press, 2004), 24–71; and Stephen Lovell, 'Soviet Russia's Older Generations', in Lovell (ed.), *Generations in Twentieth-Century Europe* (Houndsmills, Basingstoke: Palgrave Macmillan, 2007), 205–26.

21. Susan J. Linz (ed.), *The Impact of World War II on the Soviet Union* (Totowa, NJ: Rowman & Allanhead, 1985); Sheila Fitzpatrick, 'War and Society in Soviet Context: Soviet Labor before, during, and after World War II', *International Labor and Working-Class History*, 35 (Spring 1989): 37–52; and Amir Weiner, *Making Sense of War: The Second World War and the Fate of the Bolshevik Revolution* (Princeton and Oxford: Princeton University Press, 2000).

22. Katherine Verdery, 'What was Socialism, and Why did it Fall?', in Daniel Orlovsky (ed.), *Beyond Soviet Studies* (Washington, DC: Woodrow Wilson Center Press, 1995), 27–46.

23. One need only pick up any issue of the newspaper *Veteran* in or after 1991, to immediately see the shock this breakdown caused to at least the organized veterans.

24. A. Pozdniakov, 'Vystoim', *Veteran*, 52/208 (1991), 2–3; 'Ustav Sodruzhestva (Soiuza) Organizatsii veteranov nezavisimykh gosudarstv', *Veteran*, 5/213 (1992): 8–9.

25. *Nam—45!* 28; *Veterany Mordovii. 1945–2000: Istoriia veteranskogo dvizheniia* (Saransk: Mordovskoe knizhnoe izdatel'stvo, 2000), 32; 'Ustav Vserossiiskoi organizatsii veteranov voiny, truda, vooruzhennykh sil i pravookhranitel'nykh organov', *Veteran*, 15/223–16/224 (1992): 14.

26. 'Uchreditel'naia konferentsiia Vsesoiuznoi organizatsii veteranov voiny i truda: Informatsionnoe soobshchenie', *Veteran. Biulleten' SKVV* 1 (1987): 2–26, here 3.

27. A. Pozdniakov, 'Vystoim', *Veteran*, 52/208 (1991), 2–3, here 3.

28. *Nam—45!* 28–9.

29. *Veterany Mordovii. 1945–2000*, 32–3.

30. *Moskva 2000. Telefonnyi spravochnik* (Moscow: Telefonno-adresnyi biulleten', 2000), 475–7.

31. *Rossiiskie vesti*, 8 June 1993, as quoted in *The Current Digest of the Post-Soviet Press*, 45/23 (1993): 4–5.

32. *Nam—45!* 28, 31. For more detail see Ch. 8.

33. 'Russia's Putin Blames Government, Regional Officials for Benefit Reform Chaos', *MosNews*, 18 Jan. 2005, available at www.mosnews.com/news/2005/01/18/putinst.shtml (accessed Nov. 2005).

34. On the trials and tribulations of Russian pension reform see Chandler, *Shocking Mother Russia*; on veterans' role within this history, ibid. 95, 110, 119–21.

35. Natalia Danilova, 'Veterans' Policy in Russia: A Puzzle of Creation', *Journal of Power Institutions in Post-Soviet Societies*, Pipss.org: 6/7 (2007): 'The Social and Political Role of War Veterans', http://www.pipss.org/document873.html (accessed Dec. 2007). According to Danilova, the 2005 number of survivors was 969,000 (n. 34).

36. Denise Youngblood, *Russian War Films: On the Cinema Front, 1914–2005* (Lawrence, Kan.: University Press of Kansas, 2007), 236.

# Chronology

1874: Army reforms introduce general military draft, and with it the notion of a link between citizenship and military service.

25 June 1912: Pensions for disabled soldiers created.

1914−18: First World War.

1917: Revolution.

1918−21: Civil War.

1921−4: Demobilization of Red Army.

1928−32: Stalin's revolution from above.

1936−8: Great Terror.

1939: Soviet invasion of part of Poland (Western Ukraine and Western Belorussia).

1939−40: Winter War with Finland.

22 June 1941: Germany attacks the Soviet Union: start of 'The Great Patriotic War of the Soviet Union'.

16 August 1941: Stalin's Order No. 270 introduces a hierarchy of stiff penalties for officers and soldiers surrendering to the enemy. Officers and political workers were to be treated as deserters, shot on the spot upon recovery, and their families were liable to arrest; ordinary soldiers were not threatened with execution, but their families were to be deprived of welfare payments.

28 July 1942: Stalin's Order No. 227: 'Not a Step Back!' introduces penal units and blocking detachments in order to prevent further unauthorized retreat of Red Army units. Execution was threatened for disorderly retreat without explicit order. ('Panic-mongers and cowards should be exterminated on the spot!')

15 September 1944: Central Committee Secretariat warns local party organizations that committees of war invalids are 'inappropriate'

October 1944: Creation of the Administration of the Plenipotentiary for Affairs of Repatriation.

9 May 1945: Victory Day becomes a new, popular holiday.

23 June 1945: Law on Demobilization of Oldest Age Groups starts mass-demobilization by releasing the cohorts born 1893−1905.

30 September 1946: Council of Ministers Resolution no. 2220 stresses that former POWs enlisted into worker battalions and subsequently given over as regular cadres to work in industry had the same rights as other workers. Most of the benefits of the demobilization law and the right of war invalids to leave their enterprise are applied to this group of veterans.

10 September 1947: Privileges connected to major battle decorations abolished.

December 1947: Victory Day becomes a 'working holiday' (i.e. a regular work-day).

12 February 1948: Decree of Presidium of Supreme Soviet starts demobilization of birth year 1925, which marks the end of mass-demobilization of the wartime army.

21 February 1948: Series of resolutions of Council of Ministers begins new wave of repression against people deemed to be dangerous, including those who had 'anti-Soviet connections'.

October 1948: Pension payments for group III invalids cut according to income.

1951: Decree against 'anti-social parasitic elements' starts police campaign against beggars in 1952–4.

1953: Stalin dies.

1955/6: Silent rehabilitation of former POWs.

- 17 September 1955: Pardon for collaborators with the Germans.
- 24 November 1955: All war participants freed from 'special settlement'.
- 19 April 1956: Presidium of Central Committee forms commission, headed by Zhukov, to investigate fate of former POWs.
- 29 June 1956: Central Committee Resolution condemns 'flagrant violations of legality' with regards to former POWs.
- 20 September 1956: Resolution frees all remaining former POWs, who had been imprisoned for 'treason'.

February 1956: 20th Party Congress; Khrushchev's 'secret speech' denounces 'cult of personality'—a euphemism for Stalinism; this speech marks Khrushchev's victory in the succession struggles after Stalin's death and the beginning of the so-called 'Thaw' period.

14 July 1956: Law on Pensions.

September 1956: First All-Union Congress of War Veterans; Soviet Committee of War Veterans (SKVV) formed.

October 1964: Brezhnev replaces Khrushchev as First Secretary.

25–6 February 1965: Second All-Union Conference of War Veterans decides creation of local infrastructure for veterans' movement.

18 March 1965: Regulations about Sections of the Soviet Committee of War Veterans in the Localities passed by SKVV presidium

9 May 1965: Twenty Years Victory—start of fully blown war cult; Victory Day becomes holiday again.

1971: Third Congress of Soviet War Veterans. New statutes mention representation of veterans' interests as one of the goals of the organization.

12 October 1976: Central Committee resolution 'On the further improvement of the activities of local organizations of war veterans' stops further organizational development of SKVV and ends smouldering conflict with party organizations.

1977: Campaign to comment on new constitution. Veterans participate enthusiastically.

7 October 1977: Brezhnev promises 'a couple of more privileges' to war veterans.

10 November 1978: Joint resolution of Central Committee and Council of Ministers, no. 907, 'On measures to further betterment of the material and everyday conditions of participants of the Great Patriotic War', creates 'participant of the Patriotic War' as a major status group.

1985: Gorbachev become General Secretary.

25 February 1986: Gorbachev calls for the creation of an 'all-Union societal organization of veterans of war and labour'.

25 September 1986: All-Union Organization of Veterans of War and Labour founded.

December 1988: Constitutional reform creates new Congress of People's Deputies; seventy-five deputies (3 per cent of the overall number) were sent by the veterans' organization.

1991: Soviet Union breaks apart.

1992: Line asking if one had been a POW removed from standard questionnaires (*ankety*).

1995: Law 'On Veterans'.

# Glossary

**Agitator.** A person, usually a communist or Komsomol member, who delivers speeches to small groups to inform them of policies of the regime.

**Aspirant.** Graduate student.

**Aspirantura.** Graduate school of the first level, leading to the title 'Candidate of Science' (*kandidat nauk*).

**CC.** Central Committee of the Communist Party.

**Chekist.** A member of the security services. From the original name of the Bolshevik secret police, the Cheka. By the 1940s, the Cheka had long been renamed (*see* Security Services), but the word *chekist* stuck in the popular lexicon.

**Communist.** A member or candidate member of the Communist Party (Bolsheviks).

**Council of Ministers.** *See* SNK.

**GARF.** State Archive of the Russian Federation.

**GOPANO.** Socio-political archive of Nizhnyi Novgorod Region.

**Gulag.** Literally, the Main Administration of Camps within the NKVD. Often used *pars pro toto* to refer to the concentration camp system or a single concentration camp (hence the ungrammatical plural 'gulags'). *See also* Special settlement.

**ITL.** Corrective Labour Camp.

**Kolkhoz.** Collective farm.

**Komsomol.** Communist Youth League, the youth organization of the Communist Party.

**KPK.** Party Control Commission.

**Krai.** Administrative level above raion and on a similar level as oblast'. Often at the periphery of the empire. Subdivided into raions.

**MGB.** Ministry of State Security. *See* Security Services

**MTS.** Machine tractor station. An organization administering agricultural machines for collective farm use.

**MVD.** Ministry of Internal Affairs. *See* Security Services.

**NKVD.** Commissariat of Internal Affairs. *See* Security Services.

**NKGB.** *See* Security Services.

**Oblast'.** Province or region. Administrative level below Union Republic.

**Obkom.** Party committee on the level of oblast'; regional party committee.

**Pood (pud).** Russian measure of weight, equivalent to 16.38 kg.

**Raion.** District. Administrative level below oblast' or city.

**Raikom.** District party committee.

**RGAE.** Russian State Economic Archive.

**RGANI.** Russian State Archive of Contemporary History.

**RGASPI.** Russian State Archive of Socio-Political history.

**RSFSR.** Russian Republic.

**Security Services.** The Commissariat of Internal Affairs (NKVD) was split, in 1941, into two organizations: Commissariat of Internal Affairs (NKVD) and Commissariat of State Security (NKGB). This split was undone in the same year only to be repeated in 1943. In 1946 both were renamed (like all Commissariats) into ministries: the Ministry of Internal Affairs (MVD) and the Ministry of State Security (MGB). After Stalin's death, the MGB and MVD were reunited, only to be split up again in 1954. The State Security proper now acquired the name it was famous for in the West: Committee for State Security, or KGB. During the war, the Ministry of Defence acquired its own intelligence services—the organization 'Death to Spies' (SMERSh), founded in 1943. SMERSh became part of the MGB in 1946.

**SMERSh.** Organization 'Death to Spies' (military counter-intelligence). *See* Security Services.

**SNK.** Council of People's Commissars, the highest government body. Existed both on the level of republics (e.g. Ukrainian SNK) and on Union level (SNK SSSR). In 1946 renamed Council of Ministers. If not noted otherwise, SNK refers to the Union level.

**Soviet.** A council, for example a city council (city soviet). If capitalized, the word refers to the Soviet Union as a whole, if not capitalized to these lowest governmental organization ('soviet organizations'). The Supreme Soviet was, technically, the Soviet Union's highest elected body and the legislature. In practice, the Supreme Soviet functioned also as a clearing house for letters of complaint and supplications.

**Special settlement** (*spetsposelenie*). Deportation to regions such as Siberia, but not to a concentration camp. Until 1949 called 'special resettlement' (*spetspereselenie*). 'Special settlers' remained, technically, full citizens of the Soviet Union, but without the right to choose their own place of residence.

**Stakhanovite.** A particularly accomplished worker. Named after the crack miner A. G. Stakhanov, the 'Stakhanovite movement' became a campaign for increased production quotas and rationalization in production in the 1930s. Stakhanovites had special privileges, better pay, and were hailed as role models in the press.

**Technicum.** Technical college.

**TsDNI VO.** Voronezh Regional Archive of Contemporary History.

**TsDOOSO.** Archive of Social Organizations of Voronezh Region.

**Voenkomat.** Military registration and enlistment office on city (*gorvoenkomat*) or district level (*raivoenkomat*).

**VTEK.** Labour medical board in charge of classification of disabled into one of the three groups of invalidity.

**VUZ.** Institution of tertiary education (e.g. university).

**ZAGS.** Registry office.

**Zemlianka** (plural: zemlianki). A semi-pit dwelling or dugout consisting of a hole in the ground covered with a makeshift roof. A common accommodation in the postwar Soviet Union.

# Bibliography

PRIMARY SOURCES

## Archives

### Gosudarstvennyi Archiv Rossiiskoi Federatsii (GARF)
f. A-259: Sovnarkom/Sovmin RSFSR
f. A-413: Narkom/Ministry of Social Welfare RSFSR
f. A-415; Department of State Aid to Soldiers' Families under Sovnarkom RSFSR
f. A-461: State Prosecutor of RSFSR
f. r-5446: Sovnarkom/Sovmin SSSR
f. r-5451: Central Council of Trade Unions (VTsSPS)
f. r-7523: Supreme Soviet of the Soviet Union
f. r-8009: People's Commissariat/Ministry of Health of Soviet Union
f. r-8080: Committee for Affairs of Higher Schools under Sovnarkom
f. r-8131: State Prosecutor of the Soviet Union
f. r-9396: Ministry of Higher Education of the Soviet Union
f. r-9401: Special Files (*osobye papki*) of Stalin and Molotov
f. r-9507: Ministry of Labour Reserves
f. r-9517: Committee for Accounting and Distribution of Labour Power under Sovnarkom
f. r-9526: Council for Repatriation Affairs under Sovnarkom/Sovmin
f. r-9541: Soviet Committee of War Veterans

### Gosudarstvennyi obshchestvenno-politicheskii arkhiv Nizhegorodskoi oblasti (GOPANO)
f. 431: Primary party organization of Kolkhoz Mikheevsk, Ardatovskii raion
f. 3591: Territorial primary party organization of Ardatovskii raion
f. 4968: Primary party organization of Gor'kovskii gorvoenkomat

### Rossiiskii gosudarstvennyi arkhiv ekonomiki (RGAE)
f. 1884: Ministry of Ways of Communication of Soviet Union
f. 7486: Ministry of Agriculture of Soviet Union

### Rossiiskii gosudarstvennyi arkhiv noveishei istorii (RGANI)
f. 6, op. 6: Party Control Commission
f. 5, op. 30: Central Committee, General Department

f. 77, op. 1: Central Committee, Department of Organizational-Party Work (party statistics)

*Rossiiskii gosudarstvennyi arkhiv sotsial'no-politicheskoi istorii (RGASPI)*
f. 17: Central Committee, Apparatus

*Tsentral'nyi munitsipal'nyi arkhiv Moskvy (TsMAM)*
f. 415: Zavod Imeni Stalina (ZIS)
f. 1609: Moscow State University
f. 2433, op.8: Administration for Housing Distribution of Mosgorispolkom

*Tsentr Dokumentatsii Noveishei Istorii Voronezhskoi oblasti (TsDNI VO)*
f. 3: Voronezh obkom

*Tsentr Dokumentatsii 'Narodnyi arkhiv'*
Kollektsiia 'moia zhizn"

*Tsentr dokumentatsii obshchestvennykh organizatsii Sverdlovskoi oblasti (TsDOOSO)*
f. 4: Sverdlovsk obkom

## Source Collections and Published Documents

Artizov, A., Iu. Sigachev, I. Shevchuk, and V. Khlopov, eds., *Reabilitatsiia: Kak eto bylo. Dokumenty Prezidiuma TsK KPSS i drugie materialy. Mart 1953—fevral' 1956, Rossiia XX vek. Dokumenty.* Moscow: Mezhdunarodnyi fond 'demokratiia', 2000.

Artizov, A., Iu. Sigachev, I. Shevchuk, and V. Khlopov, eds., *Reabilitatsiia: Kak eto bylo. Fevral' 1956—nachalo 80-kh godov.* Moscow: Demokratiia, 2003.

*Deputaty Verkhovnogo Soveta SSSR: Shestoi sozyv.* Moscow: Izvestiia, 1962.

Iakovlev, A. N., ed., *Georgii Zhukov: Stenogramma oktiabr'skogo (1957g.) plenuma TsK KPSS i drugie dokumenty, Rossiia XX vek. Dokumenty.* Moscow: Mezhdunarodnyi fond 'demokratiia', 2001.

*Istoricheskii arkhiv*, 2 (1995): 108–27.

Khlevniuk, O. V., ed., *Politbiuro TsK VKP(b) i Sovet Ministrov SSSR 1945–1953.* Moscow: Rosspen, 2002.

Kulakov, A. A., ed., *Zabveniiu ne podlezhit: Stranitsy nizhegorodskoi istorii (1941–1945 gody. Kniga tret'ia).* Nizhnyi Novgorod: Volgo-Viatskoe kn. izd.-vo, 1995.

*Moskva poslevoennaia 1945–1947: Arkhivnye dokumenty i materialy.* Moscow: Mosgorarkhiv, 2000.

'Nezakonchennoe srazhenie marshala Zhukova: O reabilitastii sovetskikh voenno-plennykh', *Istoricheskii arkhiv*, 2 (1995).

' "Osnovnoi kostiak podbiralsia iz prestupnikov": Banda deistvovala kak voenno-stroitel'naia organizatsiia', *Istochnik*, 4 (1996): 130–5.

'[Postanovlenie of TsK and SM SSSR of 29 June 1956 on repression of former POWs]', *Voenno-istoricheskii zhurnal*, 8 (1991): 32–4.

'[Prikaz NO. 270 and commentary]', *Voenno-istoricheskii zhurnal*, 9 (1988).

*Voenno-istoricheskii zhurnal*, 2 (1994): 96.

'Zapiski o poslevoennom ustroistve armii', *Istochnik*, 2 (1996): 103–47.

Zhukov, G. K., 'Spravka-doklad [o sokrashchenii vooruzhennykh sil]', *Voennye arkhivy Rossii*, 1 (1993): 280–1.

Zubkova, E. Iu., L. P. Kosheleva, G. A. Kuznetsova, A. I. Miniuk, and L. A. Rogovaia, eds., *Sovetskaia zhizn' 1945–1953*. Moscow: Rosspen, 2003.

## Periodicals

*Bloknot agitatora*

*Bloknot agitatora Krasnoi armii*

*Bloknot agitatora vooruzhennykh sil*

*Izvestiia*

*Krasnaia zvezda*

*Krasnyi flot*

*Krokodil*

*Literaturnaia gazeta*

*Moskovskii bolshevik*

*Moskovskii komsomolets*

*MosNews*

*Novyi mir*

*Oktiabr'*

*Pravda*

*Sobranie postanovlenii i rasporiazhenii pravitel'stva SSSR [= SP SSSR]*

*Sobranie zakonov i rasporiazhenii Raboche-Krest'ianskogo Pravitel'stva SSSR*

*The Current Digest of the Post-Soviet Press*

*The New York Times*

*Trud 7*

*Vedomosti Verkhovnogo Soveta SSSR*

*Vestnik vysshei shkoly*

*Veteran*

*Veteran voiny. Biulleten' SKVV*

*Za Stalinskuiu nauku. Organ partbiuro, rektorata, komiteta VLKSM, profkoma i mestkomov Gor'kovskogo gosuniversiteta*

*Zhurnal Moskovskoi Patriarkhii*

*Zvezda*

## Published Statistics

Andreev, Evgenii Mikhailovich, Leonid Evseevich Darskii, and Tat'iana Leonidovna Khar'kova, *Naselenie Sovetskogo Soiuza: 1922–1991*. Moscow: Nauka, 1993.

CIS Committee for Statistics and International Center for Human Values, Moscow, ed., *The Statistical Handbook of Social and Economic Indicators for the Former Soviet Union*. New York: Norman Ross Publishing Inc., 1996.

*Ekspress-informatsiia. Seriia: istoriia statistiki vyp. 3–5 ch. 1: Istoriia naseleniia SSSR 1920–1959 gg*. Moscow: Goskomstat, 1990.

Eliutin, V. P., ed., *Vysshaia shkola SSSR za 50 let*. Moscow: Vysshaia Shkola, 1967.

Gel'fand, V. S., *Naselenie SSSR za 50 let (1941–1990): Statisticheskii sbornik*. Perm': Izd-vo Permskogo universiteta, 1992.

*Itogi vsesoiuznoi perepisi naseleniia 1959 goda: SSSR (svodnyi tom)*. Moscow: Gosstatizdat, 1962.

*Itogi vsesoiuznoi perepisi naseleniia 1979 goda*, ii. *Pol, vozrast' i sostoianie v brake naseleniia SSSR, soiuznykh i avtonomnykh respublik, kraev i oblastei. Chast' 1. Statisticheskii sbornik*. Moscow: Goskomstat, 1989.

*Kolkhozy SSSR: Kratkii statisticheskii sbornik.* Moscow: Finansy i statistika, 1988.

*Kul'turnoe stroitel'stvo SSSR: Statisticheskii sbornik.* Moscow: Gosudarstvennoe statisticheskoe izdatel'stvo, 1956.

*Narodnoe khoziaistvo SSSR 1922–1972: Iubileinyi statisticheskii ezhegodnik.* Moscow: Statistika, 1972.

*Narodnoe obrazovanie, nauka i kul'tura v SSSR.* Moscow: Statistika, 1971.

*Naselenie Rossii za 100 let (1897–1997): Statisticheskii sbornik.* Moscow: Goskomstat, 1998.

*Spravochnik dlia postupaiushchikh v vysshie uchebnye zavedeniia v 1955 godu: Sostavlen po dannym na 1 ianvaria 1955 g.* Moscow: Sovetskaia nauka, 1955.

*Trud v SSSR. Statisticheskii sbornik.* Moscow: Statistika, 1968.

*Vsesoiuznaia perepis' naseleniia 1939 goda: Osnovnye itogi.* Moscow: Nauka, 1992.

## Law Collections

*Direktivy VKP(b) i postanovleniia sovetskogo pravitel'stva o narodnom obrazovanii: sbornik dokumentov za 1917–1947 gg.,* 2 vols. Moscow: Izd-vo Akademii pedagog. nauk RSFSR, 1947.

Glavnaia voennaia prokuratura Vooruzhennykh Sil SSSR, ed., *Pamiatka demobilizovannym riadovym i serzhantam Krasnoi Armii,* 2nd enlarged edn. Moscow: Voennoe Izdatel'stvo, 1946.

Glazunov, A. D., *L'goty uchastnikam voiny.* Moscow: Iuridicheskaia literatura, 1981.

Gorokhovskii, V., and I. Trefilov, *Pensionnoe obespechenie v SSSR (v voprosakh i otvetakh).* Moscow: Moskovskii rabochii, 1957.

Gorshenin, K. P., ed., *Spravochnye po zakonodatel'stvu dlia ispolnitel'nykh komitetov sovetov deputatov trudiashchikhsia,* ii. Moscow: Iur. izd.-vo, 1947.

Karev, D. S., ed., *Sbornik zakonodatel'nykh aktov o trude.* Moscow, 1956.

Movshovich, Moisei Iosofovich, ed., *Vysshaia shkola: Osnovnye postanovleniia, prikazy i instruktsii,* 2nd edn. Moscow: Sovetskaia nauka, 1948.

*Pensionnoe obespechenie v SSSR: Sbornik ofitsial'nykh materialov.* Moscow: Iuridicheskaia literatura, 1958.

*Prikazy i direktivy narodnogo komissara VMF v gody Velikoi Otechestvennoi voiny 1941–1945,* x. *Velikaia Otechestvennaia.* Moscow: Terra, 1996.

*Resheniia partii i pravitel'stva po khozaistvennym voprosam,* ii. *1929–1940.* Moscow: Politicheskaia literatura, 1967.

*Resheniia partii i pravitel'stva po khozaistvennym voprosam,* iii. *1941–1952.* Moscow: Politicheskaia literatura, 1968.

*Sbornik zakonodatel'nykh aktov o gosudarstvennykh nagradakh SSSR.* Moscow, 1987.

*Sbornik zakonov SSSR i ukazov Prezidiuma Verkhovnogo Soveta SSSR 1938–1961g.* Moscow: Izvestiia, 1961.

*Sbornik zakonov SSSR i ukazov Prezidiuma Verkhovnogo Soveta SSSR 1938–1975: V chetyrekh tomakh,* iii. Moscow: Izvestiia Sovetov Deputatov Trudiashchikhsia SSSR, 1975.

*Sbornik zakonov SSSR i ukazov Prezidiuma Verkhovnogo Soveta SSSR 1939g.-iiun' 1944 g.* Moscow: Vedomosti Verkhovnogo Soveta SSSR, 1944.

*Sbornik zakonov SSSR i ukazov Prezidiuma Verkhovnogo Soveta SSSR (1938g.—noiabr' 1958 g.).* Moscow: Iuridicheskaia literatura, 1959.

*Sbornik zakonov SSSR i ukazov Prezidiuma Verkhovnogo Soveta SSSR (1938–iiul' 1956 gg.).* Moscow: Iuridicheskaia literatura, 1956.

*Sbornik zakonov SSSR i ukazov Prezidiuma Verkhovnogo Soveta SSSR (1945–1946).* Moscow, 1947.

*Sbornik zakonov, ukazov, postanovlenii, reshenii i rasporiazhenii 1946.* Leningrad: Lenizdat, 1947.

*Sotsial'noe obespechenie v SSSR. Sbornik normativnykh aktov.* Moscow: Iuridicheskaia literatura, 1986.

*SSSR: Zakony i postanovleniia. Sbornik zakonov SSSR i ukazov (1938–1956).* Moscow, 1956.

## Memoirs

Alexeyeva, Liudmilla, and Paul Goldberg, *The Thaw Generation. Coming of Age in the Post-Stalin Era.* Boston: Little, Brown, & Co., 1990.

Baklanov, Grigorii, *Zhizn', podarennaia dvazhdy.* Moscow: Vagrius, 1999.

Bogacheva, I. E., *Dorogi zhizni. Vospominaniia i razmyshleniia voennoi medsestry.* Voronezh: Voronezhskii gosudarstvennyi universitet, 2000.

Chukhrai, Grigorii, *Moe kino.* Moscow: Algoritm, 2002.

——— *Moia voina.* Moscow: Algoritm, 2001.

D'iakov, Nikolai Fedorovich, *Mechenye: Dokumental'nye zapiski byvshego soldata,* ed. Nikolai Mitrokhin, *Dokumenty po istorii dvizheniia inakomysliashchikh.* Moscow: Informatsionno-ekspertnaia gruppa 'PANORAMA', 1999.

Dzhigurda, Ol'ga, 'Teplokhod "Kakhetiia": Zapiski voennogo vracha', *Znamia,* 1 (1948): 3–86.

Gefter, M. 'Stalin umer vchera... [interview by Gleb Pavlovskii]', in Iu. N. Afanas'ev (ed.), *Perestroika: Glasnost', demokratiia, sotsialism. Inogo ne dano. Sud'by perestroiki — Vgliadyvaias' v proshloe — Vozvrashchenie k budushchemu,* pp. 297–323. Moscow: Progress, 1988.

Gorbachev, Mikhail, *Zhizn' i reformy,* 2 vols., vol. i. Moscow: Novosti, 1995.

Gorbacheva, Raissa, 'Ia nadeius'...'. Moscow: Novosti, 1991.

Gordey, Michel, *Visa to Moscow,* tr. K. Woods. New York: Alfred A. Knopf, 1952.

Gorodnitskii, Aleksandr, *I zhit' eshche nadezhde...* Moscow: Vagrius, 2001.

Gusarov, Vladimir, *Moi papa ubil Mikhoelsa.* Frankfurt a. M.: Possev, 1978.

Gutnova, E. V., *Perezhitoe.* Moscow: Rosspen, 2001.

'"Ich habe den Eid nicht gebrochen": Protokoll eines ehemaligen sowjetischen Kriegsgefangenen', in Haus der Geschichte der Bundesrepublik Deutschland (ed.), *Kriegsgefangene — Voennoplennye: Sowjetische Kriegsgefangene in Deutschland. Deutsche Kriegsgefangene in der Sowjetunion,* pp. 192–3. Düsseldorf: Droste, 1995.

Kabo, Vladimir, *The Road to Australia: Memoirs.* Canberra: Aboriginal Studies Press, 1998.

Kasenkina, Oksana, *Leap to Freedom.* London: Hurst & Blackett, 1949.

Kovanov, V. V., *Prizvanie.* Moscow: Politicheskaia Literatura, 1970.

Malakhova, Vera Ivanovna, 'Four Years as a Frontline Physician', in Barbara
    Alpern Engel and Anastasia Posadskaya-Vanderbeck (eds.), *A Revolution of their
    Own: Voices of Women in Soviet History*, pp. 175–218. Boulder, Colo.: Westview
    Press, 1998.
Mlynarzh, Zdenek, *Moroz udaril iz Kremlia*. Moscow: Respublika, 1992.
Nekrasov, Viktor Platonovich, 'Slova "velikie" i prostye', *Iskusstvo kino*, 5 (1959):
    55–61.
Pecherkii, Andrei, 'Ia shel s evangeliem i ne boialsia…', *Rus' derzhavnaia*, 7–9/19
    (1995): 16–19.
Pirogov, Peter, *Why I Escaped: The Story of Peter Pirogov*. New York: Duell, Sloan
    & Pearce, 1950.
Prut, Iosif, *Nepoddaiushchiisia o mnogikh drugikh i koe-chto o sebe*. Moscow: Vag-
    rius, 2000.
Shakhnazarov, Georgii, *S vozhdiami i bez nikh*. Moscow: Vagrius, 2001.
Tanich, Mikhail, *Igrala muzyka v sadu…* Moscow: Vagrius, 2000.
Vanni, Ettore, *Io, Comunista in Russia*. Bologna: Cappelli Editore, 1949.

**Literary Accounts**
Abramov, Fedor, 'Dve zimy i tri leta: Roman', *Novyi Mir*, 1 (1968): 3–67; 2 (1968):
    10–69; 3 (1968): 68–132.
Babaevskii, Semen, 'Kavaler zolotoi zvezdy: Roman', In *Sobranie sochinenii*,
    pp. 123–628. Moscow: Khudozhestvennaia literatura, 1979.
Bondarev, Iurii, *Tishina: Roman*. Moscow: Sovetskii pisatel', 1962.
_____ [Bondaryev, Yuri], *Silence: A Novel*, tr. Elisaveta Fen. Boston and Cambridge:
    Riverside Press, 1966.
Ezhov, V., and G. Chukhrai, 'Ballada o soldate: Stsenarii fil'ma', in Grigorii
    Chukhrai (ed.), *Moe kino*, pp. 221–84. Moscow: Algoritm, 2002.
Gausner, Zhanna, 'Vot my i doma…', *Zvezda*, 11 (1947): 4–106.
Nekrasov, Viktor Platonovich, 'V rodnom gorode', in *Izbrannye proizvedeniia:
    Povesti, rasskazy, putevye zametki*, pp. 248–470. Moscow: Khudozhestvennaia
    literatura, 1962; orig. 1954.
Pavlenko, Petr, *Schast'e: Roman*. Moscow: Pravda, 1947.
Polevoi, Boris, *He Came Back*. Moscow: Foreign Languages Publishing House,
    n.d.; orig. 1949.
_____ *Povest' o nastoiashchem cheloveke*. Moscow: Sovetskii pisatel', 1947.
Remarque, Erich Maria, *The Road Back*. New York: Fawcett Books, 1998.
Shalamov, Varlam, 'Major Pugachev's Last Battle', in *Kolyma Tales*, pp. 89–103.
    New York and London: W. W. Norton, 1982.
Tendriakov, Vladimir, 'Okhota', *Znamia*, 9 (1988).
Trifonov, Iurii, 'Dom na naberezhnoi', *Druzhba narodov*, 1 (1976).
_____ 'Studenty: Povest'', *Novyi mir* (1950): 10: 56–175; 11: 49–82.
Tvardovskii, A. T., 'Soderzhanie mnimoe i deistvitel'noe', In *Sobranie sochinenii:
    Tom piatyi. Stat'i i zametki o literature. Rechi i vystupleniia (1933–1970)*, pp. 143–4.
    Moscow: Khudozhestvennaia literatura, 1980.

Tvardovskii, A. T.,'Terkin na tom svete', in *Sobranie sochinenii v shesti tomakh*, pp. 325–78. Moscow: Khudozhestvennaia literatura, 1978.

## SELECTED SECONDARY SOURCES

Aleksievich, Svetlana, *U voiny—ne zhenskoe litso: Poslednie svideteli*. Moscow: Sovetskii pisatel', 1987 (1988, 1998).

——[Alexiyevich, Svetlana] *War's Unwomanly Face*, tr. Keith Hammond and Lyudmila Lezhneva. Moscow: Progress Publishers, 1988.

Alexopoulos, Golfo, 'Amnesty 1945: The Revolving Door of Stalin's Gulag', *Slavic Review*, 64/2 (2005): 274–306.

Altshuler, Mordechai, 'A Note on Jews in the Red Army on the Eve of the Second World War', *Jews and Jewish Topics in the Soviet Union and Eastern Europe*, 18 (2002): 37–9.

—— 'Antisemitism in Ukraine toward the End of the Second World War', *Jews in Eastern Europe*, 3 (Winter 1993): 40–81.

American Historical Association, *Why Do Veterans Organize?* Washington DC: War Department, 1946.

Aralovets, N. A., 'Gorodskaia sem'ia v Rossii 1940–1950-e gg', in V. B. Zhiromskaia (ed.), *Naselenie Rossii v XX veke: Istoricheskie ocherki*, ii. *1940–1959*, pp. 218–42. Moscow: Rosspen, 2001.

Arutiunian, Iu. V., *Mekhanizatory sel'skogo khoziaistva SSSR v 1929–1957 gg (formirovanie kadrov massovykh kvalifikatsii)*. Moscow: Akademiia nauk, 1960.

—— *Sovetskoe krest'ianstvo v gody Velikoi Otechestvennoi voiny*, 2nd edn. Moscow: Nauka, 1970.

—— *Vozniknovenie i razvitie massovykh industrial'nykh kadrov sel'skogo khoziaistva SSSR (1929–1958 gg.) Aftoreferat disertatsii na soiskanie uchenoi stepeni doktora istoricheskikh nauk*. Moscow: Akademiia nauk SSSR, institut istorii, 1963.

Arzamaskin, Iu., *Zalozhniki Vtoroi mirovoi voiny: Repatriatsiia Sovetskikh grazhdan v 1944–1953 gg*. Moscow: Arzmaskin, 2001.

Axell, Albert, *Marshal Zhukov. The Man Who Beat Hitler*. London: Longman, 2003.

Babakov, A. A., *Vooruzhennye sily SSSR posle voiny (1945–1986 gg.) Istoriia stroitel'stva*. Moscow: Voennoe izdatel'stvo, 1987.

Bacon, Edwin, *The Gulag at War: Stalin's Forced Labour System in the Light of the Archives*. New York: New York University Press, 1994.

Barenberg, Alan, ' "For a United, Clear Pension Law": Legislating and Debating Soviet Pensions 1956–1965', MA thesis, University of Chicago, 2000.

Barnes, Steven A., 'All for the Front, All for Victory! The Mobilization of Forced Labor in the Soviet Union during World War Two', *International Labor and Working-Class History*, 58 (Fall 2000): 239–60.

—— ' "In a Manner Befitting Soviet Citizens": An Uprising in the Post-Stalin Gulag', *Slavic Review*, 64/4 (2005): 823–50.

Batov, P., 'Sovetskie veterany voiny v bor'be za mir', *Voenno-istoricheskii zhurnal*, 6 (1979): 71–5.

Belov, Fedor, *The History of a Soviet Collective Farm*. New York: Praeger, 1955.

Bennett, Michael J., *When Dreams Came True: The G.I. Bill and the Making of Modern America*. Washington, DC: Brassey's, 2000.

Berkhoff, Karel C., *Harvest of Despair: Life and Death in Ukraine under Nazi Rule*. Cambridge and London: Belknap Press of Harvard University Press, 2004.

_____ 'Was there a Religious Revival in Soviet Ukraine under the Nazi Regime?', *Slavonic and East European Review*, 78/3 (2000): 536–67.

Bonwetsch, Bernd, 'Die sowjetischen Kriegsgefangenen zwischen Stalin und Hitler', *Zeitschrift für Geschichtswissenschaft*, 41/3 (1993).

_____ ' "Ich habe an einem völlig anderen Krieg teilgenommen": Die Erinnerung an den "Großen Vaterländischen Krieg" in der Sowjetunion', in Helmut Berding, Klaus Heller, and Winfried Speitkamp (eds.), *Krieg und Erinnerung: Fallstudien zum 19. und 20. Jahrhundert*, pp. 145–68. Göttingen: Vandenhoeck & Ruprecht, 2000.

_____ 'Sowjetunion: Triumph im Elend', in Ulrich Herbert and Axel Schildt (eds.), *Kriegsende in Europa: Vom Beginn des deutschen Machtzerfalls bis zur Stabilisierung der Nachkriegsordnung 1944–1948*, pp. 52–88. Essen: Klartext, 1998.

Borisov, Iu. S., ed., *Sovetskii rabochii klass: Kratkii istoricheskii ocherk, 1917–1973*. Moscow: Politizdat, 1975.

Boterbloem, Kees, *Life and Death under Stalin: Kalinin Province*. Montreal: McGill-Queens Press, 1999.

Brooks, Jeffrey, *Thank You Comrade Stalin! Soviet Public Culture from Revolution to Cold War.* Princeton: Princeton University Press, 2000.

Bucher, Greta, *Women, the Bureaucracy and Daily Life in Postwar Moscow, 1945–1953*. Boulder, Colo.: East European Monographs, 2006.

Burton, Chris, 'Medical Welfare during Late Stalinism: A Study of Doctors and the Soviet Health System, 1945–53', Ph.D. diss., University of Chicago, 2000.

Chandler, Andrea, *Shocking Mother Russia: Democratization, Social Rights, and Pension Reform in Russia, 1990–2001*. Toronto: University of Toronto Press, 2004.

Chertoritskaia, Tat'iana Vladimirovna, *Dorogie moi veterany: Iz istorii razrabotki i priniatiia zakonodatel'stva o veteranakh*. St Petersburg: Glagol', 1995.

Cohen, Deborah, *The War Come Home: Disabled Veterans in Britain and Germany, 1914–1939*. Berkeley, Los Angeles, and London: University of California Press, 2001.

Conze, Susanne, and Beate Fieseler, 'Soviet Women as Comrades-in-Arms: A Blind Spot in the History of the War', in Robert W. Thurston and Bernd Bonwetsch (eds.), *The People's War: Responses to World War II in the Soviet Union*, pp. 211–33. Urbana and Chicago: University of Illinois Press, 2000.

Cottam, K. J., 'Soviet Women in Combat During World War II: The Rear Services, Partisans and Political Workers', *Soviet Armed Forces Review Annual*, 5 (1981): 275–94.

_____ *Women in War and Resistance: Selected Biographies of Soviet Women Soldiers*. Nepean, ON: New Military Pub., 1998.

Dallin, David J., and Boris I. Nicolaevsky, *Forced Labor in Soviet Russia*. New Haven: Yale University Press, 1947.

Danilova, Natalia, 'Veterans' Policy in Russia: A Puzzle of Creation', *Journal of Power Institutions in Post-Soviet Societies* (Pipss.org), 6/7 (2007): The Social and Political Role of War Veterans, http://www.pipss.org/document873.html (accessed Dec. 2007).

Danukin, V. P., 'Trudoustroistvo invalidov: Vid sotsial'nogo obespecheniia', in V. S. Andreev (ed.), *Sotsial'noe obespechenie v SSSR za 60 let (pravovoe aspekty)*, pp. 118–25. Moscow: Vsesoiuznyi Iuridicheskii Zaochnyi Institut, 1979.

'Demobilizatsiia', in *Velikaia Otechestvennaia voina, 1941–1945: Entsiklopediia*, pp. 237–8. Moscow: Sovetskaia entsiklopediia, 1985.

Denisov, Iurii Pavlovich, *Razvitie kolkhoznoi demokratii (1946–1970 gg.)*. Rostov n/D.: Izd-vo Rost. un-ta, 1975.

DeWitt, Nicholas, *Education and Professional Employment in the U.S.S.R.* Washington, DC: National Science Foundation, 1961.

——— *Soviet Professional Manpower: Its Education, Training and Supply*. Washington, DC: National Science Foundation, 1955.

Diehl, James M., *The Thanks of the Fatherland: German Veterans after the Second World War*. Chapel Hill, NC: University of North Carolina Press, 1993.

'Dobrovol'chestvo', in *Sovetskaia voennaia entsiklopediia*, pp. 211–12. Moscow: Voennoe izd.-vo, 1977.

Donchenko, V. N., 'Demobilizatsiia sovetskoi armii i reshenie problem kadrov v pervye poslevoennye gody', *Istoriia SSSR*, 3 (1970): 96–106.

Drobiazko, S. I., *Pod znamenami vraga: Antisovetskie formirovaniia v sostave gernamsnikh vooruzhennykh sil 1941–1945*. Moscow: Eksmo, 2005.

Drugovskaia, A. Iu., ed., *Voina i zhenskaia sud'ba*. Kursk: Administratsiia goroda Kurska, Kurskii gosudarstvennyi meditsinskii universitet, Petrovskaia akademiia nauk i iskusstv, 2000.

Dukes, Paul, 'The Social Consequences of World War II for the USSR', in Arthur Marwick (ed.), *Total War and Social Change*, pp. 45–57. New York: St Martin's Press, 1988.

Dunham, Vera, 'Images of the Disabled, Especially the War Wounded, in Soviet Literature', in William O. McCagg and Lewis Siegelbaum (eds.), *The Disabled in the Soviet Union: Past and Present, Theory and Practice*. Pittsburgh: University of Pittsburgh Press, 1989.

——— *In Stalin's Time: Middleclass Values in Soviet Fiction*, enlarged and updated edn. Durham, NC, and London: Duke University Press, 1990 [1976].

Dunn, Ethel, 'Disabled Russian War Veterans: Surviving the Collapse of the Soviet Union', in David. A. Gerber (eds.), *Disabled Veterans in History*, pp. 251–70. Ann Arbor: University of Michigan Press, 2000.

Dunn, Stephen P., and Ethel Dunn, 'Everyday Life of the Disabled in the USSR', in William O. McCagg and Lewis Siegelbaum (eds.), *The Disabled in the Soviet Union: Past and Present, Theory and Practice*, pp. 199–234. Pittsburgh: University of Pittsburgh Press, 1989.

Duskin, Eric, *Stalinist Reconstruction and the Confirmation of a New Elite, 1945–1953*. New York: Palgrave, 2001.

Edele, Mark, 'A "Generation of Victors?" Soviet Second World War Veterans from Demobilization to Organization 1941–1956', Ph.D. diss., University of Chicago, 2004.

\_\_\_\_ 'More than just Stalinists: The Political Sentiments of Victors 1945–1953', in Juliane Fürst (ed.), *Late Stalinist Russia: Society between Reconstruction and Reinvention*, pp. 167–91. London and New York: Routledge, 2006.

\_\_\_\_ 'Paper Soldiers: The World of the Soldier Hero According to Soviet Wartime Posters', *Jahrbücher für Geschichte Osteuropas*, 47/1 (1999): 89–108.

\_\_\_\_ 'Soviet Society, Social Structure, and Everyday Life: Major Frameworks Reconsidered', *Kritika: Explorations in Russian and Eurasian History*, 8/2 (2007): 349–73.

\_\_\_\_ 'Soviet Veterans as an Entitlement Group, 1945–1955', *Slavic Review*, 65/1 (2006): 111–37.

\_\_\_\_ 'Strange Young Men in Stalin's Moscow: The Birth and Life of the Stiliagi, 1945–1953', *Jahrbücher für Geschichte Osteuropas*, 50/1 (2002): 37–61.

Elie, Marc, 'Les Politiques à l'égard des libérés du Goulag: Amnistiés et réhabilités dans la région de Novosibirsk, 1953–1960', *Cahiers du Monde russe*, 47/1–2 (2006): 327–48.

Elliott, Mark R., *Pawns of Yalta: Soviet Refugees and America's Role in their Repatriation*. Urbana, Ill.: University of Illinois Press, 1982.

Ellman, Michael, 'The 1947 Soviet Famine and the Entitlement Approach to Famines', *Cambridge Journal of Economics*, 24/5 (2000).

\_\_\_\_ and S. Maksudov, 'Soviet Deaths in the Great Patriotic War: A Note', *Europe–Asia Studies*, 46/4 (1994): 671–80.

Engel, Barbara Alpern, 'The Womanly Face of War. Soviet Women Remember World War II', in Nicole Ann Dombrowski (ed.), *Women and War in the Twentieth Century: Enlisted with or without Consent*, pp. 138–59. New York and London: Garland Publishing, 1999.

Englander, David, 'Soldiers and Social Reform in the First and Second World Wars', *Historical Research: The Bulletin of the Institute of Historical Research*, 67 (1994): 318–26.

Fieseler, Beate, 'Arme Sieger: Die Invaliden des Grossen Vaterländischen Krieges', *Osteuropa*, 55/4–6 (2005): 207–17.

\_\_\_\_ 'Der Krieg der Frauen: Die ungeschriebene Geschichte', in Deutsch-Russisches Museum Berlin-Karlshorst (ed.), *Mascha + Nina + Katjuscha: Frauen in der Roten Armee 1941–1945 Zhenshchiny-voennosluzhashchie*, pp. 11–20. Berlin: Ch. Links Verlag, 2002.

\_\_\_\_ *Die Invaliden des 'Grossen Vaterländischen Krieges' der Sowjetunion: Eine politische Sozialgeschichte 1941–1991*, Habilitationsschrift, Ruhr-Universität Bochum, 2003.

\_\_\_\_ 'Innenpolitik der Nachkriegszeit 1945–1953', in Stefan Plaggenborg (ed.), *Handbuch der Geschichte Russlands. v. 1945–1991: Vom Ende des Zweiten Weltkriegs bis zum Zusammenbruch der Sowjetunion. 1. Halbband*, pp. 36–77. Stuttgart: Anton Hiersemann, 2002.

―――― 'Stimmen aus dem gesellschaftlichen Abseits: Die sowjetrussischen Kriegsinvaliden im "Tauwetter" der fünfziger Jahre', *Osteuropa*, 52/7 (2002): 945–62.

―――― 'The Bitter Legacy of the "Great Patriotic War": Red Army Disabled Soldiers under Late Stalinism', in Juliane Fürst (ed.), *Late Stalinist Russia: Society between Reconstruction and Reinvention*. London and New York: Routledge, 2006.

Filtzer, Donald, *Soviet Workers and De-Stalinization: The Consolidation of the Modern System of Soviet Production Relations, 1953–1964*. Cambridge: Cambridge University Press, 1992.

―――― *Soviet Workers and Late Stalinism: Labour and the Restoration of the Stalinist System after World War II*. Cambridge: Cambridge University Press, 2002.

―――― 'The Standard of Living of Soviet Industrial Workers in the Immediate Postwar Period, 1945–1948', *Europe–Asia Studies*, 51/6 (1999): 1013–38.

―――― 'Wirtschaft und Gesellschaft in der Nachkriegszeit', in Stefan Plaggenborg (ed.), *Handbuch der Geschichte Russlands*, v. *1945–1991: Vom Ende des Zweiten Weltkriegs bis zum Zusammenbruch der Sowjetunion. 1. Halbband*, pp. 78–130. Stuttgart: A. Hiersemann, 2002.

Fitzpatrick, Sheila, 'Ascribing Class: The Construction of Social Identity in Soviet Russia', *Journal of Modern History*, 65 (1993): 745–70.

―――― 'Postwar Soviet Society: The "Return to Normalcy," 1945–1953', in Susan J. Linz (ed.), *The Impact of World War II on the Soviet Union*, pp. 129–56. Totowa, NJ: Rowman & Allanhead, 1985.

―――― 'Social Mobility in the Late Stalin Period: Recruitment into the Intelligentsia and Access to Higher Education, 1945–1953', unpublished paper, 1978.

―――― 'Social Parasites: How Tramps, Idle Youth, and Busy Entrepreneurs Impeded the Soviet March to Communism', *Cahiers du Monde russe*, 47/1–2 (2006): 377–408.

―――― 'Stalin and the Making of a New Elite', in *The Cultural Front: Power and Culture in Revolutionary Russia*, pp. 149–82. Ithaca, NY, and London: Cornell University Press, 1992 [1978].

―――― *Tear off the Masks! Identity and Imposture in Twentieth-Century Russia*. Princeton and Oxford: Princeton University Press, 2005.

―――― 'The Civil War as a Formative Experience', in Abbott Gleason, Peter Kenez, and Richard Stites (eds.), *Bolshevik Culture: Experience and Order in the Russian Revolution*. Bloomington, Ind.: Indiana University Press, 1985.

―――― 'The Legacy of the Civil War', in William Rosenberg Diane P. Koenker, and Ronald G. Suny (eds.), *Party, State, and Soviety in the Russian Civil War: Explorations in Social History*, pp. 385–98. Bloomington and Indianapolis: Indiana University Press, 1989.

―――― 'The World of Ostap Bender: Soviet Confidence Men in the Stalin Period', *Slavic Review*, 61/3 (2002): 535–57.

_____ 'War and Society in Soviet Context: Soviet Labor before, during, and after World War II', *International Labor and Working-Class History*, 35 (Spring 1989): 37–52.

Fürst, Juliane, ed., *Late Stalinist Russia: Society between Reconstruction and Reinvention*. London and New York: Routledge, 2006.

Fussel, Paul, *Wartime: Understanding and Behavior in the Second World War*. New York and Oxford: Oxford University Press, 1989.

Galgan, Valentina Iakovlevna, *Ratnyi podvig zhenshchin v gody Velikoi Otechestvennoi voiny*. Kiev: Vyshcha shkola, 1986.

Gallagher, Matthew P., *The Soviet History of World War II: Myths, Memories, and Realities*. New York and London: Frederick A. Praeger, 1963.

Geyer, Michael, 'Ein Vorbote des Wohlfahrtsstaates: Die Kriegsopferversorgung in Frankreich, Deutschland und Großbritannien nach dem Ersten Weltkrieg', *Geschichte und Gesellschaft*, 9 (1983): 230–77.

Gibson, Cristann L., 'Patterns of Demobilization: The US and USSR after World War Two', Ph.D. diss., University of Denver, 1983.

Gitelman, Zvi, 'Soviet Jewish Veterans of World War II Remember: Listening to Oral Histories', *Michigan Jewish History* 40 (2000).

Goeken, Ulrike, 'Von Kooperation zu Konfrontation: zur Repatriierung sowjetischer Kriegsgefangener und Zwangsarbeiter nach dem Zweiten Weltkrieg', *Arbeitskreis Militärgeschichte e.V., Newsletter*, 7 (1998): 15–19.

Goeken-Haidl, Ulrike, *Der Weg zurück: Die Repatriierung sowjetischer Zwangsarbeiter und Kriegsgefangener während und nach dem Zweiten Weltkrieg*. Essen: Klartext Verlag, 2006.

_____ 'Repatriierung in den Terror? Die Rückkehr der sowjetischen Zwangsarbeiter und Kriegsgefangenen in ihre Heimat 1944–1956', *Dachauer Hefte*, 16/16 (2000): 190–209.

Golczewski, Frank, 'Ukraine: Bürgerkrieg und Resowjetisierung', in Ulrich Herbert and Axel Schildt (eds.), *Kriegsende in Europa: Vom Beginn des deutschen Machtzerfalls bis zur Stabilisierung der Nachkriegsordnung 1944–1948*, pp. 89–99. Essen: Klartext, 1998.

Gorbachev, O. V., *Na puti k gorodu: Sel'skaia migratsiia v Tsentral'noi Rossii (1946–1985 gg.) i sovetskaia model' urbanizatsii*. Moscow: Izd-vo MPGU, 2002.

Graziosi, Andrea, 'The Great Strikes of 1953 in Soviet Labor Camps in the Accounts of their Participants: A Review', *Cahiers du monde russe et sovietique*, 33 (1992): 419–46.

Greene, Thomas J., 'The End of the World Must be at Hand: The Collective Farm Peasantry and the Soviet State During the Great Patriotic War, 1941–1945', Ph.D. diss., University of Toronto, 1999.

Griesse, Anne Eliot, and Richard Stites, 'Russia: Revolution and War', in Nancy Loring Goldman (ed.), *Female Soldiers: Combatants or Noncombatants? Historical and Contemporary Perspectives*, pp. 61–84. Westport, Conn.: Greenwood Press, 1982.

Gushchin, N. Ia., T. M. Baladian, and L. I Dremova, 'Naselenie i trudovye resursy sibirskoi derevni v 1917-nachale 80-kh godov (osnovnye etapy, osobennosti izmeneniia chislennosti i sostava)', in *Naselenie i trudovye resursy sovetskoi derevni (1917–1984gg.) Materialy xx sessii vsesoiuznogo simpoziuma po izucheniiu problem agrarnoi istorii. vyp. II*, pp. 19–34. Tallin: AN ESSR, 1987.

———and V. A. Isupov, eds., *Naselenie zapadnoi Sibiri v XX veke*. Novosibirsk: Izd-vo Sibirskogo otdeleniia RAN, 1997.

Hachten, P. Charles, 'Property Relations and the Economic Organization of Soviet Russia, 1941–1948', Ph.D. diss., University of Chicago, 2005.

Harrison, Mark, *Accounting for War: Soviet Production, Employment, and the Defence Burden, 1940–1945*. Cambridge: Cambridge University Press, 1996.

Hessler, Julie, 'A Postwar Perestroika? Toward a History of Private Trade Enterprise in the USSR', *Slavic Review*, 57/3 (1998): 516–42.

———*A Social History of Soviet Trade: Trade Policy, Retail Practices, and Consumption, 1917–1953*. Princeton and Oxford: Princeton University Press, 2004.

———'Cultured Trade: The Stalinist Turn towards Consumerism', in Sheila Fitzpatrick (ed.), *Stalinism: New Directions*, pp. 182–203. London and New York: Routledge, 2000.

———'Culture of Shortages: A Social History of Soviet Trade', Ph.D. diss., University of Chicago, 1996.

———'Postwar Normalisation and its Limits in the USSR: The Case of Trade', *Europe–Asia Studies*, 53/3 (2001): 445–71.

Hoffmann, Martin, 'Der Zweite Weltkrieg in der offiziellen sowjetischen Erinnerungskultur', in Helmut Berding, Klaus Heller, and Winfried Speitkamp (eds.), *Krieg und Erinnerung: Fallstudien zum 19. und 20. Jahrhundert*, pp. 129–43. Göttingen: Vandernhoeck & Ruprecht, 2000.

Holquist, Peter, *Making War, Forging Revolution: Russia's Continuum of Crisis, 1914–1921*. Cambridge, Mass., and London, 2002.

Hough, Jerry F., 'The Changing Nature of the Kolkhoz Chairman', in James R. Millar (ed.), *The Soviet Rural Community*, pp. 103–20. Urbana, Ill.: University of Illinois Press, 1971.

*Istoriia kommunisticheskoi partii Sovetskogo Soiuza*, v. *Kommunisticheskaia partiia nakanune i v gody Velikoi Otechestvennoi voiny, v period uprocheniia i razvitiia sotsialisticheskogo obshchestva: 1938–1959 gg*. Moscow: Voennoe izd.-vo, 1980.

*Istoriia Velikoi Otechestvennoi voiny Sovetskogo Soiuza 1941–1945*, v. *Pobedonosnoe okonchanie voiny s fashistskoi Germaniei. Porazhenie imperialisticheskoi Iaponii (1945 g.)*. Moscow: Voennoe izd.-vo, 1963.

Isupov, V. A., *Demograficheskie katastrofy i krizisy v Rossii v pervoi polovine XX veka: Istoriko-demograficheskie ocherki*. Novosibirsk: Sibirskii khoronograf, 2000.

Ivanov, V. N., and L. L. Rybakovskii, eds., *Demograficheskoe razvitie SSSR v poslevoennyi period: Sovetskie doklady k frantsuzsko-sovetskomu seminaru po problemam demografii, Parizh, dekabr' 1984 g*. Moscow: Institut sotsiologicheskikh issledovanii AN SSSR, 1984.

Ivanova, Iu. N., *Khrabreishie iz prekrasnykh. Zhenshchiny Rossii v voinakh*. Moscow: Rosspen, 2002.

Ivashov, L. G., and A. S. Emelin, 'Nravstvennye i pravovye problemy plena v Otechestvennoi istorii', *Voenno-istoricheskii zhurnal*, 1 (1992): 44–9.

Jacobson, Carol, 'The Soviet G.I.'s Bill of Rights', *American Review on the Soviet Union*, 7/1 (1945): 56–63.

Jahn, Hubertus F., *Patriotic Culture in Russia during World War I*. Ithaca, NY, and London: Cornell University Press, 1995.

Jahn, Peter, ed., *Mascha + Nina + Katjuscha: Frauen in der Roten Armee 1941–1945*. Berlin: Ch. Links Verlag, 2002.

Jones, Jeffrey W. ' "In my Opinion This is All Fraud!"': Concrete, Culture, and Class in the "Reconstruction" of Rostov-on-the-Don, 1943–1948', Ph.D. diss., University of North Carolina, 2000.

Karl, Lars, 'Von Helden und Menschen: Der Zweite Weltkrieg im sowjetischen Spielfilm (1941–1965)', *Osteuropa*, 1 (2002): 67–82.

Kelly, John D., 'Diaspora and World War, Blood and Nation in Fiji and Hawai'i', *Public Culture*, 7 (1995): 475–97.

Kirschenbaum, Lisa A., ' "Our City, our Hearths, our Families": Local Loyalties and Private Life in Soviet World War II Propaganda', *Slavic Review*, 59/4 (2000): 825–47.

———— *The Legacy of the Siege of Leningrad, 1941–1995: Myth, Memories, and Monuments*. Cambridge and New York: Cambridge University Press, 2006.

Kolkowicz, Roman, *The Soviet Military and the Communist Party*. Princeton: Princeton University Press, 1967.

Kolpakov, M. Ia., and Ia. I. Borisov, eds., *Veterany ne vykhodiat v otstavku: Istoriia Omskoi oblastnoi organizatsii veteranov*. Omsk: Knizhnoe izdatel'stvo, 1998.

Kostyrchenko, G., *Tainaia politika Stalina: Vlast' i antisemitizm*. Moscow: Mezhdunarodnye otnosheniia, 2001.

———— *V plenu u krasnogo faraona*. Moscow: Mezhdunarodnye otnosheniia, 1994.

Krivosheev, G. F., ed., *Grif sekretnosti sniat: Poteri vooruzhennykh sil SSSR v voinakh, boevykh deistviiakh i voennykh konfliktakh. Statisticheskoe issledovanie*. Moscow: Voennoe izdatel'stvo, 1993.

———— 'Poteri vooruzhennykh sil SSSR', in *Liudskie poteri SSSR v period vtoroi mirovoi voiny. Sbornik statei*, pp. 71–96. St Petersburg: Blits, 1995.

———— *Rossiia i SSSR v voinakh XX veka: Poteri vooruzhennykh sil. Statisticheskoe issledovanie*. Moscow: Olma-press, 2001.

———— *Soviet Casualties and Combat Losses in the Twentieth Century*. London: Greenhill Books, 1997.

———— and M. F. Filimoshin, 'Poteri vooruzhennykh sil SSSR v Velikoi Otechestvennoi voine', in V. B. Zhiromskaia (ed.), *Naselenie Rossii v XX veke: Istoricheskie ocherki*, ii. *1940–1959*, pp. 19–39. Moscow: Rosspen, 2001.

Krylova, Anna, ' "Healers of Wounded Souls": The Crisis of Private Life in Soviet Literature, 1944–46', *Journal of Modern History*, June (2001): 307–31.

Kühne, Thomas, 'Zwischen Vernichtungskrieg und Freizeitgesellschaft: Die Veteranenkultur in der Bundesrepublik (1945–1995)', in Klaus Naumann (ed.), *Nachkrieg in Deutschland*. Hamburg: Hamburger Klaus Naumann Edition, 2001.

Lane, Christel, *The Rites of Rulers: Ritual in Industrial Society. The Soviet Case*. Cambridge: Cambridge University Press, 1981.

*Leninskii Komsomol v Velikoi Otechestvennoi voine*. Moscow: Molodaia gvardiia, 1975.

Lévesque, Jean, 'Exile and Discipline: The June 1948 Campaign Against Collective Farm Shirkers', *Carl Beck Papers in Russian and East European Studies*, 1708 (2006).

_____ '"Part-Time Peasants": Labour Discipline, Collective Farm Life, and the Fate of Soviet Socialized Agriculture after the Second World War, 1945–1953', Ph.D. diss., University of Toronto, 2003.

Linz, Susan J., ed., *The Impact of World War II on the Soviet Union*. Totowa, NJ: Rowman & Allanhead, 1985.

Lovell, Stephen, 'Soviet Russia's Older Generations', in Stephen Lovell (ed.), *Generations in Twentieth-Century Europe*, pp. 205–26. Houndsmills, Basingstoke: Palgrave Macmillan, 2007.

Luzherenko, V. K., 'Plen: Tragediia millionov', in V. A. Zolotarev and G. N. Sevost'ianov (eds.), *Velikaia Otechestvennaia voina 1941–1945: Voenno-istoricheskie ocherki. V chetyrekh knigakh*, iv. *Narod i voina*, pp. 168–204. Moscow: Nauka, 1999.

Madison, Bernice, 'Programs for the Disabled in the USSR', in William O. McCagg and Lewis Siegelbaum (eds.), *The Disabled in the Soviet Union: Past and Present, Theory and Practice*, pp. 167–98. Pittsburgh: University of Pittsburgh Press, 1989.

_____ *Social Welfare in the Soviet Union*. Stanford, Calif.: Stanford University Press, 1968.

Maksudov, S., *Poteri naseleniia SSSR*. Benson, Vt.: Chalidze Publications, 1989.

Mannheim, Karl, 'The Problem of Generations', in Paul Kecskemeti (ed.), *Essays in the Sociology of Knowledge*, pp. 276–320. London: Routledge & Kegan Paul, 1964.

Markwick, Roger D., 'Stalinism at War', *Kritika: Explorations in Russian and Eurasian History*, 3/3 (2002): 509–20.

Maslov, N. N., 'Kommunisticheskaia partiia v poslevoennyi period', in Iu. P. Sviridenko A. I. Zeveleva, and V. V. Shelokhaeva (eds.), *Politicheskie partii Rossii: Istoriia i sovremennost'. Uchebnik dlia istoricheskikh i gumanitarnykh fakul'tetov vysshikh uchebnykh zavedenii*, pp. 477–99. Moscow: Rosspen, 2000.

Merridale, Catherine, *Ivan's War: Life and Death in the Red Army, 1939–1945*. New York: Metropolitan Books, 2006.

_____ *Night of Stone: Death and Memory in Russia*. London: Granta Books, 2000.

_____ 'The Collective Mind: Trauma and Shell-Shock in Twentieth-Century Russia', *Journal of Contemporary History*, 35/1 (2000): 39–55.

Mikhailev, S. N., 'Velikaia Otechestvennaia: Demograficheskie i voenno-oper-
ativnye poteri', in *Liudskie poteri SSSR v period vtoroi mirovoi voiny: Sbornik statei*,
pp. 82–96. St Petersburg: Blits, 1995.

Mitrofanova, Avgusta Vasil'evna, *Rabochii klass SSSR v gody Velikoi Otechestvennoi
voiny*. Moscow: Nauka, 1971.

Mitrokhin, Nikolai, *Russkaia partiia: Dvizhenie russkikh natsionalistov v SSSR
1953–1985*. Moscow: Novoe literaturnoe obozrenie, 2003.

_____ 'Russkaia partiia: Fragmenty issledovaniia', *Novoe literaturnoe obozrenie*, 3
(2001): 245–97.

_____ and S. Timofeeva, *Episkopy i eparkhii Russkoi Pravoslavnoi Tserkvi po sostoianiiu
na 1 oktiabria 1997 g.* Moscow: Panorama, 1997.

'Mobilizatsiia vooruzhennykh sil SSSR', in *Velikaia Otechestvennaia Voina
1941–1945. Entsiklopediia*, p. 452. Moscow: Sovetskaia entsiklopediia, 1985.

Modorov, N. S., *V trude i v boiu: Ocherki o zhenshchinakh Gornogo Altaia*. Gorno-
Altaisk: Gorno-Altaiskoe otdelenie Altaiskogo knizhnogo izd., 1990.

Moeller, Robert G., ' "The Last Soldiers of the Great War" and Tales of Family
Reunions in the Federal Republic of Germany', *Signs: Journal of Women in
Culture and Society*, 24/1 (1998): 129–45.

Morekhina, G. G., *Partiinoe stroitel'stvo v period Velikoi Otechestvennoi voiny Sovetskogo
Soiuza 1941–1945*. Moscow: Politicheskaia literatura, 1986.

Moskoff, William, *The Bread of Affliction: The Food Supply in the USSR during World
War II*. Cambridge: Cambridge University Press, 1990.

Murmantseva, Vera Semenova, *Sovetskie zhenshchiny v Velikoi Otechestvennoi voine*,
2nd rev. and enlarged edn. Moscow: Mysl', 1979.

_____ *Sovetskie zhenshchiny v Velikoi Otechestvennoi voine*. Moscow: Mysl', 1974.

_____ *Zhenshchiny v soldatskikh shineliakh*. Moscow: Voennoe izd-vo, 1971.

Nagle, John D., 'A New Look at the Soviet Elite: A Generational Model of the
Soviet System', *Journal of Political and Military Sociology*, 3/1 (1975).

Nakachi, Mie, 'N. S. Khrushchev and the 1944 Soviet Family Law: Politics,
Reproduction, and Language', *East European Politics and Societies*, 20/1 (2006):
40–68.

_____ 'Population, Politics and Reproduction: Late Stalinism and its Legacy',
in Juliane Fürst (ed.), *Late Stalinist Russia: Society between Reconstruction and
Reinvention*, pp. 167–91. London and New York: Routledge, 2006.

Naimark, Norman M., *The Russians in Germany: A History of the Soviet Zone
of Occupation, 1945–1949*. Cambridge, Mass., and London: Harvard University
Press, 1995.

Naumov, Vladimir, and Leonid Reshin, 'Repression gegen sowjetische Kriegsgefangene und zivile Repatrianten in der UdSSR 1941–1956', in Konstantin
Kikishkin, Klaus-Dieter Müller, and Günther Wagenlehner (eds.), *Die Tragödie
der Gefangenschaft in Deutschland und in der Sowjetunion 1941–1956*, pp. 335–64.
Cologne and Weimar: Böhlau Verlag, 1998.

Naumov, V. P., 'Sud'ba voennoplennykh i deportirovannykh grazhdan SSSR: Materialy komissii po reabilitatsii zhertv politicheskikh repressi', *Novaia i noveishaia istoriia*, 2 (1996): 91–112.

Osterloh, Jörg, *Soujetische Kriegsgefangene 1941–1945 im Spiegel nationaler und internationaler Untersuchungen: Forschungsüberblick und Bibliographie*, 2nd rev. edn. Dresden: Hannah-Arendt-Institut für Totalitarismusforschung e.V. and der TU Dresden, 1996.

Pavlov, Boris Potapovich, ed., *Veterany v stroiu*. Moscow: Voenizdat, 1981.

Pennington, Reina, 'Offensive Women: Women in Combat in the Red Army', in Paul Addison and Angus Calder (eds.), *Time to Kill: The Soldier's Experience of War in the West 1939–1945*, pp. 249–62. London: Random House, 1997.

———— *Wings, Women, and War: Soviet Airwomen in World War II Combat*. Lawrence, Kan.: University Press of Kansas, 2001.

Peris, Daniel, ' "God is Now on our Side": The Religious Revival on Unoccupied Soviet Territory during World War II', *Kritika: Explorations in Russian and Eurasian History*, 1/1 (2000): 97–118.

Petrov, Iu. P., *Partiinoe stroitel'stvo v sovetskoi armii i flote: Deiatel'nost' KPSS po sozdaniiu i ukrepleniiu politorganov, partiinykh i komsomol'skikh organizatsii v vooruzhennykh silakh (1918–1961 gg.)*. Moscow: Voennoe izd-vo, 1964.

*50 Let Vooruzhennykh Sil SSSR*. Moscow: Voenizdat, 1968.

Pikhoia, R. G., *Sovetskii Soiuz: Istoriia vlasti 1945–1991*, 2nd edn. Novosibirsk: Sibirskii khoronograf, 2000; orig. 1998.

Poletaev, Vladimir Evgen'evich, ed., *Rabochii klass SSSR, 1951–1956*. Moscow: Nauka, 1969.

———— *Rabochie Moskvy na zavershaiushchem etape stoitel'stva sotsializma, 1945–1958 gg*. Moscow: Nauka, 1967.

Polian, Pavel, *Deportiert nach Hause: Soujetische Kriegsgefangene im 'Dritten Reich' und ihre Repatriierung*. Munich and Vienna: R. Oldenbourg Verlag, 2001.

———— *Zhertvy drukh diktatur: Ostarbaitery i voennoplennye v tret'em reikhe i ikh repatriatsiia*. Moscow: Vash Vybor TsIPZ, 1996.

Ponomarev, B. N., ed., *Istoriia SSSR s drevneishikh vremen do nashikh dnei*, 12 vols. vol. xi. Moscow: Nauka, 1980.

Popov, V. P., *Ekonomicheskaia politika sovetskogo gosudarstva: 1946–1953 gg*. Tambov: Izd-vo Tamb. gos. tekhn. un-ta, 2000.

———— 'Gosudarstvennyi terror v sovetskoi Rossii; 1923–1953 gg. (istochniki i ikh interpretatsiia)', *Otechestvennye arkhivy*, 2 (1992): 20–31.

———— *Krestianstvo i gosudarstvo (1945–1954)*. Paris: YMCA Press, 1992.

Popova, Nina Vasil'evna, *Zhenshchiny strany sotsializma*. Moscow: Profizdat, 1947.

Prost, Antoine, *In the Wake of War: 'Les Anciens combattants' and French Society 1914–1939*, tr. Helen McPhail. Oxford: Berg, 1992.

———— *Les Anciens Combattants et la société française: 1914–1939*, 3 vols. Paris: Presses de la Fondation nationale des sciences politiques, 1977.

Pyle, Emily E., 'Village Social Relations and the Reception of Soldiers' Family Aid Policies in Russia, 1912–1921', Ph.D. diss., University of Chicago, 1997.

Qualls, Karl D., 'Raised from Ruins: Restoring Popular Allegiance through City Planning in Sevastopol, 1943–1954', Ph.D. diss, Georgetown University, 1998.

Ramos, Henry A. J., *The American GI Forum: In Pursuit of the Dream, 1948–1983.* Houston, Tex.: Arte Publico Press, 1998.

Rauchensteiner, Manfried, *Der Sonderfall: Die Besatzungszeit in Österreich 1945 bis 1955.* Graz: Styria, 1979.

Reese, Roger R., *The Soviet Military Experience.* London and New York: Routledge, 2000.

Rezvanov, V. M., *Partiinaia rabota na sele: 1945–1959.* Moscow: Mysl', 1986.

Rigby, T. H., *Communist Party Membership in the USSR 1917–1967.* Princeton: Princeton University Press, 1968.

——— 'The Soviet Regional Leadership: The Brezhnev Generation', *Slavic Review,* 37/1 (1978): 1–24.

Rossiiskii komitet veteranov voiny i voennoi sluzhby, ed. *Nam—45!* Moscow: Mezhdunarodnyi ob"edinennyi biograficheski tsentr, 2001.

Samsonov, A. M.. 'Iz istorii veteranov voiny (fragmenty)', *Istoriia SSSR,* 2 (1985): 53–79.

Sanborn, Joshua, 'Brothers under Fire: The Development of a Front-Line Culture in the Red Army 1941–1943', MA thesis, University of Chicago, 1993.

——— *Drafting the Russian Nation: Military Conscription, Total War, and Mass Politics 1905–1925.* DeKalb, Ill.: Northern Illinois University Press, 2003.

Schapiro, Leonard, *The Communist Party of the Soviet Union.* New York: Vintage Books, 1964.

Seniavskaia, E. S., *1941–1945: Frontovoe pokolenie. Istoriko-psikhologicheskoe issledovanie.* Moscow: RAN institut Rossiiskoi istorii, 1995.

——— *Psikhologiia voiny v XX veke: Istoricheskii opyt Rossii.* Moscow: Rosspen, 1999.

Sherstianoi, E., 'Germaniia i nemtsy v pis'makh krasnoarmeitsev vesnoi 1945 g.', *Novaia i noveishaia istoriia,* 2 (2002): 137–51.

Sheviakov, Aleksei Alekseevich, 'Repatriatsiia Sovetskogo mirnogo naseleniia i voennoplennykh, okazavshikhsia v okkupatsionnykh zonakh gosudarstv Antigitlerovskoi koalitsii', in *Naselenie Rossii v 1920–1950-e gody: Chislennost' poteri, migratsii. Sbornik nauchnykh trudov,* pp. 195–222. Moscow: In-t rossiiskoi istorii RAN, 1994.

——— '"Tainy' poslevoennoi repatriatsii', *Sotsiologicheskie issledovaniia,* 5 (1993): 3–11.

Shneer, Aron, *Plen: Sovetskie voennoplennye v Germanii, 1941–1945.* Moscow and Jerusalem: Mosty kultury, Gesharim, 2005.

Skocpol, Theda, *Protecting Soldiers and Mothers: The Political Origins of Social Policy in the United States.* Cambridge, Mass.: Belknap, 1992.

Skocpol, Theda, 'The G.I. Bill and U.S. Social Policy, Past and Future', in Ellen F. Paul, Fred D. Miller, and Jeffrey Paul (eds.), *The Welfare State*, pp. 95–115. Cambridge: Cambridge University Press, 1997.

Stetsovskii, Iurii I. *Istoriia sovetskikh repressii*, vol. i. Moscow: Tasis, 1997.

Stiller, Pavel, *Sozialpolitik in der UdSSR 1950–80: Eine Analyse der quantitativen und qualitativen Zusammenhänge*. Baden-Baden: Nomos Verlagsgesellschaft, 1983.

Stishova, L. I., ed., *V tylu i na fronte: zhenshchiny-kommunisty v gody Velikoi Otechestvennoi voiny*. Moscow: politicheskaia literatura, 1984.

Stockdale, Melissa K., 'United in Gratitude. Honoring Soldiers and Defining the Nation in Russia's Great War', *Kritika: Explorations in Russian and Eurasian History*, 7/3 (2006): 459–85.

Streit, Christian, *Keine Kameraden: Die Wehrmacht und die sowjetischen Kriegsgefangenen 1941–1945*, new edn. Bonn: Dietz, 1997.

Thurston, Robert W., 'Cauldrons of Loyalty and Betrayal: Soviet Soldiers' Behavior, 1941 and 1945', in Robert W. Thurston and Bernd Bonwetsch (eds.), *The People's War: Responses to World War II in the Soviet Union*, pp. 235–57. Urbana and Chicago: University of Illinois Press, 2000.

Tiurina, Aleksandra Petrovna, *Formirovanie kadrov spetsialistov i organizatorov kolkhoznogo proizvodstva*. Moscow: Nauka, 1973.

Toman, B. A., and T. B. Toman, 'V gody Velikoi Otechestvennoi voiny', in Iu. P. Sviderenko, A. I. Zeveleva, and V. V. Shelokhaeva (eds.), *Politicheskie partii Rossii: Istoriia i sovremennost'. Uchebnik dlia istoricheskikh i gumanitarnykh fakul'tetov vysshikh uchebnykh zavedenii*, pp. 461–76. Moscow: Rosspen, 2000.

Tumarkin, Nina, *The Living and the Dead: The Rise and Fall of the Cult of World War II in Russia*. New York: Basic Books, 1994.

'Uchastniki voiny', in *Velikaia otechestvennaia voina, 1941–1945: Entsiklopediia*, p. 751. Moscow: Sovetskaia entsiklopediia, 1985.

*Ukrainskaia SSR v period postroeniia razvitogo sotsialisticheskogo obshchestva (1945–nachala 60-kh godov)*, 10 vols., ix. *Istoriia Ukrainskoi SSR*. Kiev: Naukova dumka, 1985.

Vail', Petr, and Aleksandr Genis, *60-e. Mir sovetskogo cheloveka*, 3rd edn. Moscow: Novoe literaturnoe obozrenie, 2001.

Verbitskaia, O. M., 'Izmeneniia chislennosti i sostava kolkhoznogo krest'ianstva RSFSR v pervye poslevoennye gody (1945–1950)', *Istoriia SSSR*, 5 (1980).

—— 'Liudskie poteri v gody Velikoi Otechestvennoi voiny: Territoriia i naselenie posle voiny', in *Naselenie Rossii v XX veke. Istoricheskie ocherki*. ii. *1940–1959 gg.*, pp. 128–65. Moscow: Rosspen, 2001.

—— 'O nekotorykh osobennostiakh demograficheskogo razvitiia gorodskogo i sel'skogo naseleniia v gody Velikoi Otechestvennoi voiny', in V. B. Zhiromskaia (ed.), *Naselenie Rossii v XX veke: Istoricheskie ocherki*, ii. *1940–1959 gg.* Moscow: Rosspen, 2001.

_____ 'O nekotorykh osobennostiakh demograficheskogo razvitiia gorodskogo i sel'skogo naseleniia v gody VOV', in *Liudskie poteri SSSR v period vtoroi mirovoi voiny*, pp. 147–53. St Petersburg, 1995.

_____ *Rossiiskoe krest'ianstvo: Ot Stalina k Khrushchevu*. Moscow: Nauka, 1992.

_____ 'Sel'skaia sem'ia. 1940–1950-e gg.', in V. B. Zhiromskaia (ed.), *Naselenie Rossii v XX veke: Istoricheskie ocherki*, ii. *1940–1959*, pp. 243–74. Moscow: Rosspen, 2001.

'Voinskaia obiazannost'', in *Sovetskaia voennaia entsiklopediia*, pp. 302–3. Moscow: Voennoe izd.-vo, 1976.

Volkov, I. M., 'Kolkhoznaia derevnia v pervyi poslevoennyi god', *Voprosy istorii*, 1 (1966): 15–32.

von Hagen, Mark, *Soldiers in the Proletarian Dictatorship: The Red Army and the Soviet Socialist State, 1917–1930*. Ithaca, NY, and London: Cornell University Press, 1990.

_____ 'Soviet Soldiers and Officers on the Eve of the German Invasion: Toward a Description of Social Psychology and Political Attitudes', in Robert W. Thurston and Bernd Bonwetsch (eds.), *The People's War: Responses to World War II in the Soviet Union*, pp. 186–210. Urbana and Chicago: University of Illinois Press, 2000.

Weiner, Amir, 'In the Long Shadow of War: The Second World War and the Soviet and Post-Soviet World', *Diplomatic History*, 25/3 (2001): 443–56.

_____ *Making Sense of War: The Second World War and the Fate of the Bolshevik Revolution*. Princeton and Oxford: Princeton University Press, 2000.

_____ 'Myths and Identities: The Construction of Collective Identities in the Vinnytsia Region, 1943–1975', Ph.D. diss., Columbia University, 1995.

_____ 'Saving Private Ivan: From What, Why, and How?', *Kritika: Explorations in Russian and Eurasian History*, 1/2 (2000): 305–36.

_____ 'The Empires Pay a Visit: Gulag Returnees, East European Rebellions, and Soviet Frontier Politics', *Journal of Modern History*, 78/2 (2006): 333–76.

_____ 'The Making of a Dominant Myth: The Second World War and the Construction of Political Identities within the Soviet Polity', *Russian Review*, 55 (1996).

Werth, Alexander, *Russia at War: 1941–1945*, 2nd edn. New York: Carroll & Graf, 2000; orig. 1964.

Wirtschafter, Elise K., 'Social Misfits: Veterans and Soldiers' Families in Servile Russia', *Journal of Military History*, 59/2 (1995): 215–35.

Wohl, Robert, *The Generation of 1914*. Cambridge, Mass.: Harvard University Press, 1979.

Woloch, Isser, *The French Veteran from the Revolution to the Restauration*. Chapel Hill, NC: University of North Carolina Press, 1979.

Youngblood, Denise J., *Russian War Films: On the Cinema Front, 1914–2005*. Lawrence, Kan.: University Press of Kansas, 2007.

Zavgorodnii, A. F., *Deiatel'nost' gosudarstvennykh organov i obshchestvenno-politi-cheskikh organizatsii po sotsial'noi zashchite voennosluzhashchikh Krasnoi Armii i ikh semei v mezhvoennyi period (1921-iiun' 1941 gg)*. St Petersburg: Nestor, 2001.

Zeidler, Manfred, *Kriegsende im Osten: Die Rote Armee und die Besetzung Deutschlands östlich von Oder un Neisse 1944/45*. Munich: R. Oldenburg Vlg., 1996.

Zemskov, Victor, 'Angst vor der Rückkehr: Die Repatriierung sowjetischer Staatsbürger und ihr weiteres Schicksal (1944–1956)', in Haus der Geschichte der Bundesrepublik Deutschland (ed.), *Kriegsgefangene—Voennoplennye: Sowjet-ische Kriegsgefangene in Deutschland. Deutsche Kriegsgefangene in der Sowjetunion*, pp. 157–62. Düsseldorf: Droste, 1995.

—— 'Chernye dyry istorii', *Raduga* (Tallin), 6 (1990): 42–8.

—— 'Gulag (istoriko-sotsiologicheskii aspekt), chast' 1', *Sotsiologicheskie issle-dovaniia*, 6 (1991): 10–27.

—— 'Gulag (istoriko-sotsiologicheskii aspekt), chast' 2', *Sotsiologicheskie issle-dovaniia*, 7 (1991): 3–16.

—— 'Izmeneie demograficheskogo sostava gorodskogo naseleniia RSFSR v 1939–1959 gg.', in V. B. Zhiromskaia (ed.), *Naselenie Rossii v XX veke: Istoricheskie ocherki*, ii. *1940–1959*, pp. 206–217. Moscow: Rosspen, 2001.

—— ' "Kulatskaia ssylka" nakanune i v gody Velikoi Otechestvennoi voiny', *Sotsiologicheskie issledovaniia*, 2 (1992): 3–26.

—— 'K voprosu o repatriatsii sovetskikh grazhdan 1944–1951 gg.', *Istoriia SSSR*, 4 (1990): 26–41.

—— 'Repatriatsiia sovetskikh grazhdan i ikh dal'neishaia sud'ba (1944–1956)', *Sotsiologicheskie issledovaniia*, 5 (1995): 3–13.

—— 'Repatriatsiia sovetskikh grazhdan v 1945–1946 godakh: Poiraias' na doku-menty', *Rossiia XXI*, 5 (1993): 74–81.

—— 'Spetsposelentsy (1930–1959 gg.)', in *Naselenie Rossii v 1920-e-1950-e gody: Chislennost', poteri, migratsii*, pp. 145–94. Moscow, 1994.

—— 'Sud'ba "kulatskoi ssylki" (1930–1954 gg.)', *Otechestvennaia istoriia*, 1 (1994): 118–47.

—— 'Sud'ba "kulatskoi ssylki" v poslevoennoe vremia', *Sotsiologicheskie issle-dovaniia*, 8 (1992): 18–37.

'Zhenshchiny SSSR', *Velikaia Otechestvennaia voina 1941–1945: Entsiklopediia*, pp. 269–70. Moscow: Sovetskaia entsiklopediia, 1985.

*Zhenshchiny strany sovetov: Kratkii istoricheskii ocherk*. Moscow: politicheskaia liter-atura, 1977.

Zhiromskaia, V. B., *Demograficheskaia istoriia Rossii v 1930-e gody: Vzgliad v neizvest-noe*. Moscow: Rosspen, 2001.

—— I. N. Kiselev, and Iu. A. Poliakov, *Polveka pod grifom 'sekretno': Vsesoiuznaia perepis' naseleniia 1937 goda*. Moscow: Nauka, 1996.

Zima, V. F., *Golod v SSSR 1946–1947 godov: proiskhozhdenie i posledstviia*. Moscow: Institut Rossiiskoi istorii RAN, 1996.

Zubkova, Elena, 'Malenkov, Khrushchev i "ottepel" ', *Kommunist*, 14 (Sept. 1990): 86–94.

\_\_\_\_ 'Obshchestvennaia atmosfera posle voiny (1945–1946)', *Svobodnaia mysl'*, 6 (1992): 4–14.

\_\_\_\_ 'Obshchestvennaia atmosfera posle voiny (1948–1952)', *Svobodnaia mysl'*, 9 (1992): 79–88.

\_\_\_\_ *Obshchestvo i reformy, 1945–1964*. Moscow: Rossiia molodaia, 1993.

\_\_\_\_ *Poslevoennoe sovetskoe obshchestvo: Politika i povsednevnost' 1945–1953*. Moscow: Rosspen, 2000.

\_\_\_\_ 'Reformy Khrushcheva; kul'tura politicheskogo deistviia', *Svobodnaia mysl'*, 9 (June 1993): 97–107.

\_\_\_\_ *Russia After the War: Hopes, Illusions, and Disappointments, 1945–1957*, tr. Hugh Ragsdale. Armonk and London, 1998.

# Index